PEACE HANDBOOKS.

Issued by the Historical Section
of the Foreign Office

VOL. XVIII.

GERMAN AFRICAN POSSESSIONS

(LATE)

GREENWOOD PRESS, PUBLISHERS
NEW YORK

Originally published in 1920
by H.M. Stationery Office, London

First Greenwood Reprinting 1969

SBN 8371-1475-6

Editorial Note.

In the spring of 1917 the Foreign Office, in connection with the preparation which they were making for the work of the Peace Conference, established a special section whose duty it should be to provide the British Delegates to the Peace Conference with information in the most convenient form—geographical, economic, historical, social, religious and political—respecting the different countries, districts, islands, &c., with which they might have to deal. In addition, volumes were prepared on certain general subjects, mostly of an historical nature, concerning which it appeared that a special study would be useful.

The historical information was compiled by trained writers on historical subjects, who (in most cases) gave their services without any remuneration. For the geographical sections valuable assistance was given by the Intelligence Division (Naval Staff) of the Admiralty; and for the economic sections, by the War Trade Intelligence Department, which had been established by the Foreign Office. Of the maps accompanying the series, some were prepared by the above-mentioned department of the Admiralty, but the bulk of them were the work of the Geographical Section of the General Staff (Military Intelligence Division) of the War Office.

Now that the Conference has nearly completed its task, the Foreign Office, in response to numerous enquiries and requests, has decided to issue the books for public use, believing that they will be useful to students of history, politics, economics and foreign affairs, to publicists generally and to business men and travellers. It is hardly necessary to say that some of the subjects dealt with in the series have not in fact come under discussion at the Peace Conference; but, as the books treating of them contain valuable information, it has been thought advisable to include them.

It must be understood that, although the series of volumes was prepared under the authority, and is now issued with the sanction, of the Foreign Office, that Office is not to be regarded as guaranteeing the accuracy of every statement which they contain or as identifying itself with all the opinions expressed in the several volumes; the books were not prepared in the Foreign Office itself, but are in the nature of information provided for the Foreign Office and the British Delegation.

The books are now published, with a few exceptions. substantially as they were issued for the use of the Delegates, No attempt has been made to bring them up to date, for, in the first place, such a process would have entailed a great loss of time and a prohibitive expense; and, in the second, the political and other conditions of a great part of Europe and of the Nearer and Middle East are still unsettled and in such a state of flux that any attempt to describe them would have been incorrect or misleading. The books are therefore to be taken as describing, in general, *ante-bellum* conditions, though in a few cases, where it seemed specially desirable, the account has been brought down to a later date.

G. W. PROTHERO,
General Editor and formerly
Director of the Historical Section.

January 1920.

HANDBOOKS PREPARED UNDER THE DIRECTION OF THE HISTORICAL SECTION OF THE FOREIGN OFFICE.—No. 110

TOGOLAND

TABLE OF CONTENTS

Wt. 15564/89.   1000.   8/20.   O.U.P.

PAGE

IV. ECONOMIC CONDITIONS

TABLE OF CONTENTS

I. GEOGRAPHY
PHYSICAL AND POLITICAL

(1) Position and Frontiers

Togoland extends northwards from the Gulf of Guinea for a distance of over 300 miles, as far as the plains of southern Gurma. Its width averages some 130 miles, and it occupies an area of 33,700 square miles, marching on the west with the Gold Coast, on the north with the province of Upper Senegal and Niger in French West Africa, and on the east with Dahomey. The main sea-routes all pass well to the west or south ; but before the war there was direct connexion with Hamburg, and the steamers of a number of French and English lines also called at Togoland ports.

The boundaries are defined in the following documents (see also p. 18) :

(i) Between the British Gold Coast Colony and Togoland (*a*) in the Agreement of July 1, 1890, Art. IV, modified by the Convention of Sept. 26/Dec. 2, 1901, Art. X ; (*b*) in the Convention of Nov. 14, 1899, Art. V, modified by the Convention of Sept. 26/Dec. 2, 1901, especially Art. VII ; (*c*) in the Notes exchanged June 25, 1904, and slightly modified in 1907, as the result of the labours of the Boundary Commission ;

(ii) Between the French colonies and Togoland by the Convention of July 23, 1897, and the Declaration of September 28, 1912.

The western frontier is marked to a great extent by natural features, but it is otherwise with the northern and eastern frontiers, where the boundaries are artificial lines, except in the southernmost section of the eastern frontier. In the delimitation of the boundaries little notice has been taken of ethnic or linguistic divisions.

From marks set up on the coast about two miles west of Lome, the boundary runs due north to 6° 10' north latitude. This parallel it follows westward as far as the Aka River, which it ascends as far as 6° 20' north latitude, and then follows that parallel as far as the River Shavoe (Shawo, Dchawe, Dschawoë, Jevoë). It ascends the right bank of this up to the level of the confluence of the River Dea (Dayi, Deine, Daji) with the Volta (about 6° 41' N.), to which point it then proceeds in a direct line. It then ascends the left bank of the Volta to the confluence of the Daka or Kulukpene, the course of which it follows to the junction of the Kulusulo River (about 9° 18' N.). From this point the boundary runs in a generally northerly direction till it strikes a point (11° 10' N., 0° 9' W.) on the frontier of French West Africa (Sudan).

From this point the northern boundary runs slightly south of east to the parallel of 11° north latitude, which it meets at longitude 0° 35' east, and follows as far as longitude 0° 56' east. The village of Punyo, lying on the 11th parallel, at the precise point where the boundary strikes it, is assigned to French territory.

The eastern boundary then follows an irregularly demarcated line towards the south and east till it strikes the meridian of 1° 40' east longitude about latitude 9° 8' north, and follows it as far south as 7° north. This parallel it follows west to the Monu River, the course of which it descends to the Wo lagoon. The boundary then follows the middle of the lagoon westward for 10 or 12 miles to a point a mile east of Sebe, where it finally crosses to the coast, which it reaches 2½ miles east of Anecho.

(2) SURFACE, COAST, AND RIVER SYSTEMS

Surface

Togoland is traversed from south-west to north-east by a range of mountains which both begins and ends beyond the frontiers. This range divides the country into two approximately equal triangles—the north-western region consists of the lowlands, drained by the rivers Oti and Daka and bounded on the north by the Gambaga hills, together with a narrow strip of country belonging geographically to the western Sudan ; the south-eastern region is made up of a low-lying coastal district in the south and an interior plateau, geographically a westerly continuation of the Dahomey plateau, in the north. The whole area thus falls into four main divisions : (i) the coastal region, (ii) the main south-eastern plateau, (iii) the central mountain range, (iv) the north-west lowlands, together with the Gambaga hills and a strip of the Gurma plateau.

The *coastal region* consists of four parts. First, a practically unbroken bank of sand, a few feet above sea-level and a few hundred yards broad. Secondly, a zone occupied by lagoons, marshes, and rivers ramifying into numerous channels. Behind the lagoon zone an undulating plateau rises to the north to a height of about 230–330 ft., and is cut by a number of rivers, e. g. the Haho, Shio, and Aka. Farther north this plateau sinks again to a depression, lying 100–150 ft. above sea-level.

The *south-eastern plateau* succeeds the depression just described. In places it rises abruptly to 200–300 ft., and towards the interior reaches a height of 1,300–1,600 ft. North of 7° north latitude it is characterized by the emergence of isolated hills, ranging from 150 to 650 ft.

The *central mountain range* is known in various

regions as the Agome, Akposso, Kebu, and Adele Mountains; with it are connected the Buem Mountains to the west and the Kurango and Kabure groups to the north-east.

The central chain has no great elevations, and there is no extensive plateau land. The mountains, however, fall very sharply to the plains on both sides, and form a real barrier to traffic. The chain falls into two distinct sections, each with a special character of its own. The south-western part of the range from the frontier as far as the Mo may be designated the Togo range; the north-eastern part may be called the Kara-gap region.

The Togo range consists of a central ridge with outlying lateral chains on the east and west, which merge into the main range at its north-eastern end. The lateral ranges rise abruptly from the plains to considerable heights in Mt. Agu (3,370 ft.), the highest mountain in the colony, and Mt. Adaklu (2,000 ft.). Between them and the main range there are somewhat extensive plains. In the northern part this central range broadens out into plateaux divided by ravines; and at its eastern edge it finally breaks up into isolated mountains, gradually declining towards the south-east and merging into the south-eastern plateau. In the main system the highest points are Mt. Dabo (3,180 ft.), Mt. Adeja (2,630 ft.), and the Buem Mountains (2,450 ft.).

The Kara-gap region consists of a series of broad plains, lying between isolated massifs averaging about 2,500 ft. above the sea. There is a steep descent to the Kara ravine, beyond which again there is hill country.

The *north-western lowlands* are a series of broad undulating plains, rising from 500 ft. in the south to 800 ft. in the north, and traversed from north to south by the Oti, between which and the Volta the watershed is formed by a gently inclined ridge, rising from about 650 ft. in the south to 820 ft. in the north. At the north end the lowlands are defined by the Gambaga hills, a wooded sandstone range, nearly 2,000 ft. high, running east and west. On the farther side this range falls steeply to the granite plateau of Gurma.

Coast

Togoland is unfortunate in its coast, which is moreover very short in proportion to the area of the country (32 miles to 33,700 square miles). The seaboard consists of a continuous bank of sand, backed by a region of swamps and lagoons except at the western end, where Lome is situated. Lome may thus be considered the natural port of Togoland, though there is neither there nor elsewhere any harbour or any facility for the construction of one.

River Systems

The central chain divides the rivers of Togoland into two groups, namely (i) the Volta system on the west, including the rivers Kara and Keran (Kumagu), which rise, indeed, on the eastern side of the chain, but have forced their way through the Kara-gap region ; and (ii) the rivers of the south-east, draining into coastal lagoons.

(i) *The Volta System.*—This is the most important system in the colony, as the Volta with its tributary the Daka (Kulukpene, Laka) forms a considerable part of the western frontier, and the Oti, which is a left-bank tributary of the Volta, drains the northern part of the colony and the western slopes of the central mountain range.

From the confluence of the Daka to Kete-Krachi

the Volta has a fairly rocky bed. Its breadth varies very much, being 450–500 yds. at Kete-Krachi, and 270 yds., with a depth of 3–6 ft., lower down near Kpandu. Even below Kete-Krachi rapids are fairly common, but do not prevent small vessels ascending to that place. The Daka is remarkable for the number and sharpness of its bends, and it rises extremely high during floods.

The Volta in its lower course receives three considerable tributaries on the left bank, the Asukoko, the Dea, and the Shavoe.

But the most important river of this system, so far as Togoland is concerned, is the Oti, which rises in the French Sudan, traverses the eastern part of the Salaga lowlands, and ultimately joins the Volta below Kete-Krachi. It flows between banks varying from 20 to over 300 ft. in height, has a wide flood-area, is full of rocks and shoals, and follows a course even more winding than that of the Daka. Its right-bank tributaries are insignificant, but on the left bank the Kumagu, Kara, Mo, and Bassa are considerable obstacles to land travel, especially the Kara, which is impassable during floods.

(ii) *The South-Eastern Rivers.*—Of these the chief are the Shio, Haho, and Monu. The first two in their lower middle courses have numerous channels and almost form deltas. The Monu, which is the most important of this group, and in its lower reaches marks the frontier, rises among the Chaujo mountains in the Kara-gap region. At Kpeji it is 90 yds. wide, while below this it is enlarged by tributaries to a considerable size. It rises very high during floods.

During the rainy season the rivers of Togoland are very much swollen and often prohibit communication, while during the dry season they often disappear partially or entirely, except in the mountain regions.

(3) Climate

The climate of Togoland is of a monsoon type, conditioned by the Sahara on the north and the Atlantic on the south, although local conditions modify it to a considerable extent.

Temperature.—Although Togoland lies north of the Equator, its temperature is lower in the south than in the north, except in so far as the temperature is affected by the altitude. The highest mean temperature is recorded in February and March, when it averages 82° F. (28° C.) at Kpeme on the coast, 79° F. (26° C.) at Bismarckburg in the central chain, and over 82° F. (28° C.) at Sansane-Mangu in the north. In March and April there are violent storms, marking the beginning of the rainy season, and the temperature falls. In July and August the minimum mean temperature is reached, and the average at Kpeme falls to 75° F. (24° C.) and at Bismarckburg to 70° F. (21° C.).

Rainfall.—The rainfall is least on the coast and greatest in the mountain region of the south-west, where the yearly average is about 60 in. On the coast the rainy seasons, of which there are two, extend over four or five months, the heavy rains falling between April and July, the lesser rains in September and November, while August is practically rainless. The yearly average is 26 in. (665 mm.) at Kpeme and 37 in. (943 mm.) at Sebe. In the south-west heavy rain falls between March and November, but there is usually a noticeable remission in August. Here the yearly average is 53 in. (1,353 mm.) at Kpandu and 56 in. (1,414 mm.) at Voravora. The secondary rainy season is somewhat uncertain, especially on the coast, and its failure has a markedly bad effect on production.

In the north, where there is only one rainy season,

almost all the rain falls in the period April to October. The average at Sansane-Mangu is 44 in. (1,120 mm.).

Winds.—In summer winds from the south and south-west prevail over all Togoland. On the coast these are frequent during winter also, but farther inland winds between north and east predominate. The Harmattan, a very dry north-east wind bearing red dust, blows between November and March, and there are sudden violent storms, which blow from the quarter between north-east and south-east.

(4) SANITARY CONDITIONS

The most unhealthy parts of the colony are the banks of the rivers and coastal lagoons, the least unhealthy the central mountain chain and the Gambaga hills in the north. Togoland is nowhere more than moderately healthy, and is unsuited for permanent occupation by white colonists.

The most serious disease is malaria, which occurs even in the mountains. It is at its worst in the rainy season and during the transition from the rainy season to the dry. The dry months are comparatively free from malaria; but, on the other hand, it is precisely during the dry months that cerebro-spinal meningitis is most frequent. This disease is especially prevalent in the northern parts of Togoland, where it becomes at times epidemic. Another widespread disease is dysentery, of which there are also occasional epidemics. Sleeping-sickness is endemic in certain regions of southern Togoland, but there appears to be no very great yearly death-rate from this cause. Epidemics of small-pox are common; leprosy and venereal diseases are very widespread, and there are innumerable cases of minor affections of the skin. In the central chain, the most healthy part of the colony, various pulmonary complaints, including tuberculosis, and also goitre, are prevalent. Complaints due to parasites (Guinea worm, filaria, and others) are extremely common, and there are serious or fatal diseases which are only known by their native names (*mahalabi, fadu*).

Most of these diseases can be avoided by Europeans with the exercise of proper care. In spite of the high degree of humidity of the atmosphere, which is very trying to the white man's constitution, there is ordinarily a yearly death-rate of no more than 2 to 4 per cent. among the whites, though in specially wet years or during epidemics the figure rises considerably.

The supply of water depends largely on the rains. The smaller rivers dry up entirely or are reduced to a few puddles for a portion of the year. Parts of Togoland, nearly as far south as the coast, are periodically uninhabitable for want of water. The fact that, except in the mountain regions, where the rivers have running water all the year, the supply of water is largely obtained from stagnant pools, perhaps accounts to a considerable extent for the bad hygienic conditions of the colony.

(5) Race and Language

Race

The whole of Togoland falls within the Sudan negro area, though there is a certain Hamitic admixture. Nevertheless the ethnographical map of the colony is extremely complicated.

In the south the most important people are the Ewes, who have spread across the central chain at its south-western end and reach as far north as Kpandu, Ele, and Glai. As far as latitude 7° 20′ north they have absorbed practically all the older populations, whose speech remains only in a few insignificant 'islands'. In the eastern part of the southern region, especially to the east of the Monu, the Dahomey branches of the race, with local dialects, are found.

North of the Ewes is the mixed zone. In the western part of this region are various tribes, speaking Chi dialects, grouped together under the name Nbangye, the principal tribe being known as the Guams.

North again of the central mixed zone are groups of Sudan peoples. Many of the tribes are akin to those of the Mossi kingdom, and speak languages of the same family, which is akin to the Fula (Fulbe).[1] There are also representatives of the Mandingos, the conquerors of the Mossis. These northern peoples are mainly Mohammedan. They form strong tribes, and have a tendency to centralize into warlike kingdoms. In the west, near the Oti River, is the powerful Mohammedan kingdom of Dagomba, with its capital at Yendi. This country is now divided between Togoland and the Gold Coast. The Tim group in the north-east and eastern centre must also be mentioned, while north of Dagomba lies the country occupied by the Chakosis, a settled agricultural race who extend to the borders of Gurma. The Chakosis may be considered as the aboriginal race, while the Fulas (Fulbes), the trading Hausas, the Dahomeyans, and others in the same district are intruders.

Language

In the absence of the necessary anthropological and historical data, the chief principle of ethnological division is at present afforded by language, and even of this the study is very far from being sufficiently developed. Knowledge of Ewe, the language spoken over a great part of southern Togoland, is fairly far advanced; but for the central and northern parts of

[1] See *Journal of the Royal Anthropological Institute*, 1913, pp. 388–9 ; Sir H. H. Johnston, 'Ethnography of Africa.'

the colony the evidence consists of native statements about local history and isolated words and phrases.

Hausa is in general use as a trade language in the north-west and Ewe in the south-eastern half of the colony ; intermediate is a zone where Chi is spoken in the west and Tim in the east, and these two languages somewhat overlap the Hausa and Ewe zones.   A kind of English is used to a certain extent on the coast.

(6) POPULATION

The chief causes of agglomerations of population in particular spots are opportunities for trade (e. g. Kete-Krachi and Sokode, and more recently Lome and Anecho), comparative fertility of the soil (e. g. the middle Oti), and regularity of the rains (e. g. North Togo plains) ; also facilities for refuge in the case of weak tribes (e. g. the Siu mountains), and command of communications for strong ones (e. g. Chaujo). The Hausa traders appear chiefly in the north of the colony, but they are also found as far south as the coast. The Fulas, who are keepers of stock, are confined to the north.

Europeans.—In 1913 the white population numbered 368, of whom 320 were Germans, mostly officials, traders, and missionaries ; only 2 per cent. were planters. The white population is almost completely confined to the coast.

Natives.—The numbers of the native population, arrived at partly by estimate and partly by enumeration, are said to be somewhat over 1,000,000. These figures do not include the coloured non-native population, so that presumably several thousands of Hausas and Fulas (Fulbes) must be added. The average density per square mile is thus about 30 ; but the population is by no means equally spread in all parts of the area. In 1908–9 there was reckoned to be a little under 20 per cent. of the total population in the coastal region, including the oil-palm zone, that is in 5 per cent. of the superficial area; a little over 20 per cent. in Middle Togo, 55 per cent. of the area; and the remaining 60 per cent. in the north, 40 per cent. of the area. Very little is known of the numbers of the individual tribes.

II. POLITICAL HISTORY

CHRONOLOGICAL SUMMARY

1469. First Portuguese exploration of the Gold Coast.

1482. Erection of fort at S. Jorge da Mina.

1680. Expedition sent out by Elector of Brandenburg.

1683. Foundation of Grossfriedrichsburg Fort.

1687. Brandenburg Settlement at Arguin.

1718. Sale of Brandenburg possessions to Holland.

1840. German mission founded.

1884 (January). German cruiser visits Little Popo.

1884 (July). German flag hoisted at Lome.

1885 (December). First Franco-German Boundary Agreement.

1886 (July). First Anglo-German Boundary Agreement.

1888. Expedition of K. von François to the Upper Volta.

1888 (March). Further Anglo-German Boundary Agreement. Neutral zone established.

1889. Foundation of Bismarckburg.

1890. Foundation of Misahöhe.

1890. (July 1). Western boundary of Togoland laid down in the Heligoland Treaty.

1894. Foundation of station at Kete-Krachi.

1894. Agreement with England as to a United Customs District east of the Volta.

1895. Gruner's attempt to reach the Niger.

1897. Convention with France as to eastern boundary.

1899. Boundary laid down in the 'Samoa' Treaty (neutral sphere partitioned).

1904. Lome–Palime Railway begun.

1904. Final settlement of Anglo-German boundary.

1905. Horn dismissed from Governorship.

1906. Debate in Reichstag on misgovernment.

1912. Final settlement of Franco-German boundary.

1914. Completion of wireless station at Kamina.

1914. Occupation of Togoland by British and French forces.

(1) Early History

There is little early history relating to Togoland. The name Togo is modern, belonging originally to the lake opening out of the lagoon, and to the town on its shores. In the Ewe language the name meant 'Behind the Sea', and was extended by the Germans to the whole country, owing to the fact that Nachtigal's first treaty in 1884 was made with the Chief of Togo.

(2) The Portuguese Period

The Portuguese in the fifteenth century were busy in settling and trading on the Guinea Coast. They founded S. Jorge da Mina (Elmina) in what is now the Gold Coast. 'Cape Coast Castle' was originally in Portuguese Cabo Corso. They also had intimate relations with Benin; but on the actual Togo coast they seem to have made no settlement. Yet traces of their influence and blood are found in names and physical characteristics. The name Popo, in Great and Little Popo, represents the Portuguese *povo* ('people'). Porto Seguro must also have been named by the Portuguese, and there is little doubt that the coco-nut palm was introduced on this coast by the Portuguese. But neither they nor any other of the numerous European nations who built forts or trading stations on the Guinea Coast, whether English, French, Dutch, Danes, or Brandenburgers, appear to have settled on the strip of coast between Lome and Great Popo.

(3) The Brandenburg Settlement in the Seventeenth Century

Although the Brandenburg trade settlements on the coast of Guinea do not come within the limits of Togoland, but in those of the Gold Coast Colony, they require some notice as the early though futile attempts of a State, which has since developed into the Kingdom of Prussia and the German Empire, to extend its influence to Africa. Frederick William, the 'Great Elector' of Brandenburg, acting under the advice of a Dutch shipowner named Benjamin Raule, sent out in 1680 an expedition under the Dutch captain Blonck, who made a treaty with three chiefs at Cape Three Points, by which they placed themselves and their dominions under the protection of Brandenburg, permitted the erection of a fort, and promised to trade only with the ships of Brandenburg. In 1682 the Brandenburg African Company was founded to develop this trade. In 1683 possession of the ceded lands was taken by an expedition under von der Gröben, and a fort called Grossfriedrichsburg was built. During its erection von der Gröben was attacked by the Dutch, who regarded these competitors with no complacency; but apparently one discharge of a cannon was enough to repulse them. This new dominion was afterwards extended by an entrenchment and two other forts (Sophie Louise and Taccarary). In 1687 a further settlement was made in West Africa, farther north, on the island of Arguin, south of Cape Blanco (formerly a Portuguese possession, and now in the French sphere), and the neighbouring coast.

The new undertakings did not prosper. The expenditure was greater than the income, and the opposition of the Dutch was successful. The Elector was, it seems, ready to declare war against Holland on this ground; but his death in 1688 put an end to these projects. The Company was neglected, and fell into bankruptcy. The officers employed in Africa were mainly Dutch; and, probably because they saw that no interest was taken by the new King of Prussia, Frederick William I, in this undertaking, they schemed for the sale of the Brandenburg rights to their own country. The King tried to obtain a higher price than the Dutch were willing to pay, but finally disposed of the African possessions to the Dutch West Indian Company in 1718 for 7,200 ducats and 12 negroes. Arguin was sold to the French in 1721, and thus the early Prussian undertakings in Africa came to an end.

(4) Frederick the Great's Opposition to Colonization

Frederick the Great, who could have embarked on colonial enterprises if he had chosen to do so, was opposed to them *in toto*, and rejected at once a proposal laid before him in 1762 for a settlement between Benin and Cameroon. He was more concerned with pushing German colonization on the Polish frontier.

(5) German Annexation of Togoland in 1884

As its early name of Slave Coast indicates, the district was a resort of slavers ; and in this connexion stations were established throughout the lagoons by traders of various nationalities. With the passing of the slave trade, a new generation of British, French, and German merchants arose, who about 1880 founded business houses at different points on the coast and began to build factories. Misunderstandings between the rival enterprises were frequent ; and a state of affairs came into existence which was discreditable to all the nationalities concerned.

At this point a new and dominant factor came into play. The ideas and motives that dominated the movement towards overseas expansion in Germany took definite shape in 1882 in the foundation of the *Deutscher Kolonialverein* ; and Bismarck, secure in the knowledge of a consolidated Germany, was gradually becoming inclined to listen to the new society and to the claims of the German traders and missionaries in different parts of Africa.

This, then, was the position when the Senates of Hamburg and Bremen, which were directly interested in the West African coast-trade, demanded the dispatch of a German warship for the safeguarding of German commercial interests in Togoland. The *Sophie* accordingly arrived off Little Popo on January 30, 1884, and, proceeding thence along the coast, collected native hostages and obtained from the chiefs a petition asking for German protection against England.

The various parties among the tribes had been enlisting the support of the British and German merchants respectively in a contest among competitors for the chieftainship of Togo. A disturbance which took place gave the Germans their opportunity. One of the rivals visited the *Sophie*, then anchored at Great Popo, and obtained the support of her men and guns. The hostages taken were carried away to Germany, where they were duly inoculated with the idea of German strength and greatness; and they returned with Nachtigal on the *Möwe* on July 5, 1884. A treaty was then made with the Chief of Togo, who was recognized by Germany; a German Protectorate was declared; and the German flag was hoisted on July 5 and 6 at Bagida and Lome. This was the first annexation made in Africa on behalf of the German Empire.

Negotiations with France and England followed, resulting in the next two years in the settlement of boundaries with both States.

(6) BOUNDARY WITH DAHOMEY

With France provision was made in the protocol of December 24, 1885; and the boundary between Togo and Dahomey was defined on February 1, 1887, in accordance with the recommendations of Commissioners. This arrangement carried it as far north as 9° N. latitude; and a convention of July 23, 1897,[1] extended it to 11° N. latitude. Subsequently delimitation was carried out, and was finally confirmed by a declaration of September 28, 1912. French claims on Little Popo (now called Anecho) and Porto Seguro were given up in exchange for the so-called Dembiah Colony in French Guinea, called Colinsland, after a German merchant named Colin.

(7) BOUNDARY WITH GOLD COAST COLONY

Between Togo and the Gold Coast Colony the coast boundary was fixed by a joint Commission on July 14, 1886; and recommendations for extending it inland, which carried the boundary as far north as the confluence of the Volta and Daka rivers, were sanctioned in March 1888. From this point a neutral zone was established on both sides of the Volta, which was maintained in the Treaty of July 1, 1890 (the Heligoland Treaty).[2] This treaty defined the boundary up to the neutral zone; but by a later convention of November 14, 1899 (the 'Samoa' Treaty), this neutral territory was divided between the Gold Coast Colony and Togoland as far north as 9° north latitude.[3] After some further negotiations, including the Convention of September 26/December 2, 1901, the boundary was demarcated and recognized by an exchange of Notes on June 25, 1904,[4] as far north as the southern boundary of the French Sudan, i. e. about 11° 10′ north latitude, which should be taken as a recognition by both British

---

[1] See Appendix II, p. 50.
[2] See Appendix I, p. 50.
[3] See Appendix III, p. 51.
[4] See Appendix IV, p. 52.

and German Governments of the French boundary (continuing the line laid down for the Gold Coast Colony and the French Sudan by the Anglo-French exchange of Notes of March 18/April 25, 1904).

(8) Expeditions to explore and conquer the Interior

The German Government immediately set to work to organize expeditions into the interior, with a view to securing rights and obtaining treaties from the native chiefs. These expeditions followed each other in quick succession from 1887 to 1890. All were military in character, and prepared to crush opposition. The most important of them was under K. von François, who followed the Volta River to the town of Salaga, thence to Yendi, the capital of Dagomba, and on towards the Sultanates of Mossi and Gambaga. He returned to the coast by Bismarckburg, which had in the meantime been founded by Wolff in the hill country of Adele. He had started on a second journey, when he was recalled to take command of the newly-raised force in South-West Africa. Von François' expedition was followed by the agreement with England as to the neutralization of the Dagomba country.

The expedition under Wolff began with the founding of Bismarckburg as a starting-point for the subjugation of the eastern districts. Wolff also visited Salaga, and, returning to the east, explored Chaujo as far as the northern limits of Dahomey, where he died. His successor, Kling, endeavoured to reach the Niger through Borgu, in the north of Dahomey, but could not overcome the opposition he met with, and was driven back to the coast.

Bismarckburg was soon found to be unsuitable for the site of an important centre ; and, a route towards

Kete-Krachi, from Lome over a low pass, having been discovered by Herold and secured by the post of Misahöhe, the inland centre was moved to Kete-Krachi, which soon grew into an important trading post. Disputes with the British colony as to customs duties in the Volta region led to the proclamation (in 1894) of a united customs district of all territories of both Powers which lay to the east of the Volta. This arrangement lasted for ten years, but was repudiated by Germany in 1904 ; and protective duties were set up in the interest of the trade of Lome and the Lome–Palime Railway.

(9) ATTEMPTS TO EXTEND TO THE NIGER

The movements of the French towards the interior in their Dahomey expedition of 1892–3, together with the British Ashanti expedition in 1895–6, were accompanied by further German attempts to extend the Togoland territory to the north ; and a serious endeavour was made to reach the Niger bend. This expedition in 1894 was secretly organized (' in aller Stille ', says Zimmermann), but was delayed at the outset by the unfitness of the leader first chosen. Gruner was then appointed, and nearly reached the Niger by forced marches in February 1895, making treaties with several chiefs ; but the French had been beforehand with them, and Gruner had to return to Togoland. On his march northwards in 1897 he forced his way through the neutral territory of Dagomba, by Salaga and Yendi, to Sansane-Mangu, where he founded a German station.

(10) FRONTIERS LAID DOWN IN THE TREATY OF 1899

This breach of the neutrality of Dagomba led to the termination of the agreement with England. The negotiations which followed ended with the convention known as the 'Samoa' Treaty (November 14, 1899). The neutral block was divided between the Gold Coast Colony and Togoland, the former keeping the west side of the Daka River, and the latter the east side. By this arrangement Salaga and Gambaga, north of it, which the Germans claimed, fell inside the English sphere, as well as the territory of the Mamprussi and the town of Morozugu; while Yendi, with the most important part of Dagomba, the territory of the Chakosis, and Konkomba, were recognized as within the German boundary.

The Germans were very anxious to enlarge their coast-line by the acquisition of what they called ' the Volta triangle', i. e. the country from the actual Togoland boundary up to the lower Volta and its mouth, with the port of Kwitta. Their West African merchants were eager to obtain this object by the surrender of Samoa; but the German Government would not agree to give up its hold on the Pacific, and the exchange was not made.

The fact was that the port of Kwitta gave greater facilities than any on the German coast, with its surf-beaten line of sand in front of a chain of lagoons. On the French side, too, trade was drawn away by the construction of a pier at Kotonu, the terminus of the Dahomey system of railways. To counteract this tendency, a pier was built at Lome, which was connected by a coast-line with Little Popo (Anecho), in order that the trade of the latter might not be altogether ruined. The railway from Lome to Palime was begun in 1904, and a road was constructed over the Misahöhe Pass to Kete-Krachi. The treaty for a customs union on the Gold Coast border was, as already mentioned, repudiated in this same year and a new tariff imposed.

(11) Occupation of Yendi and Chaujo

After the fighting of the Gruner expedition (in 1896–97) and of the expedition led by von Massow, Yendi, the capital of Dagomba, was taken ; and another invasion of the same territory took place, in the course of which Bafilo and Sansane-Mangu were taken ; Kabure was also taken by the army on its return march.

In effecting the submission of the more independent tribes of the eastern border, great use was made of the Chaujo (Tschaudjo) tribe, an invading race of mounted warriors who had taken possession of this hill country. Dr. Kersting had made an alliance with the chief of this tribe, and through it subdued the other indigenous races. In these hills Kersting founded the sanatorium of Alejo Kadara, about 2,500 ft. above the sea, amid very pleasant surroundings.

(12) Events of 1914

Togoland was occupied by a joint British and French force in August 1914. For purposes of administration it was temporarily divided into two portions, of which the western part, up to the Haho River and Misahöhe, which included Lome and the Volta basin, with the Kete-Krachi district and the part of the Mangu-Yendi district forming the Dagomba kingdom west of the Oti, was under British administration ; while the eastern region including the Monu basin, and also the more northern territories bordering on the French Sudan and Dahomey, were placed under that of France. The occupation of the town of Yendi, in Dagomba, on August 22, 1914, was joyfully greeted by the chiefs and people of Dagomba ; and the old King expressed the wish ' to be reunited with the Dagomba country situated in the northern territories ' (of the Gold Coast

Colony) ' under the British flag and the protection of His Majesty King George V '.[1]　The arrangements made in consequence of the Treaty of Versailles, by which Germany ceded Togoland, fall outside the scope of this series.

[1] Report on the occupation of Yendi, enclosure in No. 16 of October 10, 1914, from the Governor, Gold Coast Colony, to the Secretary of State. (*Correspondence relating to the military operations in Togoland.* Cd. 7872. April 1915.)

III. SOCIAL AND POLITICAL CONDITIONS

(1) RELIGIOUS

THE great mass of the population is heathen, and is almost entirely under the influence of fetishism. This applies more strictly to the southern and central districts. The influence and power of the fetish priests are very great. Dipongo and Dikpelen, in Adele, near Bismarckburg, are the most important centres of this influence. Mohammedanism is widespread in the north, and an active propaganda is carried on by the Hausa traders. But here too fetishism is followed by the mass of the people, who are Moslems on the surface only. There is little genuine following of Islam except among the ruling families.

In the south the Christian missions have acquired a good deal of influence. One German mission has existed in Togo since 1840. An English Wesleyan mission has also been long established ; and there is a Roman Catholic (German) mission with several stations.

(2) POLITICAL

After its first annexation Togoland was administered by Imperial Commissioners down to 1891, the post being held first by Falkenthal, and afterwards by von Zimmerer (who left to take up the Governorship of Cameroon). Von Puttkamer, afterwards notorious in Cameroon, became Commissioner in December 1891, and held the higher dignity of *Landeshauptmann* from 1893 till 1895. Togoland was then raised to a Governorship, the Governor being assisted by a secretary, an inspector of customs, and an unofficial council of seven members.

The post of Governor was held by A. Köhler (at first *Landeshauptmann* and Governor from 1898), 1895–1902 (died suddenly) ; W. Horn, 1902–5 (dismissed for misconduct) ; Count J. von Zech, 1905–10 ; E. Brechner, 1911–12 ; Duke Adolf Friedrich zu Mecklenburg, 1912. The misdeeds of Horn and Schmidt (local Governor of Atakpame) are described in *Treatment of Natives in the German Colonies*, No. 114 of this series. It was by men of this type that fear and hatred of the German Government were maintained, with the resultant steady emigration. to the Gold Coast, to which the last Governor, the Duke of Mecklenburg, who visited the Gold Coast, bore witness.

The country was divided into administrative districts in 1903, as follows : the southern districts of Lome, Misahöhe-Kpandu, and Togo ; the central districts of Atakpame, Sokode-Bassari, and Kete-Krachi ; and the northern districts of Sansane-Mangu and Yendi.

(3) Educational

A number of schools were maintained by Government and missions. The strictly Government schools were only two in number, with 312 students ; a technical school for the art of dyeing and an agricultural school at Nuatya were also maintained. The missions, supported by the Government, kept up 368 schools, with 14,653 students. They were practical in their nature, mainly devoted to training pupils as artisans. The Government schools were chiefly engaged in training pupils as clerks and interpreters. Every effort was made to inspire German feelings among the population ; everywhere the children were taught to wave German flags and sing the German National Anthem. Formerly the mission schools taught English mainly, as it was the most useful language on the Guinea Coast, but German took its place throughout. The Mohammedan propaganda in the north is sometimes accompanied by schools in which the doctrines of Islam are taught.

IV. ECONOMIC CONDITIONS

(A) MEANS OF COMMUNICATION

(1) INTERNAL

(a) *Roads, Caravan Routes, Paths, and Tracks*

LOME and Anecho are connected with the chief inland towns by good roads, some of which are metalled in places, drained, bridged, and carefully constructed. Good roads also link up the inland towns, especially in the southern part of the country. In 1913 there were in all 755 miles of road suitable for motor traffic. The chief motor roads are : (1) Lome–Atakpame–Sokode, over 200 miles ; (2) Lome–Misahöhe–Kete-Krachi–Sansane-Mangu. There are many native paths.

Except in the south, the internal trade of Togoland is carried on entirely by caravans. Some of these are local, but others are large caravans on their way across Togoland to and from the kola-nut markets of Ashanti, which do minor business within Togoland to cover the expenses of their journey.

(b) *Rivers and Lagoons*

The rivers of Togoland had not been thoroughly investigated up to the end of 1913. Small vessels can ascend the section of the Volta which touches German territory as far as Kete-Krachi. The stream itself is in British territory, and the Gold Coast Government had in 1915 seven ferries across it.

The Oti, the chief tributary of the Volta in Togoland, was thought by the Germans to be capable of development as an inland waterway. Canoes can ascend as far as Sansane-Mangu.

The Daka can be navigated by small vessels in its lower course.

The Monu is navigable for about 150 kilometres· (93 miles).

The Haho is entirely in German territory and ends in the Togo Lagoon. It is navigable at the mouth for light canoes.

There is inland water communication for canoes and small motor craft along the lagoons all the way from Anecho to Great Popo in Dahomey.

(c) *Railways*

The railways of Togoland do not at present form part of any trans-continental system; but although there does not seem to be any definite proposal so far, it is natural to suppose that its lines may eventually be connected with the French trans-Sahara system. It is not as yet in railway communication with any of the neighbouring territories.

Railways of metre gauge have been constructed (1) along the coast from Anecho to Lome (27 miles); (2) from Lome to Palime, at the foot of the ascent to Misahöhe (74 miles); (3) from Lome to Atakpame (102 miles).

These railways were built by, and leased to, the Deutsche Kolonial-Eisenbahn-Bau- und Betriebs-Gesell-schaft, Berlin. The company's lease was about to fall in at the end of 1914; and, had the Germans remained, the Government intended to assume control of the railways.

The following tables [1] show the main features of the recent working of the three railways, and also of the

---

[1] From the *Statistisches Jahrbuch*, 1915.

pier service at Lome port, which is in connexion with
them :

1912

	Lome-Anecho.	Lome-Palime.	Lome-Atakpame.	Lome Pier.
Gross Receipts, £	5,639	23,470	18,010	16,780
Working Expenses, £ . . .	3,860	8,586	12,180	11,660
Percentage of Expenses to Receipts .	68·5	36·6	67·6	69·4
Passengers carried	70,139	75,082	43,740	3,677
Tons of goods carried . . .	8,153	14,733	10,197	36,123

1913

	Lome-Anecho.	Lome-Palime.	Lome-Atakpame.	Lome Pier.
Gross Receipts, £	5,135	19,053	18,745	14,690
Working Expenses, £ . . .	3,904	8,270	11,451	8,950
Percentage of Expenses to Receipts .	76	43·4	61	60·9
Passengers carried	69,977	68,004	40,768	2,957
Tons of goods carried . . .	6,906	13,261	12,720	32,497

The volume of traffic in 1913 suffered from the falling
prices of the produce market.

The line along the coast from Lome to Anecho, which
is much used by the natives, is conspicuous on account
of its low capital cost (£2,060 per mile), and its large
passenger traffic. On the other hand, its working
expenses are heavy, and its receipts from goods traffic
are surprisingly low. This is due to the fact that
through goods are carried free over the line, and the
freights are charged on entry and departure, according
to the tariff of the pier at Lome. The inland line from
Lome to Palime shows a particularly low ratio of
expenses to receipts, viz. 43·4 per cent. It should be
noted that 1911 was the first working year for the
greater part of the Lome–Atakpame line.

The total rolling stock of the Togoland lines in
1913–14 was as follows :

Locomotives	16
Passenger coaches . . .	15
Post and parcels wagons . .	5
Covered goods wagons . . .	70
Open trucks	132

(d) Posts, Telegraphs, and Telephones

The postal service in Togoland, as in the other German colonies, was directly administered as an Imperial service by the Imperial Post Office in Berlin. At the end of 1913 there were twenty-three post offices, of which five had telephone exchanges. In 1912 the number of letters handled was half a million, and the telephone service dealt with over 50,000 messages.

At the end of 1913 the colony had 684 miles of telegraph line. Togoland is in telegraphic connexion both with the Gold Coast and with Dahomey.

(2) EXTERNAL

(a) Ports

Togoland has no harbours, but at Lome there are good landing facilities. Vessels can lie within a mile of the pier. For the greater part of the year there is a strong easterly current, and during the winter there is a very heavy surf, the *kalema*, breaking on the beach even when there is no wind. Cargo is transferred in surf-boats of from four to six tons, from which it is taken by cranes into trucks on the pier. Statistics of this traffic are given with those of the railways above.

The percentage of German shipping entering Lome increased steadily, as the following table [1] shows:

Year.	German.		Per cent.	Other Countries.		Per cent.	Total No.
	No.	Tons.		No.	Tons.		
1909 .	188	399,084	57·8	181	290,920	42·2	369
1910 .	190	365,697	63·4	135	209,798	36·6	325
1911 .	171	380,810	67·1	104	186,421	32	275
1912 .	176	414,731	72·5	82	157,101	27·5	258

There is another open anchorage at Anecho, farther east.

[1] From *Die deutsche Flagge*, 1912.

(b) *Shipping Lines*

Lome was a port of call for the Woermann, Hamburg–Amerika and Hamburg–Bremer–Afrika lines, which worked in combination.

The British share of the traffic went to the British and African Steam Navigation Co. and the African Steamship Co., both belonging to Elder, Dempster & Co.

The French share of the traffic went to Fraissinet & Co. and Faure & Co.

(c) *Telegraphic and Wireless Communication*

Togoland was the first of the German colonies to be connected by cable with the Fatherland. This took place on January 2, 1913, when the German South American Cable Company brought their cable from Monrovia ashore at Lome. Togoland is also connected by cable with Duala in Cameroon.

Before the late war the Germans had two wireless stations in Togoland, a large one inland at Kamina, and a local one at Togblekof near Lome. Togoland was in wireless communication with Germany and with the other German colonies in Africa.

(B) INDUSTRY

(1) Labour

Nothing can be said about labour supply in the north of Togoland, for the Germans had not penetrated effectively beyond the mountains. In the southern districts they relied partly upon hired and partly upon forced labour. Natives who could not pay the head-tax were required instead to give twelve days' labour a year on public works. Up to 1910 this practice was common ; but since that date the natives have tended increasingly to pay the tax in money, and the supply of labour has diminished proportionately.

(2) Agriculture

(a) *Products of Commercial Value*

Not more than 38 per cent. of Togoland is under cultivation, and the soil for the most part is poor. There are fertile areas in the river valleys and below certain hills composed of hornblende gneiss, such as Mount Agu. The greater part of the country is covered with bush, in which are found some useful wild products.

The principal *vegetable products* of economic importance are as follows :

Beans of various kinds are cultivated, especially in the north. These are mainly for local consumption, though there is a small export across the land frontiers.

Cassava (*manioc*) is obtained from the root of *Manihot utilissima*, which is widely grown by the natives, especially in the south and centre of the colony. The quantity exported in 1911 was 1,091,537 kg., value £4,452. Nearly all of this went to neighbouring territories, none to Europe.

Cocoa is grown in the Misahöhe district, and its cultivation is becoming increasingly popular. The quantity exported rose from 334,904 kg. in 1913 to 457,000 kg. in 1915.

Coco-nut palm cultivation was encouraged by the German Government. Near the coast a very large number of trees have been planted, and from Lome to Anecho there are many small plantations owned by natives. The fruit is eaten locally, and the natives use the wood and leaves for building and a variety of domestic purposes. The export of copra has been rapidly increasing, and rose from 130,792 kg. in 1913 to 351,000 kg. in 1916. About 8,000 Togoland nuts are required to produce one ton of copra.

Cotton is widely cultivated, especially in the centre of the colony along the Oti and in the south round Atakpame, Nuatya, and other centres. There are, however, only three European plantations on which cotton is grown. In 1913 there were twelve ginneries driven by machine power. Expert opinion considers that cotton could not be successfully grown in the north, and that even in the centre its cultivation is not very profitable. In fact, considering the efforts made by the Germans to develop cotton-growing, the production is disappointing. However, the quantities exported increased fairly consistently from 1906 to 1912, when they reached a total of 550,696 kg., value £25,000 ; and, though in 1913 the amount was smaller (503,368 kg.), the cotton was of better quality, and therefore the value was higher (£29,000). Almost the whole export was to Germany.

Dukhn (spiked millet), one of the most important crops of tropical Africa, is grown widely by the natives in the north.

Dura (tall millet) is grown throughout the north, along the Monu, and round Misahöhe, and is one of the principal foods of the natives.

Fruits are abundant, and Sir Harry Johnston suggests that the export of dried bananas might be profitable.

Ground-nuts are the staple product of the north, but are also grown in many other parts. The quantity exported in 1911 was 130,747 kg., value £1,176. Almost the whole export was across the land frontiers. In view of the commercial value of the ground-nut as a source of edible oil, its cultivation might with advantage be further developed.

The *kapok* tree is cultivated and also occurs in a wild state near the coast. Kapok received special attention from the German Government, especially in the north. The Sokode district seems to suit it particularly well.

The natives collected the kapok, and either paid their taxes with it or sold it to the local commissioner. The whole export before the war went to Germany, and was rising steadily. In 1913 the quantity exported was 9,627 kg., value £472.

Maize is grown everywhere except in parts of the valley of the Oti. Much is consumed in Togoland, and up to 1914 the rest went mainly to neighbouring territories. In 1916, however, large quantities were shipped from the British zone to Europe, upwards of 5,000,000 kg., value £24,000, going to the United Kingdom.

Oil-palms flourish near the coast, and are also found, though less plentifully, in the centre of the colony. About 3,000 square kilometres are devoted to their cultivation. Their oil and kernels form the most important articles of export.

Piassava fibre is obtained from the palm *Raphia vinifera*, which occurs widèly in Togoland. There was no export to Europe before the war; but Togoland should be able to produce enough to make any country possessing it independent of foreign supplies. A fibrous by-product is obtained, which would be a good substitute for coir.

Rubber grows wild in Togoland, and has also been cultivated in European plantations. Up to the end of 1913 rubber occupied about one-third of the total area of plantations. The variety most cultivated was Ceará rubber (*Manihot glaziovii*), which provided about 75 per cent. of the total produced.

The wild rubber is found in central Togoland, and also in an area near Misahöhe. It comes from the vine *Landolphia owariensis*, which gives a rubber known commercially as Adele balls, and also from *Ficus vogelii* and various lianas, which furnish *sayi*, an inferior rubber known in the market as Togo lumps. Coloured traders buy the rubber from the natives and sell it to European firms. Expert opinion considered that the production of wild rubber had reached its maximum at the end of 1913, the supplies of the more valuable sorts having been exhausted through the wasteful methods of the native collectors. The German Government, however, was anxious to encourage the planting of Ceará rubber in forest areas, and was distributing seed for this purpose. The amount of rubber exported annually has fluctuated considerably. In 1912 it amounted to 165,000 kg., value £48,700, while in the following year the quantity dropped to 90,000 kg., value £18,000. Since the occupation of Togoland by the Allies, the export has decreased considerably, and in 1916 only amounted to 41,600 kg.

The *shea* tree is widespread, and bears enormous numbers of nuts. Shea butter is used locally for cooking, and has an export value as an ingredient in soap and candle-making and the manufacture of margarine. The chief obstacle to the development of an industry is the difficulty of refining the fat ; but the Edible Nuts Committee think that, if this could be overcome, the trade in shea nuts and butter might become important. The cultivation of the tree in plantations would increase the amount and improve the quality of its products. Before the war all the shea butter exported went to other parts of Africa ; but shea nuts were sent to Germany and England in small quantities.

Sisal hemp has been grown successfully on one or two plantations.

Sugar takes a fairly important place in the domestic trade of Togoland, and there are small plantations of sugar-cane, owned by natives, in the Shio valley. No attempt to develop the industry has been made.

Animals.—There are no very reliable figures as to *cattle* in the Protectorate. Count von Zech (Governor,

1905–10) gives the following estimates for the districts in which there is any cattle industry :

1912.

District.	No. of Head.
Sokode–Bassari . . .	22,000
Mangu–Yendi	50,000
On the coast	1,500
Atakpame	2,700

The tsetse fly is the chief enemy of the cattle-breeder. It is common in the south, where it makes cattle-raising on a large scale impracticable. It becomes less frequent towards the centre, and is rare in the north. There, however, cattle suffer from other diseases, especially lung-sickness.

Except in the north, *horses* do not do well in Togo-land. They cannot live in or near the tsetse-fly belt, and such animals as there are seem to be small and somewhat scraggy in appearance.

Mule-breeding has been attempted at Sokode with fair success. Mules stand the climate better than horses, can do more work, do not require so much attention, and are generally more useful.

Pigs are kept by the pagan tribes of the south and centre, where Mohammedan influence has not asserted itself.

Sheep are kept in large numbers by the natives. Attempts have recently been made to improve the breed, especially by crossing them with imported animals from the Canary Islands. The offspring of this crossing appeared to be doing fairly well in 1913.

There are many goats and domestic fowls.

The export of cattle and small stock tended to increase rapidly in the last few years before the war. In 1912 there were exported to other parts of Africa 7,682 head of cattle and 14,002 of small stock. With the return of peace and the improvement of transport, this trade should be capable of considerable expansion. The export of hides and skins, on the other hand, is very small.

(b) *Methods of Cultivation*

Apart from Government plantations, the only three European planting companies in Togoland before the war were the Pflanzungsgesellschaft Kpeme, the Agu Pflanzungsgesellschaft, and the Togo Pflanzungs-Aktiengesellschaft. The first-named was on the coast, the two others on Mount Agu, in the Misahöhe district. In 1911 their total property was 10,860 hectares, of which only 991 hectares were cultivated.

Togoland is far better adapted for native than for European cultivation. The native's working expenses are reduced to a minimum, and his whole family, including the women, is employed in the fields. The people display fair intelligence and energy in agricultural pursuits, though their methods are wasteful. The native farmers uproot or burn trees and bushes, use the cleared land for temporary plantations, and, when in the course of a few years the soil becomes exhausted, move to another area and repeat the process. The presence of the tsetse fly in many parts renders impossible the use of animals for agricultural purposes. There are, however, certain districts which are free from this insect, and here the plough could be introduced, and the extent of land under cultivation could be more than doubled. The natives are beginning to realize that the land could be made to yield much richer harvests.

The Germans established an agricultural college at Nuatya for native students. Some, when they had completed their own studies, remained as teachers, while others were sent into the villages to give lectures and practical instruction in farming. Others again were started in settlements of their own, with subsidies from the Government. These settlements, however, proved unsuccessful, and their example had little influence on the natives in general. Nearly all the settlers were sent home, and in 1913 the college was converted into an experimental station for tropical research.

(c) *Forestry*

The subject of forestry was carefully studied by the German authorities. Virgin forest in Togoland is now confined to the river-banks and mountainous districts, and it was estimated by the Director of Forestry that it covers only about $1\frac{1}{2}$ per cent. of the total area of the colony. The rest has disappeared owing to the wasteful native clearing, and has been replaced by bush, mainly consisting of stunted trees, which covers about half the surface of Togoland. Unless strict measures are adopted, the remaining forests will be destroyed in a similar way.

From 1907 onwards the Government devoted much money and energy to afforestation. The results have been good almost everywhere, except along the coast, where the soil is sand with an admixture of iron. Teak has done particularly well, and has been planted at all the stations. At Atakpame, more than 25,000 teak seedlings have been planted since 1901, with satisfactory results. Mahogany also gives promise of being a valuable product. The variety *Khaya klaini* is indigenous near Misahöhe and in the Kunja Mountains. It has also been planted; but the variety preferred for cultivation is *Khaya senegalensis.* Experiments on a considerable scale were also being made with Rhodesian mahogany. Sasswood, whose timber is immune from termites and very valuable for bridges and piles, has been grown on six plantations.

Iroko wood (*Chlorophora excelsa*) is indigenous and has
also been cultivated ; it is used for building and for
railway sleepers. There are three small ebony plantations.

Apart from timber, the forests contain several products which have been described in the section on
vegetable products of commercial value (p. 32).

(d) *Land Tenure*

The land ordinance of February 2, 1911, definitely
annexed as State property all lands without an owner.
Ownerless (*herrenlos*) land was defined under the ordinance as including any land to which no person, family,
group of families, community, or tribal association
could show a title (*Eigentumsrecht*). Demarcation was
at once commenced, a non-native being entrusted by
the Governor with the protection of the rights of the
natives. A native, to establish his title, was expected
to prove continuous possession for ten years. The
district commissioners decided on questions of ownership, and were expected to safeguard the interests of
third parties. Their decisions were to be confirmed by
the Governor. Two years were allowed in which to
lodge appeals. The probable increase of population
was a factor to be taken into account. Either a sufficient area was to be allotted to the native farmers, or,
if the land had already come into the possession of the
Government, a portion was to be returned for their
use or as their property.

Land can be obtained in Togo by non-natives for
building-sites, planting, and other purposes. It belongs,
as a rule, not to individual natives but to the whole
tribe, and although they are willing in most cases to
give concessions or let upon long lease, they do not
like selling land outright. Sale is discountenanced,
though not entirely prohibited, by native law.

(3) Fisheries

There is considerable trade in dried fish between the coast and the inland districts. It seems probable that the sea-fishing industry could be developed, though the coast-line is very small. River fishing is carried on along the whole of the Volta and Oti, along the Shio, and at a number of points on the Monu and its tributaries.

(4) Minerals

The economic minerals of note in Togoland are iron ore, gold, chromite, bauxite, and limestone.

The most important mineral asset of Togoland is a large deposit of *iron ore* at Banyeli on Jole Mountain in the Bassari country. The ore is massive haematite. A sample gave the following results on analysis :

	Per cent.
Ferric oxide	89·51
Silica	9·47
Alumina	0·24
Manganese oxide	0·16
Phosphoric oxide	0·03
Sulphuric anhydride	trace
Loss on ignition	0·30

The analysis shows that this ore is of good quality. It is roughly estimated that not less than 20,000,000 tons [1] are available, containing at least 50 per cent. of metallic iron. The deposit, however, is far removed from existing transport facilities. Exportation of the ore to Europe is, therefore, out of the question ; but it might be possible to smelt it economically in the Protectorate. A limestone of good quality for use in

---

[1] This is Professor Koert's estimate in the *Report on Iron Resources of the World*, Stockholm, 1910. There is strong reason to believe that the figure should be much higher.

smelting occurs at Tokpli (see p. 42). A German expert in 1906 was of opinion that railway communication with the coast was essential, if the mines were to be profitably worked. As there are no shafts to be sunk, the cost of recovery would be very low. Moreover, there would be but little waste matter in the main ore-beds, and labour would be very cheap. As the natives have worked the ore themselves from time immemorial, they should easily be made into good miners ; and the district round Bassari is fairly thickly populated. Zimmermann estimated its population in 1911 at 50,000.

In 1911 the German Government again examined the beds at Banyeli, with a view to estimating their mineral value and the possibility of utilizing the neighbouring streams to supply a big power-station for recovering the ore electrically on the spot. No definite results were obtained, and the inquiry was to have been repeated.

Banyeli supplies the greater part of the back-country with the crude iron (*Roheisen*), which is worked up by the natives themselves into pots and pans, tools, and weapons. The production of iron ore in 1911 by native methods was stated to be 400 tons, value £3,600.

Gold occurs in very small amounts in the eastern part of the Protectorate in quartz veins traversing the gneisses, and in the recent alluvium resulting from the disintegration of these veins. It also occurs in the alluvial deposits of the head-waters of the Monu. Auriferous quartz veins with galena, pyrites, and chalcopyrite occur in the Atakpame and Sokode districts. In all cases hitherto investigated, however, the amount is very small, and gives no promise of profitable mining. Nevertheless, it is well to remember that precious metals have been found and mines are working in the Gold Coast, where the geological characteristics are similar.

Lead ore (*galena*) has been found near Atakpame.

Aluminium appears widely as bauxite on the slopes of the Agu Mountains, south-east of Misahöhe.

Chromite appears at Amuchu, but it contains only a small quantity of nickel.

Fossiliferous *limestone*, possibly of the Eocene age, is found at Tokpli on the Monu, about thirty miles from the coast. This limestone gave the following results on analysis :

								Per cent.
Calcium carbonate	.	.	.	.	.			95·59
Magnesium carbonate	.	.	.	.	.			0·76
Silica	.	.	.	.	.	.	.	1·50
Ferric oxide	.	.	.	.	.	.		1·16
Alumina	.	.	.	.	.	.		0·44

This analysis shows that the limestone is of good quality, and suitable for the manufacture of mortar and Portland cement. The occurrence of limestone is important, since it is very scarce in other West African colonies. The Government ovens at Tokpli were four months at work in 1911–12. The output was 260 cubic metres of limestone, at 45 marks per cubic metre, so that the total value was 11,700 marks. Eight prisoners and two paid labourers under a European limestone burner were employed. Wood fuel was used.

Sandstone occurs over a considerable part of the colony, and is used for building purposes.

No precious stones are reported, except *tourmaline*, which was found by a German geologist when exploring the little-known Monu River district. This is a semi-precious gem which possesses special optical properties. In value tourmalines range from a few shillings to £3 per carat.

(5) Manufactures

The most popular native handicraft in Togoland is pottery. The women are all experts in the use of the potter's wheel. No other native industry has been so little influenced by intercourse with Europeans.

The making of straw-plait, for roofing, fencing, pouches, satchels, hats, and baskets, is a small local industry. The gaily-patterned mats of Chaujo form an article of commerce. Rope-work is principally confined to the Agotime district; wood-carving on spoons, combs, vessels, and furniture, is practised in the Volta region ; ivory-carving is carried on in the south at Kpandu, Gbele, Gbi, and Nuatya ; and great drums and fetish idols are produced in Ahenkro.

The natives are skilful smiths. They also make leather from the skins of wild and domestic animals, but this is a crude material ; the good leather employed in the manufacture of saddles, bridles, shoes, satchels, and hats is obtained from the Hausa countries, or is made by the Hausas in Togoland.

Cotton-spinning is done by women, weaving by men, chiefly by Mohammedans in the north. Dyeing is carried on all over Togoland ; red dye is produced from cam-wood, black from charcoal, while blue is obtained from native indigo.

The further development of industry in Togoland, whether native or European, requires the introduction or the education of a class of semi-skilled native labour. An attempt towards this end is being made in the school for artisans set up by the Catholic missionaries from Steyl. In 1907 this school had already fifty scholars. This form of industrial mission could undoubtedly be further encouraged with advantage.

(C) COMMERCE

(1) Domestic

The main articles of domestic trade are palm oil, salt, dried fish, and other food-stuffs. In the north and centre these are distributed by caravan, but in the south the railways have opened a way for small native traders from the coast, who are now to be found at all the principal stopping-places on the lines. Syrians are now also trading in the interior. Four trade languages, Chi, Ewe, Tim, and Hausa, are in use, each within a fairly well-defined area.

There are regular cotton markets at Ho, Sagada, Nuatya, and Atakpame in the south, and at Kete-Krachi, Kpeji, Sokode, and Bassari in the centre.

In 1912 there were seven privileged companies in Togoland, each operating as a ' Kolonialgesellschaft '. These were the three plantation companies already mentioned (p. 37), the Deutsche West-Afrikanische Bank (1904), the Kolonialwirtschaftliches Komitee, and two general trading companies, the Deutsche West-Afrikanische Handelsgesellschaft (1904) and the Deutsche Togo-Gesellschaft (1906).

According to the German directories, there were before the war only twenty-three firms doing business in Togoland, including the Catholic Mission and the bookshop of the North German Mission. There are now (1917) seven English importing houses in Lome.

(2) Foreign

(a) *Exports*

The value of the total exports from 1909 to 1913 was as follows :

							£
1909	.	.	.	.	.	.	368,602
1910	.	.	.	.	.	.	361,106
1911	.	.	.	.	.	.	465,677
1912	.	.	.	.	.	.	497,945
1913	.	.	.	.	.	.	455,000

It must be remembered that many of the articles exported were in transit between the Gold Coast and Nigeria. In 1912 the amounts exported over the several frontiers were as follows :

		£
Seaboard frontier	. . . . .	427,630
Western frontier	. . . . .	46,613
Eastern frontier	. . . . .	23,702

The principal articles exported are palm products, rubber, cotton, live-stock, maize, and cocoa. Of these palm products are the most important. Even in 1913, when an exceptional drought had markedly decreased the output, they represented over 33 per cent. of the total value of exports, while in the previous year they amounted to over 48 per cent. Maize used at one time to be the chief export, but had several bad years before 1911. Since the occupation of Togoland by the Allies, the maize export has rapidly increased, and in 1916 reached a value of £29,000.

The following table [1] shows in round figures the value of the principal articles of export from 1911 to 1913 :

	1911 £	1912 £	1913 £
Cocoa	8,700	12,100	16,600
Cotton	27,700	25,700	29,100
Live-stock. . . .	20,900	30,700	16,700
Maize	8,700	11,500	14,400
Palm kernels . . .	178,900	168,900	127,900
Palm oil	84,400	70,600	25,900
Rubber	41,600	48,700	18,000

The bulk of the exports went to Germany, which in 1912 received goods to the value of £290,400 out of the total of £497,945, or nearly 60 per cent. France took £40,500, adjacent African states £162,600, and the United Kingdom £4,100 worth of goods.

[1] From the British Consular Report, 1912–13.

The following table shows the way in which in 1912 the principal articles of export were divided among the various countries of destination :

	Germany.	United Kingdom.	France.	Neighbouring African states.	Cameroon.
	£	£	£	£	£
Cocoa	12,100	—	—	—	—
Cotton	22,600	3,100	—	30	—
Live-stock	—	—	—	30,500	170
Maize	1,300	—	—	9,800	400
Palm kernels	168,400	—	—	500	—
Palm oil	29,600	—	39,600	1,400	—
Rubber	48,700	—	—	—	—

(b) Imports

The total value of the imports, including goods in transit between Nigeria and the Gold Coast, was as follows from 1909 to 1913 :

	£
1909	561,764
1910	573,306
1911	481,001
1912	571,391
1913	530,000

The values imported over each frontier in 1912 were as follows :

	£
Seaboard frontier	449,310
Western frontier	110,534
Eastern frontier	11,547
	571,391

The articles imported into Togoland are similar to those required in all West African states.   In 1912 cotton yarns and textiles were the most valuable ; next came iron goods, fish, spirits, and building materials, including cement, lime, and timber.

The following table [1] shows the value of the *principal* imports in 1912 and 1913 :

[1] From the British Consular Report, 1912–13 (No. 5417, Annual Series).

	1912 £	1913 £
Building materials	16,102	28,312
Cotton yarns and textiles	143,598	117,176
Fish	39,357	30,713
Iron goods	47,140	54,478
Leaf tobacco	14,371	14,048
Salt	11,974	7,221
Spirits	35,410	31,477
	307,952	283,425

The largest share in the import trade went to Germany, which in 1912 contributed £240,974, or 42 per cent., of which far the largest items were cotton and iron goods. The United Kingdom contributed only £95,513, or 16 per cent., mostly cotton goods, with a small quantity of iron goods. Neighbouring African states contributed £129,270, a large proportion of which consisted of fish; the United States £23,443, almost wholly tobacco; and France £20,783, of which about half was salt.

Imports from the Gold Coast both by sea and land increased after the outbreak of the late war.

(c) *Customs and Tariffs*

The customs tariff of Togoland as revised• in 1910 was still in force in 1914. An order restricting imports was issued in 1911, and amendments to the tariff were made in 1912, 1913, and 1914. Specific import duties were imposed on eight articles, while all other articles not specifically exempted paid an *ad valorem* duty of 10 per cent. The exemptions were of the usual kind, including Government stores, coal and coke, mining and agricultural machinery, medical and scientific instruments, printed books, and West African agricultural products. Of the articles specifically charged, spirits paid a duty varying upwards and downwards from 80 pfg. per litre, according to alcoholic strength, tobacco paid 50 pfg. on every 5 kg., salt paid 2 pfg. per kg.,

sugar 5 pfg. per kg. Dried, salted, and smoked fish
of African origin, a large element in the imports, paid
5 pfg. per kg. Lamp-oils were charged 5½ pfg. per
litre. Firearms paid 3 marks each, powder 1 mark
per kg.

(D) FINANCE

(1) *Public Finance*

Togoland was the only German colony in Africa that
did not receive financial aid from the Fatherland. The
total revenue of the Protectorate between 1904 and
1914 was almost 28 million marks, while the total
ordinary expenditure during the same period was
almost 38 million marks. In 1904 and 1905 there was
a huge excess of expenditure over revenue, but the
balance was readjusted in subsequent years. The
extraordinary expenditure from 1908–14 inclusive was
11 million marks (£500,000). Most of this was incurred
in 1909 and 1910. The expenditure of the latter year
was regarded as a Protectorate and not an Imperial loan.

The following table, taken from the *Statistisches
Jahrbuch*, shows the revenue and ordinary expenditure
for each year from 1909 to 1913:

	Revenue. Marks.	Expenditure. Marks.
1909	2,650,000	2,720,000
1910	3,240,000	2,540,000
1911	3,620,000	3,310,000
1912	3,510,000	3,310,000
1913	3,380,000	4,060,000

The most important source of revenue was the
customs duties, which in 1913 furnished 44 per cent.
of the total. Taxes contributed 17 per cent. only.
The most important of these, representing 82 per cent.
of the sum derived from taxation, was a head-tax of
6 marks. There were also charges for traders' licences
of various sorts. The profits from the railways and

from Lome pier represented only 14 per cent. of the total revenue.

The principal heads of revenue [1] in 1913 were, in round numbers, as follows :

	Marks.
Customs	1,788,000
Taxes	702,000
Administrative Services	305,000
Railways and pier	589,000
Total	3,384,000
Savings from former years	673,000
Grand Total	4,057,000

About half of the ordinary expenditure was generally devoted to civil administration. The figures for 1913 were as follows :

	Marks.
Civil administration	1,880,800
Miscellaneous	1,712,700
Non-recurring expenditure	463,500

(2) *Currency*

In place of the Imperial gold standard the silver mark was introduced on February 1, 1905.

Imperial silver coins were legal tender to any amount, copper coins only up to five marks. Foreign coinage was subject to strict regulations as regards circulation, exchange value, and public use. The English shilling piece was very largely used in Togo, chiefly because it had a slightly higher silver value than the mark.

(3) *Banking*

Under German rule a virtual monopoly of banking business was enjoyed by the Deutsche West-Afrikanische Bank. This business has passed to the Bank of British West Africa. The total volume of business of the Deutsche West-Afrikanische Bank in 1912–13 was 31 million marks.

[1] From the *Almanach de Gotha.*

APPENDIX

I

PROVISION OF ANGLO-GERMAN TREATY OF JULY 1, 1890, RELATING TO TOGOLAND

Article IV, Sec. 1.—The boundary between the German Protectorate of Togo and the British Gold Coast Colony commences on the coast at the marks set up after the negotiations between the Commissioners of the two countries of the 14th and 28th of July, 1886, and proceeds direct northwards to the 6° 10′ parallel of north latitude ; thence it runs along that parallel westwards till it reaches the left bank of the River Aka, ascends the mid-channel of that river to the 6° 20′ parallel of north latitude, runs along that parallel westwards to the right bank of the River Dchawe or Shavoe, follows that bank of the river till it reaches the parallel corresponding with the point of confluence of the River Deine with the Volta ; it runs along that parallel westward till it reaches the Volta ; from that point it ascends the left bank of the Volta till it arrives at the neutral zone established by the Agreement of 1888, which commences at the confluence of the River Dakka with the Volta.

Each Power engages to withdraw immediately after the conclusion of this Agreement all its officials and employés from territory which is assigned to the other Power by the above delimitation.

II

CONVENTION BETWEEN FRANCE AND GERMANY OF JULY 23, 1897, RELATING TO TOGOLAND

Art. I.—La frontière partira de l'intersection de la côte avec le méridien de l'Ile Bayol, se confondra avec ce méridien jusqu'à la rive sud de la lagune qu'elle suivra jusqu'à une distance de 100 mètres environ au delà de la pointe est de l'Ile Bayol, remontera ensuite directement au nord jusqu'à mi-distance de la rive sud et de la rive nord de la lagune ; puis suivra les sinuosités de la lagune à égale distance des deux rives jusqu'au thalweg du Mono, qu'elle suivra jusqu'au 7e degré de latitude nord.

De l'intersection du thalweg du Mono avec le 7e degré de latitude nord, la frontière rejoindra par ce parallèle le méridien de l'Ile Bayol, qui servira de limite jusqu'à son intersection avec le parallèle passant à égale distance de Bassila et de Penesoulou. De ce point, elle gagnera la Rivière Kara suivant une ligne équidistante des chemins de Bassila à Bafilo par Kirikri et de Penesoulou à Séméré par Aledjo, et ensuite des chemins de Sudu à Séméré et d'Aledjo à Séméré, de manière à passer à égale distance de Daboni et d'Aledjo ainsi que de Sudu et d'Aledjo. Elle descendra ensuite le thalweg de la Rivière Kara sur une longueur de 5 kilom. et de ce point remontera en ligne droite vers le nord jusqu'au 10e degré de latitude nord, Séméré devant dans tous´ les cas rester à la France.

De là, la frontière se dirigera directement sur un point situé à égale distance entre Djé et Gandou, laissant Djé à la France et Gandou à l'Allemagne et gagnera le 11e degré de latitude nord en suivant une ligne parallèle à la route de Sansanné-Mango à Pama et distante de celle-ci de 30 kilom. Elle se prolongera ensuite vers l'ouest sur le 11e degré de latitude nord jusqu'à la Volta blanche de manière à laisser en tout cas Pougno à la France et Koun-Djari à l'Allemagne, puis elle rejoindra par le thalweg de cette rivière le 10e degré de latitude nord qu'elle suivra jusqu'à son intersection avec le méridien 3° 52′ ouest de Paris (1° 32′ ouest de Greenwich).

III

Extracts from Anglo-German Convention of November 14, 1899, relating to Togoland

Article I.—   .   .   .   .

Great Britain recognizes as falling to Germany the territories in the eastern part of the Neutral Zone established by the Arrangement of 1888 in West Africa. The limits of the portion of the Neutral Zone falling to Germany are defined in Article V of the present Convention.

Article II.—   .   .   .   .

The western portion of the Neutral Zone in West Africa, as defined in Article V of the present Convention, shall also fall to the share of Great Britain.

Article V.—In the Neutral Zone the frontier between the German and English territories shall be formed by the River Daka as far as the point of its intersection with the 9th degree of north latitude ; thence the frontier shall continue to the north, leaving Morozugu to Great Britain, and shall be fixed on the spot by a mixed Commission of the two Powers, in such manner that Gambaga and all the territories of Mamprusi shall fall to Great Britain, and that Yendi and all the territories of Chakosi shall fall to Germany.

Article VI.—Germany is prepared to take into consideration, as much and as far as possible, the wishes which the Government of Great Britain may express with regard to the development of the reciprocal tariffs in the territories of Togo and the Gold Coast.

IV

Notes exchanged between Great Britain and Germany defining the Boundary between the Gold Coast and Togoland, to the North of the 9th Parallel of North Latitude, June 25, 1904.

From the 9th degree of north latitude the boundary follows the thalweg of the Daka (Kulukpene) upwards to its junction with the Kulusulo ; from thence the thalweg of the Kulusulo upwards [to a distance of 1 kilom. beyond its intersection with the road from Sambu to Sung ; then a line running west, at a distance of 1 kilom. from that road], to its intersection with a meridian which passes half-way between the most easterly and the most westerly point of intersection of the 9th degree of north latitude with the Daka (Kulukpene) ; then this meridian to the north of its intersection with the Daka (Kulukpene) ; then again the thalweg of the latter upwards to its intersection with the road from Bulugu to Nayoro (Naijoro) ; then a straight line drawn from the last-named point of intersection to the point where the road from Jebega (Djebega) to Makumboro crosses a certain stream ; then the thalweg of this stream downwards to a distance of 1 kilom. beyond its

intersection with the road from Sokelo to Somayili (Somajili) ;
then a line drawn 1 kilom. to the west of the Sokelo–Somayili
(Somajili)–Naiyoboli (Naijoboti)–Yahapa (Fahapa)–Tintaraga–
Gimbendi (Gjimbende) road to the point where it intersects
the southern boundary of Mamprussi, with the proviso that the
villages of Karvison and Narabare fall to Germany, and that
the boundary-line in the neighbourhood of these two villages
shall in each case be deflected towards the west in the arc of
a circle of 1 kilom. radius, drawn from the house of the Chief
of each village as centre.

From the last-named point of intersection the boundary runs
east along the southern boundary of Mamprussi to a point
about half-way between the villages of Tintaraga and Gimbendi (Gjimbende), which point forms the junction of the
territories of Dagomba, Chakosi (Tschakossi), and Mamprussi.

At this point a pillar has been erected by the Anglo-German
Boundary Commission, and from it the boundary proceeds in
straight lines in a northerly direction, as marked in the following manner by the posts erected by that Commission. . . .

AUTHORITIES

HISTORICAL

BUTTNER, R. *Togo*. (In *Das Ueberseeische Deutschland*.) Stuttgart, Berlin, Leipzig (n.d.).

CALVERT, A. F. *The German African Empire*. London, 1916.

ELLIS, A. B. *The Ewe-speaking Peoples of the Slave Coast*. (*Togoland*, pp. 215–84.) London, 1890.

GEHRTS, Miss M. *A Camera Actress in the Wilds of Togoland*. London, 1915.

HASSERT, K. *Deutschlands Kolonien*, 2nd edition. (*Togo*, pp. 191–234.) Leipzig, 1910.

JOHNSTON, Sir H. H. *The Colonization of Africa by Alien Races*. Cambridge, 1913.

—— *A Survey of the Ethnography of Africa*. (Journal of the Royal Anthropological Institute, 1913.)

LEWIN, EVANS. *The Germans and Africa*. London, 1915.

PASSARGE, S. *Togo*. (In H. Meyer, *Das Deutsche Kolonialreich*, vol. ii.) Leipzig and Vienna, 1914.

ROHRBACH, P. *Wie machen wir unsere Kolonien rentabel?* Halle, 1907.

TRIERENBERG, G. *Togo*. Berlin, 1914.

ZIMMERMANN, ALF. *Geschichte der Deutschen Kolonialpolitik*. Berlin, 1914.

ZÖLLER, H. *Das Togoland*. (*Togo*, pp. 82–93, 217–21, 265–71.) Stuttgart, 1885.

NOTE.—A favourable account of Togoland from a flying visit by an Australian lady some years ago is given in Mrs. Mary Gaunt's *Alone in West Africa*. London, 1911.

ECONOMIC

Deutscher Kolonialatlas mit Jahrbuch. Berlin, 1918.

Deutsches Kolonialblatt. Berlin, 1915.

Die Deutsche Flagge (Statistik des Deutschen Reichs). 1912.

Die Deutschen Schutzgebiete in Afrika und der Südsee, 1912–13. Berlin, 1914.

The Economic Resources of the German Colonies. Togoland. (Bulletin of the Imperial Institute, vol. xiii, pp. 410–22.) London, 1915.

HEYDT, VON DER. *Kolonial-Handbuch.* Berlin, 1912.

Jahrbuch über die Deutschen Kolonien. Essen, 1908–14.

PASSARGE, S. *Togo.* (In H. Meyer, *Das Deutsche Kolonial-reich*, vol. ii.) Leipzig and Vienna, 1914.

Report on the Trade and Agriculture of Togoland. (Cd. 7048–52.) London, 1913.

Report for the year 1913 *on the Trade, &c., of German Togoland.* (Cd. 7620–7.) London, 1915.

Royal Commission on the Natural Resources, Trade, and Legislation of certain portions of His Majesty's Dominions. Third Interim Report, 1914, and Final Report, 1917.

Statistisches Jahrbuch für das Deutsche Reich.

UNWIN, A. H. *Report on the Afforestation of Togo with Teak and African Timber Trees.* London, 1912.

MAPS

Togoland is covered by the War Office map (G.S.G.S. 2306), on the scale of 1 : 1,500,000 (1909, with additions to 1918) ; also by the War Office map (G.S.G.S. 2434), ' West Africa,' on the scale of 1 : 6,336,000 (1903, additions 1914, boundaries corrected 1919) ; and by sheets 61 and 73 of the Million Map of Africa (old numbering), G.S.G.S. 1539.

There is an orographical map of Togoland on the scale of 1 : 2,000,000 in *Kamerun mit Togo*, by Max Moisel and D. Reimer, published in Berlin in 1913. Two sheets (2 a and 2 b) of the *Grosser Deutscher Kolonialatlas* cover Togoland on the scale of 1 : 500,000 ; the map is by P. Sprigade and D. Reimer, and was published in Berlin in 1908. There is also a *Karte von Togo*, on the scale of 1 : 200,000, in ten sheets by P. Sprigade, and published by D. Reimer in Berlin between 1902 and 1907.

The work of the Togo–Dahomey Boundary Commission of 1908–9 is described in the *Bulletin du Comité de l'Afrique Française* for 1912, pages 413 to 415, and the only maps showing the boundary as surveyed, which have so far been published, accompany this description, and are on the scales of 1 : 1,000,000, 1 : 500,000, and 1 : 250,000.

HANDBOOKS PREPARED UNDER THE DIRECTION OF THE
HISTORICAL SECTION OF THE FOREIGN OFFICE.—No. 111

CAMEROON

TABLE OF CONTENTS

Wt. 15564/89. 1000. 8/20. O.U.P.

TABLE OF CONTENTS [No. 111

I. GEOGRAPHY PHYSICAL AND POLITICAL

(1) POSITION AND FRONTIERS

THE former German colony of Cameroon[1] stretches inland from the north-eastern corner of the Gulf of Guinea, and lies between 1° 15′ south and 13° 10′ north latitude and 8° 25′ and 18° 35′ east longitude. The area, which previous to 1911 was some 190,000 square miles, was extended by the Franco-German agreement of that year to about 292,000 square miles. The colony marches on the north-west with Nigeria, on the east and south with French Equatorial Africa, while on the west coast Spanish Guinea forms an enclave.

The boundary between Cameroon and Nigeria, from the sea at the mouth of the Akwayafe (Ifiana) river to the Benue river at about 12° 55′ east longitude, was determined by the Agreement of London, March 11, 1913.[2] It circles round east of Yola at a distance of some 30 miles, and then strikes about north-by-east to Lake Chad, which it reaches near its southern extremity.[3] The trace is only in part determined by natural features, and does not appear to be altogether

---

[1] 'Cameroon' has been adopted in this handbook as an equivalent to 'Kamerun,' the former German official designation of the colony. 'Cameroons,' which is frequently used, is an English corruption of the Portuguese *camarões* (prawns), the name given by its discoverers to the estuary of the Cameroon River, owing to the number of prawns or shrimps found there.

[2] See Cd. 7056. Previously the Rio del Rey had been the boundary, and the Bakasi peninsula British.

[3] See a paper read by Captain Nugent, before the Royal Geographical Society in March 1914.

satisfactory, since it cuts in places across native tribal and political divisions.

The boundary of Cameroon towards French territory is determined by the Convention of November 4, 1911, and the Declaration of September 28, 1912. The trace was laid down by the Boundary Commission of 1912–13, but it had apparently not been ratified before the outbreak of the late war. The boundary starts from a point on Monda Bay and runs in a generally eastern direction to Wesso along a very irregular line. The remainder of the trace chiefly follows the courses of important rivers, its most pronounced features being the southern extension, which gave the Sanga (Ssanga) basin to Germany with a frontage of a few kilometres on the north bank of the Congo, and the eastern extension to the Ubanghi between the tributaries Lobaye and Ngabo. At the northern extremity the boundary follows the Shari (Chari) river to Lake Chad, a small part of which is also included in the colony.

The boundaries of Spanish Guinea, in the south-western corner of the colony, are fixed by the Convention of June 27, 1900, as the parallels of 1° and 2° 10′ north latitude on the south and north respectively (except near the coast, where they follow river courses), and on the east the meridian of 9° east of Paris (approximately 11° 20′ east of Greenwich). At the south-eastern angle of this enclave space was allowed to Germany for the construction of a railway and a road.

(2) Surface, Coast, and River System

Surface

The surface of Cameroon falls naturally into five main divisions. These are : (1) the Cameroon plateau, the largest and most important, covering the greater part of the centre and south of the colony ; (2) the coastal region, on the western edge of this plateau, between it and the sea ; (3) the lowlands of the Sanga basin in the south-east ; (4) the hill country of middle and north Adamawa skirting the central plateau on its northern side ; (5) the Lake Chad basin together with a portion of the Logone basin in the extreme north.

The *Cameroon plateau* rises in the north, between 6" and 8° north latitude, in a mountainous arc, stretching across the middle of the colony from about 10° to 15° or 16° east longitude. These highlands rise more or less abruptly from the middle Adamawa region (1,000–2,000 ft. above the sea) to heights varying from 4,000 to 10,000 ft., the greatest heights being in the west. This northern wall, which is much broken up, falls towards the south to a series of plateaux, 3,000–5,000 ft. above sea-level and also much broken. South of these is a broad and remarkably uniform plateau some 2,000 ft. in height. In some parts this plateau is quite flat, in others it is cut into ridges and hollows, while in the south it rises again on both sides of the River Ja (Dscha) to a mountainous country, about 3,300 ft. above the sea, whence there is again a drop to the Ogowe and the Congo in French territory. The Cameroon plateau falls somewhat more evenly to the coastal region in the west. In the north the Manenguba highlands form a transition between its elevated edge and the lowlands of the coast. South of these highlands the edge of the plateau descends in two steps from heights of 3,000–6,000 ft. to the coastal plains.

The *coastal region* is divided into two unequal parts by the intrusive mass of the volcanic Cameroon Mountains (over 13,000 ft. high). To the north-west an alluvial strip, 25–30 miles wide, low, swampy, and with deep indentations, rises in the interior to a region of hills and valleys, which is in turn divided from the edge of the Cameroon plateau on the north-east by the Ossidinge depression. To the south is a similar alluvial region, narrowing from north to south past Kampo and through Spanish Guinea to Ukoko. It is traversed by considerable rivers, and has two large indentations, that of the Cameroon River and that of Rio Muni in the extreme south.

The *Sanga lowlands* are part of the Congo basin, towards which the Cameroon plateau slopes gradually to the east and descends by terraces to the south. The actual lowlands may be considered to begin on the south-east about the neighbourhood of Wesso, whence the monotonous alluvial plain, with an average height above the sea of 700–1,000 ft., stretches from the foot of the Kunabembe mountains, the last terrace of the Cameroon plateau, to the River Congo.

The *Adamawa hill country* is for the most part a fairly flat region (some 1,500–2,000 ft. above the sea), divided into two parts by the broad and low Benue depression. Out of it, however, rise high mountain blocks, comparable in height with the Cameroon plateau. South of the Benue there are several such massifs, notably along the western frontier of the colony; north of the Benue are the Mandara mountains, about 4,000 ft. above the sea. On the eastern side the district passes fairly uniformly into the low alluvial plains of the Logone and Lake Chad.

The *Lake Chad basin* consists for the most part of a great plain with a scarcely noticeable fall to the north. Along the rivers which mark the boundary run ridges which rise above the rest of the plain, and which sometimes attain a fair width. In one or two places hills and ridges emerge; for the rest, the level is broken only by flat sandy hillocks. This region becomes a shallow lake during the rainy season.

Coast

The coast, whose length is about 220 miles, is mostly low and bordered by mangrove swamps ; the deposits brought down by the rivers have formed numerous bars, which tend to form lagoons. In some places, however, e.g. between Kribi and Kampo and especially round the Cameroon Mountains, the coast is steep and rocky. The chief indentations are the Rio Muni and Monda Bay in the south and the estuaries north-west and south-east of the Cameroon Mountains in the north. In the five-fingered estuary of the Cameroon River is Duala, the best natural harbour on all this part of the West African coast. There are a number of small but well-protected bays at the foot of the Cameroon Mountains, of which Ambas Bay, though exposed to west winds, is the best. In the south Kribi is the most important port, and roads run from it into the interior. Other ports worth mentioning are Rio del Rey and Kampo. At most places, however, where a landing is feasible it must be made in boats. (For details of the ports, see pp. 45–8.)

River System

Hydrographically the five divisions of Cameroon fall into four systems : the coast-river system with the rivers Sanaga, Nyong, Kampo, and San Benito (in Spanish Guinea), and including the rivers draining south to the Ogowe ; the Lake Chad system, which consists of the Shari and its tributary, the Logone, with the affluents of the latter ; the Benue system, which drains to the Niger ; and the Congo system, which includes the Ubanghi, touched by the Cameroon at Singa, and the Sanga, with its tributary the Ja (Dscha).

The head-waters of rivers belonging to all these four systems drain from the so-called Yade (Jade) massif, in the north-eastern part of the elevated edge of the plateau. Between the coast rivers and the Congo system the watershed is in places so flat that in the rainy season water flows from the same source to both. In the north the Tuburi swamp, when swollen with rain, feeds both the Benue and the Logone. In all four areas there are rivers of considerable size, capable, after more or less regulation, of being used for transport for stretches and periods of various lengths according to the vessels employed. Many of them, particularly those which rise on the Cameroon plateau or on its edges, contain rapids or falls which might prove useful for power. In the rainy coastal region the rivers have water all the year round, and their volume is relatively constant. On the plateau, where there is a long dry season, many of the smaller rivers dry up entirely or leave only pools. In northern Adamawa even the larger rivers fail in their upper courses at times during the dry season.

(3) CLIMATE

The controlling factor of the climate of Cameroon is the movement of the heat belt. In January the sun is in the south ; and the air therefore blows from the Sahara in the north as a dry, cool, dust-laden wind, while the temperature decreases from south to north. By July the sun has moved north over the Sahara ; and the wind therefore blows from the south (being generally south-westerly, though in south Cameroon there are frequent south-easterly and easterly winds), while the temperature is highest in the north and lowest in the south.

The different features of the five main regions exercise a great influence on the temperature.

(1) On the *coast* the temperature is high, though, owing to the proximity of sea and forest, not relatively excessive. The yearly variation is small, the daily variation greater and increasing towards the interior. At Duala and Debunja (Debundscha) the warmest month is February, with a temperature of about 79°–80° F. (26·5° C.) ; the coolest, August, with under 75° F. (23·5° C.). The Cameroon Mountains form an exception to the general conditions in this region. At Buea the warmest month, March, has about 69° F. (20·5° C.) ; the coolest, August, about 64·5° F. (18° C.).

(2) On the *central plateau* the temperature is lower than on the coast, and the daily variation twice as great. The yearly variation is small. At Yaunde (Jaúnde) February, the warmest month, has 73·5° F. (23° C.), and July, the coolest, 70° F. (21° C.) ; while Bali has 66° F. (19° C.) in April, the warmest month, and 62·5° F. (17° C.) in August, the coolest.

(3) In the *Sanga lowlands* March is probably the hottest month with about 77°–79° F. (25°–26° C.), and August or September the coolest with about 75° F. (24° C.).

(4) In the *Lake Chad* basin and generally in the Adamawa lowlands the temperature is much higher, and the daily and yearly variations are both very great. A double maximum and minimum are clearly marked. The temperature is at its lowest in January, reaches its highest in April, falls to a second minimum in August, and rises to a second maximum in October. January has temperatures of 75° F. (24° C.) and 71·5° F. (22° C.) at Fort Lamy and Kukawa, just beyond the frontier to east and west respectively ; April has over 91° F. (33° C.). A temperature of about 120° F. is common in the hot season at midday. As one proceeds south the difference between the hottest and coldest months decreases.

(5) In the *mountains of Adamawa* no observations are available. Fairly even temperatures may be expected.

The rainfall, as elsewhere in the tropics, varies very much from year to year. Most of the rain is brought by south-westerly sea winds, but a certain amount comes from the Lake Chad and Congo basins. In general there is most rain on the coast, and the quantity decreases progressively towards the interior. Thus at Duala there are about 155 inches a year, at Kribi 125 inches ; on the plateau Yaunde has about 62 inches, Bali about 104 ; Garua, on the Benue, has 29, Kusseri 18, Kukawa only 13. In the Sanga lowlands about 60–70 inches may be expected. The western side of the Cameroon Mountains forms an exceptional area, and is one of the rainiest regions in the world, with 400–430 inches a year. There is a great difference between the distribution of rains in the south and the north of the colony. In the south there are two dry seasons, of which the first (about December to February) is most clearly marked, and two rainy seasons, one culminating in April, the other in September or October ; in the extreme north there is a single dry season of about 8 months, and a rainy season culminating about July or August.

(4) Sanitary Conditions

Hygienic conditions are, on the whole, unfavourable. Malaria is the most serious scourge. It is prevalent in the coast region, the forest of south Cameroon, the basin of Lake Chad, and the Benue valley, all of them places where there is an abundance of stagnant water ; it is also found in the lower parts of the hill country of middle and northern Adamawa, and even in the grass-land of the plateau. Above a height of 4,000 ft. malaria ceases, but in these high regions dysentery and pulmonary and respiratory diseases cause serious ravages.

Europeans can avoid these complaints with ordinary care.

Skin diseases are widespread. Leprosy is especially common in the mountain regions of Adamawa, and is also spread over the forest region, at any rate in the western angle of the colony. Small-pox epidemics have at times depopulated whole districts. In the Laka country (on the east side of the colony between about 7° and 9° north latitude) about 90 per cent. of the male population are said to suffer from filariasis. · Finally, the dreaded sleeping-sickness is apparently on the increase. It is common along the Nyong, the upper Sanaga, the Dume (Bumba) and its tributaries, in the Sanga basin and the Ubanghi angle, and in the forest region of the coast. It is likely to spread, since *Glossina* has been observed in districts where as yet there is no sleeping-sickness, that is, where the fly has not yet been infected.

(5) RACE AND LANGUAGE

The Cameroon area is a region where great movements of peoples have occurred. The distribution of races and tribes is therefore a very complicated problem, which, in the present state of the evidence—evidence drawn almost entirely from philological considerations and native traditions—is far from solution.

The bulk of the population consists of Sudan and Bantu negroes. The line between these corresponds fairly closely to the line between northern savannah and southern forest country, though the boundary is not very strongly marked. Intermixtures of Sudan and Bantu tribes occur, and one or two Sudan tribes, for example the Ba-ngandus near Molundu, are even found well south of this line. Nevertheless in essentials the division is clearly recognizable.

In Cameroon the *Bantus,* whose languages are much

more closely related to each other than are those of the Sudan negroes, fall into an older and a younger group. The first consists of the Bakoko and Bakundu groups in the south-west and the Maka group in the south-east ; the second, which intervenes between the two sections of the first, consists of the Fang group. The Bangalla language is widely spoken in the south-east.

The relation of the *Sudan tribes* to one another is very obscure, and their languages differ widely. At present the Sudan negroes may be classified as follows : (*a*) the group, speaking similar languages, stretching across the colony, south of Lake Chad (Margis, Vandalas or Mandaras, Gumergus, Kotokos, Musgus) ; (*b*) south of these, the Fallis and some related tribes, who seem to show language affinities with tribes of the western Sudan ; (*c*) the rest of the Sudan negro tribes, consisting partly of large tribes living in the open plains and highlands, partly of small groups who have been driven into the inaccessible parts of the mountains. Of these the relationships are not yet determined.

The so-called *Pygmies* share the forest region with the Bantus. These beings, called Bagiellis, Babingas, Bumanjoks, and Bomassas in various places, may represent the remains of an earlier population. Their numbers are insignificant and probably decreasing. Nothing is known of their language.

After the Bantu and Sudan tribes the most important peoples are the Fulbes and the Hausas.

Of the *Fulbes* (*Fulas*) two types may be distinguished : the Bororos or nomad Fulbes, who have maintained themselves fairly pure from negro admixture, and the settled Fulbes, who have a strong negro tincture. Originally the Fulbes were, it is now supposed, mainly of Hamitic stock. Their language, which is widely spoken in the area where they form the ruling class (i. e. on both sides of the north-western frontier, as far south as Tibati and as far north as Madagali), is believed to represent a Hamitic type, though now it is very much coloured by negro admixture. In numbers the Fulbes are not very strong, but they control a number of well-organized states, and their slave-raiding excursions have struck terror into the negro populations over the whole centre of the Cameroon territory.

The *Hausas*, also, are not numerically very strong. Their settlements are thickest in the Fulbe states, between Koncha in the south and Marua in the north, but they are found across the whole centre of the colony as far east and south as Nola on the Sanga. They form the middle class in the Fulbe states, and are known as skilful and adventurous traders. Their language, which is important as a trade language over all this area, is now classified as Hamitic, in spite of the fact that it contains elements which are apparently Semitic and that the vocabulary is largely Sudanese.

The *Shuas*, living south of Lake Chad, speak Arabic, though it is not certain that they are racially Arabs.

The *Kanuris* live west and south-west of the lake and seem to be a mixture of some Asiatic stock with Sudan negroes.

English is said to be spoken to a considerable extent in the western angle of the colony, and the Germans are credited with having made efforts to root it out. On the western frontier the tribes seem on the whole well disposed to the present British administration.

(6) POPULATION

The total population of Cameroon was estimated by the Germans in 1915 at over 2,649,000.[1] This figure may well be an under-estimate; but if the figures be accepted, they represent a density of over 9 persons to

---

[1] Colonial Supplement to the German Year Book for 1915.

the square mile. Taking the German administrative divisions as a basis, we find the population thinnest in the south-east and centre, densest in the north and west of the colony. In the Bare, Jang (Dschang), and Yabassi (Jabassi) districts respectively the density is as high as 112, 80, and 48 persons per square mile, while the Banyo district, the least densely inhabited, shows only 1·4 persons per square mile. In the north the average is about 18 persons per square mile. In general it is possible to say that the forest region of the south, except for the coast, and the eastern side of the south Adamawa grass country are least densely populated, and that in the Lake Chad basin and northern Adamawa, in the Benue basin, and on the banks of the Logone and the highlands and hill-slopes of the western angle of the colony the population is densest.

The typical form of settlement in the Bantu or forest area is the isolated small village, built along a street, shut at both ends by defensible buildings; in the savannah (Sudan negro area) is found the village of scattered huts (called *Haufendorf* by the Germans), often of considerable size, sometimes surrounded by a wall, or in other cases by an enceinte containing several acres of ground, which renders the villagers independent in case of siege. These large villages are distinct from the towns, not uncommon in the Moham-medan area, which often possess 10,000–20,000 inhabi-tants, and are fortified or open as considerations of security prescribe. The latter control communica-tions, serve as outposts against hostile tribes, or watch a conquered territory.

Mention must be made of the nomad Bororos and Shuas in the north of the colony, who wander with their herds and have no fixed habitation.

In 1913 there were 1,871 whites in the colony, of whom 1,643 were Germans.

II. POLITICAL HISTORY

CHRONOLOGICAL SUMMARY

1471–2. First exploration of the Cameroon River (Rio dos Camarões) by Portuguese.

1845. Settlement of English Baptist missionaries.

1851. Barth discovers the upper Benue.

1858. Baptist mission at Ambas Bay (Victoria).

1870. Exploration of Bornu and Lake Chad by Nachtigal.

1872–5. Geological exploration by Buchholz and others.

1873. Grenfell's explorations in Cameroon.

1880–3. Flegel's journeys up the Niger and Benue.

1883. German merchants acquire rights from chiefs.

1884 (July 12). German Protectorate declared by Nachtigal.

1885 (April 29–June 16). First Anglo-German arrangement.

1885 (December 24). First Franco-German agreement.

1885. Flegel's expedition up the Benue into Adamawa ends with his death. Von Soden becomes Governor.

1886–92. Zintgraff opens up routes from Duala to Adamawa.

1887. Great Britain cedes Ambas Bay to Germany.

1888. Expedition of Kundt, Tappenbeck, and Weissenbaum to Yaunde.

1889. Yaunde Station founded.

1889–91. Morgen explores the upper Sanaga.

1890. Anglo-German Treaty.

1891. Von Zimmerer becomes Governor. Expeditions given up.

1892. Failure of von Gravenreuth's and Ramsay's expeditions to Buea and the north-west coast.

1893. Anglo-German Boundary Convention.

1893. Bali station abandoned. Von Zimmerer recalled. Kleist appointed deputy.

1894. Franco-German Boundary Convention.

1895. Von Puttkamer Governor till 1907. Mutiny of native troops. Charges of cruelty against Kleist.

1898. Von Carnap's expedition from Yaunde to the Sanga and Congo.

1899. Vuta invaded, and chief killed by von Kamptz.

1899. Tibati stormed. The Emir imprisoned.

1899. The Süd-Kamerun and Nordwest-Kamerun Companies obtain exclusive concessions.

1900. French expedition against Rabbeh ends with deaths of Rabbeh and Captain Laing.

1900. English Yola expedition.

1901. Ngaundere and Garua stormed.

1901. Dominik and von Bülow defeat Sultan of Yola, and break the Fula power.

1902–13. Anglo-German agreements finally settling the boundary.

1902. Dikoa (Rabbeh's capital) becomes a German post.

1903–7. Activity of traders in the southern forests. Resistance and repression of the forest tribes. Charges of cruelty against Dominik. Financial scandals. Charges against von Puttkamer, the Governor, and von Brauchitsch, the Chief Judge.

1905. Expedition against Vuta and taking of Ngutta by Dominik.

1905. Railway construction begins.

1907. Reichstag inquiry. Dismissal of von Puttkamer.

1907. Seitz appointed Governor.

1908. Franco-German Boundary Convention.

1910. Glein appointed Governor.

1911–12. French cession of territory to German Cameroon and settlement of the boundary.

1912. Ebermeier appointed Governor.

1914. Outbreak of war.

1916. Occupation of Cameroon by the Allies.

(1) Discovery and Early History

We have no distinct account of the first discovery of the Cameroon River, but it may be presumed to have been visited about the same time as the Island of Fernando Po ; an event which probably took place about 1471, although by some placed as late as 1486. The name *Rio dos Camarões*, or Prawn River, was certainly given by one of the early Portuguese explorers, for it appears in Canerio's map of 1502 and, in the Spanish form, *Rio de los Camarones*, in Diego Ribero's map of 1529 (the second Borgian map). Although the Portuguese explored the coast, they did not make any settlement between Benin and the mouth of the Congo ; and this territory, except for visits of merchants and missionaries, did not come into the possession of any European Power before its occupation by Germany.

An English Baptist mission had been established in Cameroon since 1845 ; and in 1858 another body of members of the same mission, who had been working at Fernando Po, left that island and settled at Victoria on Ambas Bay under the Cameroon Mountains. Although this acquisition was not formally recognized by the British Government, there is little doubt that Victoria was a British possession in all but name. Ambas Bay had been visited by British ships in 1841, and had been the subject of an Admiralty report ; but its full value as a harbour was not known prior to the arrival of the Baptist missionaries.

(2) First German Annexation

In 1883 some of the German merchants on the coast, hearing that Bismarck had changed his views on the subject of colonization, and that they might expect support from their Government, began to acquire rights to property from the chiefs. In 1884 Dr. Nachtigal, the well-known traveller, was sent out as Imperial Commissioner to West Africa with the ostensible object of making arrangements to promote German trade, but, in reality, with full powers to annex whatever land he could find available. He hoisted the German flag, and proclaimed a protectorate in Togoland on July 5, and in the Cameroon River on July 12, 1884. The English Consul, Hewett, was on his way thither for a similar purpose, in order to accept an application for British protection made by certain chiefs a year and a half before. He arrived too late, and had to be content with lodging a protest. However, an agreement was arrived at next year, by which all British claims were given up in return for some purely nominal concessions by Germany. Some of the tribes, disappointed at not being taken over by Great Britain, refused to acknowledge German sovereignty. In October 1884 their villages were bombarded and they were reduced to submission with the assistance of a German squadron under Admiral Knorr. In the exchange of notes, the British Foreign Secretary declared Ambas Bay, with the settlement of Victoria upon it, to be British territory; and in the exchange of notes in 1885 the words used were: 'a reservation being specially made as to the settlement of Victoria, Ambas Bay, which will continue to be a British possession.' Lord Granville, however, at the same time expressed his willingness to cede Ambas Bay if terms could be arranged with the missionaries. This was done. The missionaries accepted a sum in payment, and handed over their work to German Protestant missionaries; but it is doubtful how far they were free agents.[1] Ambas Bay was transferred to Germany on March 28, 1887.

(3) BOUNDARIES

The German protectorate was recognized by the British Government in the British and German exchange of Notes, April 29–May 7, 1885, and by the French in the Franco-German Agreement of December

---

[1] See T. V. Tymms, *The Cameroons*, a pamphlet published by the Baptist Missionary Society, London, 1915.

24, 1885.   The boundary between British Nigeria and Cameroon was laid down in the Treaty of July 1, 1890, followed by a series of agreements of which the last was that of March 11, 1913.   As regards the frontier with the French Congo, the Agreement of December 24, 1885, was superseded by the Conventions of March 15, 1894, and April 18, 1908, and finally by the Agreement of November 4, 1911, in which a large cession of territory (107,000 square miles) was made by France to Germany, and a small area (6,500 square miles) by Germany to France, as an equivalent for the recognition by Germany of French rights in Morocco.   By the terms of this agreement Spanish Guinea became an enclave in Cameroon territory.

(4) Formation of German Government

Cameroon was formed into a regular colonial government, and von Soden was appointed first Governor in July 1885.   He occupied this post from 1885 to 1891, and with him went as Finance Minister von Puttkamer, who afterwards became Governor. The new Government began at once to open up the territory by expeditions into the interior.   The coast tribes found themselves thereby threatened with the loss of the profits which they had hitherto derived from the transit trade between the coast and the inland districts, and were opposed to all such expeditions.   The Duala and Akwa chiefs on the shores of the Cameroon River were further alienated by the appropriation of their villages without compensation for the formation of the German port of Duala.   The strong military tribes of the interior, which had had no voice in asking the Germans to enter their country, were also inclined to resist the exploring parties.   Thus all the elements of trouble were present ; and the overbearing and often cruel behaviour of the German officials tended to emphasize difficulties which might have been surmounted by tact and consideration for native customs.

(5) EXPLORATION OF THE INTERIOR

Before the German occupation the territory included in the Cameroon Protectorate had already been partly explored. The Baptist mission established on the coast had done excellent work, with which the name of the Rev. George Grenfell is identified. Grenfell is best known, however, for the discovery of the Ubanghi, a tributary of the Congo to which German territory did not extend till 1911.

The interior in the neighbourhood of Lake Chad was first visited, in 1851, by Barth, who was travelling under the auspices of the British Government. Rohlfs (1865–7) and Nachtigal (1869–74), in the course of their travels, visited part of the old Kingdom of Bornu and the territory north of the Mandara Mountains. The English explorer, Baikie, ascended the Benue River almost to Yola so early as 1854. Flegel, a German explorer, made in 1880–3 two journeys up the Benue River, during the first of which he reached Garua ; on the second occasion he visited the plateau of Ngaundere in Adamawa. In 1885 he was sent on another expedition up the Niger and the Benue, with the object of pushing German claims, not only in Adamawa, but also in the great Fula kingdom of Sokoto. In this he was not successful, as Joseph Thomson forestalled him in making a treaty with the Fula Sultan. His expedition, which had the further object of promoting German influence in Adamawa, was ended by his death.

A more successful expedition was that of Kundt, Tappenbeck, and Weissenbaum, which penetrated from

Batanga, at the mouth of the Nyong river, through the dense forest belt to the high plateau beyond it. The explorers reached Yaunde in 1888 ; and a fortified post was established there in 1889. This expedition opened the way to the navigable stream of the Nyong above the rapids which impede it. Another series of expeditions towards the north was conducted by Zintgraff between 1886 and 1892. Zintgraff began by founding a post at Barombi, north of the Cameroon Mountains (now called Johann-Albrechts-Höhe), and advanced towards Adamawa, reaching Yola by a circuitous route. His expeditions ended in disaster, for he foolishly mixed himself up with the internal wars between the tribes, taking the side of the Bali against the more numerous and powerful Bafut and Bandeng. He was involved in the defeat of the former, and lost a great part of his small force, with the result that the further exploration of Adamawa had to be abandoned. When the Government was taken over by von Zimmerer (1891), it was soon decided that these costly and unprofitable expeditions must be given up, and the advanced posts withdrawn. Zintgraff in disgust returned to Germany, and did not come back till 1896, after von Zimmerer's term of office had expired. He then went again, with Max Esser, to the Bali country, but shortly afterwards died.

Between 1889 and 1891 various expeditions were carried out by Kurt Morgen to the head-waters of the Sanaga in completion of that under Tappenbeck and Kundt, and also to Adamawa. In the course of these expeditions, Morgen overcame the resistance of the coast tribes, but was forced by the opposition which he encountered at Ngaundere to turn to the north-west, and finally reached Ibi on the Benue in British territory. In 1892 von Gravenreuth attacked the Bakwiris of the Cameroon Mountains. He intended to take

Buea and afterwards to reach Lake Chad, but was ambushed and killed on the march. His successor, Ramsay, was obliged to retire owing to a mutiny among his black troops; the station founded at Balinga was lost, and the officers in command were killed.

(6) French Expeditions

The French, meanwhile, were endeavouring to extend from Baghirmi westwards round the south of Lake Chad to the upper waters of the Benue ; and an expedition under Mizon attempted to form a French sphere of influence on that river with Yola as its centre, extending as far as Kunde, and also from Gaza to Bania. At the same time, Maistre, acting from the Ubanghi and upper Shari, pushed towards Garua by way of Lai and Lame. The English and German boundary from Yola to Lake Chad having already been defined, the two nations made a joint resistance to these French claims ; and a German vessel was allowed to ascend the Benue to Yola, carrying the expedition of von Uchtritz and Passarge. This expedition occupied Garua, Baibanjedda, and Ngaundere, and established German power in the upper Benue region. The agreement of March 1894 settled the boundary with France, who obtained access to the upper Benue by Lai and Lame. This territory she ultimately ceded in 1911.

All these expeditions, and the deaths of so many explorers and officers, produced a bad effect in Germany. Von Zimmerer, who was unpopular with the mercantile element, was recalled, and von Puttkamer appointed in his place. Before this date, the Finance Minister, Kleist, had taken over charge of the Government as von Zimmerer's deputy, and under him matters rapidly grew worse.

(7) MUTINY OF NATIVE TROOPS

The mutiny among the troops in the Cameroon Mountains expedition has already been referred to. The force (called a police force) kept up in the colony had been recruited from Liberia, Togo, and Dahomey, through the German merchants in those parts. These ' police ' were to all intents and purposes slaves sold by their chiefs. The conduct of Kleist—the Deputy-Governor of the colony—in encouraging the flogging of the soldiers' wives and other outrages led to a violent mutiny among these troops, in which they seem to have been supported by some of the coast tribes. Many officers and others were killed ; and the outbreak was only suppressed with the help of marines from a cruiser. To replace this police force, a body of Sudanese was raised in Egypt ; and an expedition was sent out to punish the Miang tribe.[1] One of the results was the removal of the police force from the control of the local Government. It was placed under the Marine Department, i. e. directly under the Emperor, and formed into a ' protective force ' after the East African model. This was followed by a great extension of the system of military outposts, and by a series of punitive expeditions carried out with much severity. The arrangement led to great friction, and was modified by a new regulation in 1896.

(8) VON PUTTKAMER'S ADMINISTRATION

Von Puttkamer began his administration with a useful measure—the introduction of Courts of Arbitration for the decision of disputes among natives, after the pattern of those in use in British Nigeria. His

---

[1] The subsequent arraignment of Kleist is described in *Treatment of Natives in the German Colonies*, No. 114 of this series, p. 34.

further conduct, however, was by no means of a creditable nature.[1] Under his administration, military expeditions again began to multiply, being in some cases brought on by the excesses and exactions of the agents of the Süd-Kamerun and the Nordwest-Kamerun Companies, which obtained concessions for the exploitation of the resources of the country. In 1898–9 an expedition under von Carnap made its way from Yaunde to Kunde and back across the Sanga. Von Carnap returned by way of the Congo, while the force returned to the coast direct. In 1899 von Kamptz led an expedition into the Vuta country north of the Sanaga ; the capital, Yoko, was stormed, and the chief killed. Von Kamptz then advanced on Tibati. The Emir of that place fled, but was captured, and died in imprisonment at Duala.

Meanwhile, the French had defeated and killed the Darfur adventurer, Rabbeh, who had established his rule south of Lake Chad (1900) ; and at the same time the English occupied Yola. The Germans immediately followed suit by attacking the strong Fula kingdom of Adamawa. Ngaundere was taken by storm in 1901 ; and Klausbrach, who was in command, followed the fugitive Sultan to Garua, where he was defeated and killed. Dominik and von Bülow defeated the Sultan of Yola at Marua, and entirely overthrew the power of the Fulas. Nevertheless, there continued to be trouble in the northern districts for some time. German officials were often attacked ; Nolte was killed at Banyo in 1902, and Count Fugger at Garua.

In the south, Plehn's force on the Sanga reached Ngoko in 1899. After his death, Stein went on, between 1900 and 1903, through the south-eastern forest region. In 1905 Dominik made a second invasion of the Vuta country, and completely subdued

---

[1] See No. 114 of this series, pp. 34–5.

it through the capture of Ngutta.   A series of expeditions was undertaken against the primitive tribes of the southern forest region, the Nyongs, Nyems, Ndsims, and Makas, by Scheunemann and Stein, which extended over the years 1903–7.

The agents of the Süd-Kamerun Gesellschaft, who penetrated the forests in search of rubber, were no doubt cruel and oppressive in their actions ; and reprisals were inevitable.   Many Germans were killed, and others had to flee for their lives.   No mercy seems to have been shown to the hostile tribes ; and gross outrages accompanied the suppression of the outbreaks. In these outrages Captain Dominik took a leading part.[1]

Bound up with these expeditions was the system of obtaining forced labour for the plantations, which, as in East Africa, led to the depopulation of the country. Another evil was the evident complicity of the Governor, von Puttkamer, and other officials, such as the Chief Judge, von Brauchitsch, in the deeds of the companies, in which they were financially interested, so that no justice could be expected from them.   There was also a systematic attempt to degrade native chiefs, so as to cause them to lose all their influence.   Risings naturally followed, which provoked repressive expeditions.   In 1901 and 1903 these were very numerous.

(9) Removal of Capital from Duala to Buea

The removal of the seat of Government from Duala to the healthy uplands of Buea in 1901 seems to have led to further troubles on the coast, perhaps because it was thought that the Governor was becoming inaccessible to complaints.   A number of chiefs sent a complaint against the administration to the Reichstag and the

[1] See No. 114 of this series, p. 37.

Chancellor in 1905. This complaint was, as Zimmermann puts it,[1] 'sent for inquiry to the very gang which was the object of the accusation.' The accused persons in their turn brought charges against the petitioners; and it was on these charges that von Puttkamer took action. The petitioners were arrested and brought before the Judge, von Brauchitsch, himself one of the persons accused, and sentenced to long terms of imprisonment with hard labour. The matter at last found its way into the Reichstag, where it was brought up by Bebel. It was found that, although some frivolous complaints and some caused by ignorance (as to sanitary measures, &c.) were included, there were real grievances of a very serious character. Von Puttkamer was ultimately directed to hold a 'disciplinary inquiry' on himself. He was reprimanded and fined a thousand marks, but his dismissal from the post of Governor was due rather to an insult to the Emperor's dignity than to his numerous other misdeeds. The Governors after von Puttkamer were T. Seitz (1907–10), O. Glein (1910–12), and K. Ebermeier, who was in power when the late war broke out in 1914.

(10) Measures taken on Declaration of War

In August 1914 the Germans were in great fear of a native rising, and took violent measures in a kind of panic. The principal chief of the Dualas, known as Rudolf Bell, who had been educated in Germany, and several other chiefs, were promptly executed; and there were wholesale massacres among the Dualas, generally, it would seem, without cause. The Hausa town at Jang was also burnt, and its inhabitants driven away. By February 1916 the Cameroon Colony was completely in the hands of the British

---

[1] *Geschichte der Deutschen Kolonialpolitik* (1914), p. 260.

and French expeditionary forces. The German force
from Yaunde escaped into the Spanish territory of
Rio Muni, where it was interned. After the operations
of war were concluded, a working arrangement for
administration was made between the British and
French Governments, according to which the country
adjoining Nigeria was to be administered by the
Governor of that colony. This country comprised the
districts of Rio del Rey, Ossidinge, Johann-Albrechts-
Höhe, Victoria (north of the Bimbia Creek), Jang (north-
west half, including the town of Jang), Bamenda, Banyo
(north-west part, including Gashaka and Koncha), Garua
(south-west part), and the portion of the Bornu
Sultanate (District of Kusseri) up to Lake Chad. The
whole of the remainder of the Cameroon Protectorate
was to be administered by the Government of the
French Congo. This includes the port of Duala and
the coast south of it.

III. SOCIAL AND POLITICAL CONDITIONS

(1) RELIGIOUS

AMONG the aboriginal populations of Cameroon there is a sharp distinction between the races of the north and those of the south (including the sea-coast). The latter, except for the parts influenced by Christian missions, are still almost entirely subject to the primitive beliefs included under the general head of 'fetishism'. Amongst the former, especially in the ancient kingdoms of Adamawa and Bornu, Islam occupies a predominant position. The powerful Fula rule extended over a considerable portion of this region, and the more primitive communities were unable to resist the influence of the Mohammedan religion brought in by them, although many large groups of Sudan negroes still adhere to their old belief, especially in the Mandara Mountains and neighbourhood. Of these the Musgus are the most important. The Mohammedan influence tends to increase, and has special attractions for the chiefs and leading men. Among the population generally, Mohammedanism consists mainly in a few outward observances, while the old fetishist beliefs and practices persist under the surface, as is the case in other parts of Africa. The extension of French power in Wadai has tended to cut off the old intercourse with the Mohammedan tribes of the north. The English missions on the coast, especially the Baptist mission at Ambas Bay, which has now moved to the Congo, formerly had an excellent influence on the Duala and other tribes. This influence may, if revived, be a great aid to progress and civilization under more favourable conditions.

(2) POLITICAL

Under the Germans, the Government was in the hands of an Imperial Governor, who was assisted by a Chancellor or Finance Minister, and a local council drawn from the mercantile community. There was also a Court presided over by a Judge.

The whole country was divided into administrative districts. Those nearest the coast were organized civil governments, while those in the interior were mainly military. The civil districts were named after their principal towns, as follows : Rio del Rey, Ossidinge, Johann-Albrechts-Höhe, Victoria, Buea, Duala, Yabassi (Jabassi), Edea, Yaunde, Kribi. The military districts, also named after their principal towns, were : Ebolova, Lomie, Dume Station, Jang (Dschang), Bamenda, Banyo. There were also two Residencies : one, the Province of Adamawa (capital, Garua) ; and the other the Lake Chad Province (capital, Kusseri). The districts formed from the extensive areas surrendered by the French in 1911 are not included in these lists.

The more organized districts were managed under a fairly regular system of civil administration, but those of the interior, whether civil or military, were independent of rules ; and in these, as Hassert says,[1] it was considered sufficient ‘ to keep the negroes to road-making and porterage, to work at the stations, and to other tasks of *kultur* ’. In several districts the natives were liable to pay what Hassert calls a ‘ moderate ’ poll-tax or hut-tax. The residents of the Lake Chad country and of Adamawa were not

---

[1] *Deutschlands Kolonien*, ed. 1910, p. 190.

supposed to interfere with the internal management of the native tribes, but to confine themselves to keeping the peace between them and maintaining German rule. How far this restriction was observed in actual practice it is not easy to say.

(3) Educational

Very little attention seems to have been paid to education in this territory. There were four Government schools, at Duala, Victoria, Yaunde, and Garua, respectively, and also several missionary schools.

IV. ECONOMIC CONDITIONS

(A) MEANS OF COMMUNICATION

(1) Internal

In Cameroon communications in the European sense are comparatively recent, and consequently of small extent compared with the area of the country. They consist of a few hundred kilometres of railway, a few hundred kilometres of motor road, and several long stretches of rivers. There are also native paths and elephant-tracks. Broad well-beaten paths that have been for years in use can be used in the dry season for rough country transport.

Owing to the difficulties and expense involved in making railways and roads, the German administration latterly turned its attention to improving the waterways, of which the natives make every possible use, carrying their light canoes over or round the many short obstructions and stretches of rapids.

(a) Roads, Paths, &c.

Cameroon contains, according to the latest report, about 400 kilometres of carriage-roads, metalled and well kept. These are all in the coast districts, where Germans have settled. They connect the following points :—(i) Victoria–Bibundi ; (ii) Victoria–Bombe ; (iii) Kampo–Kribi–Longyi : this road runs along the coast, and was to be continued inland in order to connect at Edea with the road from there to Yaunde ; (iv) Kribi–Bipindi–Lolodorf–Yaunde: in 1913 this road was 18 ft. wide and unmetalled ; it was therefore unsuitable for motor transport in the rainy season ; but according to a German report it has now been metalled as far as Yaunde ; (v) Kribi–Ebolova : this road is reported to have been completed, and over a great part of the route concrete bridges have replaced the older wooden ones. All these roads are in use by motors throughout a great part of the year, and a transport company, the Süd-Kameruner Last-Auto-mobil-Gesellschaft, had organized a regular motor service.

In the north and west of the colony, wher there is dense population with a highly developed native organization, there is a very good system of tracks and paths. The country there is less broken and less mountainous than in the interior, and lends itself more easily to communications. From Garua there is a regular route north-east, leading *via* Lere, Binder, and Marua to the Lake Chad region. A post route runs from Kusseri on the eastern frontier to Dikoa on the western, thence through Bornu to Garua, and thence to Ngaundere in the centre of the colony, from which point pathways radiate in all directions. Another main post route runs from Garua along the north-western side of the colony through Koncha, Banyo, Fumban, and Yabassi, each of which is a distributing centre. The greater part of these routes is path and not road. The best portions are those leading out from Garua.

The region towards the French frontier appears to be the least well served. The official report in 1914 points out that the only connexion with Bumo station on the Logone river is by the post track from Garua, which leaves the Binder road at Lere and passes through Fianga and Pogo—twenty-one days' march, including rests.

In the high mountain region of the interior, the first

care of the Germans was to link up new districts, as soon as they came under administrative control, with better-known localities, by improving the existing tracks and cutting roads for caravan routes for trade or Government supplies. Such a route is that from Edea to Babimbi (occupied in 1913), which was intended eventually to feed the Midland Railway line. Another is that running to the north of Somo through the rich province of Yabassi.

The whole of the southern region is covered with tropical forest, and the principal routes of communication are by water. Paths and roads require constant and expensive upkeep if they are not to be quickly overgrown. When the Germans, in 1912, suddenly cancelled their plans for a southern railway, they began planning a road system instead. The starting-points were to be Yaunde and Ebolova, which were already connected by metalled roads with the port of Kribi. From Ebolova roads were to run east to Nola, south to Oyem, and south-east to Molundu; on some sections work had already begun. The River Dume was to be connected by a short section with the River Nyong at Abong-Mbang, in order to provide a through route from Duala to the Congo river (see below, pp. 33, 35).

Enough has been said to make it clear that there are few roads in the European sense in Cameroon, although the Germans took great credit for what they had already completed, and had laid ambitious plans for further construction. Apart from the ordinary differences between tropical African conditions and those prevailing in European countries, there are in Cameroon two further special difficulties. These are the broken surface of the central regions, and the vast area of periodical swamp in the whole of the south and east and in the vicinity of Lake Chad and the Logone river.

(b) Rivers

In the greater part of the colony the river systems are the chief means of communication. One of the principal advantages that the Kolonial-Wirtschaftliches Komitee claimed, when it advocated improvements in the waterways of Cameroon in preference to the construction of railways, was the low initial cost. A railway must be practically complete before it can be utilized, whilst river improvements need only be carried out to meet the growth in traffic.

1. *Coast district rivers.*—The mouths of the rivers Kampo and Nyong, the Cameroon River, and the Rio del Rey have considerable importance for coastal trade, but none as through routes. In the interior of the coastal district the Cross River flows through some of the most fertile territory, and a lively inland traffic may be expected to develop along its course. As the lower part of this river flows through Nigeria, an agreement was made between the German and British Governments in March 1913, allowing German vessels access to the British section.

The rivers flowing to the coast fall abruptly over the edge of the Cameroon plateau, so that their upper courses cannot be reached from the sea. They are navigable below the plateau, in stretches of between 40 and 70 kilometres, throughout the year. Very little work is required to make a regular unimpeded traffic possible. German engineers were of opinion that a low-water depth of one metre would suffice for a good many years. These rivers include the Ndiam, the Meme, the Mungo, the Wuri, on which Duala lies, the Dibamba, Kwakwa Creek, the Sanaga, the Nyong, the Lokunje, and the Kampo. The navigability of the Sanaga does not seem to have been examined.

The greater part of the course of the Nyong lies in the southern inland district and is referred to below.

According to the German official report for 1912–13, the principal waterways on the German side of Muni Bay had been proved to be navigable for canoes and in parts for launches. These were the Noya and Tamboni rivers with their tributaries, on one of which, the Nguola water, clearing work was being done.

2. *Rivers of the Southern Inland Region and Congo System.*—The rivers of the southern inland region and the Congo basin, viz. the Nyong (in the upper part of its course), Dume, Kadei, Ja (Dscha), and Sanga, were carefully studied by an expedition sent out in 1913 by the Kolonial-Wirtschaftliches Komitee.

The Nyong was reported to be navigable throughout the year for stern-wheelers from Mbalmajo, the terminus of the Midland Railway, to Ajoshöhe, a distance of 225 kilometres (150 kilometres as the crow flies). Beyond Ajoshöhe the level of the water requires raising by dams at certain points, an operation which needs much care in order to prevent further flooding of the banks at high water. This would open to navigation another 103 kilometres as far as Abong-Mbang (80 kilometres as the crow flies).

For trade purposes, the chief waterway in south Cameroon is the upper Nyong. The Dume and Nyong are only separated by a narrow and easily passable watershed, and the question of connecting them has constantly been discussed. Many of the tributaries of the Nyong are navigable throughout the year for flat-bottomed launches drawing 20–30 centimetres, and the German Governor himself travelled through the district in a Government canoe propelled by a Cudell motor.

Farther south the Ivindo is navigable from Alati down to Kanyama, in French Gabun. Of its tributaries, the Jua (Dschua), which is a boundary river, is navigable from Majingo on the French side of the frontier to its confluence near Mvahdi; the Karagua from Ntam down to its confluence at Mwine; and the Nuna for the greater part of its course. This system of inland waterways amounts in all to about 600 kilometres, and lies almost wholly in Cameroon territory. It is largely used by small vessels, flat-bottomed motor-boats, and canoes, and is the principal means of local communication.

The long strip of territory in the south-east of the colony through which the Sanga flows is bounded in the greater part of its length by the Green Likwala, which joins the Sanga shortly before that river empties itself into the Congo, and the Likwala-Mossaka, a tributary of the Congo. Each of these rivers is reported to have about 200 kilometres of navigable water. The value of this southern water connexion from a commercial point of view is discounted by the fact that sea-going ships can only go up the Congo as far as Matadi. Owing to the long section of rapids above that point, all incoming goods must be transferred to the Matadi–Léopoldville Railway and re-transferred to the Congo river steamer at Stanley Pool, and *vice versa* on the outgoing journey.

The navigability of the Sanga river system as it stood in 1912 can be described briefly as follows. At the lowest water-level steamers drawing 2 metres ascend to Wesso, and those drawing from 80 centimetres to 1 metre go, with occasional difficulties, as far as Nola. At the season of high water, steamers drawing from 1 to 2 metres can ascend to Nola without difficulty. From Salo (Ssalo) to Nola navigation is open to small craft for six months in the year, but to large vessels for two months only. This main route, which covers about 1,000 kilometres from Bonga, near the junction of the Sanga with the Congo, is supplemented by three tributary waterways :

(*a*) The Mambere, which is the upper portion of the Sanga, is navigable from Nola to Bania and from Likaja to Carnot. From Nola to Bania navigation is possible for $2\frac{1}{2}$ months at most, and then only for small motor launches or flat-bottomed vessels. Between Bania and Likaya the river makes its way through a mass of rocky cliffs, and has cut in many places a narrow gorge, only a few yards across. Rapids entirely prevent navigation for $3\frac{1}{2}$ kilometres, and the overland path by which canoes are taken to avoid them is 7 kilometres long. The section from Likaya to Carnot is navigable throughout the year by small steam pinnaces. At a distance of one day's journey above Carnot great rapids close all farther navigation.

(*b*) The Kadei, from Nola to its confluence with the Dume, is not navigable at all for steamers; but above the confluence a few short sections are open to boat traffic. In 1911–12 a survey of the Dume and its tributary the Mara showed that the Dume could be made navigable only with immense labour and cost; to make the river accessible and serviceable it was recommended that the road connecting it with the Nyong at Abong-Mbang should be completed. The section of the Dume from Nyassi to its confluence with the Kadei is already navigable to a limited extent by small vessels for nine months in the year; but the current is strong, and there are many sharp bends.

(*c*) In 1913 the Ja (Dscha) was examined and found to be perfectly navigable from Wesso to Molundu, with a regular flow and great depth even at low water. The only serious obstacle to navigation, the Wilhelmina Falls, could easily be overcome. A French service of small steamers, the Messageries Fluviales du Congo, was maintained from Wesso to Ngoila (beyond Molundu), and was under contract with the German Government. Higher up, on the section between Kul and Kam, traffic is possible throughout the year for motor-boats and big canoes. The Bumba, which joins the Ja at Molundu, cannot be used for continuous navigation.

It is possible that a through route from Duala to the Congo may be developed in the future by connecting the Nyong by railway with either the Dume or the Ja; but in either case double trans-shipment and the use of flat-bottomed boats can hardly be avoided.

3. *The Benue Basin.*—The Benue and its tributaries, the Mao-Kabi and the Faro, have their sources in Cameroon; the Benue crosses the frontier just above Yola and joins the Niger at Lokoja in Nigeria. During the high-water season, steamers of 800 tons can ascend as far as Yola; but above that point shallows interfere with all but very small steamers, and in the low-water season Garua can only be reached from Yola by canoes. Under the German administration freight destined for Garua was carried by Cameroon Government steamers as far as Lokoja; above that point the small steamers or steel canoes of the Niger Company were employed.

An article of the Berlin Act of 1885 provided for the free navigation of the Niger, and for a short time a German firm ran a small river service. In later years the German Government mail was chiefly brought to Garua by a boat chartered from the Niger Company. The charter prices were probably not unreasonable, as the river was open for only a few months, and the cost of the whole year's upkeep had therefore to be recovered on the few trips made during this season. The Germans, however, considered that they could provide a less costly service themselves, and in 1914 started the Niger-Benue Transport Company.

The establishment of a water-route across Cameroon from Nigeria to French territory has frequently been discussed. The proposed route would connect the rivers Benue and Logone *via* Lere and Fianga. The intermediate section (400 kilometres) would be covered by the Mao-Kabi river and the chain of water-holes known as the Tuburi lakes. The problem first attracted the attention of the French Government. Between 1902 and 1911 there were five expeditions in the Mao-Kabi region. The last of these, that of Mercier (1911), found that the Mao-Kabi was navigable in the high-water season (July to September) for 30-ton boats between Garua and Lere, but during the rest of the year only as far as the Bipare rapids. Traffic is restricted in the dry season to steel canoes, and at the lowest state of the water to native boats. From Lere to the Logone traffic is only possible for transport canoes during three months of the year. The French administration aimed at making this a practicable water-route, and now that part of it is again in French hands the project may be revived, although it has been to some extent forestalled by the Lere–Binder–Jagua road.

4. *The Lake Chad Region.*—Of the rivers flowing to the Chad basin the most notable in German territory is the Logone. German reports upon the river up to 1913 were few and conflicting; but it seems clear that it is navigable over a large part of its course and for a great part of the year, and its direction ensures it great value as a trade highway. The political objections, that it formed the German-French frontier for part of its course and that its outlet in Lake Chad was French, no longer have force; its economic value should be investigated more closely. There was a German suggestion to link it to the Nyong river by a railway, and so through the Midland Railway to

bring Lake Chad into connexion with the sea, but no survey seems to have been carried out to find a practicable route.

The Shari river is navigable for a considerable distance for small boats, and to a certain extent probably for steamers.

Great attention has been paid to the question of waterways by the French, and more recently by the German, Government. The latter had begun to realize that, in view of the special physical conditions existing in Cameroon and the primitive stage of economic development in the greater part of the colony, it would only be through extending the use of waterways that trade intercourse could be increased.

(c) Railways

The railway development of Cameroon at the time of the outbreak of war was on a lower scale than that of any of the other German African colonies. This will be seen from the following table :

	Area in square km.	Population in 1913.	Km. of railway completed. 1909.	1913.
Togoland . .	87,200	1,003,000	190	327
Cameroon . .	756,000	2,541,000	110	310
German South-West Africa	835,100	250,000	1,600	2,104
German East Africa	995,000	7,641,000	460	1,435

Further railway construction would not be easy from the engineering point of view on account of the mountain barriers and the enormous forest and swamp areas throughout the centre and south.

In 1914 there were three railways in the colony. The oldest was the narrow-gauge light railway of the Victoria Plantations Company, connecting the plantations with the harbour at Victoria. It ran from

Victoria through Soppo to Meanja, passing close to Buea, the administrative capital, and had a branch to Molive.   Including the track in the plantations themselves, it was 52 kilometres long in 1913 and 74 in 1914. The gauge is reported to be either 60 or 75 centimetres. This railway is now in the English zone.

The other two were the Northern Railway from Bonoberi, opposite Duala, to Nkongsamba (the so-called Manenguba line), and the Midland Railway from Duala through Edea to the Nyong.   Both of these lines are now in the French zone.   Their total length was as follows at the outbreak of war :

	Length of line in operation, July 1914.	Total length of railway.	Gauge.
	Km.	Km.	Metre.
Northern Railway	160	160	1
Midland Railway	174	283 [1]	1

The Northern Railway runs from Bonoberi northwards through the forest to Lum (108 kilometres) and Nkongsamba (160 kilometres).   This line is owned by the Kamerun Eisenbahn-Gesellschaft, which was founded in June 1906 as a German colonial company to take up a concession granted to the Imperial Chancellor to construct a railway through the Manenguba Mountains.   The line, however, stopped at the foot of the rise to the plateau after piercing the thick forest belt.   Even up to that point it was very expensive to construct.   There are several excellent iron bridges, the longest of which are at Bepele and Kake. The railway was to have been continued at least as far as Bamum, which is a populous district, but up to June 1914 this extension was still only being planned, though the contracting company (the Deutsche Kolonial-

---

[1] Including 109 kilometres still under construction at the outbreak of war.

Eisenbahn-Bau- und Betriebs-Gesellschaft) had completed its survey of the extension by April 1913, and had reported most favourably upon it. The country which would be covered by this part of the line is fertile, and reported to possess a good climate. The existing line is a single track. The journey between the termini occupied 9 hours 30 minutes, and one train ran daily each way. The rolling stock on December 31, 1913, amounted to 6 locomotives, 11 passenger coaches, and 74 goods wagons. The staff included 23 white officials and 608 natives. The administrative offices were at Bonoberi.

Besides the railway, the Kamerun Eisenbahn-Gesellschaft owned a land concession of 27,500 hectares, partly let to tobacco companies, partly (3,000 hectares) planted with oil-palms, and partly exploited for its timber and fine woods, which the railway company cut and sent to Germany. The chief products carried on the railway were palm oil, palm kernels, and timber. The line served numerous plantations. The railway, which in 1913 had reached its third year of working, showed very good figures for goods traffic and receipts ; the profit of 2·71 per cent. on the capital cost was satisfactory for a tropical colonial railway in the third year of working. Of the goods carried, 14,895 tons went inland, and 25,823 tons, or 63·42 per cent., went to the coast. The percentage of the working expenses to the gross receipts was only 54·39 per cent. for 1913, as against 65·36 per cent for 1912.

The Midland Railway, which was designed to be the trunk line for the Cameroon railway system, leaves Duala in a south-easterly direction, and crosses the Sanaga at Edea. The line is planned for construction as far as Mbalmajo on the Nyong. It runs for the whole of its length through tropical forest. At the time the war began, it was under construction in sections by the Deutsche Kolonial-Eisenbahn-Bau- und Betriebs-Gesellschaft. As each section was finished, the Government made a contract for a fresh one, and meanwhile leased to the same company the operating of the completed sections. The estimates for 1914 give the total cost of constructing 300 kilometres of line as nearly 50,000,000 marks, or £12,800 per mile of line. Only the less expensive sections have so far been built.

According to the annual report of the Deutsche Kolonial-Eisenbahn-Bau- und Betriebs-Gesellschaft, published in the *Deutsches Kolonialblatt* in May 1915, the state of construction up to November 1914 was as follows. The line was finished as far as Biyoka (150 kilometres) and had been open to traffic since November 1913. A further section was under construction during 1914 from Biyoka to the Nyong, and part of this section, from kilometre 150 to kilometre 174, was completed and opened for traffic at the beginning of July. The large amount of embanking and bridge work necessary on the next portion of the section, kilometre 174 to kilometre 195, made it necessary to add a narrow-gauge auxiliary construction line, which was working at the end of June 1914. Work was continued up to November 1914, despite the military operations. Very little engineering work except the bridges over the Dibamba at Yapoma (Japoma) and over the Sanaga (north and south arms) at Edea has so far been necessary. There are no steep gradients, but several wide curves. The locomotives used by the Germans were dismantled by them before their retreat, and after the occupation two new ones were sent from other colonies to replace them.

Proposed Railway Extensions.—In July 1914 a comprehensive programme of railway extension, covering a period of ten years, and involving the construction of over 1,000 kilometres of line, was presented to the Reichstag by the Kolonial-Wirtschaftliches Komitee.

The most important feature of this programme was the plan for a trunk line across the Protectorate from Duala, roughly following the 4th degree of north latitude.   Duala, which is an excellent port, is the natural outlet for the French territories of Ubanghi-Shari and Chad.   In 1914 the points of entry and outlet for trade in these regions were at Bangui, on the Ubanghi, and at a point below the rapids of Singa in the district of the Lobaje.   Goods were there transferred to the Ubanghi river for a 1,400 kilometre journey to Brazzaville, at which point they were again transferred to Kinshasa on the Belgian side for transit by rail to the port of Matadi (about 400 kilometres).   From Matadi to Bangui up-stream took 15 days (2 days by rail and 13 by boat), with a delay, as a rule, of two days in Brazzaville.   Down-stream the journey took at least 12 days.   Dr. Zimmermann in his *Was ist uns Zentral-Afrika?* proposed that the Germans should tap this trade from Cameroon.

A study of the map shows that a line drawn from Duala through Yaunde and Dume Station and continued almost due east reaches the Ubanghi at Singa. Being of much shorter length, this would divert the trade of the French Ubanghi-Shari territories from the more cumbrous route of the Congo valley.   In the long negotiations which ended in the Franco-German Agreement of 1911, German diplomatists attached great importance to the acquisition of Singa.   Their reason for doing so is now clear.

The new line was to be a continuation of the Midland Railway through the oil-palm and rubber districts of Yaunde to the grasslands round Bertua.   At the same time marine engineering work on the Nyong was being pushed forward, so that this river could be utilized as a means of transport for railway material as soon as the Midland line reached it. A field railway was to connect the river with Bertua. From Bertua the line was to be carried eastwards down the valley of the Kadei to Nola on the Sanga. The final extension from Nola to Singa on the Ubanghi, already referred to, was set down for later construction, it being first necessary to clear the district of sleeping-sickness. The whole line was to be constructed on a scale sufficient to meet a future heavy traffic—a significant hint that it would serve strategical purposes in any future operations against the Congo.

An alternative route to the Congo was also proposed, namely, a southern extension of the Midland Railway through the Ebolova district, and thence probably *via* Akoafim to Molundu on the navigable Ja. Such a line would also pass through important oil-palm and rubber districts; but, owing perhaps to the greater engineering difficulties that would be encountered, this scheme did not receive the same measure of support as the former.

The funds for these railway developments were to be provided by means of an Imperial loan, and so at a much lower rate of interest than if provided by a Protectorate loan.

A second important feature of the programme was the construction of a main line from south to north, leaving the extended Midland line at Bertua and running through Kunde, Rei-Buba, and Marua—districts thought valuable for cotton-growing—to Mora. From Mora the line was to branch to Dikoa on the western frontier, and to Kusseri on the eastern frontier, whence traffic could pass down the Logone and Shari rivers to Lake Chad.

Three further branches westwards off this main

line were included in the Government scheme. These were to Tibati through Deng Deng, to Ngaundere, and to Garua, the last named being for traffic passing down the Benue through Nigeria to the sea. On the east, at a much later date, connexion was to be established *via* the Wina valley with the heads of navigation on the west and east Logone, meeting the frontier of French Equatorial Africa at Gore on the latter river.

As regards the Northern Railway, further construction was to be limited to its extension through Bare to the prospective cotton-bearing district of Bamum as far as Fumban. The earlier ambitious plans for a continuation north were entirely discarded in view of the expense of construction.

In 1913 the idea of a southern railway from the coast inland was definitely abandoned by the Government for reasons which they declined to publish in their parliamentary report. The Kribi coast merchants were much disappointed, as they had been encouraged to expect that a railway would be built either from Kampo or Kribi.

(d) *Posts and Telegraphs*

According to the German official report the number of post offices in Cameroon in the year 1912–13 was .37. Only 10 principal places in the Protectorate had offices conducting a full postal business. Others were limited to the sale of postage stamps, the handling of ordinary and registered letters, and the delivery of ordinary parcels. In 1913 eighteen of the post offices were also telegraph offices, and there were three additional telegraph offices which had no postal business. The postal service, as in the other German colonies, was an Imperial service directly under the control of the Reichs-Postamt in Berlin. The staff included a postmaster and inspector, assisted by 21 other officials. The native staff numbered 83.

' Flag-post ', so called on account of the badges of the runners, was introduced for pressing Government messages, and covered the greater part of the Protectorate.

European Mails.—Before the war, mails were carried by vessels belonging to the German West African combine twice a month each way, and by the joint service of the African Steamship Company and the British and African Steam Navigation Company once every four weeks. The coast was served by the Government flotilla. The postal connexion with Fernando Po was through Victoria on the mainland and Santa Isabel on the island. Mails were delivered at any of the coast points as opportunity offered, and were taken to the nearest post office inland by runners. On some sections of the coast there was postal connexion by means of canoes and pinnaces, both between coast points and between these and river post offices inland. There was a service of runners inland four times every month. Two points, Garua and Kusseri, obtained their letters *via* Nigeria, while the post office at Molundu on the Ja river was supplied through Matadi in the Belgian Congo.

The telephone system was confined to the few chief towns.

(2) External

(a) Ports

Duala harbour possesses great natural advantages. The only obstacle which used to prevent big steamers from anchoring before the town was the so-called inner bar, a clay bank lying across the river some three miles below the town, leaving only 5½ metres depth at high tide. In 1914 this bank was being dredged so as to leave a channel of sufficient depth to accommodate all ships. There is also an outer bar of soft, loose mud ; but this is no obstacle to the ships which generally use the port, and could probably be run over by larger ones. The landing quays at Duala are close alongside the Midland Railway station.

The Cameroon Government decided in 1914 thoroughly to reconstruct Duala town. Nearly 4,000,000 marks were to be spent upon the work, of which 2,250,000 appeared in the estimates for 1914. A compact and orderly town was to be constructed on European lines, canalized, and provided with a water-supply. The natives were to be removed to new settlements arranged for them elsewhere. This goes to show that the Government expected the chief development of traffic to be in Duala and not in Bonoberi, the terminus of the Northern Railway, which is only of local importance.

The town of Duala lies on an open plain 20 metres above the water-level, the two divisions Bell and Akwa being separated by a broad *nullah* (formerly a mangrove swamp), on the level floor of which the Midland Railway station has been planned. The quay forms the bank of the Wuri river, which closes the mouth of this nullah, and extension is possible along the bank in either direction. As so far planned, there was to be room for three or four ocean steamers to lie alongside and discharge their cargo at the same time. Goods are transferred by crane to the quay, from which a network of lines leads past the customs sheds either to the station direct or to the factories along the river-side. For the harbour improvements in 1914 a sum of 8,790,000 marks was set aside in the budget.

Bonoberi, the terminus of the Northern Railway, lies on the opposite side of the river on the promontory that forms the corner of the next higher reach. There was apparently no intention to develop it.

Victoria, ' the pearl of Cameroon ', lies at the end of Ambas Bay, one of the most beautiful sites in the world. It is the terminus of the Plantation Light Railway, for which it serves as a port of export ; a landing bridge is available for handling cargo. One of the senior Nigerian marine officers states that as a naval station Ambas Bay has great possibilities, although it is somewhat exposed to west winds. There is deep water close inshore ; but owing to the nature of its back-country Victoria is badly situated for a commercial port, and in order to make a naval station of it heavy expenditure would be necessary.

Rio del Rey lies at the end of a marshy gulf. Its unhealthy conditions caused it to be deserted by factory owners in 1902.

Bibundi, at the foot of the Cameroon Mountains, has a deep but exposed anchorage.

Kribi, though quite a small place, was at one time the largest port of export for forest products from south Cameroon ; in more recent years, owing to the exploitation of the forest areas extending inland and farther east, it has had to share the export of this produce with Molundu. It was strongly advocated as a terminus of a southern railway, but was rejected by the German Government as not likely to make a good port.

There are two notable inland ports: Garua, on the Benue, the port of entry from Nigeria, and Molundu, on the Ja, the port of entry from the Belgian Congo. The value of these ports lies in the fact that they are situated near the boundary lines of Cameroon ; should these be shifted, the ports would lose much of their importance.

In 1910 *Garua* was the Government centre of German Adamawa. The total number of white residents was 17. There was a Government school, a hospital, and a dispensary, all free for the natives. The garrison consisted of 100 native soldiers. Garua is only open as a port for six weeks in the year. It is reported that steamers can lie alongside the river bank at a stone quay.

Molundu is a station built on a slightly undulating plain, on which the trees have been cut down and replaced by banana and cassava plantations, which provide work for the numerous convicts brought from all parts of the colony. It is served by the shipping companies of the Congo river system. The German interest was limited, in 1912, to the Süd-Kamerun Gesellschaft and the firm of Walther Karl. The Süd-Kamerun Gesellschaft had two small steamers of 30 and 50 tons respectively. These took from 2 to $2\frac{1}{2}$ weeks to reach Molundu from Kinshasa, and $1-1\frac{1}{2}$ weeks for the return, which was timed to connect with the Belgian mail steamers. The firm of Walther Karl, which had been taken over by Woermann & Co., had only one 25-ton steamer. At the outbreak of war in 1914 the services in operation on the Sanga river were in the hands of the Compagnie Belgo-Allemande, which was a development of the Walther Karl and Woermann companies, and the Neu-Kamerun Schiff-fahrts-Gesellschaft, which was formed under a friendly arrangement between the Süd-Kamerun Gesellschaft and a French company, the Messageries Fluviales du Congo.

Nature and Volume of Trade.—According to the German Government statistics for 1912, shipping in Cameroon had been steadily increasing for some years past, both in number of ships and tonnage. The following table illustrates this, and shows further that about 75 per cent. of the shipping (if Government vessels are included) was under the German flag :

Year.	Ocean-going vessels under German flag.		Cameroon Government coasting vessels.		Vessels not under German flag.		Total.	
	No.	Reg. tons net.	No.	Reg. tons net.	No.	Reg. tons net.	No.	Reg. tons.
10	217	933,468	144	57,796	168	303,565	529	1,294,829
11	242	1,126,206	140	56,000	154	368,852	536	1,551,058
12	254	1,254,250	187	74,800	156	403,980	597	1,733,030

Victoria and Duala are the most important ports in respect of entrances and clearances, the next in importance being Kampo, Kribi, and Rio del Rey.

(b) *Shipping Lines*

The oversea shipping of Cameroon had been a practical monopoly of the Woermann firm, whose activity in the West African shipping world dates back more than thirty years. In 1907 the Woermann Linie formed a combine with the two other German companies interested in the West African service, the Hamburg-Bremer Afrika Linie and the Hamburg-Amerika Linie, in order to compete with the British combination of the African Steamship Company and the British and African Steam Navigation Company, formed by Elder, Dempster & Co. The British combine maintained a weekly service from Liverpool to Rio del Rey, Victoria, Duala, Kribi, Batanga, and Elobey (Spanish). The German combine had a fortnightly mail service —the Kamerun Haupt-Linie—from Hamburg to Victoria, Duala, Kribi, Plantation, and Longyi, and a monthly service—the Kamerun Linie II—from Hamburg, calling at the Cameroon ports and those of Fernando Po, Spanish Guinea, and French Gabun.

The Government flotilla which served the coast of the Protectorate, acting as feeder for the Woermann Mail Line, consisted of two sea-going steamers and four river boats. The service must be counted as one of the failures of German administration. The ships were ill-designed and uncomfortable, while their service was irregular and caused bitter complaints from the white settlers. The Governor in 1910 tried to sell the vessels, offering them to the German South-West Africa Government, for which they would have been even less suitable, but as he was himself transferred there the sale fell through. A fortnightly mail service to the coast ports, including Rio Muni, was maintained.

(c) *Cable and Wireless Communication*

Until the end of 1912 cable communication with the Protectorate was *via* Bonny, in southern Nigeria. In January 1913, however, the Deutsche Südamerikanische Telegraphen-Gesellschaft completed a new cable from Monrovia to Duala.

According to the report of the Reichs-Postamt in March 1915, a wireless station on the Telefunken system was opened at Duala on March 5, 1913. This station was in connexion in the same year with the Telefunken Company's station at Santa Isabel in Fernando Po, with the station in Togoland, and with sea-going ships. It was controlled by the German Government, but was open to the general public for correspondence at 35 centimes a word. The normal range was 600 nautical miles.

(B) INDUSTRY

(1) LABOUR SUPPLY AND CONDITIONS

Cameroon is not a white man's country, and its development must therefore depend on the capacity of the native population and the possibility of their being stimulated to undertake and carry on plantation, agriculture, stock-breeding, and the like, under European superintendence. In this respect the outlook is not unpromising.

There is great agricultural activity throughout Cameroon. In the forest area the natives seem to cultivate more than they themselves require only when there is some special demand or some special opportunity for gain. In the savannah country, on the other hand, they show themselves in some localities active and intelligent agriculturists.

Before the war the Germans were finding considerable difficulty in securing the amount of labour needed for public works and for the cultivation of the plantations in the coastal regions; as labour was attracted to railway construction, the plantations especially felt the shortage. This condition of affairs persisted under the Allied administration. The Germans attempted to meet the difficulty by the institution of a kind of forced labour. They levied a tax of six shillings on every male, and if this was not paid the defaulter was obliged to do sixteen days' labour for the State, his services being utilized for such public works as might be going on. Should there not be public work available, the defaulter could be leased to private firms or planters, who supplied the labourer with his daily rations only. British observers considered this system unsatisfactory both in its accompaniments and its results; and the Germans were meditating the importation of Chinese labour. There is at present, generally speaking, no economic inducement to the Central African native to work as a wage labourer on a white man's estate; and it is probable that a system of plantations owned and administered by white men is inappropriate. But it has been found in the neighbouring colony of Nigeria that the natives are not at all averse to developing the agricultural resources of the country on their own behalf under European guidance, especially as their economic needs begin to increase.

(2) Agriculture

(a) *Methods of Cultivation*

Throughout the whole colony the natives cultivate the soil.   In the south agriculture is their chief means of subsistence, apart from hunting and fishing and the collection of rubber ; in the grass country towards the north there is a good deal of stock-raising as well. The hoe is the native implement ; the plough, formerly common among the highly civilized Kanuris of Bornu, has disappeared.   This is chiefly due to the prevalence of the tsetse fly, which makes the employment of cattle impossible.   In the bush and forest districts the ground is prepared by burning off the bush and scrub, whose ashes are used as manure, large trees being allowed to stand ; after some five years the land is abandoned and another plot prepared. Owing to the absence of mineral plant-food in most of the soil, intermittent fallow is necessary.   The natives prefer for agriculture land which is submerged during the rainy season. The agricultural work, as opposed to the preliminary work of clearing the land, is done by women.   A certain amount of artificial irrigation is practised in the dry season.

In general the production of wealth in Cameroon is still in the hands of the natives, apart from the very small, though fertile and valuable, area of plantations near Buea and Victoria.   In the case of cotton and rice, which grow on a large scale only in the remote north, it is unlikely that European plantation will under present conditions supersede native production.   In the case of rubber and palm oil, on the other hand, the plantation product may in time oust the wild ; rubber especially was being collected by wasteful methods, and in certain districts the supply was being exhausted. The following table [1] shows the area of plantation

[1] From the *Bulletin of the Imperial Institute*, 1915.

land from 1909 to 1912, and the proportion devoted to various crops :

	On Jan. 1, 1909.	On Jan. 1, 1910.	On Jan. 1, 1911.	On Jan. 1, 1912.
	Acres.	Acres.	Acres.	Acres.
Total area of plantation .	205,765	208,245	237,833	248,891
Area actually planted .	28,265	31,978	37,810	54,490
Area under cocoa . .	18,945	21,023	23,958	26,635
Area under *Funtumia* .	6,668	7,515	10,475	10,550
Area under *Hevea* . .	673	988	5,473	7,010
Oil-palms . . .	[124,800] [1]	[109,400]	2,388	4,790
Bananas. . . .	[240,000]	[409,000]	1,788	4,493

These plantations are all situated on the west, south, and east slopes of the Cameroon Mountains. They have very good European quarters, and are traversed by broad ways, mostly with light trolley lines along them.

(b) *Products of Commercial Value*

As regards agriculture in the narrower sense, native cultivation, though general, has not been very extensive, the demands of the natives being in most districts easily satisfied.   Food crops are, however, raised more extensively for special demands, such as arise near railways, administrative stations, the larger towns, and the chief places on the caravan routes and rivers ; in these neighbourhoods the native raises rice, maize, plantains, bananas, yams, cassava, sweet-potatoes, and ground-nuts, as well as sorghum (*dura* or *dari*) in the northern districts, and some kola and sesame in isolated places.   In several districts a certain amount of tobacco is planted ; there is also some little fruit-raising, notably in the villages of the Ambam.   In the highlands of Oshang, and in other places such as Ebolova and Yaunde, new crops such as the English potato, black bush-beans, and turnips have been

---

[1] The figures in brackets denote the number of trees ; the acreage for 1909 and 1910 is not available.

introduced, and the climate seems suited to these crops.

The main products of commercial importance are rubber, palm oil and palm kernels, and cocoa.

Before the late war *rubber* was the most important export from the colony—the value of the quantity exported in 1912 being 11,472,223 marks (about half the total value of the exports), of which only 170,552 marks represented plantation rubber. The greater part is collected by the natives from wild trees and vines, which grow in enormous quantities all over the forest region of the west and south and also in the savannahs of south Adamawa and elsewhere. The chief varieties are the *Landolphia* vine and the tree *Funtumia elastica* (*Kickxia*). Almost the entire population of Lomie, Molundu, Dume, and Geng-Deng is engaged in the collection of rubber ; there were, in 1910–11, over a thousand coloured middlemen buying rubber from the natives and selling to the dealers, of whom there were about 50, owning some 230 purchasing stations. There are at present indications that the supplies of the west districts are becoming exhausted ; but the Ngaundere plateau and the Sarri Hills contain supplies of rubber hitherto untapped.

The future of wild rubber, however, is very uncertain. It is usually dirty and not of uniform quality, and is disliked by merchants, especially for the latter reason. Further, in 1913, after the heavy fall in prices, the cost of production of wild *Kickxia* rubber was considerably in excess of the price obtainable in Hamburg. Rubber, which in December 1912 was worth 7 marks a kg., sank in 1913 to 3·40 marks a kg. and even lower. Every attempt was made to reduce the cost of production by establishing direct relations with the producers and avoiding the native middlemen ; also by the reduction of the cost of transport and by improving the quality of the rubber. But it appeared impossible to reduce the cost below 4·40 marks a kg. On the other hand, it must be borne in mind that the industry was re-established in the Belgian Congo by drastic reduction of the cost of production to 3·50 francs a kg. in 1913, and by the improvement of the quality. There, however, the problem of transport is somewhat simpler.

It is therefore impossible to predict the future of wild rubber; but it must be borne in mind that competent German authorities had decided that it could not be regarded for much longer as an asset of the colony. It will, however, always have a market until the world's demand can be satisfied by plantation rubber.

Plantation rubber, as has been seen, is still in its infancy. Owing to a fear that cocoa might not be successful, planters were induced to undertake the cultivation of rubber on a considerable scale. Results have not been particularly encouraging. A beginning was made with *Funtumia elastica*, but this tree is now being discarded, as it is deep-rooted and therefore unsuitable to the volcanic soil of the Cameroon Mountains. In its place *Hevea brasiliensis* (Pará rubber) was before the war being planted everywhere, as it is better suited to the soil and to cultivation side by side with cocoa, though it is said to suffer from an unspecified root disease. The cost of production was about 3 marks a kg. (in 1912) as against 5 to 6 marks in the case of *Funtumia*. There seems no reason why these plantations should not in due course be remunerative, though the opinion has been expressed that the cost of production of plantation rubber will always be higher in Africa than in the East Indies, and that it will be necessary to combine it with other forms of cultivation in order to distribute the cost.

Palm oil and palm kernels.—The oil-palm (*Elaeis guineensis*) grows abundantly on the edge of the

Cameroon plateau and also in the south-east of the colony. Some plantations have also been made. The export of palm oil and palm kernels is increasing in importance and value throughout West Africa. Kernel oil is used in the manufacture of soap, vegetable lard, and margarine. In the process of extracting the oil, palm-kernel cake is produced—an excellent cattle food, much in demand in Germany. Palm oil, which is prepared from the pericarp surrounding the kernel, is used for the manufacture of soap and for other industrial purposes, but is not at present suitable as an ingredient for food-stuffs, though it is possible that it could be made so by a slight alteration in the process of manufacture. The oil and kernels are collected by the natives, though the Germans had begun to instal machinery for treating the nuts in order to avoid the waste and adulteration inseparable from the native methods of treatment.

Before the war, no less than three-quarters of the total production of palm kernels in West Africa, of which the greater part came from British possessions, went to Germany to be milled. Latterly attempts have been made to divert the trade to Great Britain, and crushing machinery has been installed at Hull and Liverpool. The demand for vegetable oils and fats is almost inexhaustible ; but the success of the industry in England is dependent on the popularization of the palm-kernel cake as a feeding stuff for cattle. There seems little doubt, however, that this can be achieved.

Cocoa in Cameroon should have a prosperous future. The quality of the cocoa is equal, if not superior, to that of the best produced on the Gold Coast. Under German administration the acreage under cocoa increased from 18,945 in 1909 to 26,635 in 1912 ; and, since the conquest of the country by the Allies, the acreage under cocoa has again been largely increased, and the demand for Cameroon cocoa has been good.   Under the Germans a large majority of the plantations were owned by Europeans ; and of a total shipment of 4,479 tons in 1912 only 701 tons were grown by natives.   It is believed, however, that the native planters were discouraged by the Germans, for native-grown cocoa on the Gold Coast has made rapid progress.   The native plantations are mainly to be found in the low-lying country of the Mungo, Wuri, and Sanaga rivers, the districts of Duala, Yabassi, and Edea near these rivers, and in parts of the slope of the Cameroon Mountains, though in the last-mentioned area the taking up of land for European plantations has prevented an extension of native cultivation.

Cotton has long been cultivated by the natives to some extent, but as a result of the importation of European cotton yarns the industry has fallen more or less into desuetude.   The Germans took up the question in 1911 and sent experts to report on the suitability of various districts for cotton-growing, viz. Bamenda, Banyo, Adamawa, and parts of the country round Lake Chad and Tikar.   The reports were on the whole very favourable, and two experimental stations were established, one in the Bamenda country and the other in the Adamawa country.   The results of experiments made during the first year were various ; but it has been established that it is possible to grow cotton of good quality successfully.   If, however, an industry is ever to be developed on any considerable scale, serious problems of transport and labour will have to be overcome.   It must be borne in mind that in the neighbouring colony of Nigeria, where a cotton industry is gradually being developed some distance inland, facilities for transport by water, rail, and roads are comparatively good.

The export of *kola nuts* has largely increased owing

to their employment in the chemical industry. *Njabi nuts* and *shea nuts* are also exported in comparatively small quantities.

Tobacco, the export of which was valued at over 24,000 marks in 1911, fell almost to zero in 1912. Cultivation proved to be expensive and difficult on account of the dampness of the climate. The Germans, however, persistently encouraged the cultivation of tobacco in their colonies by guaranteed prices, and, notwithstanding previous failures, there were 383 acres under tobacco in 1912. The largest plantation, near Duala, was entirely destroyed when the Germans evacuated that town.

Successful experiments on a small scale have been made in the cultivation of *tea, spices*, and certain *fibre plants*.

The only *animal products* of importance are ivory, ostrich feathers, honey, and wax. Elephants are still numerous in the forest region east of Ngaundere and in the Lake Chad country, though they are gradually dying out. In some places the Germans began to preserve them. The recent fighting seems to have caused great movements of the herds, which may have disappeared completely from their original haunts. The total exports of ivory appear to be diminishing, though the process is irregular.

Ostriches are farmed, and the feathers are exported in small quantities by the Arabs in Bornu. All the Malem tribes keep bees; and honey and wax are plentiful in north Adamawa, Banyo, the Dume district, and other parts.

Of *domestic animals*, cattle are kept all over the north and centre of the colony; but south of the Sanaga the tsetse fly makes general stock-farming impossible. The whole of the north and the grasslands of the Adamawa district afford excellent grazing. Some tribes, however, are reluctant to keep so valuable a possession as cattle, because they are then exposed to raids.   Cattle-breeding in the strict sense is only found among the natives in Adamawa, Banyo, and the Lake Chad region.   From these districts there was at one time an active export of cattle to the neighbouring British and French possessions, but this has diminished of late years owing to a large export duty.   The best cattle are owned by the Bororos, or nomad Fulbes (Fulas), who are particularly expert herdsmen.   The Shuas also have large herds, and, though themselves dirty, keep their cattle clean.

The Germans had begun to show an interest in cattle-breeding, and had started several experimental stations, the chief being at Buea, Jang, and Yaunde.

Horses are found in the north (especially among the Shuas) and west centre, but they cannot be kept in the forest or even in the south savannah region. Sheep and goats are kept everywhere.   Pigs, which are supposed to have been introduced by Europeans, are kept by the tribes of the west near the coast.   Fowls and dogs are universal.

(c) Forestry

The tropical forest area of the south is rich in mahogany, ebony, teak, and woods useful for building. The cutting is done chiefly by the natives.   The development of timber-cutting for export is hampered by the absence of waterways in the interior and the lack of labour.   The trees stand isolated and are troublesome to float.   Something has been done by the introduction of transportable saws, which reduce the trunks to planks on the spot.   The export of mahogany is considerable, and the advance of the exportation of this and ebony is likely to be maintained.   The value of the export of mahogany and ebony in 1912 was 69,600 and 184,189 marks respectively, as against 380,000 and 138,324 marks in 1911.

There are many trees of local importance. Among these may be mentioned the kola trees in the forest area, the bamboo palm (*Raphia vinifera*) in the marshy regions, gum-producing acacias in the extreme north, fibre-producing plants (*Ceiba pentandra*) in the forest area, 'gabai' and others in the Lake Chad basin.

Afforestation was attempted at Johann-Albrechts-Höhe, and a number of forest reserves have been made in the Yabassi, Edea, and ·Jang districts. A forestry school was established at Jang.

(d) *Land Tenure*

Under the German administration, land could be obtained from the Government on lease, or bought outright from the natives, subject to the securing of a certain minimum to each native family.

(3) FISHERIES

Fishing is pursued by the natives in all parts of the colony, but on an important scale only by the tribes of the north, who inhabit the shores and islands of Lake Chad and the Shari and Logone rivers. Here the dense population live mainly upon fish.

Fishing is also practised along the coast, especially at Batanga. Attempts were made by the Germans to develop the industry. At present the natives only fish to satisfy their own needs.

(4) MINERALS

No mineral deposits of any considerable value have been discovered, but the resources of the Protectorate in this respect have as yet been very superficially investigated.

A thin stratum of *coal* (with 48 per cent. of ash) has

been found in the Cross River bed a little above Ossidinge.

Galena occurs in the cretaceous sandstone of the Ossidinge district, but no argentiferous lead or zinc ores comparable with those in Nigeria have been discovered.

Traces of *gold*, in unimportant quantities, have been reported between Ossidinge and Tinto. The country immediately north of the Cameroon River is reported to contain gold and silver veins of no great importance. Gold is also stated to occur in the neighbourhood of the Edea station. In the years before the war, two English companies, one of them working with German capital, prospected for gold and tin on the Sabri massif and near Gashaka, in the Banyo district. Alluvial gold and deposits of tin were found, but did not justify exploitation.

Graphite is found in the hills of Baibokum.

Magnetic and red *iron ores* have been found in several places near the Sanaga and in the vicinity of Yabassi, but not at present in quantities to repay working. They are also found in Laka and among the Mandara mountains. Iron ores formed by the decomposition of basalt occur on the hill slopes between Bali and Bamenda. These ores are reported to be present in considerable quantities, and, if suitable transport facilities were available, they might repay working.

Mica of good quality has been found in the Ossidinge district and also farther north in the Kentu district.

Petroleum has been found in the estuary of the Cameroon River, near Duala, but numerous borings failed to produce satisfactory results. There is bituminous shale near Ossidinge.

There are numerous *salt* springs in the Ossidinge district. The natives obtain salt from these by condensation, and trade with it in the interior. Skilled native labour is available, and a high proportion of sodium chloride in the samples of brine taken (5 to 8 per cent.) suggests the possibility of salt beds beneath the surface. There are other salt springs near Galim and perhaps in the Ebolova district.

Tourmaline is found in the region north of Duala and in the Jang district.

Prospecting for *wolframite* has hitherto been unsuccessful.

With regard to *building materials*, clays and loams suitable for brick-making are abundant in Cameroon. Limestones, however, are scarce, and those so far discovered are not of suitable quality either for cement-making or for fluxing purposes in smelting iron ore.

To sum up, the country shows promising indications of the existence of a number of economic minerals, but no definite results have as yet been obtained.

(5) MANUFACTURES

No manufactured goods were exported overseas, except in so far as the preparation of the agricultural products to which reference has been made can be regarded as manufacture.

Native industries are not of much importance, but in all parts of the country pottery-making (almost exclusively by women) and work in leather and metal are practised, and considerable skill is shown. In various parts of the country mats and coloured stuffs are woven from palm-fibre. Cotton is grown and woven in the mountainous district of south-western Adamawa, the stuffs being coloured with indigo and red and yellow dyes. Iron is extracted and forged in various parts; it is also worked up into agricultural implements, ornaments, and household objects. Brass-founding is not unknown.

(6) Power

No mechanical power, on any considerable scale, has been established in the colony. A great deal of hydro-electric power would be available from the rivers, more especially in the higher districts.

(C) COMMERCE

(1) Domestic

(a) *Principal Branches of Trade*

In the early days of the occupation of Cameroon, German influence scarcely extended beyond the coast area, and trade was carried on at the various coast towns on the so-called ' trust system ', i. e. natives were provided with goods, and entered into an agreement to bring in exchange specified amounts of the various commodities of the country. This system was obviously merely provisional. In due course trading stations (*Faktoreien*) began to be established up-country. The Nordwest-Kamerun Gesellschaft, which was entrusted with the development of a vague area north of the Sanaga, established a large number of stations, using the Cross River for transport. Progress was slow, as the Cross River is largely in British territory, and the British, by subsidizing transport, were able to offer better prices to the natives. Nevertheless, trading stations were gradually being established in the high country to the north-east ; Bamum and Banyo were becoming especially important centres.

In the Cameroon estuary the system of trading stations did not reach beyond the navigable points of the rivers, i. e. Mundame and Yabassi. The southern forest country, however, was energetically developed by the Süd-Kamerun Gesellschaft. Hausa trade had already penetrated this part of the country, and there was considerable trading connexion with Kribi. The company established its head-quarters at Molundu, even farther south than the Hausa influence had reached; but it had an uphill task, and was forced in 1914 to reduce its sphere of working to a district between the rivers Njue, Bumba, Bange, Ja, and Mbede—a country rich in rubber. This district was made over to the company freehold, except for certain Government rights as regards roads, river stations, &c. Expenses were, however, considerable, and dividends were small and infrequent. Native middlemen were also serious rivals to the company, especially during the rubber boom. Kribi was the chief centre of export. Attempts were made to send goods by the Congo route, but this was usually found to be considerably more expensive.

Central and north Adamawa formed another trading district. The caravan routes radiated mainly from the Benue. Trading stations were found as far north as Lake Chad.

Trading conditions varied a good deal in different parts of the colony. In the south there were European merchants operating from the chief stations on the coast through up-country stations managed by white men, who again were in touch with small bush stations, mostly native, whence the travelling buyers of rubber and ivory went out. Except, however, in the south, the Hausas, who are natural traders, played the chief part in the trade of the interior; they were able to carry goods more cheaply than white agents, and consequently up-country stations under white men were considerably fewer.

(b) Towns, Markets, Fairs, &c.

Trade relations in the southern forest country were naturally primitive; there were few settlements of any size and each was independent.

Markets were, however, established in neutral ground, and there was a certain amount of exchange of food-stuffs, products of domestic industry, cattle, and salt. Certain tribes, in fact, devoted themselves to the business of exchange. In the savannah country to the north, which was commercially under Hausa influence, trade was much brisker. In the larger towns, such as Bamum, there was a daily market, and a connexion was maintained with the Mohammedan peoples to the north; communications, however, remained primitive. Farther north, conditions were still more developed ; this part of the country, under Hausa and Kanuri influence, was connected with the great caravan routes which reach across Africa from Senegal to the Red Sea. Merchandise from distant countries came into the markets, which were held in all the larger towns.

As regards trade at the towns on the frontier and in the interior, Molundu, the centre for the trade on the Congo, was the most active—in 1912 its imports were valued at 594,800 marks, and its exports at 835,000. Next in importance came Garua, the centre for trade through Nigeria on the Benue, with an import and export trade of 598,000 and 494,000 marks respectively. Trade with Nigeria through Nsanakang on the Cross River amounted in the same year only to 291,900 marks in all.

(c) *British Interests*

Most of the important West African firms were established in Cameroon, and the transit trade of Duala is said to have owed a good deal to British development. The chief British firms were as follows : John Holt & Co., Herschell & Co., Wood & Co., Hatton & Cookson, Ambas Bay Trading Co., Ltd., all of Liverpool ; Nyong Rubber Plantations, of London ; King & Co., of Bristol, and the Niger Co.

(2) FOREIGN

(a) *Exports and Imports*

The total value of exports and imports for each year from 1902 to 1912 was as follows :

	Exports.	Imports.
	(In thousands of marks.)	
1902	6,264	13,275
1903	7,139	9,425
1904	8,020	9,378
1905	9,315	13,467
1906	9,945	13,305
1907	15,866	17,296
1908	12,163	16,788
1909	15,448	17,722
1910	19,924	25,580
1911	21,251	29,317
1912	23,336	34,241

It will be seen from the above that since 1909 the imports have doubled and the exports have increased by over 50 per cent. This increase was spread over all the chief articles of export. Cotton in 1912 had increased by 25 per cent. over the total for 1911 ; but the most remarkable increase was in timber, the value in 1912 being nearly 696,000 marks as against 388,000 marks in 1911. The export of kola nuts rose from 19,063 marks in 1911 to 166,962 marks in 1912. Ivory showed a slight drop. Detailed figures for previous years are not available.

The following table shows the value of the chief exports in 1912 :

	Marks.
Bananas	17,591
Cocoa	4,242,271
Ivory	536,193
Kola nuts	166,962
Palm kernels	4,406,151
Palm oil	1,622,387
Rubber (plantation) . . .	170,552
Rubber (wild)	11,301,671
Timber	695,851

About 50 per cent. of the export trade went through Kribi, 35 per cent. through Duala, and 15 per cent. through Victoria.

Of the total exports for 1912, value 23,336,212 marks, goods to the value of 19,840,972 marks went to Germany. Nearly all the remainder went to England, the value being 3,072,091 marks. The chief articles exported to England were cocoa, ivory, palm kernels, palm oil, rubber, and timber.

The following table shows the value of the chief imports in 1912 :

	Marks.
Biscuits	291,223
Butter, eggs, &c.	461,917
Fish (dried and preserved)	2,321,398
Meal	150,575
Meat	853,349
Potatoes	53,274
Rice	1,737,450
Salt	544,452
Sugar	140,084
Vegetables and fruit	252,970
Wine and spirits	941,836
Tobacco, cigars, and cigarettes	1,134,247
Drugs, &c.	925,070
Furniture	92,561
Leather goods (including boots and shoes)	531,193
Textiles (including clothing)	9,584,727
Cement	334,332
Glass	402,852
Iron and manufactured metal goods	3,989,937
Machinery	235,825
Paper, &c.	271,283
Railway lines and sleepers	422,648
Boats, &c.	279,306
Conveyances	184,762
Coal	271,139
Petroleum	161,106

Of the total imports for 1912, value 34,241,582 marks, goods to the value of 27,216,176 marks came from Germany. Of the remainder the greater part, value

5,522,829 marks, came from England. The chief articles sent from England were rice, biscuits, tobacco, spirits, preserved meat and fish, salt, manufactured iron goods, and textiles.

(b) *Customs and Tariffs*

Import duties were as follows :

Spirits, liqueurs, wine, and perfumes containing alcohol . .	from 1 to 3 marks per litre.
Fire-arms	2·50 marks each.
Gunpowder . . .	50 pfennigs per kg.
Salt	60 marks per ton.
Rice	20 marks per ton.
Tobacco, unmanufactured . .	1·50 marks per kg.
Cigars	10 marks per thousand.
Cigarettes	1 mark per thousand.

All other goods not expressly mentioned as exempt from duty paid 10 per cent. *ad valorem*, with the exception of textiles and iron of all kinds, which paid respectively 15 per cent. and 20 per cent.

There were a number of goods exempt from import duty, e.g. Government stores, live animals, cattle-food, plants, and means of transport of every description.

Export duties were as follows :

Ivory and rubber . . .	10 per cent. *ad valorem*.
Earth - nuts, coffee, red copal, white copal, palm oil, palm nuts, and sesame . . .	5 per cent. *ad valorem*.

(D) FINANCE

(1) *Public Finance*

The budget of 1913 balanced at 13,345,000 marks. Details were as follows :

Receipts.

	Marks.
Taxes	2,962,000
Customs, &c.	4,524,000
Dues of various kinds	1,364,000
Receipts from the Midland Railway	3,000
Contributions from the natives for Hospitals	5,000
Interest on Invested Loans	40,000
Contributions from Togoland	3,000
Imperial Contribution towards Military Establishment	2,804,000
Savings from previous years	1,640,000
Total	13,345,000

Expenditure.

	Marks.
Ordinary Expenditure for the year	10,853,000
Adjustment Fund	38,000
Reserve Fund	2,454,000
Total	13,345,000

Besides ordinary receipts, the sum of 1,817,000 marks from the Colonial Loan appears under the heading of Extraordinary Receipts, and a similar, though usually considerably larger, item appears every year since 1908. There is also under Extraordinary Receipts in 1913 an item of 183,000 marks of savings from previous years.

The total amount of public debt up to 1914 appears to have been 49,209,000 marks.

(2) *Currency*

The currency in use in the colony was German. Trade in the interior was carried on largely by means of barter, except in the north where conditions were somewhat more advanced, and cowrie shells, brass and gold tokens, and Maria Theresa dollars were in use.

(3) *Banking*

There was a branch of the German West African Bank in Duala. According to the last figures available before the war, the total turnover was about 65,000,000 marks ; Government deposits were about 13,000,000 marks ; deposits by natives amounted to 85,000 marks. An agricultural bank had been established early in 1913.

(E) GENERAL REMARKS

Cameroon is to a large extent an unknown and undeveloped country, and it is too early to be able to estimate its value with any certainty. Hitherto its wealth has consisted almost wholly in the export of wild rubber and palm products. The future of wild rubber is, as has been seen, more than doubtful owing to its poor quality, the fall in the price of rubber, and the increasing supplies of plantation rubber. Palm products, on the other hand, have, so far as can be seen, an assured future before them ; there is little doubt that vegetable oils and fats will become much more important in the future, and the number of oil-palms in the colony is very considerable. At present the greater part of the palm products is obtained from wild trees, but it is likely that in the future the plantation system will prevail. The industry is not an arduous one and the natives take to it readily.

For the rest, the development of the resources of the country is still in an experimental stage. It is known that cotton, cocoa, tobacco, plantation rubber, maize, and other less important tropical products can be grown successfully, but whether and where they can best be cultivated on a large scale is a question that it is not yet possible to answer. It must be remembered, too, that until railways are constructed, it is scarcely possible to develop the country beyond the coast districts. There is little doubt that some of the best land, and certainly the best labour, is to be found in the north towards Lake Chad. It would, however, be useless without railway communications to attempt to grow cotton or tobacco, to which this neighbourhood is said to be especially suited.

There is some probability that cattle ranching on a large scale could be established in the high grassland of the Adamawa district; but the forest district is infested by the tsetse fly, and railway transport would be needed to convey the cattle rapidly to the coast.

No mineral resources of any exploitable value are at present known, but the country has scarcely been prospected at all and the possibility of the discovery of some such valuable deposits as the tin and coal in Nigeria cannot be ignored.

APPENDIX

I

ANGLO-GERMAN AGREEMENT OF NOVEMBER 15, 1893

The Undersigned,

1. Mr. Martin Gosselin, Her Britannic Majesty's Chargé d'Affaires ;

2. Baron von Marschall, Actual Privy Councillor, Imperial German Secretary of State for Foreign Affairs ;

After discussion of points connected with the question of the delimitation of the boundary between the territories under the influence of their respective Governments in the region extending into the interior from the Gulf of Guinea, which question has already been partially determined by the Anglo-German Agreements of April 29/May 7, 1885, July 27/August 2, 1886. July 1, 1890, and April 14, 1893, have come to the following Agreement on behalf of their respective Governments :

ARTICLE 1

The above-quoted Agreement of 1886 having stipulated that the point where the boundary shall reach the River Benue shall be fixed to (*sic*) such a point to the east of and close to Yola as may be found on examination to be practically suited for the demarcation of a boundary, that point shall be fixed as follows :—

The boundary, drawn from the point on the right bank of the Old Calabar or Cross River, about 9° 8′ of longitude east of Greenwich, marked ' Rapids ' in the English Admiralty Chart referred to in the above-quoted Agreement of 1885, shall follow a straight line directed towards the centre of the present town of Yola.

From that centre, a measuring line shall be drawn to a point on the left bank of the River Benue five kilometres below the centre of the main mouth of River Faro ; from the latter point the circumference of a circle, the centre of which is that of the present town of Yola, and the radius of which is the aforesaid measuring line, shall be described, south of the Benue, continuing till it shall meet the straight line drawn from the Old Calabar or Cross River.   The boundary, deflecting from that straight line at this point of intersection, shall follow the circumference of the circle till it shall arrive at the point where the circumference reaches the Benue.   This point on the Benue shall henceforth be accepted as the point to the east of, and close to, Yola, mentioned in the Agreement of 1886.

ARTICLE 2

The boundary determined in the preceding Article shall be continued northward as follows :—

A line shall be drawn from the point on the left bank of the River Benue fixed in that Article, which, crossing the river, shall go direct to the point where the 13th degree of longitude east of Greenwich is intersected by the 10th degree of north latitude.   From that point it shall go direct to a point on the southern shore of Lake Chad, situated 35 minutes east of the meridian of the centre of the town of Kuka, this being the distance between the meridian of Kuka and the 14th meridian east of Greenwich measured on the map [by Kiepert] published in the German Kolonialatlas of 1892.

In the event of future surveys showing that a point so fixed assigns to the British sphere a less proportion of the southern shore of Lake Chad than is shown in the aforesaid map, a new terminal point making good such deficiency, and as far as possible in accordance with that at present indicated, shall be fixed as soon as possible by mutual agreement.   Until such agreement is arrived at, the point on the southern shore of Lake Chad situated 35 minutes east of the meridian of the centre of the town of Kuka shall be the terminal point.

ARTICLE 3

Any part of the line of demarcation traced in this Agreement, and in the preceding Agreements above quoted, shall be subject to rectification by agreement between the two Powers.

ARTICLE 4

The territories to the west of the boundary-line traced in the present Agreement, and in the preceding above-quoted Agreements, shall fall within the British sphere of influence ; those to the east of the line shall fall within the German sphere of interest.

It is, however, agreed that the influence of Germany in respect to her relations with Great Britain shall not extend eastwards beyond the basin of the River Shari, and that Darfur, Kordofan, and Bahr-el-Ghazal, as defined in the map published in October 1891 by Justus Perthes, shall be excluded from her influence, even if affluents of the Shari shall be found to lie within them.

Article 5

The two Powers take, as regards the extended spheres of influence traced in the present Agreement, a similar engagement, as regards their respective spheres, to that taken in the preceding above-quoted Agreements.

They agree that neither will interfere with the sphere of influence of the other, and that one Power will not, in the sphere of the other, make acquisitions, conclude Treaties, accept sovereign rights or Protectorates, or hinder or dispute the influence of the other.

Article 6

Great Britain recognizes her obligation to apply, as regards the portion of the waters of the Niger and its affluents under her sovereignty or protection, the provision relating to freedom of navigation enumerated in Articles 26, 27, 28, 29, 30, and 33 of the Act of Berlin of February 26, 1885. Germany on her side recognizes her obligation, under the 32nd Article, to be bound by those provisions as regards the portion of the waters under her control.

Berlin, November 15, 1893.

Martin Gosselin.
Frhr. von Marschall.

II

FRANCO-GERMAN CONVENTION OF NOVEMBER 4, 1911[1]

1. *Convention entre l'Allemagne et la France relative à leurs possessions dans l'Afrique Équatoriale*

ARTICLE 1

La France cède à l'Allemagne les territoires dont la limite est fixée comme il suit : La frontière partira du côté de l'Atlantique d'un point à fixer sur la rive orientale de la baie de Monda, vers l'embouchure de la Massolié. Se dirigeant vers le nord-est la frontière obliquera vers l'angle sud-est de la Guinée espagnole. Elle coupera la rivière Ivondo à son confluent avec la Djoua, suivra cette rivière jusqu'à Madjingo (qui restera français) et de ce point se dirigera vers l'est, pour aboutir au confluent de la Ngoko et·de la Sangha au nord d'Ouesso.

La frontière partira ensuite de la rivière Sangha à un point situé au sud du centre d'Ouesso (qui reste français) à une distance de 6 kilomètres au moins et de 12 kilomètres au plus de cette localité, suivant la disposition géographique des lieux. Elle obliquera vers le sud-ouest, pour rejoindre la vallée de la Kandéko, jusqu'à son confluent avec la Bokiba. Elle descendra celle-ci et la Likouala jusqu'à la rive droite du fleuve Congo. Elle suivra le fleuve Congo jusqu'à l'embouchure de la Sangha, et de façon à occuper sur la rive du Congo une étendue de 6 à 12 kilomètres, qui sera fixée suivant les conditions géographiques. Elle remontera la Sangha jusqu'à la Likouala-aux-herbes qu'elle suivra ensuite jusqu'à Botungo. Elle continuera ensuite du sud au nord, selon une direction à peu près droite, jusqu'à Béra Ngoko. Elle s'infléchira ensuite dans la direction du confluent de la Bodingué et de la Lobaye et descendra le cours de la Lobaye jusqu'à l'Oubanghi au nord de Mongoumba.

Sur la rive droite de l'Oubanghi et suivant la disposition géographique des lieux, le territoire allemand sera déterminé de façon à s'étendre sur un espace de 6 kilomètres au moins et de 12 kilomètres au plus ; la frontière remontera ensuite oblique-

[1] From B. and F. S. P. (1911), pp. 956 *et seq.* To the German translation, printed in Appendix to Karl Ritter's *Neu-Kamerun* (Jena, 1912), is appended a note as follows : ' The French text is alone decisive for the interpretation [of the Treaty].'

ment vers le nord-ouest, d'une façon à gagner la rivière Pama en point à déterminer à l'ouest de son confluent avec le Mbi, remontera la vallée de la Pama, puis rejoindra le Logone oriental, à peu près à l'endroit où cette rivière rencontre le huitième parallèle à la hauteur de Goré. Elle suivra ensuite le cours du Logone vers le nord jusqu'à son confluent avec le Chari.

Article 2

L'Allemagne cède à la France les territoires situés au nord de la limite actuelle des possessions françaises dans les territoires du Tchad et compris entre le Chari à l'est et le Logone à l'ouest.

Article 4

La commission technique et les agents chargés de l'abornement dont il est parlé dans l'article précédent, pourront tenir compte d'un commun accord de la configuration du terrain et des circonstances locales, telles que par exemple la facilité de la surveillance de la frontière ou la communauté de race de la population. Ils devront autant que possible faire suivre à la frontière les limites naturelles indiquées par les cours d'eau, et dans le cas où la frontière couperait la direction des rivières, lui faire suivre la ligne du partage des eaux.

Les procès-verbaux de la commission technique et ceux des agents d'abornement ne seront définitifs qu'après ratification des deux Gouvernements.

Article 5

Les présents échanges de territoires sont faits dans les conditions où ces territoires se comportent au moment de la conclusion du présent accord, c'est-à-dire à charge pour les deux Gouvernements de respecter les concessions publiques et particulières qui ont pu être consenties par chacun d'eux. Les deux Gouvernements se communiqueront le texte des actes par lesquels ces concessions ont été accordées.

Le Gouvernement allemand est substitué au Gouvernement de la République Française dans tous les avantages, droits et obligations résultant des actes dont il est parlé ci-dessus au regard des sociétés concessionaires qui passeront sous la souveraineté, l'autorité et la juridiction de l'État allemand. Une convention spéciale réglera l'application des dispositions ci-dessus.

Il en sera de même pour l'État français au regard des concessions qui seraient situées dans les territoires qui passeront sous sa souveraineté, son autorité et sa juridiction.

ARTICLE 6

Le Gouvernement allemand n'apportera aucun obstacle à l'exploitation, à l'entretien et aux travaux de réparation et de réfection de la ligne télégraphique française existant actuellement le long de l'Oubanghi et qui restera française sur son parcours au travers du territoire allemand.· Les autorités allemandes pourront transmettre leurs communications par cette ligne dans des conditions qui seront réglées ultérieurement.

ARTICLE 7

Si le Gouvernement français désire continuer au travers du territoire allemand un chemin de fer entre le Gabon et le Moyen Congo et entre cette dernière colonie et l'Oubanghi Chari, le Gouvernement allemand n'y mettra pas obstacle. Les études ainsi que les travaux se poursuivront suivant les arrangements qui seront faits, le moment venu, entre les deux Gouvernements, le Gouvernement allemand se réservant de faire connaître s'il voudrait prendre une part dans l'exécution de ces travaux sur son territoire.

Si le Gouvernement allemand désire continuer sur le territoire français un chemin de fer établi au Cameroun, le Gouvernement français n'y mettra pas obstacle. Les études ainsi que les travaux se poursuivront suivant les arrangements qui seront faits, le moment venu, entre les deux Gouvernements, le Gouvernement français se réservant de faire connaître s'il voudrait prendre une part dans l'exécution de ces travaux sur son territoire.

ARTICLE 8

Le Gouvernement Impérial cédera à bail au Gouvernement français, dans des conditions à déterminer dans un acte spécial, et en bordure sur la Bénoué, le Mayo Kébi et en deça dans la direction du Logone, des terrains à choisir en vue de l'établissement de postes de ravitaillement et de magasins destinés à constituer une route d'étapes.

Chacun de ces terrains dont la longueur sur le fleuve aux hautes eaux devra être au plus de 500 mètres, aura une superficie qui ne pourra pas dépasser 50 hectares. L'emplacement de ces terrains sera fixé suivant la disposition des lieux.

Si dans l'avenir le Gouvernement français voulait établir entre le Bénoué et le Logone au-dessus ou au-dessous du Mayo Kébi une route ou une voie ferrée, le Gouvernement Impérial n'y ferait pas obstacle. Le Gouvernement allemand et le Gouvernement français s'entendront sur les conditions dans lesquelles ce travail pourrait être accompli.

ARTICLE 9

L'Allemagne et la France, désirant affirmer leur bons rapports dans leurs possessions de l'Afrique Centrale, s'engagent à n'élever aucun ouvrage fortifié le long des cours d'eau qui doivent servir à la navigation commune. Cette prescription ne s'appliquera pas aux ouvrages de simple sûreté destinés à abriter les postes contre les incursions des indigènes.

ARTICLE 10

Les Gouvernements allemand et français s'entendront pour les travaux à exécuter en vue de faciliter la circulation des bateaux et embarcations sur les cours d'eau dont la navigation leur sera commune.

ARTICLE 11

En cas d'arrêt de la navigation sur le Congo ou l'Oubanghi la liberté de passage sera assurée à l'Allemagne et à la France sur les territoires appartenant à l'autre nation aux points où ceux-ci toucheront ces fleuves.

ARTICLE 12

Les deux Gouvernements d'Allemagne et de France renouvellent les déclarations contenues dans l'acte de Berlin du 26 février 1885 et assurant la liberté commerciale et la liberté de navigation sur le Congo et les affluents de ce fleuve ainsi que sur ceux du Niger. En conséquence les marchandises allemandes transitant au travers du territoire français situé à l'ouest de l'Oubanghi et les marchandises françaises transitant à travers les territoires cédés à l'Allemagne ou suivant les routes indiquées à l'Article 8. seront affranchies de tout droit.

Un accord conclu entre les deux Gouvernements déterminera les conditions de ce transit et les points de pénétration.

ARTICLE 13

Le Gouvernement allemand n'apportera aucune entrave au passage des troupes françaises, de leur armes ou munitions, ainsi que de leur matériel de ravitaillement par le Congo, l'Oubanghi, la Bénoué, le Mayo Kébi, ainsi que par le chemin de fer à construire éventuellement dans le nord du Cameroun.

Le Gouvernement français n'apportera aucune entrave au passage des troupes allemandes, de leurs armes et munitions, ainsi que de leur matériel de ravitaillement par le Congo, l'Oubanghi, la Bénoué, le Mayo Kébi, et le chemin de fer à construire éventuellement de la côte à Brazzaville.

Dans l'un et l'autre cas, les troupes, si elles sont purement indigènes, devront toujours être accompagnées par un gradé européen, et le Gouvernement sur le territoire duquel les troupes passeront, prendra toutes les mesures nécessaires pour éviter qu'aucune difficulté soit opposée à leur passage et pourra au besoin déléguer un agent pour les accompagner. Les autorités locales régleront les conditions dans lesquelles les passages de troupes se feront.

ARTICLE 14

L'égalité de traitement pour le transport des personnes ou des marchandises sera assurée aux ressortissants des deux nations sur les chemins de fer de leurs possessions du Congo et du Cameroun.

ARTICLE 15

Le Gouvernement allemand et le Gouvernement français cesseront, à partir du jour de la cession réciproque des territoires concédés à l'Allemagne par la France et à la France par l'Allemagne, d'exercer aucune sorte de protection et d'autorité sur les indigènes des territoires respectivement cédés par eux.

ARTICLE 16

Dans le cas où le statut territorial du bassin conventionnel du Congo tel qu'il est défini par l'acte de Berlin du 26 fevrier 1885, viendrait à être modifié du fait de l'une ou de l'autre des parties contractantes, celles-ci devraient en conférer entre elles, comme aussi avec les autres Puissances signataires dudit acte de Berlin.

ARTICLE 17.

La présente convention sera ratifiée et les ratifications seront échangées, à Paris, aussitôt que faire se pourra.

Fait à Berlin, le 4 novembre 1911 en double exemplaire.

KIDERLEN   JULES CAMBON.

2. *M. de Kiderlen-Waechter, Secrétaire d'État des Affaires Étrangères de l'Empire d'Allemagne, à M. Jules Cambon, Ambassadeur de la République française à Berlin.*

Berlin, le 4 novembre 1911.

Pour bien préciser l'esprit dans lequel sera appliquée la Convention que nous venons de signer relativement aux échanges territoriaux dans l'Afrique équatoriale, il est entendue entre les deux Gouvernements que les différends qui viendraient à s'élever entre les parties contractantes, au sujet de l'interprétation et de l'application des dispositions de cette Convention, seront soumis à un tribunal arbitral constitué dans les termes de la Convention de La Haye du 18 octobre, 1907. Un compromis devra être dressé et il sera procédé suivant les règles de la même Convention en tant qu'il n'y serait pas dérogé par un accord exprès au moment du litige.

Cependant, si des malentendus s'élevaient entre les membres de la Commission technique chargée de fixer la délimitation de la frontière, ces agents seraient départagés par un arbitre désigné d'un commun accord entre les deux Gouvernements et appartenant à une tierce Puissance.

Le Gouvernement allemand sera toujours heureux de voir des associations d'intérêt se produire entre les ressortissants des deux pays pour les affaires qu'ils entreprendraient dans les possessions françaises et allemandes qui font l'objet de la Convention de ce jour.

Il est entendu que l'application de ladite Convention sera faite suivant les règles prévues pour celle de la Convention franco-allemande du 18 avril, 1908, sur la frontière Congo-Cameroun par les protocoles qui y sont annexés.

KIDERLEN.

AUTHORITIES

Historical

ALEXANDER, LIEUT. BOYD. *From the Niger to the Nile.* 2 vols. London, 1907.

BURTON, SIR R. F. *Abeokuta and the Camaroons Mountains.* 2 vols. London, 1863.

CALVERT, A. F. *The Cameroons.* London, 1917.

DOMINIK, H. *Kamerun. Sechs Kriegs- und Friedensjahre.* Berlin, 1901.

—— *Vom Atlantik zum Tschadsee. Kriegs- und Forschungsfahrten in Kamerun.* Berlin, 1908.

FROBENIUS, L. *The Voice of Africa. Travels of the German Inner African Exploration Expedition,* 1910–12. Translated [from *Und Afrika sprach*]. 2 vols. London, 1913.

HAASE, L. *Durch unbekannte Kamerun.* Berlin, 1915.

HASSERT, K. *Deutschlands Kolonien* (*Kamerun*, pp. 128–90), 2nd ed. Leipzig, 1910.

HUTTER, F. *Wanderungen und Forschungen im Nord-Hinterland von Kamerun.* Brunswick, 1902.

—— *Kamerun* [in *Das Ueberseeische Deutschland* (1903)]. Stuttgart, Berlin, Leipzig.

JOHNSTON, SIR H. H. *George Grenfell and the Congo, &c.* 2 vols. London, 1908.

—— *Pioneers in West Africa.* London, 1912.

—— *A History of the Colonization of Africa.* Cambridge, 1913.

—— *Survey of the Ethnography of Africa* (Journal of the Royal Anthropological Institute, 1913).

LEWIN, EVANS. *The Germans and Africa.* London, 1915.

MORGEN, K. VON. *Durch Kamerun von Süd nach Nord. Reisen und Forschungen im Hinterlande 1889 bis 1891.* Berlin, 1893.

Notes on the Cameroons. By a member of the West African Frontier Force. (Geographical Journal, November 1916.)

PASSARGE, S. *Kamerun* [in H. Meyer, *Das deutsche Kolonialreich*, vol. i, pt. 2]. Leipzig and Vienna, 1914.

PASSARGE, S. *Adamáua. Bericht über die Expedition des deutschen Kamerunkomitees*, 1893–94. Berlin, 1895.

PUTTKAMER, J. VON. *Gouverneursjahre in Kamerun*. Berlin, 1912.

RITTER, K. *Neu-Kamerun*. Jena, 1912.

ROHRBACH, P. *Wie machen wir unsere Kolonien rentabel?* Halle, 1907.

SEMBRITSKI, E. *Kamerun*. Berlin, 1909.

TYMMS, REV. T. V. *The Cameroons*. London [1915].

W. A. A. F. *Another Side-Show : The Cameroons* (Blackwood's Magazine, December 1916).

ZIMMERMANN, ALF. *Geschichte der deutschen Kolonialpolitik* (*Kamerun*, pp. 82–93, 205–10, 256–65). Berlin, 1914.

ZIMMERMANN, EMIL. *Neukamerun. Reise-erlebnisse und wirtschaftspolitische Untersuchungen*. Berlin, 1913.

ZINTGRAFF, E. *Nord-Kamerun*. Berlin, 1895.

ECONOMIC

Official

Der Baumwollbau in den deutschen Schutzgebieten : seine Entwickelung seit dem Jahre 1910. German Colonial Office.

Deutsches Kolonialblatt. German Colonial Office. Berlin, 1914.

Die deutschen Schutzgebiete in Afrika und der Südsee. Berlin, 1912–13.

Final Report of the Royal Commission on the Natural Resources, Trade and Legislation of certain portions of His Majesty's Dominions. 1917.

German Official Report on the German Colonies. 1911–12.

Verhandlungen der Kautschuk-Kommission des kolonialwirtschaftlichen Komitees. Berlin, 1913.

General

BONN, PROF. M. *German Colonial Policy* (Journal of the Royal Colonial Institute, 1914, p. 127).

CALVERT, A. F. *The Cameroons*. London, 1917.

Economic Resources of the German Colonies (Bulletin of the Imperial Institute, vol. xiii, p. 392).

HAMILTON, L. *German Colonies*, 1912–13 (Journal of the Royal Colonial Institute, 1914, p. 493).

Journal of the African Society, 1915–17

LEONARD, MAJOR A. G. *Commercial Development in German Kamerun* (Journal of the Royal Colonial Institute, 1914, p. 327).

MARQUARDSEN, H. *Mitteilungen aus den deutschen Schutzgebieten* (vol. xxv, no. 1). Berlin, 1912.

METCALFE, SIR C. *Railway Development of Africa, Present and Future* (Geographical Journal, vol. xlvii, p. 3. 1916).

Notes on the Cameroons. By a member of the West African Frontier Force (Geographical Journal, November 1916).

NUGENT, CAPT. W. V. *The Geographical Results of the Nigeria Kamerun Boundary Demarcation Commission* (Geographical Journal, vol. xliii, p. 360. 1914).

PASSARGE, S. *Kamerun* [in H. Meyer, *Das deutsche Kolonialreich*, vol. i, pt. 2]. Leipzig and Vienna, 1914.

MAPS

The general German map of Cameroon is in 31 complete and 3 incomplete sheets, on the scale of 1 : 300,000. It is a compilation from route traverses and sketches, and was published by D. Reimer in Berlin between 1910 and 1913.

The territories ceded by France to Germany in 1911 are covered by a French map, on the scale of 1 : 1,000,000, prepared by the Service Géographique de l'Afrique Équatoriale Française and published by Challamel in Paris between 1910 and 1913 ; this map is also a compilation. The orographical map of Cameroon by Max Moisel, published in one sheet at Berlin in *Mitteilungen aus den deutschen Schutzgebieten*, 1913, is on the scale of 1 : 2,000,000, and gives additional information for these territories.

The War Office map of Cameroon (G.S.G.S. 2793) was published in 1915, and is also on the scale of 1 : 2,000,000.

The colony is also covered by the General War Office map of West Africa (G.S.G.S. 2434) on the scale of 1 : 6,336,000 (1903 ; additions and corrections, 1914, 1919). The western and southern parts of Cameroon are covered by sheets 74, 82, and 83 of the War Office map of Africa, on the scale of 1 : 1,000,000 (G.S.G.S. 1539).

HANDBOOKS PREPARED UNDER THE DIRECTION OF THE HISTORICAL SECTION OF THE FOREIGN OFFICE.—No. 112

SOUTH-WEST AFRICA

TABLE OF CONTENTS

TABLE OF CONTENTS

I. GEOGRAPHY PHYSICAL AND POLITICAL

(1) Position and Frontiers

THE former German Colony of South-West Africa lies on the coast between 17° and 29° south latitude, and 11° 45′ and 25° 15′ east longitude, though the main body of the territory does not extend east of longitude 21° east. It has an area of about 322,200 square miles, and marches on the north with Angola and Northern Rhodesia, on the south with Cape Colony, and on the east with Bechuanaland. About the middle of the coast, extending south from the Swakop River, between about 22° 40′ and 23° 12′ south latitude, and west of about 14° 41′ east longitude, lay the British enclave of Walvisch Bay.

On the south and east the boundary follows the north bank of the Orange River to 20° east longitude, this meridian to 22° south latitude, this parallel to 21° east longitude, and this meridian to a point between about 18° 10′ and 18° 20′ south latitude, the determination of which depends on the interpretation of inconsistent clauses in the Agreement of July 1, 1890. The boundary here turns due east, and follows a straight line to the Kwando (Chobe, or Linyanti) River, which it descends to its confluence with the Zambezi.

The northern boundary, defined by a Declaration of December 30. 1886, ascends the Kunene River from its mouth as far as the falls some 60 miles below Humbe in about 17° 17′ south latitude, proceeding thence due east (along a line concerning which there is some difference of interpretation) to the Okowango (Kubango) River. This it descends to Fort Mucasso (18° south latitude) near the village of Andara or Libebe, continuing thence along a straight line drawn slightly north of east, crossing the Kwando River and reaching the Zambezi at the Katima–Molilo rapids shortly above Katongo. It finally descends the Zambezi to the confluence of the Kwando or Linyanti, thus meeting the eastern frontier and completing the eastern extension known as the Caprivizipfel.

(2) Surface, Coast, and River System

Surface

The surface of this territory falls into three main natural divisions. On the west is a coastal strip, rising gradually to a highland region or plateau averaging between 3,000 and 5,000 ft. high. The highland sinks in its turn to the Kalahari depression, which occupies all the eastern part of the territory and extends far beyond its borders.

The Coastal Strip, or Namib, is a monotonous desert region, which varies in breadth from about 30 to 80 miles. It consists largely of sand-dunes, from which in various places emerge rocky or gravelly hills, with gravel plains and sandy undulating flats. The belt of dunes is widest and most continuous south of the Swakop, some of them here reaching a height of more than 500 ft. North of the Swakop the dunes are at once much less continuous and much lower; the country east of them is more broken. The northern Namib is further distinguished from the southern by the presence of watercourses which have kept an open channel to the sea.

The Interior Plateau.—In the north the Namib rises through a district of hilly country to a chain of table-topped hills reaching an elevation of about 5,000 ft., and stretching north-west to south-east through the highland region of the Kaokoveld, at a distance of 25-40 miles from the coast. Still farther to the east, the north-eastern Kaokoveld consists of an elevated plain, sloping abruptly towards the Kunene and Amboland; from it hills emerge to the south and west. There is a general decrease in height towards the south of the Kaokoveld. This southern part, a country of steep, rocky hills with narrow valleys, passes over to the east into a region characterised by the formations associated with dolomitic limestone.

This Karst region is for the greater part a wide plain sloping gently towards the Etosha Pan. The usual features of this kind of country—sink holes, subterranean caverns and springs, and the absence of defined waterways, due to the porous character of the surface covering—are met with.

To the south of the Karst district is northern Damaraland, a region of extensive grass plains from which emerge isolated mountains and a few mountain chains. Here the greatest heights in the territory are found, the double peak of Omataka reaching nearly 9,000 ft. Farther south, in southern Damaraland and the north of Great Namaqualand, mountain massifs form the predominant feature. Great valleys and gorges, widely extended plains, and high peaks are characteristic of this central portion of the territory; and the whole southern part is dominated by two longitudinal trenches, that of the Konkip to the west, that of the Great Fish River to the east. West of the former is a series of mountain ranges and elevated plateaux, among them being the Tsaris (Zaris) and Tiras mountains and the Huib plateau; while to the east of it is the Hanam plateau. Still farther to the east, beyond the Great Fish River, is the Urinanib plateau, which overlooks the Kalahari region. In the south-east the isolated Great and Little Karas mountains rise to considerable heights; but the country is for the greater part flat or rolling.

The Kalahari region, which falls away to the east of the regions above described, is for the most part a monotonous region of sand and dunes. The dunes are sparsely covered in the south, but become more wooded towards the north, and the country is intersected by a considerable number of watercourses (*omurambas*). Amboland (or Ovamboland), which shares the characteristics of the Kalahari region, is a slightly undulating sandy plain, intersected by a number of shallow watercourses filled by the Kunene overflow and draining to the Etosha Pan.

Coast

From the Kunene to the Orange River the coast-line measures about 830 miles. It is generally low, almost unbroken by bays or promontories, and beaten all the year round by a heavy surf. The only harbours worth mentioning are Swakopmund, Walvisch Bay (formerly a British enclave in German territory), and Lüderitz Bay (Angra Pequena). Swakopmund is merely an open roadstead, which is gradually silting up, where steamers must anchor about 2 miles off-shore. Walvisch Bay, about 20 miles south of Swakopmund, is a bay facing north with a large, sheltered anchorage. At present landing facilities are poor. Lüderitz Bay, which is the port serving the south of the colony, is said to be one of the best-sheltered harbours in South Africa. The landing facilities could easily be so improved as to allow large vessels to come alongside a quay.

River System

Except for those rivers that form part of the northern and southern frontiers of the territory, there are practically none which carry surface water all the year round. Almost all are simply watercourses which become torrents for a short period after rain, and for the rest of the time have water only below the bed or in pools.

The watercourses may be grouped into three drainage systems: (*a*) those draining directly to the Atlantic in the west, of which the chief are the Kuiseb, Swakop, and Ugab; (*b*) those draining to the Orange River in the south, of which the chief are the Konkip, the Great Fish River (Oub), and the Hom; and (*c*) those draining eastwards and losing themselves in the Kalahari Desert, the longest being the Omatako (Chuob). To these must be added the small portion of the Zambezi system in the north-east of the country, which contains the only navigable stretches of water in the whole territory.

The rivers of the west run largely in deep canyons eroded in the high plateau, those of the east in broad and shallow depressions (*omurambas*) or broad channels deeply cut in the superficial strata (*reviers*).

Water is not the scarce commodity that might be imagined from the absence of regular rivers and the smallness of the rainfall. It is found not only under the dry river beds and in standing pools for some time after rain, but, in many parts of the country, is provided by springs, sometimes thermal. Something had already been done, and further projects were on foot before the late war, for increasing the supply by borings and by impounding the run-off by dams, reservoirs, and similar works.

(3) Climate

Although the northern half of the territory falls within the tropic of Capricorn, the climate is on the whole temperate rather than tropical. The extreme north and north-east are hot and trying to Europeans, but on the central plateau the dryness of the air makes the heat easily supportable. Two seasons may be distinguished, one dry and cool, the other rainy and hot, the latter normally extending from November to April. Both the setting in of the rainy season and the quantity of rain that falls, however, are subject to great variations. In general, both rainfall and temperature increase from south to north and from west to east. There is a great difference between the climate of the coast and that of the interior.

The coastal region is dominated by cool winds from south and south-west for about 50 miles inland, although there are occasional very hot winds from the east during the dry season. It is practically rainless, but there are frequent heavy mists in that part of the

country which borders on the sea. The temperature of
the coastal region is fairly constant. The mean yearly
temperature at Walvisch Bay is 62° F. (16½° C.); at
Swakopmund 59° F. (15° C.). The hottest month is
March (average: Walvisch Bay, 67° F., 19½° C.;
Swakopmund, 63° F., 17° C.), the coolest is August
(average: Walvisch Bay, 57° F., 14° C.; Swakopmund,
55° F., 12½° C.).

The climate of the interior contrasts strongly with
that of the coastal zone. During the dry season the
prevailing winds come from the south-east or south-
west, but the predominant winds during the rainy
season are east or north-east.

Both the yearly and daily ranges of temperature are
much greater on the plateau than in the coast region.
The nights are cold, and in the dry season frosts at
night are not uncommon. The mean yearly temperature of Windhoek, which is in about the same latitude
as Swakopmund, is 67° F. (19½° C.); the hottest month
is January, with an average of 74½° F. (23½° C.), the
coolest June, with 56° F. (13½° C.).

As has been said, the amount of rain increases normally from west to east and from south to north, as does
also the number of rainy days. Bethany has an average
fall of 4·37 in. (111 mm.); Hasuur, 7·28 in. (185 mm.);
Windhoek, 14·80 in. (376 mm.); Gobabis, 16·18 in. (411
mm.); Zesfontein, 3·97 in. (101 mm.); Grootfontein,
23·53 in. (598 mm.). Figures for Amboland and the
Caprivizipfel show a corresponding increase.

Severe hailstorms sometimes cause much damage.

(4) Sanitary Conditions

The health conditions of the territory are as a whole
not unfavourable. Malaria occurs, indeed, over the
whole area, but not to any great extent except in the
north and north-west, where it is prevalent after heavy
rains. Blackwater fever also occurs in the north.

Rheumatic complaints are fairly common, especially
on the seaboard, as also are intestinal diseases, due

largely to the lack of a good supply of pure drinking
water and the eating of half-raw meat.   Ailments
especially prevalent among the natives are inflamma-
tion of the lungs, affections of the eyes, and venereal
diseases.

In spite of its tropical situation, the territory has
regions adapted to European colonization, and healthy
children can be reared.   The death-rate in 1913 was
only 11·3 per thousand among the white population.

(5) RACE AND LANGUAGE

The chief native races are the Bantus, the Hottentots,
and the Berg-Damaras.   There are also various mixed
races formed by the crossing of the above peoples with
each other and with whites.

The chief Bantu races are the Ovambos, and most of
the inhabitants of the Caprivizipfel in the north, the
Ovahereros, or Hereros (Damaras), and Ovambanjerus
in the centre, and the Ovatyimbas in the north-west.

The Hottentots (Koikoins) are chiefly found in the
south, although there are a few in the northern Namib
and southern Kaokoveld.   Their racial affinities are
quite uncertain, and their language is possibly of
Hamitic origin.   A considerable portion of the
Hottentots now speak a corrupt form of Cape Dutch
or English.

The Bushmen are found chiefly in the West Kalahari
region, and may possibly represent the remains of a
primitive race once inhabiting the whole country.
Their language may, it is thought, be connected with
the Sudan tongues.

The Berg-Damaras live scattered about the northern
half of the territory.   They speak the same language as
the Hottentots, but anthropologically are quite distinct
from them.

Of the mixed races the only one worth mention is
the Bastards, formed by a crossing of Cape Dutch and
Hottentots, who are found in various places in the
southern half of the territory, chiefly round Rehoboth.

(6) Population

The total native population was estimated in 1912 at 239,000, but at the census taken in 1913 the number of natives actually counted was 69,003, and the estimated total not quite 79,000. These figures excluded Amboland (or Ovamboland, pop. upwards of 150,000) and the Caprivizipfel (pop. about 10,000). The area of the territory is estimated at about 322,200 square miles, and the density of the population is therefore very low—less than 1 per square mile. It is, in fact, in most regions far less, since Amboland, which includes not more than about 5 per cent. of the whole superficial area, contributes more than 50 per cent. of the population.

The white population at the beginning of 1913 was just under 15,000.

The chief centres of population are Windhoek, Swakopmund, and Lüderitz Bay, but there are also a number of other smaller towns and villages in the interior with white populations varying between 150 and 700.

II. POLITICAL HISTORY

Chronological Summary

1482 First discovery of the coast by the Portuguese.
1685 Dutch expedition to Namaqualand.
1836 Alexander's exploration.
1842 Settlement of Rhenish (Barmen) missionaries at Bethany.
1850-52 Journey of Galton and Andersson.
1863 War between Hereros and Namaquas begins.
1867 Despatch of British vessels to Walvisch Bay.
      Annexation of islands on coast.
1875 Palgrave sent as Commissioner from the Cape.
1878 Walvisch Bay annexed by British.
1883 Lüderitz settlement at Angra Pequena.
1884 (Aug. 15) German Protectorate declared over the Lüderitz
          Bay settlement.
      (Sept. 8) German Protectorate declared for coast between
          Orange River and Cape Frio.
      (Oct. 18) German Protectorate declared over Great
          Namaqualand.
1885-92 Administration of the German South-West Africa
          Colonial Society.
1885 (Sept. 2) German Protectorate over Red Nation.
      (Oct. 21) Hereros agree to Protectorate over Damaraland.
1886 Treaty defining boundary with Portuguese Angola.
1888 First rising of Hereros.
1890 Treaty defining boundary with British territories.
1892 Imperial Commissioner appointed.
1893 Witbooi's rising.
1894 Von Leutwein appointed Governor.
1898 Swakopmund harbour founded.
1904 (Jan.) 1905. Herero rebellion.
1904 (Oct.) Von Leutwein superseded in the military command
          by Von Trotha.
1905 (Nov.) Von Lindequist becomes Governor.
1911 (May) Walvisch Bay boundary arbitration award.

(1) *Early Exploration*

The Portuguese first discovered this coast in 1482,
when Diogo Cão sailed southwards from the mouth of
the Congo as far as Cape Cross (22° S.), where he

erected one of the stone columns (*padrões*) with which he marked notable points in his journeys. This column was still standing at Cape Cross till a few years ago, when the Germans carried it away to the Kiel Museum. Other names which commemorate the Portuguese explorations are Cape Frio and Angra Pequena (or the Little Bay). No colonization was attempted on this part of the coast by the Portuguese or any other European race till modern times.

The first journey into the interior was probably that of Van der Stell, Dutch Governor of the Cape, who made his way into Namaqualand in 1685. Another exploring party passed through Namaqualand and reached Angra Pequena in the middle of the eighteenth century. In the early part of the nineteenth century several missions began to enter the country, and many of the missionaries stayed for some years. The first permanent settlement, however, was that of the Rhenish missionaries in 1842, who established themselves at Bethany, and gradually obtained much influence, combining trade with evangelization. A considerable part of the country had already (in 1836) been explored by Captain Sir J. Alexander, while a later and notable journey was that of Galton and Andersson in 1850-52.

(2) *Action of British and Cape Governments*

As more became known of the territory, efforts were made to induce the British Government to extend the limits of the Cape Colony northwards along the coast, a summary of which will be found in Lord Derby's despatch of December 4, 1884 (C. 4265, December 1884). In the years 1861, 1866, and 1867 possession was taken of twelve small islands off the coast; but the mainland was not touched, the Duke of Buckingham, Secretary of State for the Colonies, writing, in August 1867, that the British Government was not prepared to take the responsibility of sovereignty over an extensive territory without stronger evidence than was then forthcoming of the necessity for such a course. In

1863 a war had broken out between the Namaquas and the Hereros, which led to constant attacks upon the stations of the German missionaries, even Walvisch Bay being plundered.   In 1868 the Rhenish Missionary Society, supported by Bismarck, then Chancellor of the North German Confederation, urged British intervention, and asked that the whole of Damaraland might be declared British territory.   But no such step was taken, though a British man-of-war was sent to Walvisch Bay, and the good offices of the Governor of the Cape Colony brought about peace among the natives in 1870.   In 1875 Mr. J. C. Palgrave, who knew the country well, went as a special commissioner from the Cape Government to report upon it.   He was sent in pursuance of a resolution of the Cape Parliament that the limits of the Colony should be extended so as to include Walvisch Bay and so much of the country inland as might be thought advisable.   Both natives and whites, traders and missionaries, gave evidence of desiring British protection, the missionaries being German and the majority of the traders Germans or Swedes.

(3) *German Protectorate Established*

In 1877 Sir Bartle Frere, then Governor of Cape Colony and High Commissioner for South Africa, recommended the annexation of the coast as far as the Portuguese boundary; but the only result was the annexation of Walvisch Bay and a small patch of country near it on March 12, 1878.   It is possible that the restricted action then taken, coupled as it was with the appointment of a Resident at Okahandya and a Special Commissioner in the southern province, might have developed into a more definite and extensive occupation had it not been for questions of expense at issue between the Home and Colonial Governments. The tribal war broke out again in 1880; neither Government was willing to assume the responsibility of an advance; and Lord Kimberley, as Secretary of State for the Colonies, definitely pronounced against extending British responsibilities in the north-west beyond the Orange River.

These circumstances were turned to account by the Colonial party which had been growing up in Germany, as affording a good opportunity for establishing a German colony in South Africa; and the result of the Transvaal War of 1880-81 probably encouraged the hope of combining with the Dutch element in South Africa against the British. In 1880 Sir Bartle Frere called attention to a remarkable article by Ernst von Weber, published in the previous November in the Berlin *Geographische Nachrichten*, which advocated a German colony or colonies in South or South-Central Africa; but the British Government were informed by their Ambassador at Berlin that such a scheme would not be supported either by the German Government or by the German Parliament.[1] In February 1883 the German Embassy in London informed the British Foreign Office that a Bremen merchant was about to establish a factory on the coast north of the Orange River, and had asked for the protection of the German Government in case of need. They enquired whether the British Government exercised any authority in that locality; if so, they would be glad if British protection could be extended to the German factory; if not, they would do their best to give such German protection as was given to German subjects in remote parts of the world, "but without having the least design to establish any footing in South Africa."

In July 1883 it was learnt in London that a German named Vogelsang had landed at Angra Pequena as agent for a Bremen merchant named Lüderitz. Through the help of the German missionaries at Bethany, Vogelsang obtained from a local chief a cession of 215 square miles at Angra Pequena, and there hoisted the German flag. Since that date the place has been called by the Germans Lüderitzbucht (i.e., Lüderitz Bay). Attempts to assert British rights without asserting British sovereignty were of no avail. Both the

____
[1] C. 4190, August 1884, pp. 1-9.

Imperial Government and the Cape Government procrastinated, and the German Government, after repeatedly asking whether there was any title to British sovereignty, and receiving no affirmative reply, notified the British in April 1884 that the settlement "was under the protection of the Empire."[1] A German Protectorate was formally declared on August 16 (? 15), 1884.

During the remainder of 1884 and through 1885 a series of treaties was concluded with native tribes, by means of which the German Protectorate was extended to the whole of the territory included within its limits. The coast, from the Orange River northwards to Cape Frio (of course omitting Walvisch Bay), was declared to be a Protectorate on September 8, 1884, and Great Namaqualand on October 18, 1884. On September 2, 1885, a treaty with the Geikous, or " Red Nation," a branch of the Namaquas of the south, was signed, which extended the Protectorate to their country; and on September 15 of the same year a similar treaty was made with the Bastards. Finally on October 21 the Hereros of Damaraland accepted the German Protectorate. These territories had no settled limits, but they corresponded roughly with the present boundaries, which were definitely fixed by the treaties of December 30, 1886, and July 1, 1890, with Portugal and Great Britain respectively.[2] On September 14, 1892, a Protectorate was proclaimed over what was styled by the German Government " the unclaimed district lying between Herero and Ovamboland, within the German sphere of interest in South-West Africa."

(4) *Concessions to Companies*

In 1885 the German South-West African Colonial Society, which had acquired the rights of Lüderitz, was placed in possession of the country, and was charged with the administration. In 1892 the Society

---

[1] *Ibid.* and C. 4265, December 1884.
[2] **See Appendix.**

was relieved of this responsibility, and an Imperial Commissioner was appointed to carry on the government. Concessions were made to various other companies also, mainly of mineral rights which had been acquired from native chiefs. All these companies were brought under a uniform rule by the Mining Ordinances of 1905.

(5) *A Military Force Established*

A small native military force was first formed in 1887 to protect the gold workings of the German South-West African Colonial Society at the Pot and Anawood Mines. This force was disbanded soon afterwards during the first Herero rising of 1888, and was replaced by a small European force, which gradually grew in strength. At the time of the Herero rebellion (1904) this force was greatly increased, many British and Dutch from the Cape Colony serving in it. After the rising had been subdued, a considerable body of men, provided with artillery and machine guns, was maintained. Estimates as to its strength vary greatly, some putting it as high as 10,000. It was thoroughly equipped, and rested on strong bases, with good stocks of artillery, supported by a system of strategical railways, so planned as to give easy access to the British territories, which were obviously aimed at. This object is clearly set forth by Dr. P. Samassa in the passage (dated 1905) quoted on p. **122** of Evans Lewin's *The Germans and Africa.*

The greatest military arsenal was at Keetmanshoop, which has now been connected with the Cape system of railways.

(6) *Von Leutwein's Governorship, 1894–1905, and the Herero Rising*

Von Leutwein, who governed the colony from 1894 to 1905, seems to have endeavoured to manage the native tribes with some regard to their own customs. On the other hand, suspicion was raised by the perpetual endeavours of German colonists to acquire possession of tribal lands, and to make it impossible for the pastoral population to graze their cattle over them. The most important of the tribes affected was the Herero, a numerous pastoral race, who depended entirely on their large herds of cattle. There was great friction between them and the colonists. They saw themselves deprived of the liberty which they had formerly enjoyed of wandering unrestrained over the whole country; and came to believe that all their rights would be forfeited, and that even if they kept their herds they would be confined to small reservations.

Other tribes also had been previously involved in risings. Among them were the Hottentots of the south, near the Orange River and Gibeon. The Witbooi tribe of Hottentots, under their old chief, Hendrik Witbooi, a man of great ability, had with difficulty been induced to submit in 1893, but had continued since that time to observe all their agreements. At the end of 1903 there was an outbreak of another Hottentot tribe, the Bondelzwarts, who occupied the country in the extreme south. This rising was suppressed with difficulty, the garrisons being withdrawn from the Herero country for the purpose. The Herero chief, Samuel Maherero, thereupon seized the opportunity to rise. He tried to obtain the co-operation of the Witbooi chief; but, owing to the interception of a message, Hendrik Witbooi did not strike till six months later.

The main outbreak took place in January 1904. It began with an attack on the scattered farms of the colonists, all who could not escape being massacred. The chief made a proclamation declaring formal war against the Germans, adding an order that no Englishmen, Boers, Bastards, Berg-Damaras, or Hottentots were to be touched; and von Leutwein considers that the chief intended also to protect women and children. Many were, however, killed, as well as some Boers.[1]

The military posts were with difficulty held; and

[1] Von Leutwein, *Elf Jahre Gouverneur in Deutsch-Südwestafrika*, p. 467.

the whole colony was in danger until reinforcements began to arrive from Germany. Ultimately two German columns were formed, one operating in the east towards the British frontier and the Kalahari Desert, whose object was to prevent the Hereros from crossing the border, and to head them northwards; the other column co-operating from the west. By these means the southern gathering of Hereros in the Oujati mountains was gradually driven north towards the Waterberg mountains, and the tribe was finally hemmed in. Brought to action at the foot of the steep rocky range, the whole body, men, women, and children, with their wagons and cattle, fled, after desperate fighting, westwards, pursued by the Germans. The greater part of them perished miserably in the desert, though the leaders escaped into British territory, where they were disarmed and interned. The number of Hereros who were killed or died of thirst and starvation is uncertain, but has been estimated at about 60,000.[1]

As a result of the war, Professor Bonn told the Royal Colonial Institute in January 1914 that the Herero tribe and what remained of the Hottentots were practically exterminated. Their lands were confiscated, and partly settled by German farmers; but the immigration of white settlers was inadequate to take their place.

The native population of the territory was so much reduced that the colonists afterwards had cause to lament the lack of labour. Von Leutwein, who was accused in Germany of having provoked the rebellion by his endeavour to govern the natives in too lenient a manner, was deprived of his military command in October 1904 (von Trotha taking his place), and in the following year was superseded in the Civil Government by von Lindequist.

[1] A vivid picture of the flight and destruction will be found in Gustav Frenssen's *Peter Moors Fahrt nach Südwestafrika*, in which the story is given as a soldier's narrative. See below, p. 44, for statistics of the Hereros and Hottentots before and after the rebellion

III. SOCIAL AND POLITICAL CONDITIONS

(1) RELIGIOUS

IN South-West Africa the principal point requiring consideration is the relations between Christianity and the pagan or half-converted races. The Mohammedan question, so important in the northern protectorates, does not arise here.

The establishment of German Missions in the first half of the nineteenth century, and other influences from the side of the Cape Colony, have led to the growth of a considerable population which is nominally Christian. The most important of these societies (the Rhenish (Barmen) Mission), established in 1842, has made the greater number of converts. A Finnish society has been at work among the Ovambos in the north, and a Roman Catholic (Oblate) society in the south. The majority of the natives profess some form of Christianity, although their conversion is often quite superficial. Primitive African beliefs prevail among the remainder, and have great influence even among the nominal Christians.

(2) POLITICAL

The Government rested in the hands of an Imperial Governor, who had extensive powers, exercised through the officials in charge of the districts into which the German Protectorate was divided. These districts were : Windhoek, the capital; the coast districts of Swakopmund and Lüderitz Bay; the northern districts of Karibib, Okahandya, Gobabis, Omaruru, Waterberg, Otyo, and Grootfontein; the southern districts of Rehoboth, Gibeon, and Keetmanshoop.

The Governor was assisted by an advisory council, consisting partly of nominated and partly of elected members, who were chosen by the German settlers in the respective districts. The Regulation of 1909 gave more extended powers to the council, and was regarded as a distinct step towards self-government. How far the advance had gone it is not easy to say. It is evident that the system of government was not popular, that officials were far too numerous, and rules and regulations too stringent for a thinly inhabited and gradually developing colony.

(3) EDUCATIONAL

Among the aboriginal populations the arrangements for education have rested mainly in the hands of the Missions, which have maintained a large number of successful schools. A knowledge of reading and writing (mainly in the Cape Dutch brought in by Boers and Bastards) is widely diffused. Technical schools giving instruction in handicrafts and the minor arts of civilization have also been maintained. The Rhenish or Barmen Mission had also two training schools for teachers. Primary and secondary schools for Europeans were also maintained wherever required for the settlers.

GENERAL OBSERVATIONS

German South-West Africa could have been included in the British Empire, not only without objection from, but with the active goodwill of, Germany. That it ever passed into German hands was due to the continued inaction of the Home Government and the Government of the Cape Colony. It is geographically inseparable from the rest of South Africa.

The extent to which the Protectorate, organized with a complete system of railways and cleared of its pastoral tribes, succeeded in attracting the surplus population of Germany may be judged from the fact

that in 1913 the total European population amounted
to 14,830, of which 12,292 were German, the remainder
being mainly drawn from the Cape Colony. In spite
of many experiments in the growth of cotton, vines,
and tobacco, agriculture did not flourish. Very large
areas were employed, by the Hereros and others, almost
entirely for stock-raising. The somewhat shifty policy
followed by the German Government does not seem to
have met with the approval either of the colonists or of
the merchants; but, while the general system of
administration, with numerous officials and irritating
regulations, was not calculated to encourage private
enterprise, on the other hand the systematic development of communications was here, as elsewhere in the
German colonies, a feature in their policy which others
might copy with advantage. The railways were, as has
been stated above, constructed on strategical lines; but,
at the same time, being supplemented by roads and
bridges, they served the purpose of developing the
country.

IV. ECONOMIC CONDITIONS

(A) MEANS OF COMMUNICATION

(1) INTERNAL

(a) Roads

THERE are few roads of any kind in South-West Africa, and there is none that can be called good. In particular, the routes across the frontiers to the interior are all subject to severely adverse conditions of surface and climate, and interstate road transport has consequently been small in amount.

From the three ports of Swakopmund, Walvisch Bay and Lüderitz Bay ran the old transport roads which served the Germans as routes of penetration. The four alternative tracks from Swakopmund and Walvisch Bay to Windhoek crossed a broad belt of soft, dry sand, which made traction so difficult that since the construction of the railway to Windhoek wagon transport has been discontinued. Similarly, the rough road leading east from Lüderitz Bay over patches of rock and through stretches of sand to Aus and thence to Keetmanshoop has as a channel of traffic been replaced by the Southern Railway.

Three so-called main tracks lead up to the Angola border through much sand and scrub, while the approaches to the Caprivizipfel are along the dry bed (omuramba) of the Omatako, and afterwards through the waterless Hukwe Veld. The routes across the Kalahari on the eastern frontier are merely the lines of the main watercourses, dry except immediately after rains.   A dozen routes lead into the south-east of the territory from points on the road between Upington and Rietfontein in Gordonia. These were extensively used for the transport of supplies during the native wars (1904-7).   On the south there are feasible routes leading to some sixteen fords or 'drifts' across the Orange River.   The chief of these are Olijvenhout's Drift, at Upington, in the Cape Province; Schuit Drift, close to the eastern limit of the southern frontier; and Raman's Drift, with a wagon track leading to Steinkopf on the Port Nolloth railway.

In recent years a good deal of attention and labour had been given to improving the wagon tracks connecting the more important towns and stations throughout the territory; but even now the best roads of the interior can only be described as 'well-defined main tracks,' on which numerous stretches occur of stony ground, heavy sand, and steep gradients. The necessity for good roads, however, has to some extent been obviated by an active policy of railway construction.

In the chief towns main streets are provided with pavements and with narrow-gauge rails, on which trollies are drawn by horse or mule.

To sum up, it may be said that, great as are the difficulties of surface and gradient almost everywhere, the chief hindrance to movement by road is the insufficiency of water for any considerable number of animals.   A careful survey of such water facilities as exist appears to be a necessary preliminary to any development of communications in the territory.

(b) Waterways

Within the territory there are no navigable waterways, nor any that from an economic point of view can be made navigable for steam vessels.   The Okowango river, which forms the boundary on the north-east, is in its upper course a deep, clear river with an average width of about 300 feet, and contains reaches navigable by light craft.   Stretches of navigable water occur also along the loop formed by the Kwando (Chobe or Linyanti) and Zambezi Rivers across the Caprivizipfel and along its southern and eastern extremities.

(c) Railways

The existing railway system: mileage, construction cost.—Railway construction in South-West Africa necessarily proceeded from the seaports inland. From Swakopmund two lines were laid—the Otavi Railway north-east to Otavi, Tsumeb and Grootfontein, and the State (or Northern) Railway eastward to Windhoek, with a northerly curve *via* Karibib and Okahandya. From Lüderitz Bay the Southern Railway was constructed eastward to Keetmanshoop, with a branch line from Seeheim to Kalkfontein. Windhoek and Keetmanshoop, the inland termini of the two Government lines, were next linked up by the North-South Railway.

In 1915 the Government of the Union of South Africa extended the Prieska line in the Cape Province *via* Upington to the Southern Railway at Kalkfontein, introduced the Cape gauge on the Otavi Railway from Karibib to Swakopmund, and built a line connecting Swakopmund with Walvisch Bay. The direction and control of the South-West African Railways —which under the German regime had been vested in a Railway Board comprising two representatives of agriculture, two of commerce, two of industrial and other professions, one of the Protectorate troops and one of the Governor's staff—have now passed to the Administration of the South African Railways.

1. *State (or Northern) Railway.*—This line, the first in the territory, was commenced in 1897 and finished in 1902. Its primary object, partly political, partly economic, was to connect the seaport, Swakopmund, with the capital, Windhoek. Its length was

121 miles from Swakopmund to Karibib, and 117 miles from Karibib to Windhoek—about 238 miles in all. A small branch line, 10 miles long, was run out from Jakalswater to carry water from the Swakop river at Riet. The total cost of construction is apparently not on record.

The gauge of this line was originally 2 feet, but the advantages offered by the Cape gauge (3 feet 6 inches), which was used on the railways south of Windhoek, led in 1911 to the broadening, at a cost of £550,000, of the section between Windhoek and Karibib.

About the same time the coastward section, Karibib to Swakopmund, was practically abandoned in favour of the alternative route provided by the Otavi Railway. By 1917 it had ceased to exist; for the whole line between Karibib and Rossing (95½ miles), the 10-mile branch from Jakalswater, and the Kubas military line, 4½ miles long, were lifted and removed, to provide material for Tanganyika and the Union of South Africa.

On this, the coastward section of the State Railway, the maximum gradient was 1 in 21, and the minimum radius of curves 225 feet. There were iron girder bridges at Khan River, Dorst River and Kubas. Water supply was good and plentiful only at Swakopmund and Karibib. The rails were bulb tee-section, weighing 19 lb. to the yard, and were laid on iron sleepers.

On the Windhoek-Karibib section, which is now of Cape gauge, the maximum gradient is 1 in 66. The sand embankment on which the track is laid makes indifferent ballast, and is liable to washaways during the rainy season. The Swakop River at Okahandya is spanned by a bridge 350 feet long, and there is a smaller bridge at Otyihavera. The water supply is good, especially at Karibib, Johann Albrechtshöhe, Waldau and Okahandya.

2. *Otavi Railway.*—The Otavi Railway was built by the Anglo-German syndicate which owns the copper mines at Otavi and Tsumeb, for the purpose of transporting ores from its mines to the seaport, and

generally developing its mining and land concessions. Begun in 1903, the construction of the line was delayed by the Herero War, and was not completed till August 1906. Branch lines were subsequently laid from Otavi to Grootfontein (59½ miles) and from Ongoati to Karibib station on the State Railway (12½ miles). The main line, Swakopmund-Tsumeb, is 356¼ miles long. The railway with its two branch lines cost approximately £1,000,000 to build. It was purchased by the Government in 1910 for £1,250,000, but the management was left in the hands of the Otavi Company under a 30 years' lease terminable after 10 years.

The Otavi Railway, like the State Railway, was built to a 2-feet gauge, though the difference of 1 centimetre in the wheel gauges prevented the interchange of rolling-stock. The broadening of the gauge between Swakopmund and Omaruru had been voted by the German Railway Board; but it was the Union forces who in 1915, in the course of the invasion of German South-West Africa, laid a Cape-gauge line for 100 miles inland from Swakopmund along the track of the original line, which the Germans had wrecked in their retreat. The construction of a new section, of similar gauge, from Kranzberg to Karibib, again connected the Otavi Railway with the State (Northern) Railway, and for the first time gave continuous communication of uniform gauge from Swakopmund to Windhoek and the south. The present mileage on the Otavi Railway system is therefore about 113 of Cape-gauge line on the coastward section, and 316 miles of 2-feet gauge further inland. There are also two lengths of branch lines which are meanwhile disused—the 7-mile Kalkfeld Iron Line and the 22 miles of track from Otyivarongo towards Otyo, on the projected Ovamboland Line (see p. 29).

Connected with the Otavi Railway are three small private lines. From Arendis Station a line 6¾ miles long runs down to the Khan Mine; the marble quarry near Karibib is connected with the main railroad by a track 7½ miles long; and the private lines of the Otavi Mining Company are 9⅔ miles in length.

The ruling gradient on the Otavi Railway is 1 in 67. Between Ongoati and Usakos the line falls 690 feet in 13 miles. The last 40 miles, down to Swakopmund, can be run by gravitation. Although the line winds considerably, there are no very sharp curves, the standard radius of curves being 150 metres (nearly 500 feet). The narrow-gauge rails are 30 feet long, weigh 30 lb. to the yard, and are borne on iron sleepers. The permanent way is well ballasted, and occasional damage done by heavy rains does not seriously interfere with the traffic. The difficulty formerly experienced in procuring suitable water for locomotive boilers has now been overcome. Usakos in particular has a good and abundant water supply. The rolling-stock in 1913 included 31 engines and 379 cars and trucks.

3. *Walvisch Bay—Swakopmund Line.*—The Cape-gauge line from Walvisch Bay to Swakopmund was laid during the war by the Union Government, and was opened in March 1915. The line, 21¼ miles long, lies almost wholly outside the limits of the former German Protectorate; but it forms part of the South-West African railway system, and, with the latter, is under the control of the Union Administration. It provides the northern and central railway systems with their natural terminus at the best seaport on the coast.

Before this line was built the jetty at Walvisch Bay was connected with the village by a shaky line of 2½-feet gauge, which at one time extended to Rooibank, 12 miles distant. The greater part of it had been derelict and buried in sand for some years.

4. *North-South Railway.*—The construction of this railway was undertaken chiefly for military reasons, to expedite the movement of troops and supplies; but the linking-up of Windhoek and Keetmanshoop, the inland termini of existing railways, was an inevitable development, justifiable on economic grounds.

Work was commenced in March 1910 from both ends of the projected line simultaneously. The contractors for the northern section, Windhoek to Kub, were the Bechstein-Koppel Co., who also effected the conversion to Cape gauge of the Windhoek-Karibib line. The southern portion, Keetmanshoop to Kub, was built by Lenz and Co., the contractors for the Southern Railway. The cost of construction was £2,000,000. Short branch lines were planned to the towns of Gibeon and Rehoboth. A line 7½ miles was actually built to Rehoboth, opened in 1913, and let to a contractor to work; latterly it has not been used.

The main line is 317 miles in length, and is laid to the Cape gauge of 3 feet 6 inches. The track is single except at stations, and is carried on iron sleepers. The sand of the embankment on which most of the permanent way is laid is liable to be washed off in the rainy season and to be blown away by the violent winds prevalent in the dry months. There is one tunnel, 50 yards long, through the Aus mountains, about 10 miles south of Windhoek. The rolling-stock in 1912 comprised 12 engines, 150 goods vehicles, and 4 passenger coaches.

5. *Southern Railway.*—In December 1905, during the native rebellion, the pressure on the line of communication from the coast to the southern theatre of operations and the difficulty of crossing the Namib Desert necessitated the construction of a railway from Lüderitz Bay to Aus, a distance of 87½ miles. The following year, when this, the first section of the Southern Railway, was completed, the Government authorized the extension of the line from Aus to Keetmanshoop on economic as well as military grounds. The extension was finished in 1908, and a branch line from Seeheim to Kalkfontein (South) was constructed by the middle of 1909.

In 1915, in the course of the invasion of German South-West Africa, the Union Government extended the Prieska line to Upington and the Gordonia frontier,

and thence for some 84 miles through the Protectorate
to Kalkfontein, where it joined the Southern Railway
The main system of South-West African railways,
being of uniform gauge with the Union lines, was thus
made available for the passage of Union rolling-stock;
and the length of Cape-gauge line was further
increased, as has been shown, by the conversion of the
Karibib-Swakopmund section of the Otavi Railway
and the building of the line from Swakopmund to
Walvisch Bay.

The main line of the Southern Railway is 227 miles
in length between Lüderitz Bay and Keetmanshoop,
and the branch line, Seeheim to Kalkfontein, 112
miles. The total cost of construction was £2,100,000;
the contractors were Lenz and Co., who worked the
railway for the Government until 1913.

Near the coast the shifting sand-dunes through
which the railway passes seriously hinder the maintenance of the permanent way, and expedients such as
the erection of palings and jute mats, and the planting
of grasses and other vegetation, have met with little
success. The ballast is chiefly stone, 6 in. to 8 in. deep,
and the rails, running 40 lb. to the yard, are supported
on iron sleepers weighing 67 lb. each. Water supply
is difficult near the coast, and for 50 miles inland has
to be maintained by special water trains. Farther east
there are ten water stations, and the Seeheim-Kalkfon-
tein branch has an ample supply.

6. *Kolmanskop-Bogenfels Line.*—Kolmanskop, 10
miles from Lüderitz Bay along the Southern Railway,
is the starting-point of a private railway of 2-feet
gauge, owned and operated by the Koloniale Bergbau-
Gesellschaft. This line, 74 miles in length, serves the
coast diamond fields, running south to Elizabeth
Bay and thence to Bogenfels. Several of the mines
have short branch lines. The locomotives are driven
by electricity generated on the engines, benzol being
used as fuel. The line was not being worked in 1916.

Financial Considerations.—The financial position of

the Government Railways of South-West Africa may be judged from the figures given below for the year 1912-13 :—

	State Railway.	Southern Railway.	Otavi Railway.	Totals.
	Marks.	Marks.	Marks.	Marks.
Traffic Receipts ..	1,625,291	2,029,171	4,921,287	8,575,749
Construction .. Transport	219,022	..	..	219,022
Working Expenses	1,371,691	1,629,850	2,429,156	5,430,697
Net profit ..	253,600	399,321	2,492,131	3,145,052
Percentage Ratio of Expenses to Receipts	84·4	80·3	49·4	63·3

On the State Railways expenses appear to have been relatively high in this year, for in 1911-12 and 1913-14, the ratios of expenses to receipts were only 64·8 and 67 respectively. The high percentage of working expenses on the Southern Railway was due largely to special difficulties of supplying water and removing sand. On the Otavi Railway the ratio had fallen from 56·5 per cent. in 1911-12 to 44·6 per cent. in 1913-14 and the profits realized on the working of this line in recent years must have averaged 10 per cent. of capital expenditure.

Adequacy to Economic Needs.—Now that the South-West African railways have been linked up with the South African system it may be expected that the volume of traffic will steadily increase. The rates on the German lines have in the past been higher than those obtaining in South Africa, and the Union Administration had not in 1916 seen fit to reduce them, though it had instituted special rates for through over-land traffic, and also for fruit, vegetables, and potatoes consigned from the Union.

In addition to traffic expansion and reduction in tariffs, other advantages are likely to follow from the connexion of the two systems. The German locomotives are for the most part obsolete, and the rest of the rolling-stock is inferior in design and condition. It may be assumed that the whole of the rolling-stock will in course of time be brought up to Union standards, and that services will improve both in speed and in frequency. Between January and December of 1916 the time occupied on the journey from De Aar to Walvisch Bay had been reduced from 101 hours to 72 hours 10 minutes. Passenger trains ran twice weekly from De Aar to Windhoek and Walvisch Bay, and made connection with Lüderitz Bay.

The requirements of internal traffic in German South-West Africa were efficiently met by the railways in operation before the war. The mileage of State-owned lines, which then totalled 770 of Cape gauge and 560 of 2-feet gauge, gave an average of 4·1 miles per thousand square miles of territory—a high proportion, considering that construction began so recently as 1897. Until 1915, however, the territory was practically isolated, and had no railway communication with its neighbours. Now that its railways are connected with those of South Africa it will play its natural part in the commercial activities of the sub-continent, and other lines will probably be constructed to open direct routes to the Transvaal, Rhodesia, and Angola.

Possibilities of expansion.—Proposals for a number of new lines had been considered by the Railway Board before 1914, and several had been approved.

1. *Ovamboland Line.*—The first aim of the railway to Ovamboland was to provide Ovambo labour for the south. The Landesrat in November 1913 approved a line of 2-feet gauge, on earthworks and bridges wide enough for a Cape-gauge track, to run from Otyivarongo on the Otavi Railway to Otyo and Okahakana. A sum of £450,000 was allowed for this in the Loan Estimates for 1914-15. The first section, including the 55 miles from Otyivarongo to Amiab Poort, was to cost £250,000. Construction was begun, and the line was laid for 22 miles before the outbreak of hostilities.

2. *Waterberg Line.*—The Landesrat is said to have intended to construct a line from Otyivarongo on the

Otavi Railway through Waterberg to Okahandya on the Northern Railway.

The completion of the Ovamboland and Waterberg lines and their connexion with the North-South Railway at Okahandya would give a continuous railway route from north to south right down the centre of the territory. A southward prolongation of this route was anticipated by the suggested extension of the North-South Railway from Kalkfontein to Warmbad

3. *Swakop Valley Line.*—In November 1913 the settlers in the district obtained the promise of a short line from Swakopmund to the Swakop Valley. The material of the disused State line between Swakopmund and Kubas (92 miles) was to have been used for this purpose, but has since then been removed, part to Tanganyika, part to the Union (see p. 23).

4. *Gobabis Line.*—A line from Windhoek to Gobabis was under consideration, and a flying survey was ordered by the Landesrat in November 1913.

5. *South-West Africa–Union Lines.*—The Railway Board had also considered the following schemes for railway connexion between South-West Africa and the Union :—

(*a*) The proposed Windhoek-Gobabis line, if continued across the Kalahari Desert, would strike the South African system at Palapye in the Bechuanaland Protectorate, and thus give a trans-continental line either northwards through Buluwayo to the port of Beira, or southwards through Pretoria to Lourenço Marques. It is not clear whether a railroad which would traverse some 500 miles of reputed desert country is likely to earn profits.

(*b*) A second line across the Kalahari, alternative or additional to the former, was to run from Keetmanshoop to Hasuur by a route which had been surveyed before March 1909. It was then to cross the Kalahari along or below the valley of the Molopo, and. joining the Cape railways near Vryburg, effect a connexion *via* Mafeking with Johannesburg and Lourenço Marques. The proposed line would measure about 450 miles, and would give the most direct communication with the Rand and the East Coast.

(*c*) The third suggested route was from Kalkfontein
to Ukamas and thence across the Gordonia frontier to
link up with the Cape railways. This was approximately the route actually followed, though construction
proceeded from the other end, when the Union Government in 1915 built a line from Prieska to Upington and
Kalkfontein (see p. 26).

6. *South-West Africa–Angola Lines*.—For the
connexion of South-West Africa with Angola a
number of schemes have been advanced from time to
time.

(*a*) The earliest project was that of Cecil Rhodes
who in 1899 proposed the construction of a line from
Port Alexander in Angola, *via* the first cataract of
the Kunene River, to Waterberg, and thence through
Gobabis to Bechuanaland.

(*b*) An alternative route suggested for a continental
railway is from Great Fish Bay (Tiger Bay) across
Ovamboland and through the Caprivizipfel, to join the
Rhodesian system on the Zambezi above the Victoria
Falls.

(*c*) An extension of the Otavi Railway from Tsumeb
to Port Alexander was contemplated at one time, and
the route is said to have been surveyed in 1909.
Nothing more has been heard of this scheme, and it was
probably abandoned in favour of the alternative extension from Otyivarongo.

(*d*) The Ovamboland Railway was planned, as has
been shown, to run from Otyivarongo to Otyo and
Okahakana. It is probable that the Germans intended
to push this line northward to the Kunene River, and
would have found occasion to carry it across Portuguese Ovamboland to Great Fish Bay (Tiger Bay) or
Port Alexander.

(*e*) A fifth possible connexion, along a route much
nearer to and roughly parallel with the coast, was indicated by an announcement made in the *Leipziger
Neueste Nachrichten* of May 31, 1914. According to
this, it was reported that, after lengthy discussions with

the Government, a syndicate for the purpose of building railways in German South-West Africa had been formed, with an initial capital of 50,000,000 marks. The syndicate was said to include the Hamburg-Amerika-Linie, the Norddeutscher Lloyd, the Woermann-Linie, the Deutsche Bank, the Disconto-Gesellschaft, Bankhaus Bleichröder in Berlin, and Bankhaus Sal. Oppenheim und Gesellschaft in Köln. The first railway to be built was to be a line "along the coast of German South-West Africa to the Angola Province, traversing the Mossamedes Company's territory."

Early in 1914 the Bernardino Machado Cabinet in Lisbon had sanctioned the despatch to Southern Angola of a party of German engineers by the Hamburg-Bremer-Afrika Gesellschaft, which is an offshoot of the Norddeutscher Lloyd, supported financially by the Deutsche Bank. The expedition was then called a mixed German and Portuguese mission. But in June 1914 the *Kölnische Zeitung* declared the Southern Angola mission and its projects to be exclusively German undertakings, and added that the Imperial Government was prepared to give the proposed railway a kilometric guarantee. The Governor of German South-West Africa in the early part of 1914 toured the northern part of the Protectorate, and is said to have gone as far as Great Fish Bay, in connexion with possible railway construction in the near future. These facts, the statements made in the German press, the financial support given by the Berlin banks to the Mossamedes Company, and the known German aspirations to the company's concessions, all go to prove that in this instance, as in so many others, German plans of railway expansion contemplated the economic penetration and ultimately the political absorption of foreign territory. The economic factors are not in themselves strong enough to account for the extension of the railway into Angola. The labour supply which the Germans were entitled to use lay to the south of the Kunene. The mineral resources which a Kaokoland line would have tapped lie, with few exceptions, nearer to the Otavi

Railway and nearer even to Swakopmund than to Port Alexander.   Part of Ovamboland, however, lies in Angola, and the natural outlet for all Ovamboland seems to be either Great Fish Bay (Tiger Bay) or the more serviceable harbour of Port Alexander.   The two harbours provided a plausible solution for the alleged difficulty of railway connexion with the Kaokoland mines, and the scheme of railway extension veiled the plan of economic penetration.

(d) Posts, Telegraphs, and Telephones

Posts.—During the German occupation the Imperial posts and telegraphs were administered from the Post-Office at Windhoek under a Director of Posts, who was responsible to the Imperial Post-Office at Berlin.   The service was thus independent of both the German Colonial and Protectorate Governments.   In April 1913 there were in all 70 postal establishments, of which 3 were full Imperial Post-Offices, 25 ordinary post-offices, and 42 sub-offices.   Fifty out of the 70 postal establishments were connected with the tele-graph circuit; there were also 32 telegraph agencies which gave no postal facilities.   The Imperial Post-Offices and 14 of the larger post-offices were in charge of postal officials sent out from Germany, the re-mainder being under railway officials, police, and troops, or in some cases private persons.   In 1902 there were only 13 Post-Office officials in the country; in April 1913 there were 73.   Natives were largely used as postal messengers, and their numbers rose from 8 in 1902 to 81 in 1909 and 91 (including one native tele-graphist) in 1913.

Mails were either despatched by the Deutsche Ost Afrika-Linie or by the joint Woermann Hamburg-Amerika sérvice, or sent to Cape Town by sea or over-land across the Orange River *viä* Raman's Drift.   The various routes together provided a weekly service in wards and outwards.

Telegraphs.—Besides a short line in the hands of the police (Otyivarongo-Waterberg), there were three telegraph systems in the territory, viz., the Imperial postal telegraph circuit, the military (field) lines, and the railway telegraphs.

The principal telegraph lines followed generally the railway and main road systems; the central " backbone " being between Windhoek and Keetmanshoop, with two main transverse lines crossing it at right angles from Swakopmund to Windhoek and Gobabis and from Lüderitz Bay to Keetmanshoop and Hasuur, and with northern and southern extensions from Karibib to Tsumeb and from Keetmanshoop to Raman's Drift respectively.

These main lines had numerous branches and subsidiary transverse lines.   The ends of the main transverse lines were connected, on the west by the wireless stations at Swakopmund and Lüderitz Bay, on the east by the field telegraph line Gobabis-Hasuur-Stolzenfels. Visual signalling lines were used to connect up various telegraph stations not in communication by telegraph. It will be seen that the whole telegraph system was very complete and well arranged—primarily, however, for military purposes.   There were two lines on each of the main   telegraph   routes,   Swakopmund–Windhoek, Lüderitz Bay–Keetmanshoop; and all railways were provided with telegraphic communication (railway telegraph system) throughout.   The railway telegraph poles were used to carry the Imperial telegraph wires when the routes coincided.

The length of telegraph circuit in South-West Africa in April 1913 was 3,964 kilometres, and the total length of line was 6,487 kilometres.   These figures cover the Imperial postal telegraph circuit, but do not include the extensive military (field) lines.

Telephones.—The telephone system was also extensive.   It embraced 28 towns and villages, and there were telephones in nearly all hotels and officers' quarters.   Detached posts were connected by telephone to their headquarters; even outlying farms situated near a telegraph station had telephonic communication.

The telephone wires were usually carried on the telegraph poles; in some cases the telegraph wires themselves were used.

In April 1913 there were 28 local telephone exchanges, with 954 subscribers in all. The total length
of line was 1,078 kilometres.

(2) EXTERNAL

(a) Ports

Accommodation and Equipment.—The Protectorate
had only two ports, Lüderitz Bay Harbour and Swakopmund Roads; Walvisch Bay now makes the third.

Swakopmund, the port for the middle and northern
part of the colony, and the terminus of the Otavi Railway, is a desolate looking place, built on a sandy flat at
the mouth of the Swakop River. Except in a few
private gardens there is not a speck of green to be
seen.

Swakopmund being an open roadstead, steamers used
to anchor about 2 miles from the shore. A boat harbour was completed in 1913, but two years afterwards
it was entirely silted up owing to the Benguella current
and the surf. A wooden jetty 1,200 feet long was then
built, and is still in existence. In 1911 the construction of an iron jetty was begun, and 850 feet out of a
total of 2,035 were completed by 1914.

Swakopmund is a bad port, nor does it appear that
it can ever be made a good one.

Lüderitz Bay, or Angra Pequena, the terminus of
the Southern Railway, is the port serving the south.
The harbour is well sheltered from all but east winds,
and the anchorage is good. A serious disadvantage is
the absence of fresh water in the neighbourhood;
drinking water has to be condensed or brought by train.
The sand blown from the dunes which surround the
town causes much inconvenience and annoyance, and
has made it necessary for business purposes to run a
light tramway with mule transport along each street,
with a branch line into each yard.

Although landing and embarking are not, as at
Swakopmund, frequently interrupted by bad weather,

there were at Lüderitz Bay in 1913 no facilities for discharging cargo direct on to the quay, except from small coasting steamers. From larger vessels cargo had to be landed from lighters towed by tugs. There is a proposal to build on the side of Haifisch (Shark) Island a quay where steamers could lie alongside. If this were constructed and provided with railway connexions and the necessary storage accommodation, the port would become one of the best on the West Coast of Africa.

Walvisch Bay is an excellent deep-water harbour, with sheltered anchorage close to the shore. Had it lain within the German Protectorate it would doubtless have been selected as the northern port and equipped with the landing facilities which it has hitherto lacked.

Volume of Trade.—The tonnage of shipping entering South-West Africa ports is shown in the table below. The figures given are the German official figures for the years 1907 to 1912, and do not include Government steamers. It is remarkable that during these years there was practically no increase in the total tonnage, and very little in the number of ships. The tonnage was 1,331,000 at the beginning and 1,417,000 at the close of the period; the number of ships, 383 and 430.

The table specifies the tonnage of Lüderitz Bay and that of Swakopmund. A little more than half of the total fell to Swakopmund, and this proportion was very evenly maintained over the whole of the years 1907-1912.

The table also distinguishes between steamships under the German flag, steamships not under the German flag, and sailing ships. The figures illustrate significantly the effect of German colonial trade methods, for whereas in 1907 83·7 per cent. of the total tonnage was German and 15·1 per cent. sailed under other flags, by 1912 the latter class had dwindled to 2·4 per cent. and the German tonnage had risen to 97·3 per cent. of the total. Thus practically the whole of the Protectorate trade was carried in German ships and passed through German hands only. A measure which was largely instrumental in achieving a result so desirable from the German point of view was the monopoly granted to the Woermann Company of the landing and shipping business of both ports.

In 1912 a new contract was concluded, to remain in force until the new pier at Swakopmund was completed or until March 31, 1915. By the terms of this agreement, which was published in the *Deutsches Kolonialblatt*, the monopoly was maintained, ordinary charges were slightly reduced, uniformity secured in the landing regulations at both ports, and power reserved to the Government to expropriate the tugs, lighters, and landing appliances of the Woermann-Linie. Although it was entered into ostensibly in the interests of national defence and for the better regulation of the traffic at the ports for the benefit alike of the private trader and of the Government, the contract nevertheless proved in practice a most powerful instrument of economic boycott. It is a fair and just inference that in the Protectorate, as in German East Africa, the landing rights monopoly was designed and dictated primarily in the interest of the Hamburg merchants and shipowners.

VESSELS ENTERING PORTS OF GERMAN SOUTH-WEST AFRICA.

| Year. | Steamers. | | | | Sailing ships. | |
| | Under German flag. | | Not under German flag. | | | |
	No.	Net registered tons.	No.	Net registered tons.	No.	Net registered tons.
ALL PORTS.						
1912 ..	368	1,378,929	41	34,747	21	3,554
1911 ..	323	1,194,335	52	86,765	26	14,698
1910 ..	347	1,174,877	74	138,657	62	14,822
1909 ..	261	987,973	81	223,710	70	20,144
1908 ..	260	935.620	51	179,109	28	11,840
1907 ..	296	1,115,061	65	200,981	22	15 491

Year.	Steamers.				Sailing ships.	
	Under German flag.		Not under German flag.			
	No.	Net registered tons.	No.	Net registered tons.	No.	Net registered tons.
SWAKOPMUND ONLY.						
1912 ..	156	702,778	31	21,656	13	269
1911 ..	129	597,726	21	43,569	10	2,587
1910 ..	170	621,390	21	52,758	—	—
1909 ..	144	522,888	30	78,102	6	1,584
1908 ..	159	536,608	18	55,694	14	252
1907 ..	177	679,816	17	49.200	8	3,166
LÜDERITZ BAY ONLY.						
1912 ..	149	601,543	10	13,091	3	3,190
1911 ..	131	515,849	31	43,196	8	11,077
1910 ..	134	495,206	51	85,550	10	13,974
1909 ..	108	434,385	50	145,308	19	17,857
1908 ..	98	389,960	33	123,415	14	11,588
1907 ..	117	429,473	48	151,781	14	12,325

(b) *Shipping Lines*

The German service between Hamburg and South-West Africa by the western route was maintained by the Deutsche Ost-Afrika-Linie in combination with the Woermann-Linie and the African Service of the Hamburg-Amerika-Linie.

The Imperial mail steamers called at Bremerhaven, Antwerp, and Southampton on the outward voyage to Swakopmund and Lüderitz Bay, where they stayed a few hours only before passing on to Capetown and returning round Africa by the east coast route. There was a fortnightly service in 1914. The time occupied on the voyage between Hamburg and Swakopmund was twenty-five days. Fares were 250 marks (£12 10s.) for steerage, and double and treble this sum for second-class and first-class passages respectively.

The Deutsche Ost-Afrika-Linie had also a three-weekly passenger service by the east coast route. The ships called at Rotterdam, Southampton, Lisbon, Tangier, Marseilles, Naples, Port Said, Suez, Aden, Kilindini, Tanga, Dar es-Salaam, Beira, Lourenço Marques, East London, and Capetown, and continued round the west of Africa after visiting the Protectorate ports. The fares charged for passages to the Protectorate by this route were one and a-half times to twice the rates on the western or Atlantic route.

In 1914 the Hamburg-Amerika Afrikadienst ran steamers once a month to the Protectorate *via* Antwerp, Las Palmas, Monrovia, and the Portuguese West Africa ports.

Freight from Germany to the Protectorate was taken by a fortnightly joint service of the three combined German lines, Woermann, Hamburg-Amerika (Afrikadienst), and Hamburg-Bremer Afrika, calling at Las Palmas and Monrovia on the outward voyage. In this service the so-called Swakopmund-Linie took twenty-five days from Hamburg to Swakopmund, and the so-called Lüderitzbucht-Linie took thirty-three days to Lüderitz Bay. They called at coast ports on the return journey. Each line ran a monthly service in 1914.

The English steamships of the Union-Castle Mail Line had a weekly service from Southampton to the Cape, where passengers to the Protectorate transshipped to vessels of the three local lines mentioned below. The time taken on this route was sixteen days from Southampton, *via* Madeira, to Capetown, and three to five days from Capetown to Swakopmund.

The three chief lines connecting Capetown by local service with the South-West Africa ports were: (*a*) the passenger steamers of the combined German lines already mentioned, which took no freight; (*b*) the coasting steamers of the Woermann-Linie, which ran every other week, carrying both passengers and freight, and calling at Walvisch Bay and at Port Nolloth in Cape Province; and (*c*) the service of the

Houston Steamship Line, which was maintained almost wholly by freight steamers touching at all four ports, but was discontinued before 1914.

To reach the so-called diamond stations—Conception Bay, Spencer Bay, Princes Bay, &c.—it was necessary to trans-ship at Lüderitz Bay to the small steam-vessel "Linda Woermann," of the Woermann-Linie.

Connexion with New York in 1914 was maintained by a regular bi-monthly service in either direction. The three German lines—Woermann, Hamburg-Amerika (Afrikadienst), and Hamburg-Bremer Afrika —ran this service jointly with Elder, Dempster and Co.

(c) *Telegraphs—Overland, Submarine, and Wireless*

Land Lines.—The Protectorate was in telegraphic communication with foreign countries through Capetown by the overland route.

Cable.—The Eastern and South African Telegraph Company's submarine cable between Capetown and Europe has a "T-piece" to Swakopmund, which is brought ashore to a cable junction near Walvisch Bay and carried as a land cable to Swakopmund. The staff was not under German control. An annual subsidy of £4,500 to the Cable Company formed a charge on the revenues of the Protectorate.

Wireless.—Before the war there were wireless telegraph stations at Swakopmund, Lüderitz Bay, and Windhoek. The last is said to have been able—occasionally, at least—to communicate direct with Nauen in Germany. It was blown up by the Germans in 1915.

With the completion of the so-called African triangle, consisting of the stations at Windhoek, Tabora (German East Africa), and Atakpame (Togoland), with the latter of which Duala (Cameroon) was in communication, the whole German African Empire was connected internally and with the Fatherland by wireless communication.

The stations at the ports, in addition to communicating with ships, are at all times in communication with each other. The Swakopmund station, under favourable conditions, has been able to get into touch with the stations in Cameroon; and Lüderitz Bay can communicate with Slangkop, in the Cape Peninsula.

(B) INDUSTRY

(1) LABOUR

(a) *Immigration.*—For the last twenty years there has been very little emigration from Germany, and in South-West Africa there were no special inducements to attract large numbers of settlers. Few even of the garrison elected to remain. The density of population in the Protectorate in recent years was only 0·046 of whites per square mile and 0·85 of all races, as against 0·289 and 1·93 in adjacent Bechuanaland, and 0·553 and 1·22 in the eleven north-west districts of the Cape Province.

The annual total of adult male residents of European descent showed a decrease in 1912, when the railway construction was completed, though the renewed activity in diamond mining in that year partly counteracted the loss. The increase in later years in the total number of Europeans was due to the influx of women and children. The number of British and non-German immigrants had fallen steadily year after year. There was an obvious desire to reduce to a minimum the number of British subjects in the Protectorate.

During the South African War (1899-1902) the Germans encouraged the immigration of Boers, in the belief that, owing to their Teutonic origin, they would easily be assimilated. They had latterly revised the opinion and modified the policy. The Boer immigrants, numbers of whom had settled in the country, were not encouraged to remain, and many were expelled on various grounds.

Although South-West Africa holds out no higher attractions than the territories of the Union, it seems capable, with its large tracts of unoccupied land, of supporting a greatly increased white population; and this might possibly be secured if immigration were encouraged by the offer of land on favourable terms.

The native tribes were, in several cases, practically annihilated during the native wars, and the policy of the Government and the inhabitants generally towards the natives had neither the aim nor the result of attracting others to fill up the vacant territories.

(b) *Native Labour and German Policy*.—The policy followed by the Germans between 1900 and 1908 in their treatment of most of the native races of the Protectorate may fairly be described as a policy of extermination. It was never formally withdrawn or reversed; but with the discovery of diamonds in the sandfields of the Namib it became clear to the German Administration that if the policy were not discontinued they would have no native labour left for the work of recovering the diamonds, nor would they obtain any from other States.

Between 1908 and 1914 the policy adopted towards the survivors seems to have been to make every native dependent for a living upon employment by Europeans. If any native tried to live otherwise he was treated practically as a vagabond. That is shown in the clearest way by the notorious Ordinance No. 82, *Massregeln zur Kontrolle der Eingeborenen*, issued by the Governor on August 18, 1907 (*Kolonialblatt*, p. 1181), and strictly enforced.

Under the first clause natives were prohibited from acquiring rights over or titles to land. They could acquire such rights or titles only with the sanction of the Governor. By the second clause they were similarly debarred from owning animals for riding purposes or cattle, the small tribe of Bastards of Rehoboth alone being excepted. Thus dispossessed of the land they had owned, of their horses and herds, and even their sacred cattle, they were denied the freedom of a nomadic life, and made liable, as vagrants, to penalties specified in the later clauses of the Ordi-

nance.   In such circumstances it is not surprising that
the question of native labour was one of much difficulty.

(*c*) *Labour for* (i) *Agriculture*, (ii) *Mines and Railways*.—Work on the farms was done usually by Hereros, Hottentots, Berg-Damaras, and Bastards. A few Bushmen were also employed, but neither Bushmen nor Hereros take kindly to the work as a rule. Further, it appears that in many cases the arrangements for housing and feeding native labourers left much to be desired. It is significant that the Official Report for 1908-09 states that farmers who treat their men well were usually able to obtain labour, a statement corroborated by H.B.M. Consul E. Müller in his report for 1913. The difficulty for the farmers was, however, increased by the high wages offered in the mines.

Some 6,500 Cape-Kaffirs and Bastards were employed in 1911, chiefly for railway construction and work in the mines. Their recruiting received a severe check in that year as a result of the " Wilhelmstal incident," when a number of strikers (Cape boys) were shot down by the troops. After the completion of the North-South Railway the number of these imported labourers largely diminished.

Application was made in 1911 for native labour from Cameroon and German East Africa, but was refused by the Governments of those Protectorates. A proposal then made to obtain 1,000 natives of India for work in South-West Africa was not proceeded with.

The main source of labour supply for both railway work and mines has hitherto been Ovamboland. For this reason it was laid down in the 1913 session of the Landesrat that Ovambos were to be employed on these two classes of work only.

The supply of Ovambo labour is at times precarious. It depends largely on the harvest and on the season for sowing in the natives' own country. Large numbers come down after their harvest, but most of them have to be at their homes in the sowing season, in order to provide food for the families they leave behind when they go to work. Contracts for Ovambo labour were, therefore, drawn for the half-year only. Special regulations, enacted in recent years, controlled the re cruiting, the movement of labourers from their terri tory to the railway, and their housing and sanitation.

Another factor affecting the supply of Ovambo labour is the existence or cessation of tribal warfare in Ovamboland. Thus, in 1912, the defeat of Mandume, the paramount chief of the Ovakwanyamas, in a conflict with another tribe, caused a temporary but serious diminution in the supply.

(*d*) *The Labour Reservoir—Native Tribes.*—The Ovambo tribes of South-West Africa were estimated by Major Pritchard in 1915 to number 156,000. A few labourers are also supplied by the smaller tribes of the northern districts—the Ovatyimbas of the Kaokoveld, the Ovakwangaris of the Okovango Valley, and scattered contingents of Bushmen.

The three other principal races are the Hereros, Hottentots, and Berg-Damaras. Their numbers in 1904 were estimated to be, at the lowest figure, 80,000, 20,000, and 30,000 respectively. In 1911, after the repression of the last rebellion, the census showed that they had fallen to 15,130, 9,781, and 12,831 respectively, a total of 37,742 instead of 130,000.

The Bushmen of the Grootfontein district were recently estimated at 7,000 or 8,000, and those of the northern areas at over 10,000. The German farmers declared that Bushmen were too weak for agricultural work, and would not remain on the farms; but this was denied in a report submitted to the German Governor by the District Chief of Grootfontein in 1912. His opinion was :—" It is remarkable to observe how the Bushmen serve the purpose of farm labourers. They learn to plough, to cultivate tobacco, to control oxen transport, and whatever else a farm labourer must do. Many remain for long years on the farms, and become indispensable assistants to the farmers." The testimony of this broad-minded official is valuable, since, with the unhappy diminution in the numbers of the

Herero, Hottentot, and Damara tribes, the Bushmen constitute an important source of labour for the immigrant white settlers of the future. Should there be any considerable influx of these, the problem of finding native labour for agricultural work will present much less difficulty.

(2) AGRICULTURE

(a) *General Conditions: Government Assistance*

Agriculture in South-West Africa labours under many difficulties, of which the chief are want of water, scarcity of labour, and the ravages of locusts. Lack of a large market and insufficient road communications have also tended to restrict development. The figures for 1913 show that out of a total holding of 1,331 farms, covering 33,484,015 acres, only 13,000 acres were cultivated, the chief items of culture being maize, potatoes, and pumpkins. The proportion of cultivated land is certain to increase in the future, especially when irrigation and dry-farming are practised on a larger scale. Parts of the country have soil admirably suited for crops. In Eastern Ovamboland, in the more rainy region to the north, the plains are covered with a rich deep loam, and are capable of yielding large returns when malaria, faults of soil and other evils have been overcome by cultivation and drainage. In Ovamboland generally and in the neighbouring districts native agriculture alone has been practised in the past, as the country was for political reasons closed to Europeans and accessible only by road. Should the political settlement result in the formation of a protected Ovambo State and the opening up of the country by railways, native agriculture might be successfully stimulated by methods such as those followed in Uganda, on the Gold Coast, and in the Belgian Congo. The climate is tropical, and the Ovambos are an agricultural people. The rainfall in Ovamboland, though higher on the average than farther south, is not constant, and in 1915 there had been a severe drought of three years' duration, which caused great distress and high mortality among the natives.

Speaking generally, the territory is predominantly a grazing country. Even in Ovamboland cattle breeding is one of the leading native pursuits alongside of agriculture. The same mixture of occupations is found in the Caprivizipfel. In Damaraland the Berg-Damaras, the subject race, are agricultural; while the Hereros, the ruling race, are keen and successful cattle breeders. Farther south again, in Namaqualand, the Hottentots own sheep and cattle, and cultivate very little land.

Native agriculture is thus practically confined to the northern and central regions. As regards stock, sheep predominate in the south, cattle in the north.

The German Government showed its interest in the progress of agriculture by many practical measures. A Veterinary Research Division was established at two stations, Gamams and Friedrichsfelde, the annual cost of which was approximately £4,500 in addition to the salaries of the veterinary surgeons. Experts were appointed—an orchardist at Grootfontein, a tobacco expert at Okahandya, a wool expert at Windhoek, a stock farming expert, a forester, and an agronomist. The number of officials employed in these services was 44 in 1914, and the annual expenditure on experimental farms and plantations was about £10,000. There was a stud farm at Naukhas, a camel farm at Kalkfontein (North), an ostrich farm at Otyitwezu, a sheep farm near Windhoek, a tobacco station at Okahandya, and an experimental tillage farm at Neudamm, near Windhoek.

Government grants were made for the destruction of vermin, the eradication of pests, and the investigation of diseases. The commonest animal diseases were horse-sickness, biliary fever, mange, and glanders among horses; lung-sickness and lamziekte among cattle; scab and sheep-pox among sheep.

Large sums were spent annually on the purchase and maintenance of live-stock, on fencing, and on the erection of shelters. Grants were made to agricultural and horse-breeding societies, and the Government paid the expenses of the Agricultural Advisory Board established by an Ordinance in 1913.

(b) Products and Live-stock

Plant Production.—The products to which most attention was devoted are *maize* and *potatoes*, but even of these the supply was insufficient to make them cheap. Irrigation has been employed in the cultivation of *lucerne*, which is used for feeding stock. *Sorghum*, *food-melons*, and *beans* are also cultivated.

With the help of experiments made at the Government station at Okahandya, *tobacco* is being grown, mainly on the small farms of Osona. The variety chiefly cultivated is pipe-tobacco; but experimental crops have been grown with the aim of producing a cigarette tobacco of Turkish flavour.

Cotton, although trial crops are reported to have proved successful, has not yet been cultivated on a commercial scale. Parts of Ovamboland are said to be suitable for its cultivation, and it is grown by natives on the Kunene River.

Several varieties of *fruit*, including peaches, apricots, and apples, have produced abundant crops, not perhaps of the highest quality. Cherries and pears have hitherto proved unsuccessful. Citrus fruits appear to offer good prospects. Over 1,000 orange trees were planted in 1909 by farmers near Grootfontein, and oranges have been exported since the British occupation. *Vegetables*, as well as fruit, are grown with pronounced success on the small holdings along the Nossob and Swakop rivers.

The *grape-vine* has been cultivated, usually with the aid of irrigation, and there are possibilities of wine-making. The wine farmer, however, will have to face the competition of the Cape, with its more favourable conditions, physical and economic.

Live-stock.—In spite of the dryness of the climate
and the scanty water supply, the territory is capable
of providing grazing for large numbers of stock.
Stock farms, however, have to be very extensive, as 25
to 45 acres are required per head of large stock, and
from 2 to 5 acres per head of small stock.   The
reason for this is that the grasses and so-called forage
bush grow in isolated clumps with bare ground between
them.   A further reason is the occurrence of rainless
years, such as 1911, during which the grasses are
unable to renew their growth; the farmer is therefore
obliged to keep a portion of his grazing land un-
touched, as a reserve.

Parts of the territory in which good grazing is
to be found after rain are in the district of Gibeon,
round Aus and Kubub, east of Kanus and between
Kanus and the Little Karas mountains.   Towards the
west, in Lüderitz Bay district, there are grasslands on
either side of the Southern Railway from the Tiras
Mountains as far south as Obib.   Central Namaqualand, however, consists largely of bare rocky plain.
Towards the east, the Kalahari is good grass country,
where formerly large herds of game grazed, and where
shortage of forage is scarcely ever experienced.

Between the Kalahari and Central Namaqualand
there are chalky plateaux which produce many bushes
suitable for forage, and also a variety of Bushman-
grass used by the farmers as reserve fodder.   Large
sections of Ovamboland are eminently suitable for cattle
raising.

The total numbers of the different classes of live-
stock in the territory (excluding Ovamboland) during
the years 1910-1913, are shown in the following
table.   It will be observed that there had been a steady
increase in all varieties except camels:—

	1910.	1911.	1912.	1913.
Cattle	121,139	144,445	171,784	205,643
Merino sheep	29,201	32,209	46,901	53,691
Persian sheep	—	—	12,588	17,171
Karakul sheep	—	427	341	776
Karakul sheep (half bred)	—	—	3,753	10,418
Native sheep	343,989	381,240	435,069	472,585
Angora goats (full bred) ..	—	—	10,044	13,340
Angora goats (half bred)..	8,095	10,257	10,387	18,163
Native goats	319,000	384,986	448,279	485,401
Horses	10,661	12,683	13,340	15,916
Mules and donkeys ..	12,693	9,994	11,894	13,618
Pigs	5,208	7,761	7,195	7,772
Camels	954	847	789	709
Ostriches	334	642	1,277	1,507

Horses.—The best districts for horses are Windhoek, Rehoboth, and Keetmanshoop, and second to these are the Warmbad, Hasuur, Maltahöhe, and Karibib districts. Horse-breeding is still in a backward state, owing to the prevalence of horse-sickness, to losses during the native wars, and to careless methods of breeding. So few were the horses of good substance and quality that the Government had to spend £20,000 annually on the importation of remounts for troops and police.

Special measures were adopted in order to improve the breed. A Government Stud Farm was established at Naukhas; well-bred stallions were made available; and under a "Selection Ordinance" promulgated in 1912 action was taken to limit breeding to horses that had been approved by a Government Commission.

Mules.—Mule-breeding has hitherto been less profitable than horse-breeding, and has further been retarded by lack of mares. A mule-breeding farm has been in existence for some years at Gobas, near Keetmanshoop, and in 1911 the Government assisted mule breeders by providing imported jack-asses at less than cost price. Mules were latterly imported direct from South America, and no longer from South Africa.

Donkeys.—Donkeys have increased in numbers in recent years. They are popular for slow transport work because of their hardiness and immunity from horse-sickness.

Camels.—Camels had been imported privately in 1898 as an experiment, but were first introduced in large numbers in the course of the native war. Five hundred were imported from the Canary Islands, 2,000 from Somaliland. The latter were smaller, slower, and more expensive than those from the Canary Islands. They were employed chiefly for transport, and proved very useful, though many died, probably through mismanagement. The camel-farm, managed by a veterinary lieutenant, was at Kalkfontein (North), where water is plentiful and the veld sweet. Camels are fed chiefly on alfalfa grass, chaff, and barley, but can get good grazing on the grass and bush of the country. Breeding was successful, but the total number of camels declined latterly, because private owners found them difficult to handle and the military authorities considered them awkward on muddy or rocky ground.

Cattle.—At the time when the Germans first occupied the territory, the natives owned cattle belonging to three distinct breeds, the Herero, the Ovambo, and the Afrikander. The Herero or Damara cattle are medium-sized, long-legged, well-built, and suitable for draught. The Ovambo breed is short-legged and plump, not quite so good for draught purposes. The Afrikander or Bastard represents a cross between Dutch and native cattle, and is useful for heavy draught work, but slower and less enduring than the Herero variety.

The natives of tribes other than the Ovambo were not allowed to own cattle without special permission. Great numbers of their animals passed into German hands by confiscation or in return for merely nominal payments. Only in Ovamboland are cattle, valued here at £4 to £5 per head, still owned by most of the natives, while the chiefs are said to have enormous herds. The total number of cattle in this region has never been ascertained.

In the earlier years of the German occupation settlers and natives alike endeavoured to increase the numbers of their cattle without regard to breed; but the establishment of Government cattle-breeding farms and the attention paid to the improvement of breed by the Government advisers have led not only to the discovery of the best districts for cattle, but to the practice of more discriminating methods of breeding. Since 1900 stud cattle have been imported from Europe and from Argentina in order to improve the local breeds. A number of animals were also imported from South Africa; but the prevalence of East Coast fever in the Cape Province made it necessary to prohibit importation.

In the light of the results of many experiments the Government cattle-breeders at the outbreak of war were endeavouring to produce an improved strain by crossing with selected varieties of the Afrikander breed. Expert opinion generally favoured the so-called Red Afrikander variety, which, when crossed with Friesland or Holland cattle, was expected to produce a type of fuller form, better breeding quality, and higher working power. In the northern districts a cross between Afrikander and German lowland cattle has given a useful dairying type. Mornheim cattle proved useful for cross-breeding in the mountain districts. The East Forestland breed was expected to give a cross useful for milk and also for meat, and several English breeds promised the best results for meat alone.

Dairying was an industry still in its infancy before the war. A co-operative creamery was started in 1913 at Tugab, 35 miles west of Windhoek. Stock-raising for slaughter purposes is likely to prove highly successful. There is a very considerable market in the Union, now linked with the territory by railway; and, when South African requirements have been satisfied, the establishment of a cold storage depot will make it possible to export the surplus of meat to Europe, where the demand increases yearly.

Large interests in the territory have been acquired by the Liebig Company and by Brauss, Mahn and Co.

Small Stock.—All varieties of small stock, except pigs, have increased in recent years. Pure-bred Karakul sheep have been imported from Russia. In 1913 the pure-bred Karakul sheep in the country numbered 776, and the total number of half-breeds had risen to 10,418. The Karakul variety is said to be the best for the country; it is very hardy, and superior to the Afrikander as a mutton sheep. In 1913 1,400 high-class flock sheep were imported from Australia, the Government paying the cost of transport and distributing them to farmers at the Australian cost price. Merinos were also imported from Germany and in large numbers from the Union.

The territory does not appear to provide the conditions essential for a yield of the finer kinds of wool, and it is unlikely that the Cape range of qualities will be surpassed.

In mohair, also, the most that the territory is likely to accomplish is to equal the standards and possibly the output of the Cape Province, from which large numbers of Angora goats have been obtained.

Ostriches.—The future of the ostrich-feather industry is too uncertain to assure the success of ostrich farming or its prosecution on a large scale.

(c) Special Methods of Cultivation

Dry Farming.—The scantiness of the rainfall in this country of high temperatures accounts for the concentration of the efforts of agriculturists upon the discovery of the best methods of utilizing the natural water supply of each locality, and the best methods of supplementing local surface supplies either by boring for water or by diverting river-water into irrigation channels. The question of the water supply in general is the most important of all for the economic prosperity of the territory, and is therefore discussed at some length below under the heading of Irrigation. Another method of cultivation, however, alternative or complementary to the usual methods followed with the help of irrigation, has in recent years received much attention, especially in suitable areas in the south of the territory. This is the so-called "dry farming" practised here on Campbell's principles.

For the success of cultivation according to this method it seems essential to have not only suitable underground conditions of soil and drainage, but also a reliable average rainfall of 12 in. Where the rainfall ranges between 7 and 12 in., the whole surface should be cultivated, but sown only by halves in alternate years. The ground is ploughed deep, and the surface kept open in order to retain the maximum of moisture below; and, as long periods of heat and drought have to be faced, plants are selected for their depth of root and other drought-resisting qualities. One of the circumstances that militate against the success of the method is the great difficulty of providing wind screens for the selected areas. With such obstacles to contend against and with a very limited market for the produce cultivated under such disadvantages, the dry farmer will probably be satisfied if he finds himself able to grow lucerne, maize, and forage plants in quantities sufficient for purely local needs.

Irrigation.—The sources of water supply in the territory have been described in Part I of this volume, and need only be summarized here. The rainfall is least along the coast-line, and increases from west to east and from south to north. The only perennial streams are the rivers along the northern and southern boundaries, and no other river-bed shows any surface water except during the rainy season or at places where the existence of perennial pools indicates that the underground water is dammed by dykes of impervious rock or other natural obstructions. Such pools are fairly numerous, especially in narrow side-valleys where there is some shelter from sun and wind. Springs are not common; they are most plentiful in the region of highest rainfall, towards the north-east. Thermal springs are found in several localities, yielding water slightly charged with sulphuretted hydrogen and carbon dioxide. Sheets of standing water, known as pans or *vleys*, form during the rainy season in depressions in level country. They are very shallow and salt, and are most numerous in Damaraland and in the eastern districts towards the Kalahari; the largest is the Etosha Pan, on the border of Ovamboland. The natural rock reservoirs of the highlands of Central Damaraland contain useful accumulations of rain-water, the sole supply on some of the farms.

Where natural reservoirs are absent or inadequate, the first resource of the farmer is to prevent the total waste of flood-water by constructing dams to retain as much as possible. In Damaraland, in particular, there are several large storage dams, and suitable sites for many more. The enterprise of individual farmers in this direction had been somewhat dis-- couraged by frequent washaways, but in 1913 the German Government resolved to make a start with similar operations on a very large scale by building a series of reservoirs and underground barriers along the course of the Fish River and its tributaries. The first great dam, to contain 110,000,000 cubic metres. was to be constructed at Komatsas, near Mariental; the second, holding 130,000,000 cubic metres, below the junction of the Leber River; the third, to contain 200,000,000 cubic metres, at Hons, just above Seeheim. The three together would, it was anticipated, impound practically the whole annual run-off of the Fish River. The water retained in the dams was to be employed in irrigating large areas of riparian land, and also in supplying the motive power for pumping-stations where these were required for the irrigation of further areas. The river thus controlled would no longer be liable to torrential floods, and the riparian farmers,

relieved of their dread of washaways, would, in their
own interest, construct numerous subsidiary weirs and
underground barriers.   The whole scheme was to be
only the first of a large number of similar enterprises
in other parts of the country and especially in the
neighbourhood of Windhoek.

In localities where a surface supply did not exist,
or could not, for technical reasons, be impounded,
successful results were obtained in many instances
from boring operations.   It appears, indeed, that,
except in the Namib and certain parts of the Kalahari
regions, fair supplies of underground water may
everywhere be tapped at moderate depths.   Even in
the Namib, boreholes sunk in some of the sand and
detritus-choked river valleys have produced copious
supplies; at Garub, for example, the boreholes yield
140,000 gallons per diem.   The farmers have naturally
been active in sinking wells, especially in or near the
dry river-beds throughout the territory.   In some
cases water was easily obtained at shallow depths;
but, where boring was necessary, it involved heavy
expenditure for the individual, even when assisted by
Government, since the normal depth at which water
is reached is from 130 to 160 ft. in the more favourable
localities, and the cost of boring averages nearly 10s.
per foot of depth.   The German Government, therefore, took measures to assist progressive farmers by
advancing money for boring at 4 per cent., repayable
in ten yearly instalments.   It also maintained two
boring columns, which in 1911 were working nine sets
of boring machinery.   The total annual cost of the
columns was then about £20,000, but by 1913 the
annual grant had risen to £45,000.   At this date there
were 24 private drills at work in the country.

Artesian supplies have been obtained from one bore-
hole near Keetmanshoop, from two in the neighbourhood of Stampriet, and from nine wells sunk in the
Auob Valley in the German Kalahari.   The geological
conditions which determine these supplies and warrant
the probability of further discoveries are fully des-

cribed in Dr. Wagner's *Report on the Geology and Mineral Industry of South-West Africa.*

The construction of waterworks at Osona, at Aub, in the Aris Valley, and near Omaruru was contemplated, and the Landesrat in November 1913 resolved that the preliminary surveys and investigations should be carried out, and that in 1914-15 a sum of £50,000 should be made available, partly for this purpose, partly as grants-in-aid to farmers for dam-making and water-boring. By votes of this kind and by other measures already described the Government showed how fully it realized the urgency of the problem of water supply for the whole territory.

Most of the chief towns have now secured reliable supplies. At Windhoek, the supply obtained from the hot springs and from new boreholes is estimated now to be sufficient to warrant an underground drainage scheme. Karibib is supplied by three wells, about 100 ft. deep, from which a volume of 21,560 gallons per diem is obtained by three pumps operated severally by a windmill, an electric motor, and an oil engine. The bed of the Swakop River near its mouth provides Swakopmund with a plentiful supply of slightly brackish water, obtained at three pumping stations and distributed by 9-in. mains laid under the streets. Lüderitz Bay has hitherto depended for its supplies upon condensers, which were unreliable and inadequate for a town of this size. In 1913 the water used for household purposes was brought 60 miles by rail from Garub, and sold at 15s. per 250 gallons. A plentiful supply was struck by boring in the valley of the Kuichab River near Aus, and provision was made in the 1914-15 Estimates for the construction of reservoirs and the laying of a pipe-line to Lüderitz Bay. Keetmanshoop is supplied from the copious artesian well near the village, Omaruru from the periodical river of the same name, Otavi and Grootfontein from neighbouring springs found in the Otavi dolomite beds.

The most ambitious scheme hitherto proposed for

improving the water supplies of South-West Africa
and the Kalahari was suggested recently by Professor
Schwartz, and has been debated in the Union Parliament. The proposal aims at nothing less than
restoring to the Kalahari and all the country adjoining it the climatic conditions of moisture and fertility
which these regions appear to have lost in the last
300 years, and which have appreciably diminished
even since the days of Livingstone. To effect this, it
is proposed to weir up the Chobe River at a point
above its junction with the Zambezi and thus divert
the waters of the Chobe and Okowango into the Ngami
depression. Further, a weir thrown across the Kunene
would turn that river back into its old channel as a
feeder of the Etosha Pan, and prevent the waste of the
water which now hurries uselessly to the sea. The
surplus water from the Etosha Pan would in turn
find its way along the Omatako into the Okowango.
Fed by the combined streams of the Kunene, Okowango,
and Chobe, Lake Ngami would regain its former
dimensions, and its overflow would fill up the Makari-
kari depression round the Ntetwe and Soa Pans, and
would recreate the fertility of the whole Molopo
basin. "No more hot winds would blow from the
desert, no more locusts would hatch out there undis-
turbed, for the ground, so long fallow, would be rich
as the best in the world, and would be occupied and
tilled." Incidentally, a waterway of 1,000 miles would
be created, with only one break, where the Okowango
below Andara has a waterfall of 20 ft., surmountable
by a lock. Professor Schwartz estimates the total cost
of the scheme at £250,000, and claims that the rainfall of the entire region would be augmented by the
evaporation and subsequent condensation of moisture
from the area of some 40,000 square miles covered by
the reconstituted lakes. On a scheme of these propor-
tions the verdict of expert engineers must be awaited.

(d) Forestry

As there was very little timber actually under German control in the territory, the Government in earlier years pursued no active policy with regard to forestry, but in 1914 a trained forestry official was sent out in order to examine the forest and timber supplies of the northern districts, to consider the question of reafforestation, and to draw up a programme for the establishment of a forestry service. Reafforestation in the greater part of the territory must await the satisfactory solution of the problem of water supply. The timber resources of Ovamboland should be one of the first questions taken in hand by the new Government.

Under the conditions obtaining in the settled districts of South-West Africa all that had been done was to establish forest nurseries, in order to provide young trees for distribution at Windhoek, Okahandya, Grootfontein, Gobabis, and Gibeon. The number of young trees sent out from these nurseries in 1912-13 was over 46,000, of which nearly one-third came from Windhoek. There is, in addition, a forest station at Ukuib, which specializes in date-palm cultivation.

(e) Land Tenure

Tribal territories.—Before the German occupation the Namib on the west and the German Kalahari to the east were occupied by Bushmen and Berg-Damaras, with the Ovatyimba Hereros in the north - west. The Ovambos at that time held the territory which they still occupy. The Topnaar and Zwartbooi Hottentots had pushed northwards past the central districts held by the Hereros, but all the other Hottentot tribes were south of the line of the Swakop and Epikiro Rivers. Three smaller bodies of Hottentots, the Khogeis (or Amiraal), Ogeis (or Grote Doden), and the Gunugus (or Lowlanders), had previously been absorbed by the stronger tribes, as had also the once powerful Afrikaner tribe of Eik-hams, after suffering defeat by the Hereros and Witboois in turn. The Hottentot tribes were at that time twelve in number, viz., the Koweses or Witboois; the Khauas (Gei-Khauas) or Gobabis; the Hei-Khauas or Berseba tribe; the Amas or Amans of Bethany; the Eicha-ais or Afrikaners; the Gaminus or Bondelzwarts; the Khora-gei-Khois or Fransman tribe; the Geikous or Red Nation; the Khau-Goas or Zwartboois; the Kharo-oas or Tseib tribe; the Habobes or Veldschoendragers; and the Topnaar Hottentots of the Zesfontein district and Walvisch Bay.

By 1906, within sixteen years from the date when the tribes were taken under the protection of the German Government, very few of the surviving remnants retained either land or chiefs or tribal organization. The exceptions to this rule were the fortunate tribes who were too remote or too numerous for full administration, or too poor to invite aggression. The Ovambo tribes have preserved their lands because their conquest would have been a matter of too great difficulty. The territories of the less warlike Ovakwangari tribes of the Okowango valley, and the Bantu tribes of the Caprivizipfel have hitherto been practically inaccessible for European settlers. The Ovatyimbas of the Kaokoveld inhabit a plateau which is included in the land concessions claimed, if not yet occupied, by the Kaoko Company. Their neighbours, the Topnaar and the Zwartbooi Hottentots, lived beyond the area of the Hottentot War (1904-07) on lands afterwards included in the concessions of the Kaoko Company and German Colonial Company. Of the Hottentots further south the Hei-Khauas of Berseba were the only tribe, besides the Rehoboth Bastards, that had not been driven into rebellion. They alone had escaped the universal confiscation of land and of live-stock that was the lot of the other Hottentots and of all the Hereros. The essential character of the German land-policy was candidly and justly summarized by Dr. Paul Rohrbach, who had in 1890 occupied a high position in the German Colonial Office :—'' The decision to colonize in South-West Africa could, after all, mean nothing else but that the native tribes would have to give up their lands on which they had previously grazed their stock in order that the white man might have the land for the grazing of his stock.''[1]

Land companies.—The briefest summary of the steps by which so much of the land passed into the hands of European owners is all that can be attempted here. The validity of such titles as have been acquired is a problem which presents many difficulties and on which no opinion can be hazarded in general terms.

The Hottentots and Hereros alike regarded their land as the communal property of the tribe and therefore inalienable. But the customs and rights of the tribal communities were never regarded seriously by adventurers who were eager to acquire land, and justified their purchases by flimsy pretexts of legal processes. The earliest acquisitions of land were made by the German missionaries, who by the year 1870 had established numerous stations, and, in addition to their professional duties, carried on an active barter trade, receiving cattle and sheep and native products in exchange for goods, clothing, arms, and ammunition. The possession of flocks and herds may account for the missionaries' extensive purchases of land. Among the first of the more purely commercial ventures was that of the firm De Pas, Spence & Co., who acquired from the Hottentots territory in the neighbourhood of the Pomona Mine, and afterwards sold the right to mine diamonds to Herr Scholtz and the Pomona Company. The nominal purchase by Adolf Lüderitz of the coastal belt from the Orange River to Cape Frio (excluding British territory at Walvisch Bay) is described on p. 12 of this volume. With reference to the deeds of sale by which this territory was acquired, it is sufficient to note, first,

---

[1] *Deutsche Kolonialwirtschaft*, vol. 1, p. 286.

that the tribes of Aman and Topnaar Hottentots, of
which Piet Heibib and Joseph Frederiks were chiefs,
had never owned more than one-fourth of the land
which was transferred; second, that their action in
selling any lands which belonged to their tribes con-
travened the principle that such tribal territory was
not alienable.

Concession-hunting was frequent during the early
years of the Protectorate, and the mining or land
rights then acquired were usually transferred at an
enhanced price to one or other of the greater companies. For instance, the Kharaskhoma Syndicate had
before 1893 secured very extensive mining and grazing
rights in South Namaqualand; its interests were
subsequently transferred to The South African
Territories, Ltd., which has in recent years sold
considerable blocks of land. The latter company.
registered in London in 1895 with a capital of
£500,000 and an Anglo-German directorate, acquired
from the Syndicate the Government concession of
mineral rights over 30,000 square miles and ownership
of 128 freehold farms. 2,700,000 acres (4,220 square
miles) in extent. Its claim, in terms of the original
concession, to a second grant of 128 farms of the same
acreage, appears to depend on the German Government's title to the lands in question, and on its own
discharge of its legal obligations to the Bondelzwart,
Zwartsmodder, and Veldschoendrager tribes of this
region.

The South-West Africa Company is an Anglo-
German association, which in 1892 received large
concessions in Damaraland. Its holding comprised
freehold occupation of 4,500 square miles, included
within an area of 22,000 square miles, over which
it enjoyed mining rights, and further both freehold
and mining rights over a strip of land 6 miles broad
on either side of any railway built by it north of the
Tropic of Capricorn. An offshoot of this company,
the Otavi Minen- und Eisenbahn-Gesellschaft, held
rights granted by Government over about 23,000 square

miles in Ovamboland, in consideration of the surrender of some of its railway privileges.

The Kaoko Land- und Minen-Gesellschaft is another offshoot of the South-West Africa Company. Its capital of half a million pounds is held in Germany, and the extent of its mining areas, almost all of which it claimed as freehold, was more than 37,000 square miles, and covered the greater part of the Kaokoveld.

The Anglo-German Territories, Ltd., was registered in London in 1891, with a capital of £300,000. It took over the former property of the Orange River Estates Company, Ltd., said to amount to 2,000 square miles in German territory and a somewhat similar area south of the Orange River.

There were apparently two Hanseatic companies, one solely, and the second primarily, interested in mining. The Hanseatische Minen-Gesellschaft, formed in 1910 with a capital of £50,000, had mining rights over some 15,000 square miles in two blocks in the middle of the territory near Rehoboth. The Hanseatische Land-, Minen- und Handels-Gesellschaft für Deutsch-Südwest-Afrika has a capital of £132,000. Its interests, too, were at Rehoboth, and as it has the same address in Berlin, it is probably closely connected with the other company.

The Windhuker Farmgesellschaft in 1907 acquired the Siedelungsgesellschaft für Deutsch-Südwest-afrika, and in 1912 owned five farms totalling 137,000 acres (214 square miles), and, in addition, some 400 square miles held for it by the German Government.

The Gibeon Schürf- und Handels-Gesellschaft had concessions in the districts of Gibeon and Keetmans-hoop.

The Deutsche Kolonial-Gesellschaft für Südwest-Afrika was the first in the field of all the land and mining companies. It was constituted in 1885, with a capital of £15,000, to take over the concessions acquired by Adolf Lüderitz. At the time of the German occupation it was granted mining rights over the whole Protectorate, and was charged with its administration under the suzerainty of the German Empire. Its ownership of land was presumably limited by the rights of the natives to the territories they occupied, and also by the concessions previously acquired by individuals or by other associations. In 1889 the company was deprived of its monopoly of mining rights, and in 1892 it was relieved of the burden of administration. Finally, in terms of agreements made in 1908 and 1910, the company transferred to the Government all its landed property except nine small districts near Swakopmund and Lüderitz Bay. It retained control of a coast strip, 100 kilometres deep, between 26° south and the Orange River, so long as diamond extraction and mining should be prosecuted on a large scale. The area transferred to the Government was nearly 12,000 square miles, less such portions as had been sold or leased.

It may be added here that the company's capital was gradually increased until it amounted to £100,000, and this was doubled in 1909 by the issue of 6 per cent. cumulative preference shares. Dividends between 1885 and 1905 were nil, but in the years 1906 to 1911 were successively 20, 20, 20, 25, 64, and 50 per cent. The rise in profits was no doubt mainly due to the company's holdings of diamond claims and to its interest in several mining companies. It held four-fifths of the capital of the Deutsche Diamanten-Gesellschaft, and considerable interests in the Südwestafrikanisches Minen-Syndikat, Lüderitzbucht-Gesellschaft L. Scholtz & Co., Deutsch-Südwestafrikanische Wollzüchterei, Deutsche Walfang-Gesellschaft "Sturmvogel," and Diamanten-Régie des Südwestafrikanischen Schutzgebiets.

If the claims made by these various land companies can be proved to rest on valid titles, it would follow from the figures quoted that the freehold land owned by them amounts in all to nearly 64,000 square miles of the best land, out of the total Protectorate area of 322,200 square miles. The land available for European settlement includes, in addition, all the territories confiscated by the Government from the Herero and Hottentot tribes who had been goaded into rebellion. The 1,331 farms which had been taken up by 1913, and of which 193 were then lying idle, occupied a total area of 33,484,015 acres, or about 52,320 square miles. Thus, approximately one-sixth of the surface of the Protectorate was then occupied by European settlers, who numbered 1,587 all told. The average size of a farm was over 21,000 acres.

Settlement.—The land companies, except the South-West Africa Company, had done little to attract settlers; but it was the policy of the German Government in later years to acquire all possible land rights with a view to offering land on easy terms to farmers of the right type and nationality. Non-Germans complained that the Government officials took every chance of contesting their titles, so as to dispossess them in favour of more amenable German settlers. In the sale of new farms preference was given to Germans who had performed their military service and had capital enough (£300) to start cattle farming with State assistance, which was given both in money and by free prospecting for water on their properties. To such settlers the large land-owning companies were induced by the Government to offer farms at fixed prices. The lowest prices for land bought from the Government in 1912 were 1·20 marks per hectare (2·47 acres) in the North; 1 mark in the Rehoboth and Gibeon districts; and 50 pfennigs in the South—in the Keetmanshoop, Warmbad, and Hasuur districts. In that year the Government sold 60 farms, of 943,279 acres, and leased 26, of 577,220 acres; while the land companies sold 19 farms, of 529,700 acres, and leased 10, of 629,580 acres. Generally speaking, the country does not offer advantages sufficient to attract a large influx of settlers, nor have there hitherto been openings for white men as farm officials, since even the biggest cattle farms were worked mainly by natives.

The Government Land Bank had not been long

enough established before the outbreak of war to influence the transfer of property appreciably.

(3) FISHERIES

Sea-fishing in the ordinary sense is an unimportant industry. Fish of various kinds exist in abundance, but have formidable enemies in the countless sea-birds that congregate on the guano islands off the coast. Crayfish are common along the coast, but are not caught for canning, as at the Cape. The fish which is most frequently offered for sale seems to be the snoek.

The taking of fish, however, was only a secondary aim of the solitary fishing enterprise, the Lüderitz-buchter Robbenfang- und Fischerei-Gesellschaft, which was founded in 1912, with a capital of £1,000. It engaged in sealing throughout the sealing season, and in 1912-13 took 1,769 seals, the skins of which were sold for £2,078. The question at issue between the Protectorate and Union Governments as to the sealing (and diamond) rights on the islands along the coast had not been settled in 1913.

There were two whaling companies at work before the war. The Whaling Company, of Walvisch Bay, is said to have secured 700 whales in less than a year. The Deutsche Walfang-Gesellschaft "Sturmvogel," founded at Bremen in 1912, with a capital of £46,000, built a station at Sturmvogel Bay in 1912-13, and began its operations in 1913 with a staff of 20 white and 100 native employees. The results of the first year's working were considered disappointing.

(4) Minerals

Output.—In 1913 the mineral output of South-West Africa was as follows :—

	£
Diamonds	3,084,581
Copper (including lead ore and copper matte)	396,436
Tin ore	31,568
Other ore and minerals ...	3,316
Marble	1,450
	3,517,351

These figures show clearly that only copper and diamonds were exploited on a large scale. Although the country as a whole is highly mineralized, the other minerals that occur are relatively unimportant and call for the briefest notice.

Less important minerals.—The chief mineral products are indicated on the map attached to Mr. Tönnesen's useful article in the *Geographical Journal* for April 1917. Commercial value cannot be claimed for the known deposits of asbestos, fluor-spar, mica, molybdenite, sulphur, tantalite, and vanadium; and no attempt had been made before the war to work the more promising finds of graphite or to quarry on a large scale the useful building-stone found in many localities. Attempts made to work deposits of galena and veins carrying aquamarine, beryl, and heliodore had not proved remunerative.

Auriferous quartz veins occur in the Kaokoveld, but neither there nor elsewhere has gold been found in workable quantity. Lead, as well as copper, was mined by the Otavi Company, which exported, between 1910 and 1912, 2,616 tons of lead valued at £71,700. The ore shipped from the Otavi mines contained about 24 per cent. of lead, and a small percentage of silver. Silver was at one time mined near Pomona Island. Iron ore is found at a number of points on the Kaokoveld and also near Kalkfeld. The ore extracted at Okovakwatyivi is employed at Tsumeb as a flux for the locally smelted copper ores. Coal has been reported in recent years in various parts; a seam is said to have been located near Keetmanshoop, and a deposit of gilsonite near Gibeon; but no seam had been worked with success before the war. The discovery of kimberlite in Gibeon district excited high hopes; but investigation has hitherto failed to reveal the presence of diamonds in any of the 40 known pipes, dykes, and chonoliths. Veins carrying wolframite in rich patches were opened at Nakeis, in Great Namaqualand, but owing to interposed stretches of barren quartz proved too poor to reward exploitation.

Some miles from the coast, near Elizabeth Bay, there is an extensive bed of rock salt, containing a high percentage of sodium chloride. Since the British occupation rock salt has also been discovered in immense quantities close to the railway line at Nonidas Siding, 8 miles from Swakopmund. The only saltpan of note is at Aminuis; of the numerous others the best seem to occur west of the Etosha Pan. The pans along the coast are spoiled by the presence of wind-blown sand. Accumulations of guano are found not only on the Guano Islands, belonging to the Union of South Africa, but also at intervals along the coast of the mainland. Limestone is common, and lime-kilns have been worked in many localities.

Marble.—In the neighbourhood of Karibib, and of Swakopmund and Walvisch Bay, there exist vast quantities of marble of every hue, texture, and pattern, which, if not pure enough or homogeneous enough to compete with Carrara rock, is yet suitable for architectural purposes. The handsome appearance and vast extent of the Karibib deposits led to the formation in 1910 of the Afrika Marmor Kolonialgesellschaft, Hamburg, with a capital of 3,000,000 marks. This company absorbed the smaller Afrika Marmor-Syndikat, which had taken over the interests of the Deutsch-Südwestafrikanische Marmorgesellschaft. The latter company had been formed by H. C. F. Smidt, of Swakopmund, with a nominal capital of 442,000 marks, but after a run of two years it went into liquidation at the end of 1911. The Afrika Marmor Kolonialgesellschaft opened up several large quarries, connected them with Karibib by narrow-gauge railway, and installed large cranes and transporters on the jetty at Swakopmund. Unfortunately, freight-age to Europe was so high that export at a profit proved impossible, and all quarrying had to be suspended. The future of the industry seems to depend on the market which may yet offer itself in the Union, and on improved harbour facilities at Walvisch Bay, which may so reduce the cost of transport to Europe as to leave a margin of profit.

Tin.—Deposits of cassiterite are found at Orab, Gokhas, and Persip, but the majority of occurrences are located between the Khan and Ugab rivers, especially on the Erongo mountains. The tin recovered hitherto has been obtained from the alluvial deposits, which are of considerable extent, and not from the reefs of pegmatite and quartz, in which the tin content is apparently too irregular and patchy to be profitable.

The export of tin began in 1911 with consignments of 9 tons, valued at £470. By 1913 it had risen to 200 tons, of a value of £31,600. The first tin-mining company was the Erongo Zinn-Gesellschaft, of Ameib, formed locally in December 1910, with a capital of £10,250. Its preliminary operations were considered promising enough to warrant the introduction of more capital. Failing to obtain German backing, the syndicate eventually obtained in the Union sufficient support to create in 1911 a new company, The Ameib Exploration Company, of Capetown, which had a capital of £175,000, and took over the Erongo properties, $3\frac{1}{2}$ square miles in extent. The Ameib venture was not specially successful, but its example led to further prospecting and development work on the better class tin claims which are held by the Anglo-German Tins Syndicate, the De Beers Company, the Otavi Exploring Syndicate, and the South-West Africa Company. A smaller company, the German African Tins, Ltd., had ceased work on its claims by 1913. In 1912 a number of claims of uncertain value were purchased from prospectors by three wholly German companies, the Hamburger Schürfsyndikat, Woermann, Brock & Co., and the Koloniale Bank. The latter is probably the banking section of the Deutsche Kolonial-Gesellschaft für Südwest-Afrika.

Copper.—Copper ranks second to diamonds in importance among the minerals of the territory. It is found at a great many points throughout the country, but the chief deposits are those in the dolomite rocks of the Otavi district, in which copper is usually associated with lead. Next to these come the output of the Khan and Ida mines in the Swakopmund district, and the Sinclair mine in the north-east of the Lüderitz Bay district. The two main areas are served by the Otavi Railway and its branches.

The only mines which were worked at a clear profit appear to have been the Tsumeb, Groot Otavi, Asis East, Guchab, and Bubus mines of the Grootfontein district, the Khan and Sinclair mines mentioned above, and the Otyisongati mine, 30 miles east of Okahandya. The most productive of all is the Tsumeb mine.

The total quantities of ores extracted in the Tsumeb-Otavi-Grootfontein district, and shipped from Swakopmund since the completion of the railway and the beginning of systematic mining, were as follows:—

Year.	Copper and Lead Ores.	Copper Matte.	Metallic Lead.
	Tons.	Tons.	Tons.
1907-08	16,800	1,000	700
1908-09	27.700	3,150	3,000
1909-10	33.500	2,940	2,732
1910-11	31,600	2,220	2,040
1911-12	29,600	991	913
1912-13	44,550	655	400
1913-14	50,070	1,179	..

During the same years the output from all the other
districts together was less than 5 per cent. of the whole
total.   The value of the combined exports of copper
and copper ore for each of the years 1910-13 was
£284,860, £187,685, £326,170, and £396,435.

Sir Francis Galton, in his journal, reported that in
the course of his trip to Ovamboland, in 1851, he had
met caravans of Bushmen conveying copper ore from
Tsumeb to the skilled metal-workers of the Ondonga
tribe of Ovambos; but the value of the deposits was
first realized in 1901, as the result of an expedition
sent out by the South-West Africa Company.   This
company transferred its mineral rights to the Otavi
Minen- und Eisenbahn-Gesellschaft, which had been
registered in Germany in 1888, with a capital of
£200,000.   It at once proceeded to link up Tsumeb
with Swakopmund by the Otavi narrow-gauge railway, completing it in 1906.   Until recently it retained
an area of 15 kilometres in diameter round the Tsumeb
mine, and areas of 4 kilometres in diameter round the
Guchab and Great Asis mines, but its prospecting
rights over the rest of its concession of 1,000 square
miles had been passed on for a term of 10 years to
the Otavi Exploring Syndicate, Limited, founded in
London in 1909 with a capital of £63,000.   This
syndicate conducted development work as well as prospecting, and in recent years shipped considerable
quantities of copper ore from Groot Otavi and Bubus

mines, as well as trial consignments of mottramite from Nosib.

The Khan copper mine was owned and worked by the Khan Kupfergrube Gesellschaft, which was formed at Duisburg in 1909, with a capital of £50,000. The company's production of ore was 2,000 tons in 1911, 1,000 tons in 1912. New machinery electrically driven was installed in 1914, and was expected to treat 50 tons of ore per diem.

Otyisongati appears in the titles of two companies. One of these, the Otjozonjati-Minen-Syndikat, is a small concern, constituted at Windhoek in 1907 with a capital of £5,000, and directed by four local men. The other, the Otjozonjati-Kupferminen-Gesellschaft, was formed in Berlin in 1906 by a number of German officials and merchants, who controlled its operations. Its capital was £10,000, and its annual output from the Otyisongati mines between 1907 and 1912 was just over 500 tons. The guiding spirit in this enterprise was Dr. Max Schoeller, of Burg Birgel, who directed groups of similar ventures in both East and South-West Africa. Included in his South-West Africa group were the Onjati-Kupferminen-Gesellschaft, the Stanley-Minen-Gesellschaft, and the Deutsche-Süd-westafrikanische Kupfer-Gesellschaft Gorobminen, all registered in Berlin. The Onjati-Kupferminen-Gesellschaft, formed in 1907 with a capital of £9,250, took over 30 claims for a consortium headed by Otto Peycke, a Hamburg merchant. The Stanley-Minen-Gesellschaft also dates from 1907. With a capital of £15,650, it took over concessions granted by the German Colonial Company to Messrs. J. W. Stanley and W. Tripmacker. The Onjati and Stanley companies, which own properties adjoining the Otyisongati mine, were being liquidated in 1912 by Dr. Schoeller and Paul Henning, of Berlin. The Gorob Company was founded in 1907, with a capital of £20,000, to work copper and graphite discoveries on 39 claims located near Gorob in the Swakopmund Namib.

The Sinclair Mine was acquired in 1913 by the Koloniale Bergbau-Gesellschaft, a prominent diamond combination.

The Bergbaugesellschaft Namaqua was constituted in Keetmanshoop in 1909 by two local merchants, Robert Blank and Jean Neuneier, with a capital of £8,000. It worked copper and other minerals on its property, and also exploited the coal discoveries near Aurus.

Diamonds.—The diamondiferous deposits of South-West Africa were first made known in April 1908. In 1913 they yielded over 20 per cent. by value of the total diamond output of the world. The production between 1908 and 1913 is indicated in the following table:—

Year.	Carats.	Value.	Value per carat	Average number of stones to the carat.
		£	s. d.	
1908	38,275	55,898	29 2	.
1909	483,266	705,629	28 2·8	5·0
1910	846,695	1,109,643	26 2·5	5·75
1911	773,308	969,065	25 0·7	6·5
1912	1,051,177	1,511,600	28 8·8	6·09
1913	1,470,000	3,084,581	41 11·5	4·97
Total .	4,662,721	£7,436,416	..	..

Of the 1913 yield 1,284,727 carats, valued at £2,698,500, had been sold before the outbreak of war. The total output up to August 1914 was 5,400,000 carats, of the value of £9,250,000. These figures are sufficient to show the immense importance of the diamond industry to the economic development of the territory.

The diamonds found on the south-western coast are quite unlike any of the diamonds found in the Union of South Africa. In point of hardness and of brilliancy they more closely resemble Brazilian stones.

They are of all hues, and, although small in size, show uniform good quality. The largest stone hitherto discovered weighed 34½ carats; it was found on the Lüderitzfelder, just south of the Pomona boundary. The average size of the diamonds recovered in 1913 was almost exactly one-fifth carat.

All the deposits occur along the coast at intervals between Conception Bay and Marmora, opposite Sinclair Island. Those which lie north of Dogger Fels are relatively unimportant, and in few cases repay working. The whole of the higher value holdings are found on the southern section, between Dogger Fels and Marmora.

No diamonds have yet been discovered at a greater distance from the coast than 15 miles. This fact, taken in conjunction with the occurrence on Possession Island of diamondiferous gravel of identical character, proves that the deposits are in some way related to the sea.

It is not yet known whether diamonds occur under the sea off this coast, and the problem of the origin of the diamonds still awaits solution. A statement of the conflicting theories may be found in Dr. Wagner's *Report on the Geology and Mineral Industry of South-West Africa* (Pretoria, 1916).

One feature in the distribution of the diamonds is that the average size of the stones increases steadily from north to south until it reaches its maximum at Ida valley in the Pomona area.

The deposits are of two distinct types—(1) marine, and (2) eluvial or residual. The former have in a number of instances proved to be worth exploiting, but the total output from them is negligible in comparison with the yield of the eluvial deposits. The latter are composed of fine sand and coarser particles in ratios varying between 3·2 and 9·1, and probably averaging 4·1. The layer of diamond-bearing material is usually 4 to 6 inches thick, but in places between Lüderitz Bay and Elizabeth Bay it attains a depth of 25 and even 30 feet.

There is a wide variation in the diamond content of the " gravel " at different parts of the fields. On the Bogenfels claims considerable patches occurred which averaged over 10 carats of diamonds per cubic metre, and in the Ida valley yields running up to 200 carats per cubic metre have been recorded.

The cost of production per carat varies widely on different holdings, and is relative to the diamond content of the " gravel," the depth of the deposit worked, the distance from railway and from power plant, the scale of operations, rates of pay, and other factors. In 1913 the cost per carat on the Pomona property was only 2s. 2d., as compared with 35s. on some of the poorer and more distant holdings. Transport expenses were greatly reduced by the construction of the narrow-gauge railway to Bogenfels.

Water supply is a problem of considerable difficulty; the necessary minimum has been obtained either from wells or by condensing sea-water. Power is supplied to the holdings near Lüderitz Bay from a large electric generating station equipped with suction gas-engines. The current, transmitted at a pressure of 30,000 volts, costs 4d. per kilowatt-hour, or less to large consumers. The more remote claims derive their power from their own oil-engines. The labour employed before the war was about 500 white men, and 5,000 coloured labourers. Of the latter some 2,000 were Cape boys, paid at the rate of £3 per month, and the rest were Ovambos, drawing 25s.

Prospecting was carried on vigorously between 1910 and 1914; but no further discoveries of any importance were made, and it seems unlikely that the area of the diamond field will be increased. On the main holdings, such as the Ida valley at Pomona, the richest and most accessible stretches have already been worked out. Large resources doubtless remain in the form of lower-grade material, and the working of these will be profitable for a considerable term of years. The diminution of output, due to the exhaustion of the richer deposits, will be only partially balanced by the introduction of

improved methods for recovering the smallest stones;
and the average size, as well as the quality, of the
diamonds recovered seems bound to fall off, unless
further investigations should disclose more diamondiferous areas, or unexpectedly reveal the common
source of all the littoral deposits. In 1913 it was considered sanguine to estimate the life of the fields at
twelve to fifteen years; the output would probably remain undiminished for five years, but after that period
might be expected to decrease rapidly.

Government supervision of diamond mining was
exercised by the Department of Mines, the staff of
which included two inspectors of mines, two geologists,
and one scientist for the mining laboratory. The diamond tax was originally 10 marks per carat, but in 1909
was changed to an *ad valorem* duty of $33\frac{1}{3}$ per cent.;
this change rendered the poorer workings unremunerative. A new system was, therefore, introduced in
December 1912. The assessment was fixed at 66 per
cent. of the selling price of the diamonds, less 70 per
cent. of the total cost of production. The sliding
scale thus created exempted from taxation the output
of the poorest claims, and nearly doubled the previous
rate on cheaply recovered yields from the deposits of
highest value. The result was that latterly the poorer
deposits were once more being exploited, development
was encouraged, and experimental work was being
carried on in the doubtful grounds of the northern
area. The estimated revenue from the diamond tax
in 1913-14 was £330,000; the actual receipts were
£800,000 in excess of this figure. For 1914-15 the
receipts were expected to realize £689,500, an estimate
which under normal conditions would again have been
largely exceeded.

The German Government at an early stage took
control of the sale of the diamonds. A company called
the Diamond Régie (Diamanten-Régie des südwestafrikanischen Schutzgebiets) was formed in 1909, with
a capital of £100,000, for the purpose of placing the
output on the market, and distributing the proceeds

among the companies, after deducting taxes, royalties, and commission. This company was granted the disposal of all diamonds mined in the Protectorate, and the sales were made at the discretion of the German bankers, who were the chief shareholders. Producers were dissatisfied with prices obtained; and eventually they secured from Government in 1913 a share in the control of the company. Tenders were then invited for the purchase of the next year's output, with the result that the prices offered by the successful tenderers, the Antwerp Syndicate, were 15 per cent. higher than in 1912.

The contract was presently found to be subject to a proviso that the Syndicate would not have to take delivery of more diamonds than it required; and, although output was averaging 130,000 carats per month, the rate of delivery was at once reduced to about 100,000 carats. Emphatic protests were recorded by the producers, who had not been aware of the condition, but the German Government quashed their opposition. It took over all the bankers' shares in the Régie, and, having thus secured a majority of votes, it then proclaimed its intention of assuming the functions of the Régie, which no longer existed in its original form. In December 1913 a Government Ordinance appeared, announcing that from the beginning of 1914 Government would determine the total amount of diamonds to be sold in each year, as well as the quota of each individual company. The total fixed for 1914 was 1,038,000 carats, or 86,500 carats per month, and each company was informed what its share was to be. The producers resented this somewhat high-handed measure and instituted legal proceedings, but after negotiations they agreed to the principle of restriction, and Government reorganized the Régie and gave the producers four members out of the eight that compose the board. Government and producers are alike interested in the revenue derived from the sale of diamonds, and the arrangement arrived at in 1914 seemed likely to maintain profits, encourage development, and secure community of action for the purpose of keeping the market steady.

The economic importance of the industry justifies a brief account of the more important diamond-mining companies. The number of these increased from 51 in 1912 to 79 in 1913, when the total capital invested amounted to 29,987,100 marks, or nearly £1,500,000.

(1) The German Government had holdings which were leased in 1909 to the *Diamanten-Pacht Gesellschaft*, of Berlin, whose capital is £125,000. The lease was to run for 15 years, with extension if necessary for 10 years more, and Government was to receive three-fourths of the net profits. The Diamanten-Pacht-Gesellschaft in turn made an agreement with the *Koloniale Bergbau-Gesellschaft*, by which the latter undertook the management of the mining operations to the end of 1919, with possible extension to 1924, in return for half of the other company's profits during this period. The output from the Government claims was 158,356 carats in 1912, 119,920 carats in 1913. For 1914 the quota allotted under the Government arrangement with the Diamond Régie was 109,000 carats.

Of the Government claims, what is known as the Government Block was owned by the Government, while the other claims were held under a fifty years' lease from the Deutsche Kolonial-Gesellschaft für Südwestafrika, which held the mineral rights over the so-called Sperrgebiet (Reserve), a tract of land 65 miles deep from the coast, between the Orange River and 26° south latitude. The only claims in the southern region which were not similarly held under a fifty years' lease from the Deutsche Kolonial-Gesellschaft were those bordering on the railway and the holdings of the Deutsche Diamanten-Gesellschaft.

(2) The *Kolmanskop Diamond Mines, Ltd.*, floated in Capetown in 1909, with a capital of £125,000, leases a property of about 10,000 acres 6 miles east of Lüderitz Bay. Its output was 122,525 carats in 1912, 106,879 carats in 1913, and its quota for 1914 was to be

89,500. The company's dividends in five years had amounted to nearly twice its capital. Its richest claims are now exhausted, and the material remaining for treatment consists mainly of deep deposits of low-grade gravel.

(3) The holdings of the *Koloniale Bergbau-Gesell-schaft* are among the most valuable in the whole area. The company produced 368,867 carats in 1912, 316,774 carats in 1913 and was allotted a quota of 245,000 carats for 1914. In the four years 1910 to 1913 it paid dividends of 24, 25, 38, and 25 times the amount of its capital, which is £5,025. These dividends, distributed after payment of the heavy Government taxes, probably constitute a world's record.

(4) The *Deutsche Diamanten-Gesellschaft*, with a capital of £125,000, owned a number of claims in the vicinity of Lüderitz Bay, and very large areas further south, between Pomona and Marmora. Its claims near Bogenfels have proved to be particularly valuable, and between Bogenfels and Pomona extensive tracts of profitable gravel occur. The company's production rose from 158,158 carats in 1912 to 172,710 carats in 1913; and its allotted quota for 1914 was 118,500 carats.

(5) The *Pomona Diamanten-Gesellschaft* was floated in May 1912 with a capital of £150,000, and commenced work in August 1912. The yield of diamonds for 1912 was 124,412 carats, and for the complete year 1913 it amounted to 512,384 carats, and resulted in a dividend of 175 per cent. A quota of 350,000 carats was allotted for 1914.

Among the best claims on the company's holdings are those of the Ida valley, the Scheibe, Anna, and Märchen valleys, and the Kaukansib valley.

(6) The *Vereinigte Diamantminen-Gesellschaft* has a capital of £100,000. Its best holdings appear to have been the Rohrbach, Komet and Reichenstein claims, all on the large southern block. The company also hoped to obtain an area of 1,294 acres on the Marmora farm, which was the subject of litigation in 1914,

The output from the company's holdings was 33,715 carats in 1912, and 51,478 carats in 1913; the output assigned for 1914 was 50,000 carats.

(7) The *Diamanten Aktien-Gesellschaft* was constituted in 1912, with a capital of £25,000, to acquire the holdings of Weiss, De Meillon & Co. It produced 21,765 carats in 1913, and was assigned a quota of 18,500 carats for 1914.

(8) The *Diamanten Abbau-Gesellschaft* has a capital of £3,000, held largely by the German South-West African Diamond Investment Company, of Capetown. Its output from April to November 1913 was 13,347 carats, and its quota for 1914 was 12,500 carats. It also leased the claims of (9) the *Diamant-Gesellschaft Grillental*, which was assigned a quota of 6,500 carats for 1914.

(10) The *Lüderitzbuchter Bergbau-Gesellschaft* was formed in March 1913 with a capital of £1,050. It took over 5 claims from the Swakopmunder Diamant-Gesellschaft, produced 8,550 carats of diamonds in 1913, and was assigned a quota of 7,500 carats for 1914.

(11) The *Neue Nautilus Gesellschaft* and (12) the *Keetmanshooper Diamantgesellschaft* appear to have suspended operations on their holdings long before the outbreak of war.

Narrow strips of diamond-bearing ground on either side of the railway were left free from the restrictions attaching to the Government Block, and were secured by three small companies: (13) the *Bahnfelder Diamantgesellschaft*, (14) the *Bahnfelder Abbau-Gesellschaft*, and (15) the *Kolmanskoppe Bahnfelder Gesellschaft*. The combined output of the three companies in 1913 was about 16,000 carats, and the respective quotas allotted them for 1914 were 9,000, 3,000, and 3,000 carats.

(16) The *Halbescheide Gesellschaft* was formed in 1914, the Government providing half of the capital of £30,000. The company originated in the agreement made in 1910 between the Imperial German Govern-

ment and the Deutsche Diamanten-Gesellschaft, in accordance with which prospecting for minerals in the Sperrgebiet (Reserve area) would be reserved to the company after April 1, 1911. The prime object of the company was to ascertain the source of the diamonds distributed over the fields.

(17) The *Allgemeine Schürfgesellschaft* appears on the list of producing companies, and was assigned a quota of 6,000 carats for 1914. It was formed at Windhoek in 1910 with a capital of £8,750.

The companies which worked the shallow and patchy deposits of the Conception Bay fields were five in number. (18) The *Holsatia Diamantgesellschaft* and (19) the *Charlottenfelder Aktien-Gesellschaft* appear to have been unsuccessful. (20) The *Hansa-Diamant-gesellschaft* and (21) the *Gewerkschaft " Kyffhäuser "* must have succeeded moderately well. The quotas allotted them for 1914 were 4,000 and 6,000 carats respectively. The claims of (22) the *Diamantfelder-verwertungsgesellschaft* were worked by the Koloniale Bergbau-Gesellschaft, which engaged to run a light railway and a pipe-line to the claims at an estimated expenditure of £15,000, and in return was to receive 55 per cent. of the net profits. Between May 1913 and August 1914 the output was at the rate of about 2,000 carats per month, and the diamonds produced, though very small, were of excellent quality.

(5) MANUFACTURES

Manufacturing industries were just beginning to make their appearance before the war. The first sea-going steam-vessel, the "Angola," was built at Lüderitz Bay in 1913. It was 16 metres long, and was designed for coast-fishing and sealing. The railway workshops at Usakos and Keetmanshoop were able in 1916 to cope with considerable heavy and light repairs to German and Union engines, and all castings for the territory were made in the foundry which has been installed in Usakos since the British occupation. Highly successful breweries had been established at Windhoek and Swakopmund, with the result that imported beer had been driven out of the local market.

The development of the minor industries and trades can be roughly estimated from the following list, reproduced from the German Official Report, 1914, which gives the state as on April 1, 1913. This list indicates, as might be expected, that the businesses connected with the supply of food easily outnumbered all the others, those connected with construction and transport coming next in importance.

List showing the number of industries and minor trades in South-West Africa as on the 1st April, 1913 (from the Annual Official Report, 1914).

Kind of Trade.	Total No. of Employers.	No. of persons employed.	
		White.	Coloured
Apothecaries	2	1	2
Bakers	35	39	88
Barbers	10	4	6
Bootblacks	3	1	1
Breweries	4	5	25
Brush Factory	1	..	1
Builders	26	98	289
Butchers	23	23	78
Carpenters	2	..	2

List showing the number of industries and minor trades in South-West Africa as on the 1st April, 1913 (from the Annual Official Report, 1914)— Continued.

Kind of Trade.	Total No. of Employers.	No. of persons employed.	
		White.	Coloured.
Carpet Factory	1	1	2
Confectioner	1	2	3
Distilleries	2	5	11
Dye Works	1	1	3
Gardeners	4	5	29
Gunsmiths	2	..	1
Hotel-keepers	121	247	537
Ice Plant	1	1	11
Iron and Metal Factory	1	1	2
Jam Factory	1	4	6
Joiners	22	26	39
Key Makers	9	11	24
Laundries	7	5	18
Lime-kiln	1	2	3
Lime Works	1	2	25
Machine Shop	1	12	14
Masons	4	2	5
Milliners	13	9	8
Painters' and Artists' Sundries	15	17	24
Photographers	7	4	5
Refinery	1	2	6
Saddlers	7	5	8
Sausage Factories	2	5	7
Shoemakers	20	6	13
Shopfitters	1	1	1
Smiths	8	8	18
Soap Boiler	1		2
Soda-Water Makers	9	7	41
Tile Makers	2	1	15
Tinkers	6	6	8
Transport Agents	17	12	180
Wagon Builders	18	54	96
Watchmakers and Goldsmiths	8	6	4
Water Engineers	4	..	5
White Beer Breweries	3	2	17
Total	428	643	1,683

(C) COMMERCE

(1) DOMESTIC

(a) *Principal Branches of Trade*

Domestic commerce in South-West Africa was on a
very modest scale, as is indicated by the list of
industries on p. 81. The chief commodities in which
trade was carried on are foodstuffs and clothing for
Europeans and for native labourers; spirits, wines,
and beer; building materials, furniture, and household
requisites; agricultural implements and other equipment required by the large stock-raising farms or
ranches. The import lists show as their principal
categories foodstuffs, machinery and hardware,
textiles and timber; and the chief exports from the
country, as has already been indicated, were diamonds,
copper and other minerals, guano, and animal
products. In the years preceding the war the numbers
of cattle and sheep in the Protectorate were increasing
at a faster rate than the population, and the farmers
found difficulty in marketing stock beyond what was
required for local needs. The result was a pronounced
fall in the prices of beef and mutton. At Windhoek
the former was $7\frac{1}{2}d$. per lb. in 1908 and $3\frac{3}{4}d$. per lb. in
1913, while mutton dropped from $6d$. to $3\frac{1}{2}d$. per lb. in
the same period. The opening of the Union markets
may be expected to benefit the farmers in the future.

(b) *Towns and Markets*

The insignificance of the internal trade is an index
of the smallness of the population. Windhoek, Lüderitz Bay, Swakopmund, and Keetmanshoop are the
only towns in which the European residents number
over 1,000, and only in Windhoek do they exceed
2,000. There are about a dozen villages with white
inhabitants numbering between 300 and 1,000. In
these the European buildings, solidly constructed and
including as a rule an hotel, a few stores, officials'

quarters, and public offices, give an impression of well-being; but it is obvious that they cannot represent a large purchasing power or indicate any considerable market. The native population in the vicinity of the villages outnumbers the whites in ratios varying from 150 to 2,000 per cent., but has attained neither such wealth nor such standards of living as to influence appreciably the volume of internal trade.

(c) *Organizations to promote Commerce*

Numerous organizations existed in Germany for assisting trade and industry in overseas protectorates. By these the whole field of commercial opportunities was carefully mapped out, every section covered, and all large-scale enterprises systematically interlocked. Most of these organizations had their head-quarters either in Berlin or in Hamburg. The great propaganda institution, the German Colonial Society (*Deutsche Kolonial-gesellschaft*), with its subsidiary body the Colonial Economic Association (*Kolonial-Wirtschaft-liches Komitee*), has been discussed in the book on *Tanganyika*, No. 113 of this series, p. 86. Second only to the Imperial Government in its anxiety to foster German trade in South-West Africa was the Senate of Hamburg, which lent support both to individual firms and to commercial bodies. The shipping interests of the Protectorate were in the hands of the big Hamburg lines, and landing rights at the ports were a monopoly of the Woermann-Linie. Hamburg also exercised its influence through the *Hamburgisches Kolonialinstitut*, which was both a colonial training college and a research institute, and was closely linked up with the Central Intelligence Bureau.

The rivalry between the Hamburg Institute, backed by the Senate, merchants, and shippers of Hamburg, and the German Colonial Society with its offshoots and various subsidiary Intelligence Bureaux, all supported by the Imperial Colonial Office at Berlin, was often acute. The German Government knew well how to make the rivalry between the two centres serve its purpose when circumstances seemed to call for a vigorous colonial policy, and how to repress their activities when continental expansion was considered to be in Germany's best interest.

Within the Protectorate the chief organizations which helped to promote trade were the Chambers of Commerce, the Chamber of Mines, the Agricultural Advisory Board, the Stock Exchanges, the Co-operative Associations, and the Diamond Régie.

Chambers of Commerce existed at Windhoek, Swakopmund, and Lüderitz Bay. All of these did useful work in dealing with matters affecting trade and industry.

The Chamber of Mines was formed at Lüderitz Bay in 1910. It handled such questions as the supply of labour, the reform of the Régie, and the regulation of taxes of all kinds levied on the diamond industry. It was also active in pressing for alterations in the Mining Ordinances.

The Agricultural Advisory Board was constituted in terms of an Ordinance of 1913, to replace the three farmers' associations which had previously existed for the three districts, northern, middle, and southern. The new Board, composed of members elected by the German farmers in each division, was commissioned to advise the Government on agricultural matters. At the first meeting, fixed for March 1914, the Government experts were to submit for the Board's consideration draft laws on animal diseases, fencing, and water rights. Expenses up to about £400 per annum were met by the Government.

The opening up of the diamond fields led to the creation of a fairly active local market for stocks and shares. A few brokers did considerable business, and the banks made arrangements for purchasing stock for clients on the European and neighbouring African Exchanges. The largest of the Protectorate Exchanges was at Lüderitz Bay and was founded by the local Stock Exchange Association (*Börsen-Verein*).

Several co-operative produce-associations had been started before the war by private enterprise among the farmers.   These included the *Ein- und Verkaufsgenossenschaft, Windhuk*; the *Ein- und Verkaufsgenossenschaft in Grootfontein* and the *Grootfonteiner Verwertungs-Gesellschaft*; and the *Verwertungsgenossenschaft Okahandja*.   Of these the Windhoek company carried on a slaughterhouse business, and marketed dairy and farm produce.   Its business grew steadily and rapidly.   The produce handled was valued at £13,118 in 1910, £19,631 in 1911, and £22,073 in 1912.   In 1911 its liabilities were £5,200 and its capital £2,450.   Of the two Grootfontein associations the former was closed down by 1912, and the latter was then formed by the local farmers in order to supply the mining community at Tsumeb.   The Okahandya association was engaged solely in slaughterhouse business.

The function performed by the Diamond Régie in marketing the diamonds recovered on the Protectorate fields has been described on p. 76.   That the position held by the reconstituted Régie was recognized as authoritative is shown by the fact that it was officially represented in London in July 1914, at the joint meeting held by the various diamond industries of the world.

(d) *Non-German Interests*

Foreign interests have not been attracted to the Protectorate in any large measure, although a certain proportion of the capital invested in the various companies was drawn from the United Kingdom and from the Union of South Africa.   The proportion of British subjects in 1913 was 12·2 per cent., while other foreigners represented 4·9 per cent. of the total white population.   The total number of British subjects had declined from 1,866 in 1911 to 1,799 in 1913.   Boers and British owned a number of farms, about 10 per cent. of the Protectorate total, between the Orange River and the northern limits of the Hasuur district, more especially in the neighbourhood of Klipdam.

The Boer settlers were neither popular nor contented with the German Administration, which, contrary to its pledges, had denied them separate Dutch schools and had not released them from the obligation of military service.

(e) *Economic Penetration*

The Germans were not more skilful in penetrating foreign territories than they were in limiting foreign influences in their own protectorates. German South-West Africa was well guarded even by its physical features; for not only were the land frontiers practically closed by natural barriers such as the native states of Ovamboland in the north and the wide stretch of the Kalahari towards the east, but the seaboard facilities were limited to two small and unfavourable ports, Swakopmund and Lüderitz Bay. These natural defences were strengthened deliberately and skilfully. The necessary excuse for handicapping foreign trade was discovered in the alleged difficulty of providing harbour facilities. It was argued that the interests of shippers and traders alike required the careful regulation of the loading and discharging of cargo; and on this pretext an elaborate contract was drawn up, by which the Government granted the Woermann-Linie a practical monopoly of the landing rights for a number of years. British and other foreign firms were thus debarred from employing agents of their own nationality, and all trade, whether of German origin or not, was compelled to pass through German channels. Further, although, in the absence of manufacturing industries within the country, the imports extended over a very wide range, including almost all the essentials of food-stuffs, clothing, house and farm equipment, machinery, and materials for building and construction, the heavy taxes imposed on non-resident commercial travellers under the German regime made it practically impossible for outsiders, canvassing for foreign firms, to compete with the local German merchants.

(2) Foreign

(a) *General Remarks*

Although the detailed trade statistics of German South-West Africa before the war will be of value to traders dealing with the country in the near future, they are not a clear index to the trade prosperity of the colony. One might even say that they are as likely to mislead as to instruct. The reason is that the diamonds and copper, which constitute almost the entire exports, are produced by outside capital, and the profits are consequently spent in other countries, serving to stimulate internal trade only to a limited extent, and perhaps only temporarily. Against this, it may still be argued that these two industries may some day develop on a very large scale. As has happened in South Africa, towns must spring up round mines; and such towns create a demand for agricultural produce and for manufactured articles, thereby causing an increase in the trading and agricultural communities, and eventually, though very much later, bringing about the introduction of manufacturing interests. This is a question which is constantly discussed in the neighbouring territories of the Union, especially in its application to the gold mines of the Rand and the great diamond mines of Kimberley. For South-West Africa the contingency is too remote to need more than a mention here.

When the figures of export and import for the seven years before the war are subjected to closer examination, it becomes clear that the trade balance which appears to have been so satisfactorily established is in reality wholly dependent upon the copper output, which was growing, and the diamonds recovered, which were stationary in value. As the Deutsche Afrika Bank pointed out in 1913, the export of copper ores benefits the colony directly only to the extent of that proportion of the wages of officials and labourers which is expended in the colony itself. As both of these classes to a great extent were recruited from other countries, to which they periodically returned—the officials every few years and the labourers for the most part every year—the total amount of wages available for local dispersal is heavily discounted. This is true of the diamond fields also. But the two industries contributed materially, if indirectly, to the economic progress of the Protectorate. The Otavi copper mines, lying far inland, were the original cause and are still the mainstay of a narrow-gauge railway line, 400 miles long. They have thus effectively assisted the agricultural and commercial development of the districts opened up by the railway. The same claim cannot be made on behalf of the diamond fields. The light line which serves them is only seventy miles long, and the country traversed is a barren waste of gravelly sand incapable of agricultural production. But the high taxes paid by the diamond companies to the Government sufficed to cover the whole of the Budget and to provide an appreciable surplus, which was available for development work elsewhere in the Protectorate, and thus ultimately stimulated its commercial prosperity.

In respect of the investment of capital in the Protectorate and of income arising from such investments, it may be said that at the outbreak of war one set of people in Germany was drawing a considerable income from the dividends of the diamond and copper companies, whilst quite another set was annually investing considerable sums in South-West Africa farms, which could be expected only very gradually to return a regular income.

With reference to the foreign trade proper, although four other countries are shown as participating, nearly seven-eighths of the total was with Germany, as may be seen from the distribution statistics given below under 'Imports' and 'Exports.' As the Union Government's Memorandum points out, the policy of the German Government was obviously to keep both import and export trade in German hands. The exceptional position of the United States of America in 1912 was doubtless due to the existence of direct steamer communication with that country. The introduction of foreign steamship services would have done something to foster trade with other countries; but the real reason why Germany secured such a large proportion of the trade is that practically all merchants and traders were Germans, and that the Government had ensured for German exporters facilities which were not enjoyed by the merchants and manufacturers of other countries.

(b) *Export and Import Trade*

Values of exports and imports.—Statistics show that practically all the trade in pre-war years entered or left the Protectorate through the German seaports. Less than 2 per cent. of imports in 1911 and less than 1 per cent. in 1912 crossed the other frontiers— the southern frontier almost exclusively. Of exports a still more insignificant percentage followed these routes. The railway connexion now established with the Union seems certain to lead in future to a large development of trade. Before the war the export trade with South Africa was inconsiderable, while imports included live-stock, agricultural produce and seeds, groceries, fruit, vegetables, textiles, machinery, metals, and hardware. Since the British occupation, moderate consignments of alcoholic liquors, grain, sugar, fats, and other food-stuffs, boots, soap, and tobacco have been imported from the Union. The table given below shows the values of exports and imports from German South-West Africa from 1900 to 1913. For the years previous to 1909 the figures are given to the nearest thousand. In earlier years they cover only private goods, but from 1906 onward goods purchased on Government account are included. Imports were exceptionally high in 1906 owing to the large importation of Government stores and ammunition for military use in the Herero War, which lasted

from June 1904 to March 1907. The war was also
responsible for the shrinkage of exports by more than
90 per cent. during the years 1904–6. The discovery
of diamonds led to the sudden and remarkable rise in
export values from 1908 onward.

Values of Imports and Exports of German South-West Africa for 1900–13

Year.				Imports.	Exports.	Total Trade.
				Marks.	Marks.	Marks.
1900	..	..	..	6,968,000	908,000	7,876,000
1901	..	..	..	10,075,000	1,242,000	11,317,000
1902	..	..	..	8,568,000	2,213,000	10,781,000
1903	..	..	..	7,931,000	3,444,000	11,375,000
1904	..	..	..	10,057,000	299,000	10,356,000
1905	..	..	..	23,632,000	216,000	23,848,000
1906	..	..	..	68,626,000	383,000	69,009,000
1907	..	..	..	32,396,000	1,616,000	34,012,000
1908	..	..	..	33,179,000	7,795,000	40,974,000
1909	..	..	..	34,713,448	22,070,904	56,784,352
1910	..	..	..	44,344,280	34,691,331	79,035,611
1911	..	..	..	45,301,955	28,573,244	73,875,199
1912	..	..	..	32,498,899	39,035,340	71,534,239
1913	..	..	..	43,424,806	70,302,830	113,727,636

Nature and destination of exports.—The principal
items of export in 1913 were as follows :

	£
Diamonds	2,945,475
Copper and copper ore	396,436
Tin, lead and other ores	54,751
Horns, hides and skins	31,415
Ostrich feathers	6,204
Wool	6,814
Cattle, small stock, and meat	15,669

The diamonds all went to Germany in the first
instance; but the bulk of the copper was shipped to
other than German ports, and a considerable amount
went to the United States. A more detailed analysis
of the exports for the years 1911 and 1912 is given in
the following tables :

Summary of Exports during the Years
1911 and 1912

	1911. Marks.	1912. Marks.
Products of agriculture and forestry ..	4,345	28,368
Live stock	45,515	53,414
Animal products	525,795	739,515
Raw minerals and fossils	27,173,079	37,215,380
Manufactures, curios, &c.	824,510	998,663
Total exports	28,573,244	39,035,340

Chief Articles of Export during the Years
1911 and 1912

	1911. Marks.	1912. Marks.
Cattle	21,600	16,519
Small stock	1,890	18,345
Meat..	14,544	28,974
Horns	24,526	24,003
Hides, goat- and sheep-skins	246,417	297,787
Skins of wild animals	34,051	29,575
Sealskins	43,543	41,569
Ostrich feathers	79,804	97,012
Wool..	74,172	149,658
Marble	1,232	19,968
Other stones and earths	9,184	5,485
Rough diamonds	23,034,146	30,414,078
Copper	325,000	229,850
Copper ores..	3,428,703	6,293,408
Tin ore	—	9,400
Other ores	28,946	15,064
Lead..	345,868	228,127
Leather and leather ware	14,863	18,535
Photographs	27,158	8,671
Curios and miscellaneous articles.. ..	115,378	154,397
Packing cases, materials re-exported ..	667,111	817,060
Mohair	—	17,617
Wood and forestry products	779	14,154

The distribution of the exports, in respect of their values,[1] among the different countries of destination, was as follows in the years 1910–12 :

	1910. Per cent.	£	1911. Per cent.	£	1912. Per cent.
Germany	82·6	1,197,683	85·2	1,595,661	83·2
Union of South Africa ..	0·6	10,779	0·8	17,555	0·9
United Kingdom	0·1	4,643	0·3	4,074	0·2
France	—	84	—	15	—
United States	7·1	34,755	2·5	103,870	5·4
Other countries	9·6	156,904	11·2	198,058	10·3

[1] The total values of exports, as quoted here from British official sources, differ to a slight extent from the German official figures quoted on p. 91.

Nature and origin of imports.—The table given above on p. 91 shows the values of imports, which may be said to have averaged £2,000,000 per annum in recent years. In 1912, in consequence of a depression in diamond mining in 1911, and of the cessation of work on the railway lines, which had then been completed, they were abnormally low. The following year, however, they had almost regained their former level.

The different classes of imports are shown in the following analysis of the returns for 1911 and 1912. It will be seen that the imports cover the usual wide range of the needs of a young country.

Imports during the Years 1911 and 1912

	1911. *Marks.*	1912. *Marks.*
Products of agriculture and articles pertaining to these (including grain and cereals, vegetables and fruit, groceries, provisions and beverages, seeds, living plants and products of forestry)	15,162,379	11,797,118
Animals and animal products	4,068,644	2,752,462
Raw minerals, fossils and mineral oils	2,804 693	2,335,676
Oils, fats, resins. &c.	533,576	370,605
Chemical and pharmaceutical products	705,254	646,639
Textiles	4,936,759	4,196,520
Leather and leather wares, oilcloths and furs	1,570,332	1,110,479
Indiarubber and gutta-percha goods	73,755	67,680
Wooden, plaited, and carved articles	823,787	688,480
Paper, cardboard, printed matter, works of art, &c.	585,739	471,045
Earthen, stone and glass ware	425,769	312,202
Metals and hardware (excluding instruments, machinery, and firearms) :—		
(*a*) Unwrought metals and metals partly manufactured	3,572,425	637,262
(*b*) Manufactured	4,644,584	3,769,152
Instruments, machinery and locomotives	4,457,679	2,698,054
Guns and ammunition	528,429	375,392
Articles imported for the military, as guns, ammunition, &c. (excluding provisions)	-	270,133
Specie	408,151	—
Total imports	45,301,955	32,498,899

In the following table the imports for 1910–12 are classified according to countries of origin :

	1910.		1911.		1912.
	Per cent.	£	Per cent.	£	Per cent.
Germany..	77·6	1,831,885	82·2	1,300,038	81·37
Union of South Africa ..	14·8	301,819	13·6	194,953	12·20
United Kingdom ..	1·8	29,742	1·3	15,681	0·98
France	0·1	310	0·1	157	—
United States	0·2	13,751	0·6	53,841	3·37
Other countries	5·5	49,829	2·2	33,190	2·08

(c) Customs and Excise

The Protectorate was not subject to the German Imperial Customs Regulations, but had its own tariff —the Customs Tariff of 1908, with subsequent amendments. Under a Director of Customs at Windhoek there were chief customs-offices at Windhoek, Swakopmund, Lüderitz Bay, and Keetmanshoop. Minor customs-houses existed at Davignab, Hasuur, Ukamas, Stolzenfels (Schuit Drift), Raman's Drift, Sandwich Harbour, Ururas (near Walvisch Bay), Haigamkhab, Outyo, Grootfontein, and Gobabis. There was an excise station for brandy at Osona (near Okahandya), and a postal customs-house at Usakos.

The Estimates for 1914–15 provided for the following officials : a director of customs, a controller of the central warehouse, 4 controllers of customs-houses, 10 inspectors of customs, 23 customs officers and tide-waiters, and one storeman.

The imports on which customs were levied were tobacco, liquors, slaughter cattle and sheep, fresh meat, milk, butter, margarine, sugar, arms and ammunition, matches, chemicals, and drugs. Export dues were payable on female cattle, hides, guano, and diamonds.

The estimated revenue under the head of customs in 1913–14 and 1914–15 was :

	1913–14.	1914–15.
	£	£
Import duties	115,000	100,000
Export duties	50	50
Sundry revenue	1,650	1,500
Total	116,700	101,550

Excise was levied on beer and on brandy. The estimated excise revenue for three years was as follows :

	1912–13.	1913–14.	1914–15.
	£	£	£
Excise on beer	3,000	2,500	2,500
Excise on spirits	3,000	2,000	2,000
Total	6,000	4,500	4,500

Details of the customs tariff in force before the war are given in the Consular Report for 1910. If this tariff is compared with the Union tariff it will be found that in nearly every instance the Protectorate rate was the lower; and it is clear that the recent application of the Union tariff to South-West Africa will, under normal conditions, result in a considerable increase of revenue. This measure was announced in a Proclamation (No. 6 of 1917) extending to South-West Africa the duties specified in the Union of South Africa's Customs and Excise Duties Act, 1917.

(d) Commercial Treaties

There was, prior to the war, no commercial treaty in existence between the United Kingdom and Germany. The treaty formerly in force had been terminated in 1898, and subsequent attempts to conclude an arrangement acceptable to both sides had failed. The recent state of war, therefore, has not had the effect of abrogating any instrument of first importance. Germany had rightly understood that, so far as the United Kingdom was concerned, it was not proposed to introduce any change of practice to her detriment; and on her side she procured the assent of the German Bundesrat at regular intervals to enactments extending most-favoured-nation treatment to all our dominions, colonies, and possessions without exception.

There were, however, one or two instruments affecting commercial intercourse between the United Kingdom and Germany in force at the outbreak of war. One was a Declaration of 1869, providing for the free admission into the respective countries, subject to certain conditions, of patterns and samples brought by commercial travellers. Another was a

Declaration of 1874, granting joint-stock companies and other commercial, industrial, and financial associations established in the territories of one country the privilege of access to the tribunals and of exercising their rights in the territories of the other. An Āgreement, supplementing the Declaration of 1869, provided certain facilities for expediting the passage of commercial travellers' samples through the custom-houses of the respective countries; and a further Agreement of 1913 extended the Declaration of 1874 to cover the Protectorate and Consular Court Districts of both parties thereto. Beyond these there was nothing affecting the British Empire except arrangements relating to Protectorates in Africa and the western Pacific.

On January 1, 1909, Germany adhered on behalf of the Protectorate to the Berne Copyright Convention of September 9, 1886, and to the Additional Act and Declaration signed at Paris on May 4, 1896. The Protectorate, as such, would also appear to be a party to a number of other recent international conventions.

In the absence of a commercial treaty, commercial relations between Germany and Great Britain were established by Acts renewed from time to time and published in England every two years. Nevertheless, as a matter of fact, British shipping and British trade were effectively boycotted in the Protectorate. The boycott was carried on by the co-operation of the German Government with the financial and shipping interests of Berlin and Hamburg; and this was done, it must be remembered, under cover of admirably drawn paper agreements.

The Portuguese Government concluded an agreement with Germany on December 30, 1886. This was embodied in a Declaration containing two economic articles, No. IV and No. V, as follows:

Art. IV. Portuguese subjects in the German Possessions of Africa, and German subjects in the Portuguese Possessions, shall enjoy in respect to the protection of their persons and goods, with the acquisition and transfer of personal and real property, and to the exercise of their industry, the same treatment without any difference whatever, and the same rights as the subjects of the nation exercising sovereignty or protection.

Art. V. The Portuguese and Imperial Governments reserve to themselves the right of concluding further Agreements to facilitate commerce and navigation, as well as to regulate the frontier traffic in the African Possessions on both sides.[1]

H.M. Government protested against this treaty on August 15, 1887, on the ground that it arrogated to Portugal large territories between Angola and Mozambique in which there was no sign of Portuguese jurisdiction or authority.

(D) FINANCE

(1) *Public Finance*

The chief features of the financial administration of the Protectorate will be easily grasped from the following table giving estimates of revenue and expenditure for the years ending March 31, 1913–15:

REVENUE

	1914–15. £		1914–15. £	1913–14. £	1912–13. £
A. Ordinary Revenue:					
1. Taxation:					
Diamonds	689,500				
Licences, Land Tax, Transfer Duty, &c.	27,150				
			716,650	357,150	388,775
2. Customs			101,550	116,700	131,500
3. Fines, Forfeitures, Fees of Office, and Departmental Receipts			98,242	82,500	69,495
4. Mining Department:					
Government Diamonds ..	37,875				
Other	3,290				
			41,165	49,900	145,376
5. Railways:					
State	73,360				
Otavi	82,875				
Southern	11,500				
			167,735	151,745	110,900
6. Harbours:					
Swakopmund	24,650				
Lüderitz Bay	6,750				
			31,400	31,400	34,250
7. Interest and Adjustment of Account			130	130	—
8. Military Medical Services and sales of Cast Animals, &c.			8,100	4,655	—
Total Ordinary Revenue ..			1,164,972	794,180	880,296

[1] Hertslet: *Map of Africa by Treaty*, vol. ii, pp. 703–5.

	1914–15.	1913–14.	1912–13.
	£	£	£
B. Non-Recurrent Revenue :			
1. Savings and Surplus ex 1912, 1911, 1910 ..	225,000	114,061	229,252
2. Imperial Contribution towards Military Expenditure ..	681,185	731,342	691,417
Total Revenue ..	2,071,157	1,639,583	1.800,965

EXPENDITURE

A. Ordinary Expenditure :

	1914–15.	1913–14.	1912–13.
1. Salaries of fixed Establishment ..	88,150	80,942	82,973
2. Salaries of non-fixed Establishment	48,257	50,204	74,975
3. Native Employees' Wages	3,580	4,940	10,408
4. Pensions, Gratuities, &c.	7,468	6,825	5,569
5. Public Health, Hospitals, &c. ..	12,350	10,850	9,500
6. Public Worship and Schools ..	12,300	10,300	8,550
7. Upkeep of Government Buildings, Lands, Furniture	28,650	26,160	25,475
8. Upkeep of Live Stock, including Stud Stock and Stock for Bacteriological and Veterinary Researches	16,175	16,675	45,420
9. Agriculture and Surveys	47,300	35,705	9,800
10. Transport and Sundry Expenditure	59,193	58,426	93,521
11. Police Vote	185,670	185,875	143,380
12. Military Expenditure	689,285	691,203	714,485
13. Railways and Harbours	123,960	99,300	42,350
14. Interest and Sinking Fund on Public Debt	182,425	165,925	132,900
15. Equalization Fund	17,984	—	10,000
Total Ordinary Expenditure ..	1,522,747	1,443,330	1,409,306

B. Extraordinary Expenditure :

1. Civil Administration, including :

	£			
Public Works	50,000			
Waterworks, Wells, and Roads	52,900			
Payment of Revenue Contribution towards Railway Construction	350,000			
Contribution towards the upkeep of Garrison ..	54,786			
Grants-in-aid, Eradication of Pests, &c...	24,122			

	1914–15.	1913–14.	1912–13.
	531,808	146,678	335,000
2. Police—Buildings and Allowances ..	5,600	4,780	—
3. Deficit, 1911, 1910, 1909	11,002	44,793	60,755
Total Extraordinary Expenditure	548,410	196,251	395,755
Total Expenditure	2,071,157	1,639,581	1,805,061

These figures call for some comment. In the first place, it is to be noted that they constitute a statement of estimates, not of actual receipts and disbursements. Details of realized revenue and expenditure were not accessible to the author of the Union Memorandum on South-West Africa, from which the statistics given in this paragraph are mainly drawn, but a surplus was apparently recorded in each of the five years immediately preceding the war. This is said to have amounted to £230,000 in 1910; £114,000 in 1911; £225,000 in 1912; £350,000 in 1913; and £800,000 in 1914.

Of the ordinary revenue three-fifths was drawn from the tax on diamonds, the annual profits of the Government diamond claims (£25,000), and the Government share in the profits of the Deutsche Diamanten-Gesellschaft (£12,525). The railway earnings come second, and the customs receipts third in order of value. The receipts and expenditure on posts and telegraphs were not included in the Protectorate figures, as this service was controlled by the Imperial Government. Receipts from dog-taxes and from spirit and other trading licences were assigned to the local government authorities. Commercial travellers' licences cost from £10 to £12 10s. per quarter for each fiscal division in which business was transacted.

The non-recurrent revenue includes two items. One of these consists of the surplus revenue from the third year before. The second item is the Imperial grant-in-aid, which represented in recent years nearly two-fifths of the total revenue. This contribution was latterly assigned to the maintenance of the garrison, but in earlier years it was both greater in amount and more general in character, as the very large deficits which were recorded annually were all made good by the Imperial Government. Further, all the expenditure in connexion with the Herero War, 1904–7, was met by special Imperial subsidies. The total sums provided up to 1912 under these two heads were as follows:

(a) Grants-in-Aid		(b) Native War Expenditure	
	£		£
1904	40,100	1904	5,406,800
1905	2,220,000	1905	6,112,300
1906	297,500	1906	6,423,100
1907	3,740,750	1907	3,253,550
1908	5,332,000	1908	1,903,300
1909	1,387,500		
1910	1,508,900		
1911	721,300		
1912	570,800		
Total	15,782,850	Total	23,099,050

The Imperial authorities apparently anticipated that at some future date the Protectorate might accept responsibility for a part at least of this debt; but latterly, it would appear, they had realized that Empire as well as Protectorate would benefit if surplus revenue were devoted to internal development—to the construction of railways, harbours, and public buildings, and the prosecution of water-boring and irrigation schemes. The surplus revenues were therefore credited annually to a Reserve or Equalization Fund, and employed in subsequent years to meet the amounts voted under the head of Extraordinary Expenditure. The objects for which they were employed were the construction of piers and jetties, roads, wells, and water-works, hospitals and a quarantine station, the upkeep of the garrison, the Fish River Irrigation Scheme (first instalment), the purchase, at £1 each, of 50,000 shares in the Diamond Régie, and—most important of all—the construction or relaying of railways. The items of Ordinary Expenditure are self-explanatory.

The loans outstanding against the Protectorate in 1914 amounted apparently to nearly £3,000,000. The Imperial Treasury granted loans of £390,000 and £180,000 in 1907 and 1908 respectively, and the Reichstag a few years later sanctioned the raising of an Imperial Protectorates Loan, of which the share assigned to German South-West Africa was £5,000,000. Of this amount about £2,100,000, raised at 4½ per cent., had been taken up at the end of 1913.

Against it were debited £1,250,000 for the Otavi Railway, about £1,000,000 for the other railways, £117,500 for the Swakopmund Pier, £250,000 for the capital of the Land Bank, and (probably) the cost of the completed sections of the Otyivarongo–Okahakana line.

(2) *Currency*

The monetary standard in the Protectorate was the same as that of Germany, the unit of legal tender being the mark. The denominations of metal currency were the same, and so too were those of the paper currency *Reichsbanknoten* and *Reichskassenscheine*. Notes of the German issuing banks other than the Reichsbank were not accepted by Government cashiers except at a considerable discount—an important consideration in a very thinly populated country. Both English sovereigns and South African pound notes were freely used, the sovereign being exchanged at 20 marks. The postal service was so widespread that within the Protectorate (following a custom much in favour in Germany itself) money was generally transferred by postal orders. The growth of the banking system, however, was latterly causing these to be displaced, in respect of larger amounts, by bank drafts and cheques.

It may be noted that weights and measures were the same as in Germany.

(3) *Banking*

Since the British occupation, the Standard Bank of South Africa and the National Bank of South Africa have established themselves in the territory. Both have branches in Windhoek, Swakopmund, and Lüderitz Bay, and the National Bank has also a branch at Keetmanshoop and agencies at Walvisch Bay, Usakos, and Karibib.

Under the German regime there were eight banks: the Deutsche Afrika-Bank, the banking department of the Deutsche Kolonial-Gesellschaft für Südwest-

Afrika, the Deutsch-Südwestafrikanische Genossen-schaftsbank, the Swakopmunder Bank-Verein, the Spar- und Darlehnskasse, the Südwestafrikanische Boden-Kredit-Gesellschaft, the Omaruru Farmers' Bank, and the Government Land Bank.

The *Deutsche Afrika-Bank*, whose annual reports form a record of the progress of trade in the Protectorate, had its head-quarters in Hamburg. Its capital was found by the Norddeutsche Bank in Hamburg, the Disconto-Gesellschaft in Berlin, C. Woermann and Octavio Schröder of Hamburg. It was established in 1906 to take over the banking business of the Damara und Namaqua Handelsgesellschaft in Windhoek, Swakopmund, and Lüderitz Bay, and had also an agency in the Canary Islands. Its original capital of £50,000 was raised in 1913 to £100,000, and dividends of 8 per cent. were paid for several years up to and including 1913.

The *Deutsche Kolonial-Gesellschaft für Südwest-Afrika* conducted a banking section in Swakopmund. In Germany it was represented by the company's head-quarters in Berlin.

The *Deutsch-Südwestafrikanische Genossenschafts-bank* was a co-operative bank formed in Windhoek in 1908 by 26 farmers. Farmers' requirements were met by the issue of small short-term loans. The number of members had increased to 125 in 1911 and 131 in 1912. The capital was then £25,000 and liabilities £32,500. Dividends of 5 per cent. had been paid for a number of years. The bank was represented in Germany by the Reichsgenossenschaftsbank of Frankfort and Hamburg, which has a network of affiliated co-operative agencies in other German towns.

The *Swakopmunder Bank-Verein* was a co-operative bank founded in 1911 by industrial workers. Its liabilities had grown from £13,500 in 1911 to £39,000 in 1912, and the number of members was 56 in 1912, 68 in 1913. For its first business year the association declared dividends amounting to 20·94 per cent.

The *Spar- und Darlehnskasse* was an unlimited liability association, which was founded by farmers and business men in Gibeon in 1902 and conducted a loan bank and a trading store. Its business, which was purely local, increased largely in consequence of the completion of the railway through Gibeon. In 1913 it had 44 members.

The *Südwestafrikanische Boden-Kredit-Gesellschaft* was established in 1912, with a capital of £50,000, and was the first bank in the Protectorate to perform all the ordinary functions of a bank. Loan operations, in respect of taking up mortgages and making advances, were at first restricted to communal bodies, but afterwards extended to owners of town properties. Country loans were regarded as involving risks which required a special Land Bank supported by the Government. The Südwestafrikanische Boden-Kredit-Gesellschaft was not allowed to acquire land itself except for its business premises or in order to save loss on its mortgages.

The report, issued in June 1914, on the first year's work, showed that 39 mortgage loans were issued, of a total value of £44,115. Twenty-two of these, of a total value of £15,240, were held in Swakopmund; 8, of £11,975 in Lüderitz Bay; 7, of £15,500, in Windhoek; and 2, of £1,400, in Keetmanshoop. As the number of loans applied for was 73, and the value £78,350, it appears that rather more than half of the applications were successful. Loans of values not exceeding £500 might be granted without reference to Berlin.

The original head-quarters of the association were at Swakopmund, but branches were very soon established at Lüderitz Bay and Windhoek, and official sanction was obtained at intervals to extend operations to other towns. As the original capital of £50,000 was likely to be exhausted at the close of the first year, 5 per cent. debentures, of the total value of £150,000, were issued in 1914.

When war broke out the bank had not been long

enough in existence to establish a profitable balance between the interest charged on mortgages and the interest it had itself to pay on its debentures, and was therefore content to cover the first costs of organization and management from the current receipts.

The *Omaruru Bank* was founded in December 1913 by a number of farmers, who obtained the promise of support from the newly established Land Bank on condition of accepting its complete control, of furnishing a membership of at least 100 shareholders, each guaranteeing £250, and of observing prescribed limits in the total of loans advanced.

The *Land Bank* was established, with head-quarters in Windhoek, under an Imperial Ordinance dated June 9, 1913. The Protectorate Government was required to provide the initial capital of £500,000, but further capital might be raised subsequently by debentures. The bank was empowered to make advances to farmers, on mortgage of land, for the purpose of making improvements, such as waterworks, buildings, fences, cattle and sheep dips, and the laying out of orchards and vineyards. The rate of interest was fixed at 6 per cent., which, with the amortization at $1\frac{1}{2}$ per cent., compared favourably with previous rates of 8 per cent. or more, on bonds liable to be called up on short notice. During its first year the bank advanced £67,464 for farm improvements, such as dam-making, water-boring, wells, fencing, and buildings.

The urgent need for the establishment of a Land Bank had been made clear by the state of credit prevailing in the country for several years previous to 1913. In Britain and in the British dominions it is customary to find traders with very small means who operate on a bank account, but in Germany such individuals usually resort to a savings bank or a co-operative bank. The tradition survived in South-West Africa to this extent, that the banks were used by a comparatively small number of the merchants in the chief towns, while throughout the rest of the country the leading merchants of each district acted as bankers for the farmers and small traders. This led inevitably to a system of long credits, the natural result of which was to divert the capital of the merchants from its proper uses, hamper commercial development, and maintain high prices. The farmers also suffered, for they were so deeply involved that, when they had slaughter stock to dispose of, they found themselves compelled to sell it to the merchants at unduly low prices in part payment of their debt.

The general financial position was reflected in the mortgage returns. In 1911 mortgages amounting to £387,000 were passed on 866 farm properties. In these circumstances the banking institutions were naturally enough extremely cautious in issuing credit. The Genossenschaftsbank in Windhoek was the only bank that made an effort to grant loans to the limit of the funds available, but even so it confined itself to advancing money as working capital for short terms only, and chiefly to farmers. The other banks required the usual bankers' securities for loans, and these, naturally enough in a new country, were rarely forthcoming. The banks can hardly be blamed for their policy, because, in a young country and with unsettled conditions, free lending would have involved great risk of losses.

By 1913, owing to the scarcity of ready money among the country people, matters were approaching a climax, and general disaster might have overtaken merchants and farmers alike but for the prospect of the introduction of fresh capital through the establishment of the proposed Land Bank. Creditors and debtors were willing to hold out, in hope of relief, and it seems that the whole situation would have gradually improved in the course of a few years. The Land Bank had not had time before the outbreak of war to effect a marked change; in fact, it had not even matured its organization for dealing with the important matter of loans for dams and waterworks.

(4) *Foreign Capital*

The details given in the earlier sections of this volume have made it clear that of the capital invested in the land companies and in the mining and agricultural enterprises of the Protectorate by far the greater part was drawn from Germany, although appreciable amounts were also subscribed in Britain and in the Union of South Africa. The measures devised by the Protectorate and Imperial authorities had been successful in keeping practically the whole of the trade of the country, internal and foreign, in German hands; and the influence of non-German investments in furthering foreign infiltration may be said to have been conspicuously absent. The landward isolation of the Protectorate was a bulwark against economic penetration, and the oversea carrying trade was, as has been shown, a German monopoly. The British occupation, with the railway developments already described, has destroyed these barriers; but it is scarcely possible to predict the strength of the economic forces that will in future invade this quondam preserve of the commercial interests of Berlin and Hamburg.

(5) *Principal Fields of Investment*

The four main fields of investment are railways, copper, diamonds, and the cattle industry. Each of these has been treated in detail in earlier parts of this report, but a few general remarks upon their financial aspect may be added.

Before the war, railways were passing under the administration of the German Government, and now form part of a complex system owned and managed by the Union Government. They have already proved profitable investments. The Southern Railway has such difficulties to contend with in the lack of water and superabundance of sand that its net earnings have not yet equalled, and will probably never equal, those of the main system, much less those of the Otavi

Railway. The latter has been extraordinarily successful; the ratios of its net profits to gross receipts for
the years 1911–14 were 42·4 per cent., 43·5 per cent.,
50·6 per cent., and 53·4 per cent.

The Otavi Minen- und Eisenbahn-Gesellschaft retained the management of the Otavi Railway, even
after selling it to the Government, and to this department of its activities owed about three-fourths of its
net profits. These were such as to warrant the payment, in the years 1912–14, of dividends of 30 per
cent., 40 per cent., and 45 per cent. respectively per
ordinary share, and 25 per cent., 35 per cent., and
40 per cent. per deferred share. The remainder of the
company's profits were derived from copper mining,
and represented a dividend value of $11\frac{1}{4}$ per cent. on
ordinary and 10 per cent. on deferred shares. The
Otavi Company was probably the most successful
of all the companies engaged in copper mining—an
enterprise in which there was a considerable element of
speculation.

If copper mining was speculative, the diamond
industry of the Protectorate was peculiarly so. The
occurrence of diamonds in the sand-fields is due to
causes not yet ascertained, so that neither can the life
of the deposits be predicted nor can further discoveries
be confidently expected. Further, many of the
companies were new and lacking in experience. The
principal companies made extraordinary profits, others
did well, but a considerable number failed to make
good their expenses, and some never even reached the
producing stage.

When compared with the dividends yielded by the
best of the diamond companies, the profits hitherto
achieved by the cattle-raising companies have been
insignificant. The Windhuker Farmgesellschaft paid
8 per cent. in 1911, 8 per cent. in 1912, and 10 per
cent. in 1913, and its shares remained fairly steady at
10 per cent. to 30 per cent. above par. The Südwest-
Afrikanische Schäferei-Gesellschaft, founded in 1901,
had a capital of £33,500 in 1912, when it owned

112,593 hectares divided into less than a dozen farms. It had paid no dividends up to 1913.

The most important farming companies hitherto established in the Protectorate were the international firm of Liebig and the German firm of Brauss, Mahn and Company. The former operated locally under the title of the Deutsche Farmgesellschaft (A.-G. Düsseldorf), formed in 1907 with a capital of £250,000. It was engaged in cattle-breeding and intended to set up a meat-packing factory as soon as the number of cattle in the Protectorate was sufficiently large. Its holdings between the Swakop and Husab Rivers, mainly on hill country suitable for cattle and sheep, amount to 532,000 hectares, and it had also acquired about 160,000 hectares in the Okahandya and Gobabis districts. Its farms were well watered, and most of them well fenced and stocked. In 1913 it employed 23 white men and 329 natives, and its stock included about 500 horses, mules, and donkeys, 900 head of cattle, 11,000 sheep and goats, and a few ostriches.

Other large companies engaged in the meat industry in different parts of the world may be expected to establish similar ranches in the territory. Until the country is developed to the point where water-supply is easy and certain and local markets are sufficient, it is unlikely that farming on a small scale will be more profitable than the big ranches. The great companies are much better able to stand the risk of loss during the experimental period of cattle-breeding and during epidemics of cattle diseases. Nevertheless, Government assistance may well be extended, as far as possible, to the individual owner, the permanent occupier; and limits might reasonably be imposed upon attempts by large firms, especially by firms of alien complexion, to secure a preponderant share of the best lands for cattle-raising.

(E) GENERAL REMARKS

The chief features of the economic position of the territory have been fully discussed under the headings of Railways, Industry, and Commerce, and need not be recapitulated here. An unqualified reversion to pre-war conditions is scarcely possible, for the railway connexion alone must create new currents of trade and bring the country into closer touch with the rest of South Africa. It may be doubted whether the Germans had made, or would ever have been able to make, a financial success of their colony. Its administration since 1904 had cost the Imperial Government more than £40,000,000; and the economic results, direct and indirect, can scarcely have equalled this total. Even with the help in recent years of the funds derived from diamond taxation, the country's revenues were insufficient to meet the whole cost of administration; and the life of the diamond fields, it must be remembered, may terminate within a few years.

APPENDIX

EXTRACTS FROM TREATIES, Etc.

I.—PROCLAMATION ANNOUNCING A GERMAN PROTECTORATE OVER THE COAST OF NAMAQUALAND AND DAMARALAND, August 16 (? 15), 1884.

His Majesty the German Emperor William I, King of Prussia, has commanded me to proceed to Angra Pequena with His Majesty's two-decked corvette, the *Elisabeth*, to place under the direct protection of His Majesty the territory belonging to M. A. Lüderitz, on the West Coast of Africa.

The territory of M. A. Lüderitz will, according to official communication, be taken to extend from the north bank of the Orange River to the 26° south latitude, 20 geographical miles inland, including the Islands belonging thereto by the Law of Nations.

In carrying out His Majesty's commands I herewith hoist the Imperial German flag, and thus place the above-mentioned territory under the protection and sovereignty of His Majesty the Emperor William I, and call upon all present to give three cheers for His Majesty.

Long live His Majesty the Emperor William I.

> Schering, *Captain at Sea, and Commandant of His Imperial Majesty's ship* Elisabeth.

II.—DECLARATION BETWEEN GERMANY AND PORTUGAL, December 30, 1886.

Art. I.—The Boundary line which shall separate the Portuguese and German Possessions in South-West Africa follows the course of the River Kunene from its mouth to the waterfalls which are formed to the south of the Humbe by the Kunene breaking through the Serra Canna. From this point the line runs along the parallel of latitude to the River Kubango, then along the course of that river to the village of Andara, which is to remain in the German sphere of influence, and from thence in a straight line eastwards to the rapids of Catima, on the Zambesi.

III.—AGREEMENT BETWEEN THE BRITISH AND GERMAN GOVERNMENTS RESPECTING AFRICA AND HELIGOLAND, July 1, 1890.

Art. III.—In South-West Africa the sphere in which the exercise of influence is reserved to Germany is bounded—

1. To the south by a line commencing at the mouth of the Orange River, and ascending the north bank of that river to the point of its intersection by the 20th degree of east longitude.

2. To the east by a line commencing at the above-named point, and following the 20th degree of east longitude to the point of its intersection by the 22nd parallel of south latitude, it runs eastward along that parallel to the point of its intersection by the 21st degree of east longitude; thence it follows that degree northward to the point of its intersection by the 18th parallel of south latitude; it runs eastward along that parallel till it reaches the River Chobe; and descends the centre of the main channel of that river to its junction with the Zambesi, where it terminates.

It is understood that under this arrangement Germany shall have free access from her Protectorate to the Zambesi by a strip of territory which shall at no point be less than 20 English miles in width.

The sphere in which the exercise of influence is reserved to Great Britain is bounded to - the west and north-west by the above-mentioned line.

It includes Lake Ngami.

The course of the above boundary is traced in general accordance with a map officially prepared for the British Government in 1889.

The delimitation of the southern boundary of the British territory of Walfisch Bay is reserved for arbitration, unless it shall be settled by the consent of the two Powers within two years from the date of the conclusion of this Agreement. The two Powers agree that, pending such settlement, the passage of the subjects and transit of goods of both Powers through the territory now in dispute shall be free; and the treatment of their subjects in that territory shall be in all respects equal. No dues shall be levied on goods in transit. Until a settlement shall be effected the territory shall be considered neutral.

AUTHORITIES

1. OFFICIAL AND SEMI-OFFICIAL PUBLICATIONS

Africa Pilot, part ii, 6th ed., 1910, with revised supplement, 1917. London.

Bulletin of the Imperial Institute, vol. xiii. London, 1915.

Deutsches Handels-Archiv: Zeitschrift für Handel und Gewerbe. Berlin, 1917.

Deutsches Kolonialblatt: Amtsblatt für die Schutzgebiete in Afrika und in der Südsee, herausgegeben im Reichs-Kolonialamt. Berlin, 1913, 1914.

Die deutschen Schutzgebiete in Afrika und in der Südsee, 1911-12, 1912-13. Jahresberichte, herausgegeben vom Reichs-Kolonialamt. Berlin.

Diplomatic and Consular Reports: Reports on the Trade of the Consular District of German South-West Africa, Annual Series. **London.**

Jahrbuch über die deutschen Kolonien, Jahrg. 1 (1908); 4 (1911) and 7 (1914). Essen.

Memorandum on the Country known as German South-West Africa. Pretoria, 1915.

Parliamentary Papers. Union of South Africa. Cd. 7873; 1915. Cd. 8371; 1916. Cd. 9146; 1918. *Department of Overseas Trade. Report on Trade Conditions and Prospects in the Protectorate of South-West Africa.* Cmd 842; 1920.

Report of the Royal Commission on the Natural Resources, Trade, and Legislation of certain portions of His Majesty's Dominions, Cd. 8462. London, 1917.

Report on a Tour to Ovamboland, by Major S. M. Pritchard. Pretoria, 1915.

South African Railways and Harbours: Report for the year ended 31st December, 1916. Pretoria, 1917.

Statesman's Year Book, 1918, edited by Sir J. Scott Keltie, LL.D. London.

Taschenbuch für Südwestafrika, 1912, Teil 1, edited by Kurt Schwabe. Berlin.

The Geology and Mineral Industry of South-West Africa, by Percy Albert Wagner. Pretoria, 1916.

U.S.A. Consular and Trade Reports, No. 218, December 11, 1913, September 17, 1914, and September 23, 1914. Washington.

Von der Heydt's Kolonial-Handbuch: Jahrbuch der deutschen Kolonial- und Uebersee-Unternehmungen. Jahrg. 6 (1912). Berlin.

2. Periodicals and Newspapers

Board of Trade Journal: issues of August 2 and December 13, 1917, and May 2, 1918. London.

Der Tropenpflanzer: Nos. 4 and 5, 1914. Berlin.

Geographical Journal: issues of September 1915, January and February 1916, and April 1917. London.

Journal of the African Society: issues of January and July 1915, January 1916, January, April, and July 1917. London.

Revue Économique Internationale, October 15 and 20, 1909. Brussels.

South Africa (weekly journal): issue of July 21, 1917. London.

South African Journal of Industries: issue of March 1918. Pretoria.

The African World: issues of August 11, August 25, September 22, November 3, and December 8, 1917; January 19, February 3, February 9, and February 16, 1918. London.

The Colonial Journal: issues of January and April 1915, and January 1916. London.

The Times: issues of May 29 and 31, 1917. London.

United Empire (Journal of the Royal Colonial Institute): issue of August 1917. London.

3. Historical and Descriptive Works

Brown, A. S., and Brown, Gordon G. *Guide to South and East Africa.* London, 1918.

Bülow, F. J. von. *Deutsch Südwestafrika,* 2nd edn. Berlin, 1899.

Calvert, A. F. *South-West Africa during the German Occupation,* 1884-1914. London, 1915.

—— *The German African Empire.* London, 1916.

Dove, Professor K. *Die deutschen Kolonien.* IV. *Südwestafrika.* Berlin and Leipzig, 1913.

Eveleigh, W. *South-West Africa.* London, 1915.

François, H. von. *Nama und Damara. Deutsch Süd-West-Afrika.* Magdeburg [1896].

Frenssen, Gustav. *Peter Moors Fahrt nach Südwestafrika.* Berlin, 1906. English translation, *Peter Moor's Journey to South-West Africa.* London, 1908.

Hassert, K. *Deutschlands Kolonien* (Südwestafrika, pp. 55-127), 2nd edn. Leipzig, 1910.

Irle, I. *Die Herero.* Gütersloh, 1906.

Leutwein, T. G. von. *Elf Jahre Gouverneur in Deutsch Südwestafrika.* Berlin, 1910.

Lewin, Evans. *The Germans and Africa.* London, 1915.

Opitz, W. *In Südwestafrika.* Leipzig, 1909.

ROHRBACH, P. *Deutsche Kolonialwirtschaft*, vol, i, *Südwest-afrika*. Berlin, 1907.

—— *Wie machen wir unsere Kolonien rentabel?* Halle, 1907.

SCHULTZE, PROFESSOR L. *Das deutsche Kolonialreich*. II. Band, ii. Teil: *Südwestafrika*. Leipzig and Vienna, 1914.

SCHWABE, K. *Im deutschen Diamantenland*. Berlin, 1909.

TONNELAT, E. *L'Expansion allemande hors d'Europe*. Paris, 1908.

TÖNNESEN, T. *The South-West Africa Protectorate*. (Geographical Journal, April 1917.)

ZIMMERMANN, A. *Geschichte der deutschen Kolonialpolitik*. Berlin, 1914.

MAPS

German South-West Africa is covered by the War Office Map (G.S.G.S. Provisional Map No. 2133), "German South-West Africa," on the scale of 1:3,000,000 (1914); also by sheets 113-115, 119, 120, 123, 124, 127-8 (old numbering) of the War Office Map of Africa (G.S.G.S. 1539).

War Office Maps (G.S.G.S. Nos 2914 *a*, *b*, and *c*) show, respectively, the disposition of the tribes in 1890, the rights of the principal land and mining companies, and the principal claim-holdings on the diamond fields of Lüderitz Bay.

HANDBOOKS PREPARED UNDER THE DIRECTION OF THE HISTORICAL SECTION OF THE FOREIGN OFFICE.—No. 113

TANGANYIKA

(GERMAN EAST AFRICA)

TABLE OF CONTENTS

TABLE OF CONTENTS

TABLE OF CONTENTS

PAGE

(D) FINANCE

(E) GENERAL REMARKS

APPENDIX

EXTRACTS FROM TREATIES.

AUTHORITIES

MAPS

Note.—In this book the name Tanganyika, now adopted for the British portion of what was German East Africa, has generally been used, excepting where conditions prevailing under German rule are in question. The western portion of German East Africa, consisting of the greater part of the districts of Ruanda and Urundi, which under present arrangements are to be administered by Belgium, is included in the survey as being formerly German territory.

I. GEOGRAPHY PHYSICAL AND POLITICAL

(1) POSITION AND FRONTIERS

TANGANYIKA lies between 1° and 11° 44′ S. latitude, and about 28° 50′ and 40° 35′ E. longitude; it marches with Kenya and Uganda in the north, with the Belgian Congo in the west, with Northern Rhodesia and Nyasaland in the south-west, and with Mozambique in the south. Its area is about 384,000 sq. miles.

From the mouth of the Umba the boundary between Kenya and Uganda, and Tanganyika, runs in a north-westerly direction towards Victoria Nyanza, but bends so as to pass north of Mount Kilimanjaro. It reaches the east shore of Victoria Nyanza at 1° south latitude and, after crossing the lake, continues along that parallel until it reaches the northern bend of the River Kagera, the course of which it follows as far as the Kakitumba confluence. It then turns south-west, leaving Mpororo in Uganda, and, after skirting the Mfumbiro region, joins the Belgian frontier on the summit of Mount Sabinio. From this point the boundary runs by Mounts Karisimbi and Hehu to the northern shore of Lake Kivu at a point half-way between Ngoma and Kissenyi. From here it proceeds south, leaving the islands of Kwijiri and Iwinje, with Gombo (formerly German), in the possession of Belgium. From Lake Kivu the boundary follows the valley of the River Rusizi, keeping to the chief western branch of its delta as far as Lake Tanganyika. It then follows the middle of Lake Tanganyika to the mouth of the River Kalambo at the southern end of the lake.

From this point the south-western boundary of Tanganyika follows a somewhat irregular course east-south-east to Lake Nyasa at the point where the River Songwe flows into the lake, and continues south-wards down the middle of Lake Nyasa to about 11° 34′

south latitude. The southern boundary, which divides Tanganyika from the Portuguese province of Mozambique, leaves the shore of Lake Nyasa in latitude 11° 34' 30" south and follows in general that parallel to the River Rovuma, a distance of about 34 miles. Thence the Rovuma forms the boundary to within about 30 miles of its mouth; there the frontier leaves the river and, after running parallel to its course for a short distance, turns due east, reaching the coast at Cape Delgado, leaving the lowest ford and the mouth in Tanganyika.

(2) Surface, Coast, River System, and Lakes

Surface

The territory of what was German East Africa has a varied surface, and for purposes of description may conveniently be considered under the following six headings: (1) the coastal region, (2) the Rand Mountains, (3) Kilimanjaro and Meru, (4) the East African plateau, (5) the Victoria Nyanza region, and (6) the region of the Western Rift.

(1) The *coastal region* occupies a narrow strip of country in the north of the territory between the Rand Mountains and the sea, and widens as it proceeds south until, in the country north of the Rovuma, it occupies the greater part of the territory. Its surface is broken by small plateaux, abrupt rocky *inselberge*, and considerable hill ranges. Both in climate and in vegetation the area is clearly divided into two sections: (*a*) the extensive region which includes the valley of the Rufiyi and stretches south to the Rovuma, and (*b*) the narrower strip north of the Rufiyi between the coast and the Nguru and Usambara mountains.

(*a*) The southern district is occupied by a series of small plateaux, of which the Makonde plateau is the most important, reaching an altitude of between 2,000 and 2,600 ft. These plateaux are badly watered and covered with dense bush. Farther north, in the neighbourhood of Kilwa, are the Matumbi hills, whose eastern slopes are well watered and fertile.

West of the Makonde and Mweru plateaux lies a badly watered country covered with myombo wood, which extends over the whole of the interior between the Rovuma and the Ubena. The Rovuma valley itself is rocky above the mouth.

In the north-west of this region lies the Mahenge district, which includes the Upogoro hills and the broad Ulanga depression. The low-lying alluvial plains of the River Ulanga are extremely fertile.

The plains north of the Rufiyi towards Kisaki have similar characteristics, but are covered with bush, and almost uninhabited. Farther down the river cultivation increases, and the alluvial lands of the delta are fairly well populated, though there is much jungle and mangrove swamp.

(*b*) The northern section of the coastal region includes the important district of the somewhat isolated Uluguru mountains. On the north-west these mountains rise abruptly above the surrounding plains to a height of 8,200 ft. Their surface is extraordinarily broken, and, except on the west, their slopes are covered with forest.

(2) The *Rand Mountains*, which form the eastern edge of the East African plateau, are divided into three sections by the rivers Ruaha and Pangani. To the south-west lie the highlands of Ungoni, Ubena, and Uhehe; between the Ruaha and the Pangani is the Central Plateau, fringed by the Nguru and Usagara mountains, and to the north lie the Usambara and Pare ranges.

(*a*) The Ungoni Highlands rise gradually from the upper Rovuma towards the Nyasa watershed, and consist of a well-watered fertile plateau lying at an altitude of 3,200 to 4,600 ft. They were formerly one of the best cultivated districts of the territory, and have been named "the granary of German East Africa;" but the population was enormously reduced by the suppression of the rising of 1905, and large districts are now covered with bush. From the Ungoni plateau the thinly-peopled but fertile Matumbi hills stretch northwards to the Ruhuje. These heights are lower than the northern part of the Ungoni plateau.

Beyond the Ruhuje rise the high plateaux of Ubena and Uhehe. These lie at a general altitude of 5,000 to 5,500 ft., but in parts of Uhehe especially considerably greater heights are attained. The plateaux consist for the most part of open grass-lands.

On the north-west the Uhehe plateau falls away to the Usungu depression, through which flows the Great Ruaha. This region suffers from drought in the dry season, and from inundation during the rains. The southern parts consist of open grass plains, and in the north there is open forest alternating with stretches of bush.

(b) Beyond the Ruaha depression, the Usagara—Nguru section of the Rand mountains runs north-west till it is broken by the Masai Steppe and the Pangani valley. It consists of three ranges, which are divided by the broad valleys of the Mukondokwa and the Mkundi. On the east the ranges rise abruptly out of the Useguha-Wami plains, and on the west slope gradually down to the Ugogo plateau and the Masai Steppe. The whole region contains much fertile land.

(c) The Usambara-Pare Range forms a wedge-shaped mountain mass which runs inland in a north-westerly direction from the Tanga-Pangani coast towards Kilimanjaro. It rises sheer on all sides from the surrounding plains, and has been cut into a number of different ranges by deep and broad valleys, of which the most important is that of the Mkomazi.

In the well-watered districts the vegetation is exceptionally rich, and the tropical rain forest of eastern Usambara is one of the most valuable forest regions of the Protectorate.

(3) The district of *Kilimanjaro and Meru* belongs to the southern extension of the volcanic region of British East Africa. The two mountains rise from the isolated level plateau. Kilimanjaro (Kilima-Njaro), which

consists of two peaks united by a saddle, is the highest mountain in Africa (19,391 ft.), and Meru (Mweru), which lies about 43 miles east-south-east, has an altitude of 14,960 ft. The mountain region consequently embraces every degree of climate from tropical to polar, and the middle zone might be suited to European settlement.

On both mountains the tropical rain-forest reaches up to a height of 6,500 ft. to 9,500 ft., but on Meru there is also a belt of forest of a much finer type between 4,600 and 6,000 ft.

(4) The *East African Plateau*, which occupies the greater part of the territory, is divided by the Rand mountains into two regions, namely (*a*) the interior region of the Masai Steppe and the Eastern Rift, and (*b*) the Unyamwezi or Central Plateau in the west.

(*a*) In Tanganyika the Eastern Rift loses much of its valley character; south of Lake Natron (Magad) the eastern wall falls away, and, past Lake Manyara as far as latitude 6° south, the western wall alone remains defined. West of this main depression are other smaller ones, the most important of which are those occupied by Lake Eyasi and Lake Hohenlohe.

The greater part of the region east of the Rift consists of dry steppe country covered with thorn scrub, which in some districts, e.g., the Masai Steppe and the Marenga-Makali plain, approaches desert conditions. Characteristic of the whole region are the salt lakes and swamps, such as the Wembere and the North Ugogo Steppes, in which the rivers lose themselves.

The only district which is sufficiently watered is the strip of highland country lying immediately to the west of the Eastern Rift, which has an altitude of between 5,000 and 11,000 ft. It attains its highest point in the Winter Highland south of Lake Natron, where the volcano of Lengai (Denyo-Ngai) is still active. The lower slopes of these highlands are covered with rain forest of the same type as that of Kilimanjaro, but above 6,500 ft. the wood gives place to high pastures, which are said to be suitable for European stock-raising.

(*b*) The Unyamwezi, or Central Plateau, extends from the watershed of Victoria Nyanza to the Rukwa depression, and from the western limits of the Eastern Rift region to the mountains east of Lake Tanganyika. It lies at an altitude of 3,600 to 4,300 ft. above the sea, and forms the water-parting between the rivers flowing towards the Atlantic and those flowing into the Indian Ocean. The climate is hot and dry, and the region possesses but one perennial river, the Malagarazi. The whole region is a great undulating plain broken by frequent granite tors and by occasional *inselberge*.

The north-western districts of Usumbwa and Uha represent a transition from the conditions of the plateau to those of the lake. The climate is equatorial, like that of the lake region, not of the trade-wind type which prevails in Unyamwezi.

(5) In the *Victoria Nyanza region* the plateau which stretches westwards through Karagwe, Ruanda, and Urundi to the Western Rift, falls abruptly to the western shores of Lakes Kivu and Tanganyika; transition from the plateau to Victoria Nyanza is gradual and broken in places by groups of hills.

To the east of the lake the grass-lands end in the barren Masai Steppe, but Ushashi and Usukuma are fertile. Usinja, south-west of the lake, is hilly and covered with myombo wood, and in the southern parts there is much dense bush. Beyond Usinja the Western Plateau rises immediately above the lake, and there is no low coastal strip. The only important island in the southern portion of the lake is Ukereve.

The western highlands rise in successive ranges from Victoria Nyanza towards Lake Kivu and the volcanic region to the north of it, and attain an altitude of over 9,000 ft. in the western part of the Ruanda highlands, while in Urundi, south of Ruanda, the hills are even higher. There is much virgin forest in the mountain districts of south-west Ruanda.

(6) The western frontier of the territory follows the line of the *Central African Rift* (Western Rift)

from the north end of Lake Kivu to the middle of Lake Nyasa, and this district may be considered as forming two sections, those of Kivu—Tanganyika to the north, and Rukwa—Nyasa to the south.

The region of the Western Rift consists of a very narrow lowland strip, which in some districts vanishes entirely, and a region of mountains and high broken plateaux which separate the Rift from the Central Plateau.

(*a*) Kivu—Tanganyika Section.—In the extreme north the mountains of western Ruanda descend abruptly to the narrow but fertile and well-peopled eastern shore of Lake Kivu, which is the highest lake of the Western Rift valley.

The coastal strip east of Lake Tanganyika is broader than that on the Belgian side of the lake. North of the Mlagarazi, the Urundi plateau rises above the lake, and to the south are the picturesque highlands of Utongwe and Uwende. On the south-east the Ufipa plateau, consisting of well-watered and fertile grasslands, rises steeply between Lake Tanganyika and the Rukwa depression, and is continued southward by the Urungu plateau into Nyasaland.

(*b*) Rukwa—Nyasa Section.—The Rukwa depression has a length of about 180 miles and a breadth of 15 to 37 miles. Lake Rukwa occupies the southern part of this and fluctuates considerably in area. South-east of the lake lies the mountainous district of Ukimbu. It is dry, and covered by a light steppe forest. The great Nyasa depression is bordered on the north-east by the Livingstone Mountains (highest altitude about 9,840 ft.), which descend sheer to the lake. North of Lake Nyasa is the alluvial Konde plain, which is blocked by a great mountain mass from which rises the peak of Rungwe, the highest mountain in Nyasaland.[1] Between the Konde mountains and the River Songwe rise the Bundali uplands.

---

[1] The height of this mountain has been variously given by different authorities as 9,850, 10,416, and 14,000 ft.

Thus practically the whole of this section consists of highland country, and mountain pasture is the predominant type of vegetation, the only important exception being the fruitful Konde plain. The Konde and Bundali uplands are also fertile, and support a very large population. On Rungwe and the other important heights there is a zone of virgin forest above the limit of native settlement (about 5,000 ft.).

The northern section of the Livingstone Mountains has a cool and moderately dry climate, and is said to be suitable for European settlement, Buanyi, the district east of the Elton plateau, being particularly healthy.

Coast

The coast, about 470 miles in length, is uniformly difficult to approach owing to its shelving character, to the numerous coral reefs, and to the changing bars at the mouths of the rivers. There are, however, several good natural harbours, notably Kilwa Kisivani or Old Kilwa, about 15 miles south of Kilwa Kivinje, and Mikindani Bay, 40 miles south-east of Lindi. Neither of these has up to the present been much used. Tanga and Dar es-Salaam are the only large ports which possess really good harbours.

There are three large islands off the coast: Zanzibar, which is the natural centre for the trade of the territory, Pemba, and Mafia. Of these, Mafia, which alone forms part of Tanganyika, is a low island, fringed with mangrove swamps, about 27 miles long and with a maximum width of 9 miles. Besides these there are numerous small coral islands.

The low shore of the mainland is either sandy or fringed with mangroves; behind it rises a coral terrace from 30 to 80 ft. high, and at a comparatively short distance from the sea the surface rises again sharply to the region of the coastal back-country.

River System

The coastal drainage area, to which all the impor- tant rivers belong, consists of the coastal region described above, together with the Rand mountains. It is therefore comparatively narrow in the north of the territory, and widens out greatly south and west of Usagara. In the south it comes at many points within a few miles of Lake Nyasa.

By far the most important of the coast rivers is the Rufiyi, which includes in its basin about one quarter of the whole territory. In spite, however, of the vast area of its drainage system and the size of its delta, the volume of water in the dry season is not great, and the river is of little value for navigation. The river consists of two main branches, of which the northern is formed by the junction of the Kizigo and the Ruaha, and the southern, known in part of its course as the Ulanga, is formed by the junction of the Kilimbero and the Luvegu. The first branch drains Ubena, Usunga, Usagara, and the south-eastern part of the Central Plateau; the second Mahenge and a part of Ungoni and Uhehe.

The Rovuma, which rises in the Ungoni highlands near Songea, forms for the greater part of its course the frontier between the territory and Portuguese East Africa (Mozambique), but the mouth is entirely in Tanganyika. Its chief drainage area lies to the south in Portuguese Nyasaland.

The most important river in the north of the territory is the Pangani or Ruvu, which rises on the slopes of Kilimanjaro, and flows to the sea between the Masai Steppe and the Pare-Usambara mountains.

Farther south the Wami waters northern Usagara and the neighbouring districts, and the Kingani drains the Uluguru mountains and Uzaramo. Owing to the large rainfall in these districts, the latter is an important river in spite of its small drainage area. The other coast rivers, e.g., the Matandu, the Mbemkuru, and the Lukuledi, are intermittent in flow, except in the lower parts of their courses.

The rivers belonging to the region of the East African Rift are of little importance, owing to the low rainfall which prevails in that district. They either flow into the lakes of the Rift Valley or lose themselves in the steppes.

There are a certain number of rivers which flow into the various great lakes. Of these the chief is the Kagera, a large and very important river, head of the Nile system, which drains the greater part of the Ruanda and Urundi regions, and finally flows into the western side of Victoria Nyanza, just over the border of Uganda. Many of the smaller lakes to the west of Victoria Nyanza (see below) also communicate with the Kagera, and feed its upper waters.

Lake Tanganyika has one important affluent, the Mlagarazi, which drains south-western Urundi and the Uha and Uvinza districts. Its eastern and southern tributaries drain the greater part of the Unyamwezi plateau, but these are only of importance during the rainy season. Lake Tanganyika is intermittently connected with the Congo system by the small river Lukuga.

The only important affluent of Lake Nyasa is the Ruhuhu, which drains a part of the Ungoni highlands.

Lakes

Victoria Nyanza, the largest lake in Africa, occupies an area of about 27,000 square miles (including islands), and has a length and breadth of about 220 miles, with a depth of about 228 ft. It possesses few good harbours, and the best anchorages are on the low and broken southern coast. The most important port situated in Tanganyika is Mwanza, at the southern extremity of the lake.

In the plateau west of Victoria Nyanza there are numerous small lakes which lie in three groups: (1) north-west on either side of the Uganda frontier; (2) in the Kisaka district and East Ruanda; and (3) in Karagwe. Most of these communicate with the Kagera River, but Lake Mohazi in the Kisaka group and Lake Ikimba in Karagwe are without outlets.

Lake Kivu, which lies at an altitude of 4,920 ft.

above the sea, has a length of about 60 miles and a maximum breadth of 30 miles. Its coast is excessively broken. It drains into Lake Tanganyika, 74 miles to the south, by the River Rusizi.

Lake Tanganyika is about 400 miles long, with a maximum breadth of 56 miles, and a maximum depth of 4,758 ft. Its area as measured on the best maps varies from 12,300 to 12,400 square miles, and earlier estimates appear to be excessive. The coast is often precipitous and the harbours are few and poor. The waters of the lake are brackish, owing to the salt brought down by the Mlagarazi.

Lake Rukwa, a small and shallow lake of very variable dimensions, is without outlet, and drains a considerable tract of country in the south of the Central Plateau. The water is brackish.

Lake Nyasa, the third largest lake in Africa, has a length of about 360 miles, a width of from 50 to 15 miles, and a greatest known depth of 2,316 ft. The section of the lake bordered by Tanganyika is badly provided with harbours.

The region of the Eastern Rift contains three important lakes : the *Natron (Magad)*, *Eyasi (Nyarasa)*, and *Manyara*. All of these are very salt and have no outlets.

(3) CLIMATE

The climate of Tanganyika is determined by its latitude and its position relatively to the Indian Ocean, which is considerably warmer than the Atlantic. Generally speaking the rainfall is low for a tropical country and varies greatly from year to year, while in some years there are great droughts. Three types of climate are to be distinguished : (1) the Indian or trade-wind type, which prevails over the greater part of the country; (2) the monsoon type, which prevails in the north-east; (3) the equatorial type, which prevails in the north-west.

(1) The first type of climate is influenced primarily

by the south-east trade-winds. It has only one rainy season in the year, and its hottest period is at the end of November, immediately before the beginning of the rainy season. The coolest and driest period of the year is from June to August, when the south-east trade-winds blow. Thereafter it becomes increasingly warmer until the rainy season, which lasts from December till April, with the heaviest rainfall from December to February. The winds during the rainy season are weak, and vary from north-east to south.

(2) The region where the monsoon type of climate prevails is bounded by a line running from the mouth of the Rufiyi through the territory to the north-west, including the countries of Uluguru and Unguru, together with most of the smaller northern lakes except Eyasi (Nyarasa). Usagara, Ugogo, South Unyamwezi, and Tabora are included in this region.

The monsoon type of climate has two rainy seasons. The south-east trade-wind prevails to a great extent from June to September, but gradually turns to the south and passes into the south-west monsoon. This period, during which the winds blow from south-east to south-west, is the cool and dry season.

After the southern winter, the north-east monsoon gradually prevails. There is an interval of varying and gentle winds, which give rise to the lesser rainy season at the end of October or in November. When the north-east monsoon establishes itself there follows the driest and warmest period of the year (December to February). The hottest month is February, just before the beginning of the great rainy season.

During the interval of uncertain winds between the departure of the north-east monsoon and the return of the south-east to south-west winds, which prevail between June and September, is the greater rainy season from March to May, with extraordinarily copious rainfall. In the mountainous districts there is generally a third rainy season in July.

(3) The north-west or equatorial region is bounded roughly by a line drawn from south of Ujiji to the

southern end of Lake Manyara, and from there due north. It includes the country west of Victoria Nyanza and Victoria Nyanza itself, together with the large districts of Usukuma, North Unyamwezi, and Uha, and the country round Lake Tanganyika as far south as Ujiji.

The equatorial climate is distinguished from the other two in that it has two warmer and two cooler seasons, with two rainy seasons separated by a short abatement of the rains. The two warmer periods are October and February-March, the two cooler July and November-December, i.e., the warmer periods are when the sun is above the equator, the cooler when it is at its farthest north and south. The variation in temperature between the coolest and warmest months is slight. In Ujiji, for instance, which has an average yearly temperature of 75° F. (24° C.), the seasonal range is only about 4·5° F.

Easterly winds prevail in this district. From May to August the south-east trade-wind blows hard, and the dry season lasts from May to September (Victoria Nyanza) or even October (Tanganyika). The rainy season is from October to May (Victoria Nyanza) or November to April (Tanganyika). There is a short abatement in the middle of the rainy season about January, which divides it into two parts. The influence of the north-east monsoon does not extend so far inland, and the climate is affected considerably by the local winds in the basins of the great lakes, and by calms.

The varying heights above sea-level of different parts of the country also give rise to a considerable variety of local climates, and from this point of view we may distinguish six climatic levels:—

(1) The warm and rather damp coast-region (up to rather more than 300 ft. above sea-level). The characteristics of this part of the country are high humidity of atmosphere, moderate rainfall, and a temperature moderated by the neighbourhood of the sea. Average yearly temperature 78° F. (25·5° C.); yearly variation on the northern coast 12° to 14° F., on the

southern coast 20° F. Daily variations in the extreme months on the northern coast 11° to 16° F., on the southern coast 20° to 22° F.

(2) The hot and moderately dry zone between the coast and the ranges which bound the Central Plateau (300-1,600 ft.). Here the characteristics are low humidity of atmosphere, less rain, and a rather lower yearly temperature, but greater daily and yearly variations.

(3) The moderately warm and moist zone of the eastern slopes of the ranges which bound the central plateau (1,600-6,500 ft. and above). The characteristics are high humidity of atmosphere, heavy showers almost daily, and a somewhat lower temperature, although with greater extremes.

(4) The hot and dry zone of the Central Plateau (average height 4,000 ft.), the climate of which of course differs greatly in different places. Its prevailing characteristics are, however, very low humidity of atmosphere (at Tabora under 40 per cent.), little rainfall (at Tabora 32 in. or 810 mm.), a fairly high mean temperature (at Tabora, July, 70° F. or 21° C.), and great daily and yearly variations (at Tabora sometimes exceeding 36° F. or 20° C. daily).

(5) The cool and moist zone of the sub-alpine heights (6,000-10,000 ft.). To this belong the lower parts of the heights mentioned under (6), and the higher peaks of Usambara, Unguru, Usagara, Uluguru, Uhehe, Konde, and Ruanda, with the Livingstone mountains and the volcanic district west of the Eastern Rift. The characteristics here are high humidity of atmosphere, much mist, and fairly low yearly temperature, with great extremes.

(6) The cold and dry alpine zone above 10,000 ft. This includes Mounts Kilimanjaro, Meru, Karisimbi on the Congo border, Lomalasin, Rungwe, and a few other mountains. The characteristics of this zone are low humidity of atmosphere, little rain, snow, and a low temperature, with very great extremes.

(4) Sanitary Conditions

Malaria is prevalent throughout Tanganyika, and is the most serious obstacle to European settlement, being common even in the high districts of the interior. The coastal regions are specially affected, and the Bismarckburg district south-east of Lake Tanganyika also has a very bad reputation. There are, however, many districts, such as Usambara, the slopes of Kilimanjaro and Meru, and the volcanic highlands of Ruanda and Urundi, which are perfectly suitable for habitation by Europeans, although cases of malaria may be met with even at a height of 4,500 ft. The German Government undertook energetic measures against the disease at Dar es-Salaam and Tanga, which were attended with some degree of success.

Other diseases affecting Europeans are blackwater fever, dysentery, and recurrent fever. The last, which is often known as tick-fever, is also very common among the natives, and is carried by infection along the chief caravan routes, especially along that from Mwanza to Tabora.

Sleeping sickness occurs in two forms: (1) The form carried by the tsetse fly (*glossina palpalis*), which has been introduced on both sides of Victoria Nyanza from Uganda, and also on the east coast of Lake Tanganyika from the Congo, the latter district being especially affected. The Government attempted to stamp out the disease by segregating the infected persons in concentration camps and by destroying the breeding-places of the fly; and in the Victoria Nyanza districts the disease is now said to be well under control. (2) The Rhodesian form of the disease, which is carried by *glossina morsitans*, and occurs on the upper Rovuma.

Ankylostomiasis (hook-worm disease) is almost universal among the natives of the Protectorate, but has been combated by sanitary measures and by treatment with thymol. Much mortality among the natives has also been caused in the past by small-pox. Systematic vaccination, however, has recently been carried out, and in 1909-10 about 800,000 natives were inoculated. Leprosy is also very widespread.

Plague, which was formerly endemic at places in the Iringa district, is sometimes introduced at Mwanza and the coast ports.   The last outbreak occurred in 1914 at Dar es-Salaam.

There are two large hospitals at Dar es-Salaam and Tanga, and a fine Government sanatorium in the west Usambara mountains.

(5) Race and Language
Race

There are traces in Tanganyika of the existence of an aboriginal population of Bushman-Pygmy type, but the racial foundation of the population of the Protectorate is formed by Bantu peoples.   The different tribes are distinguished by the districts in which they dwell, as the Wanyamwezis of Unyamwezi, the Wazaramos of Uzaramo, and so on.[1]   The open character of the interior has facilitated tribal migrations, and there has been little opportunity for the evolution of strongly differentiated types.   The population have, however, been subjected to more external influences than any other portion of the Bantu race, and the invading peoples have communicated something of their blood and culture to the tribes with which they came in contact.   These invading peoples are : (1) the Wahimas (or Watusis) in the north-west; (2) the Masais in the north-east; (3) the Wangoni-Zulus in the south; (4) the Arab-Swahilis on the coast and in the centre.   Roughly speaking, the population of the whole Protectorate may therefore be divided into these four sections.

(1) The *Wahimas* or *Watusis* are a pastoral people of Hamitic race, dwelling in the region lying between the great equatorial lakes.   They are most numerous and the type is purest in the districts of Ruanda, Mpororo, and Urundi, while they are also found in smaller

[1] In Bantu *U* denotes country, *Wa* people, and *Ki* language.

numbers and much mixed with the Bantu throughout the north-western districts. The Watusis of Ruanda, and to a less extent of Urundi and Uha, have organized a strong feudal social system, in which the Bantu natives, known as Wahutus, who make up from 95 to 99 per cent. of the population, occupy a semi-servile status. In certain districts the ruling chiefs are of Watusi blood, and a considerable number of Watusi cattle-keepers are to be found throughout Unyamwezi.

(2) The *Masais*, also of Hamitic race, are warlike nomads, who formerly wandered with their herds throughout the Masai Steppe. The majority of the Masais of Tanganyika occupy a reserve south of Mount Meru. The Masais, like the Wahimas, are dolichocephalous and remarkably tall and slender, while in colour they are considerably lighter than the negro.

Two other tribes of Hamitic stock, the Wanderobbos and the Wakwafis, closely allied to the Masais, are found in the Masai Steppe. They do not possess the strong tribal organization of the Masais, and exist by hunting rather than by war and cattle-farming.

Throughout the country between the Pare mountains and Victoria Nyanza on the one hand, and the Rhodesian frontier and the south of Ugogo on the other, all the native tribes have been affected by contact and intermixture with the Masais. On the east coast of Victoria Nyanza the Wageias of Kavirondo seem to belong to the Nilotic negro race, and the Wasandawis and Wakindigas in different districts of the Eastern Rift are said to represent the aboriginal Bushman race. With these exceptions, however, the tribes of this region are Bantu, more or less modified by Hamitic blood and influence.

(3) The *Wangonis*, a Bantu people of Zulu stock, are established in the highlands east of Lake Nyasa. From this centre, which became known as Ungonis, they raided far into the interior of the territory. The Wahehes succeeded in repelling the Wangonis by

adopting their own weapons and military organisation, and in this way Wangoni influence may be said to extend to all the tribes conquered by the Wahehes as well as to those conquered by the Wangonis themselves.

The Wangonis were variously known as Magwangwaras, Mafitis, Mazitus, and Watutas in the different districts in which they raided, and these names were also applied to any tribe like the Wahehe using Zulu weapons. Owing to wholesale inter-marriage and the embodiment of conquered peoples in the Wangoni tribe, a Wangoni racial type can hardly be said to exist.

(4) *Arab-Swahilis*. Of all the external influences that have operated on the peoples of the territory, that of the Arabs has been by far the most important. Arab and Persian (Shirati) colonies have been established on the coast for a thousand years; the great period of Arab influence in the interior, however, was in the nineteenth century under the Omanian rulers of Zanzibar. The number of pure Arabs in the interior was always very small, and it is now quite negligible, but their influence survives and extends itself in the bastard Swahili race and culture.

Swahili was originally the name given to the descendants of the Arab and Persian settlers in the islands of Lamu and Patta, who spoke a mixed Arab-Bantu tongue. By degrees the name was extended to all those who spoke the language, that is to say, to all the natives who are under the influence of Arab and Mohammedan civilization. Thus practically the whole coast population is Swahili; and, as this element is naturally adapted to be the intermediary between the ruling race, whether Arab or European, and the natives, every extension of civilization and government control in the interior brings with it an increase in Swahili influence. Tabora is one of the strongest and oldest centres of Swahili influence in the interior, and Swahili traders and minor officials are to be found everywhere along the railways and in the administrative centres.

Bantu Tribes.—The most important peoples as yet not mentioned are the Wanyamwezis and Wasumbwas of the Central Plateau, from whom the bulk of the plantation labour has been drawn in the past; the Wakondes, who inhabit the fertile northern end of Lake Nyasa; and the Yaos on the Rovuma. The peoples of the coastal back-country, such as the Wamakondes and the Wamweras, are for the most part barbarous and timid, and of little value for the development of the territory.

Language

The vast majority of the inhabitants of the territory speak various forms of Bantu. The Masais and Wanderobbos have preserved their original Hamitic tongue, which has had some influence on the surrounding Bantu dialects. The Wahimas have adopted the Bantu speech of the conquered race. The Wasandawis in Ugogo and one or two other tribes farther north are said to speak a primitive non-Bantu language similar to Hottentot. Swahili is understood almost everywhere in the territory, and is the recognised language of administration and commerce.

(6) POPULATION

Distribution

The total native population was estimated to be about 7,641,800 in March 1913. It was distributed as follows among the various districts:—

District.	Population.	Density per square mile.
Ruanda	2,000,000	187
Urundi	1,500,000	132
Tanga	108,400	61
Dar es-Salaam	161,500	39
Bukoba	270,500	26

District.	Population.	Density per square mile.
Rufiyi	89,100	26
Moshi	118,300	24
Mwanza	620,000	24
Lindi	395,500	22
Pangani	98,500	18
Langenburg	195,800	17
Wilhelmstal	98,600	16
Ujiji	240,000	15·9
Morogoro	158,400	12
Bagamoyo	72,800	12
Tabora	437,500	10·6
Dodoma	299,400	10·4
Kondoa-Irangi	218,300	10·4
Mahenge	120,000	9
Arusha	84,200	6·2
Kilwa	93,000	4·1
Songea	90,300	4·1
Iringa	90,000	3·4
Bismarckburg	81,700	2·3

The total white population at the same date was
5,336, of which 4,107 were of German nationality and
90 of British. In 1912 there were 128 British and 268
" Colonial English," chiefly Boers. The coloured
population other than native was 14,933 in 1912.

As will be seen from the above statistics, population
is thickest in the north-western districts between the
lakes and in the coastal region. In Ruanda and Urundi
the chief cause of the density has been the existence of
strongly organized native states which imposed discipline on the natives and prevented depopulation by
war. In the south-west of the territory a densely populated district occurs in Kondeland at the north end of
Lake Nyasa. The coast districts owe their comparative
density of population to the presence of the coast towns
and the European plantations, which draw large
numbers of native labourers from the interior to

Usambara, &c. The thinly-peopled districts of the interior can be divided into two classes: the steppe regions and the districts depopulated by war. The former includes the Masai Steppe, Ugogo, and the country east of the Rukwa depression. Instances of the latter are the Songea district and the highlands south-west of Lake Natron. The warlike races of Tanganyika, the Masais, the Wahehes, and, above all, the Wangonis, have depopulated the districts most exposed to their raids, and the Masais themselves have been almost exterminated by the loss of their cattle from disease (*cf.* below, p. 34).

Towns and Villages

Tanganyika possesses a number of comparatively large and important towns dating from the period of the supremacy of Zanzibar. These lie along the great trade-route which crossed Lake Tanganyika from the Congo to Ujiji, and ran through Tabora, Kilimatinde, and Mpapwa to the coast at Sadani or Bagamoyo, and so to Zanzibar.

The prosperity of these places was ruined by the suppression of the slave trade and the fiscal closing of the Congo frontier, but Tabora still remains the largest town in the territory, with 40,000 inhabitants (1907); Ujiji also has a considerable population (14,000).

Few towns of any importance have grown up during the German occupation. The largest are the inland port of Mwanza on Victoria Nyanza (population about 14,000), Moshi (6,000, including 800 white men), and Wilhelmstal. Of the coast towns the largest is Dar es-Salaam, the seat of government, which has a population of 25,000, of whom about 1,000 are white men. Tanga and Bagamoyo are also important places on the coast.

Movement

The natural increase of the population of the territory has been greatly checked in the past by war. The period of native wars, which depopulated whole tracts of country, was followed by the risings against the German Government, which were suppressed with great loss of life. The most serious of these, that of 1905-7, is recent enough for its results to be still visible throughout the southern districts. The great epidemic of rinderpest in the early days of the German occupation also had a very adverse influence on the growth of the pastoral tribes, especially on that of the Masais. There has also been a tendency towards the depopulation of certain districts through labour emigration; for example in some parts of Unyamwezi and Usumbwa the decrease in population has been as much as 14 per cent. between 1910 and 1913. This is not, of course, sheer loss, but nevertheless the class of plantation labourers have a larger death-rate and a smaller birth-rate than other parts of the population, and in consequence there is a serious drain from this cause.

There has been a considerable increase in the European population of late years, but it has consisted for the most part of officials, missionaries, soldiers, and engineers. The class of true settlers, i.e., planters and farmers, numbered 758 in January 1912, and was settled principally in the Usambara and Kilimanjaro districts. This class consisted mainly of Germans, but there was also a considerable number of Boers, and many British and Greeks were settled on Kilimanjaro and Meru.

A large number of Asiatics have entered the territory as small traders, artisans, &c. In 1912 the total non-native population, excluding Europeans, amounted to 14,933. The majority of these were British Indians, but Goanese, Arabs, and Levantines are also numerous.

II. POLITICAL HISTORY

CHRONOLOGICAL SUMMARY

1505   Foundation of Kilwa fort by the Portuguese.
1587   Sack of Kilwa by Zimba.
1698   Occupation of mainland of Zanzibar by Muscat Arabs.
1784   Revolt of Mombasa against the Seyyids of Muscat.
1832   Seyyid Said subdues Mombasa and makes Zanzibar his capital.
1832-40   Extension of his rule on mainland.
1856   Death of Seyyid Said.
1858   Burton travels through Unyamwezi to Ujiji.
1858 (Aug. 3)   Speke discovers south coast of Victoria Nyanza.
1861-62   Speke's second expedition to Victoria Nyanza.
1870   Seyyid Majid dies and Bargash succeeds.
1877   Lease of the mainland offered by Bargash to Mackinnon.
1884   Peters obtains his first treaties from the natives.
1886   First agreement with England.
1887   Charter given by Germany to the German East African Association.
1888   Occupation of the coast and Arab rising.
1889   Wissmann appointed Imperial Commissioner.
        German Protectorate proclaimed (Oct. 22).
1890 (July 1)   Treaty with England.
1891 (Jan.)   Imperial Government takes over East Africa from the German East African Association.
        First Governor appointed.
        Usambara Railway begun.
        (Aug.)   Destruction of von Zelewski's expedition.
1892 (June)   Fighting at Tabora and Kilimanjaro.
1893   Tabora Boma stormed.
        Usambara Railway opened to Pongwe.
        Fighting near Kilwa.
        Exploration between Victoria Nyanza and Lake Tanganyika.
1895   Wissmann appointed Governor.
1896   Severe fighting in Uhehe. Iringa taken.
        Liebert appointed Governor.
1897   Hut-tax introduced.
1900   Steamer launched on Lake Tanganyika.
1901   Von Götzen appointed Governor.
1902   Usambara Railway opened to Korogwe.
1904   Usambara Railway reaches Mombo.

1905 Central (Dar es-Salaam to Tabora) Railway begun.
      Outbreak of great rising in the south.
1906-10 Dernburg Colonial Secretary.
1906-12 Von Rechenberg Governor.
1907 Suppression of rising.
1908 Central Railway reaches Morogoro.
1909 Central Railway reaches Kilossa.
1910 Boundary Protocol between Great Britain and Germany
      and Belgium.
1910-11 Lindequist Colonial Secretary.
1911 Dr. Solf Colonial Secretary.
1912 Usambara Railway extended to Moshi.
      Central Railway reaches Tabora.
      Schnee becomes Governor.
1914 Central Railway reaches Kigoma, on Lake Tanganyika.

i. EARLY HISTORY

FOR the early history of European dealings with this country reference may be made to *Mozambique*, No. 121 of this series, p. 22. The whole coast of Italian, British, and German East Africa was in the sixteenth century under Portuguese influence, but no permanent Portuguese post was maintained within the limits of what was lately the German colony. The fort which was built at Kilwa in 1505 was abandoned after a few years, and the government was carried on from Mozambique or Mombasa. Kilwa, however, remained an important post under Portuguese suzerainty until the end of the seventeenth century.

Kilwa was the capital of an Arab kingdom whose power extended from Sofāla, in the south, nearly to Mombasa, in the north. It was identical with Kilwa Kisivani or Island Kilwa, being situated on an island in the bay to which the name "Kilwa" properly belongs. Here are the remains of the fort already mentioned, and those of mosques and other Arab buildings.[1] The modern port of Kilwa, which was the headquarters of a German district, is about twelve miles to the north. It was

---

[1] Burton, *Zanzibar: City, Island, and Coast*, vol. ii, p. 342; Strandes, *Die Portugiesenzeit von Deutsch- und Englisch-Ostafrika*, pp. 62-65, 86, 88.

founded in the early part of the nineteenth century by fugitives driven out by Seyyid Said. Its name is properly Kilwa Kivinje, which Strandes interprets as Kilwa "of the *casuarinas*" (i.e., the *Casuarina equisetifolia*, a tree well-known on hot lowlands).

After the Portuguese conquest Kilwa remained tributary under its native rulers. In 1587 it was sacked by an invading army of Zimbas, a Bantu race of cannibals, who afterwards came into contact with Turkish invaders at Mombasa. It seems to have lost its prosperity after this time, and in 1698, with the rest of this coast, it fell into the hands of Saif bin Sultan, Imâm of Muscat.

The island of Zanzibar soon became the centre of Arab rule. The recovery of Portuguese power for a few years (*c.* 1728) was only temporary; the power of Muscat continued to increase; and when Seyyid Said left Muscat and made Zanzibar his residence, his ships were able to establish his power along the coast.

Until the time of Seyyid Said, who began to rule in 1804, the power of the Imâms was intermittent. The internal dissensions of Oman prevented any effective exertion of force in East Africa; and the attacks of the Wahhabis still further weakened the rulers. The defeat of the Wahhabis by the Government of Mehemet Ali of Egypt in 1813, and the suppression of the pirates of the Persian Gulf by the British in 1819, followed by Sir L. Smith's expedition to the Persian Gulf in 1821, relieved Sultan Said of many of his difficulties, and enabled him to turn his attention to Africa.

In 1824 Captain Owen, of the frigate *Leven*, having made a treaty with the Benu Mazruis, an Arab tribe which was in possession of Mombasa, proclaimed a British protectorate. Against this Sultan Said, as suzerain of the tribe, protested; the Government of India admitted his contention, and annulled the treaty. During the years 1829-32 Said attacked Mombasa, and eventually subdued it after desperate fighting, several times renewed. He then made Zanzibar his headquarters, and took up his residence there in 1832.   He commenced a series of expeditions against the Swahili tribes of the mainland, and attacked the ports over which his family had claimed or exercised power, until ultimately the whole coast of what became German and British East Africa accepted his rule.   Mogadishu, Barawa, and the islands of the Lamu archipelago admitted his suzerainty; and his claims (although he could not enforce them) extended to Aden, Berbera, and Zaila.   The islands of Zanzibar, Pemba, and Mafia were under his immediate rule.

Said was a good ruler of the Oriental pattern, and promoted the prosperity of his dominions.   Among other things he introduced the clove-tree into Zanzibar and Pemba, which now supply the greater part of the cloves for the whole world.   In 1856 he died; and from that time Zanzibar has been entirely separate from Muscat.   Said's fourth son, Majid, obtained the African possessions on condition of an annual payment to Thuwainy, who retained Muscat. These terms were settled by the arbitration of the Viceroy of India, whose award, dated April 2, 1861, was accepted by both parties.   It was followed on March 10, 1862, by a joint declaration of Great Britain and France, in which they reciprocally engaged to respect the independence of Zanzibar.   Majid died in 1870, and was succeeded by his brother, Bargash. Throughout the reign of these Sultans the British Agent at Zanzibar exercised great influence over the whole coast; and the Sultans, both before and after the separation from Muscat, had practically no relations with any other European Power, though certain other Powers had rights of consular jurisdiction within their dominions.

The Arab rule over the seaboard was generally admitted; but there was no agreement as to its extent inland.   The trade of the ports was mainly in the hands of British-Indian subjects, Hindu and Mohammedan; but the inland trade was almost entirely in slaves, and was worked only by

Arabs. Sir John Kirk, who long occupied the post of British Consul at Zanzibar, and exercised great influence in the time of Seyyid Bargash, held (in 1885) that—

> "the Sultan's authority is weak in this direction " [*i.e.*, in the interior], " and can only be said to be felt on the trade routes, though undoubtedly he has, through his subjects, a certain power in places far distant, as Manyema, for instance."

Considering all the circumstances of the British connection with East Africa, the British Government might at any time have proclaimed a protectorate of the whole country up to the Great Lakes, had it chosen to do so. The influence of Sir John Kirk was very great; and in commercial matters Mr. (afterwards Sir) William Mackinnon was also in a position of great power. In 1877 he was actually offered a concession and seventy years' lease of the Customs and administration of the whole area later comprised in British and German East Africa. But the Foreign Office refused its sanction, the British Government being here, as elsewhere in Africa, unwilling to increase its responsibilities.

ii. German Interests in East Africa

Before the year 1884 Germany had had no official connection with East Africa, though a German trading firm had long had its headquarters at Zanzibar. Among other German missionaries, Krapf and Rebmann had studied the races and languages of the country, and had made some journeys of exploration, discovering the mountains of Kenya and Kilimanjaro. Much information as to East Africa had thus been accumulated and made available in Germany. After the conclusion of the Franco-Prussian War in 1871 some leading Germans began to advocate tropical colonization in this and other regions. Among them may be mentioned Vice-Admiral Livonius, who recommended a protectorate of Zanzibar, and E. von Weber, who demanded the annexation of the region of the Juba river. But the French also had commercial interests on this coast, and had enquired into its history and trade, Captain Guillain, of the French Navy, being one of the principal authorities on these subjects. There was therefore no ground before 1884 for supposing that Germany had any special claims to consideration in East Africa, or that her rulers contemplated any settlement there.[1]

In that year, however, Dr. Karl Peters, Dr. Jühlke, and Count J. Pfeil found their way into the Usagara highlands, and obtained from local chiefs a number of treaties ceding extensive rights to the German Colonization Society. On the strength of these treaties the Society was granted by the German Government a charter giving it sovereign rights over the large tract of country between the dominions of Zanzibar and Lake Tanganyika.   A number of similar expeditions followed, by means of which treaties of the same nature were obtained as far south as the boundary of the Portuguese province of Mozambique, and as far inland as the shores of Lakes Tanganyika and Nyasa. To the north, other treaties were obtained from the Sultan of Witu and neighbouring chiefs, upon which claims were based not only to the coast between the Tana and Juba rivers, but also to a territory extending far inland—claims which threatened to shut off British expansion from the regions of the Upper Nile.

The Sultan of Zanzibar protested in vain against the infringement of his rights, but, not being supported by the British Government, he yielded to threats of force, accompanied by the despatch of a German squadron to Zanzibar. The British point of view was that no opposition should be offered to German expansion within certain limits; and Sir John Kirk was instructed to act in accordance with this decision.

---

[1] See also *Kenya*, No. 96 of this series p. 45,

iii. Relations and Agreements between Great Britain and Germany

After Lord Salisbury's accession to office in 1885, a joint British, French, and German Commission was appointed to determine the precise limits of the sovereignty of the Sultan of Zanzibar, the British commissioner being the future Lord Kitchener. The Commission reported in June 1886; and, following on their report, an Anglo-German Agreement was concluded on October 29/November 1, 1886, which was accepted, under pressure from the British Government, by the Sultan of Zanzibar on December 4. It recognised the Sultan's rights over the whole coast from the Portuguese border in the south to the mouth of the Tana river in the north, for a depth of 10 miles inland, and to certain other ports north of the Tana, together with the islands of Zanzibar, Pemba, Lamu, and Mafia; but his claim to the vast inland territory was not recognised. He was invited to lease to the German African Company the Customs duties at the ports of Dar es-Salaam and Pangani, in return for an annual payment by the Company; and Germany adhered to the Anglo-French Declaration of 1862, which recognised the independence of Zanzibar. The agreement drew a line of demarcation between British and German spheres of influence in East Africa. In the following July (1887) the two Governments agreed that each would discourage attempts at annexation by their citizens in the rear of the other's sphere.

As soon as the Agreement of 1886 had been concluded the German Company's agents set to work to induce the Sultan to cede his rights on the mainland; and a lease of these rights for fifty years, subject to certain payments, was obtained on April 28, 1888. A similar concession in the British sphere had been made on May 24, 1887, to the British East African Association, incorporated in 1888 by

Royal Charter as the Imperial British East Africa Company. Having obtained their concession, the German Company, incorporated by Imperial Charter in March 1887, and thenceforth known as the German East African Association, took over, on August 16, 1888, the administration of the whole of the coastal districts now included in Tanganyika.

Meanwhile, Dr. Peters had embarked on a new adventure. He proposed an expedition for the relief of Schnitzer, better known as Emin Pasha, who was isolated at Wadelai, on the Upper Nile, and obtained a promise of co-operation from Major H. Wissmann, who had crossed Africa from west to east some years before. Just at that time the outbreak among the natives of the east coast, which is mentioned below, took place. The German Consul-General, Dr. Michahelles, recommended that Wissmann should be appointed Imperial Commissioner (*Reichskommissar*) of the new territories, where signs of dis turbance were appearing. Wissmann, who was accordingly appointed in February 1889, immediately took up this work, and the relief expedition fell through for the time; it was, however, revived in 1890, though not looked on with much favour by the German Government.

That Government was then endeavouring to negotiate a general settlement of outstanding questions with England, and saw a danger in Peters' endeavours to open up a passage from the neighbourhood of Witu to the Upper Nile. The news of Stanley's success in relieving Emin Pasha was received while Peters, after evading an English squadron which was co-operating in the German blockade of the coast, was making his way into the interior. His expedition of relief fell through; but by the exercise of his peculiar gifts he was able to obtain treaties which ceded extensive rights to Germany. These were all abandoned in the ensuing Agreement with England. Bismarck had never intended any acquisitions north of the British sphere to be more than a means of bargaining—a " *Kompensa-*

tionsobjekt," as he called it.[1] He considered his pending Agreement worth more than the whole of Witu; and well he might, considering that Heligoland was one item in the bargain. Peters had arrived in Uganda when the news reached him.

The Arab and Swahili peoples of the coast had not been consulted on the question of the cession to a German Company of the rights on the coast, and greatly resented the transfer. The Germans were opposed everywhere, and their settlements were attacked. For a time all were abandoned except Dar es-Salaam and Bagamoyo, which were protected by a German squadron. The Company having shown itself incapable of administering this territory, it was taken out of their hands, and an Imperial German Protectorate was proclaimed on October 22, 1889. Meanwhile, a military force had been raised and placed under the command of Wissmann. By the middle of 1890 the country had been reduced to submission, although further outbreaks occurred in the next year.

The matters at issue between Great Britain and Germany in this and other fields were dealt with by the Agreement of July 1, 1890, generally known as the Heligoland Treaty. This Agreement, so far as it concerned East Africa, had three consequences. The first was the definition of the frontier of German East Africa, as described elsewhere (p. 1). The second was the withdrawal of the German protectorate over Witu, together with all other German claims north of the Tana river. This second result was effected by Article II of the Treaty, which ran as follows:—

" In order to render effective the delimitation recorded in the preceding Article, Germany withdraws in favour of Great Britain her Protectorate over Witu. Great Britain engages to recognise the sovereignty of the Sultan of Witu over the territory extending from Kipini to the point opposite the island of Kwyhoo, fixed as the boundary in 1887.

---

[1] Zimmermann, *Geschichte der Deutschen Kolonialpolitik*, p. 160.

> " Germany also withdraws her Protectorate over the adjoin-
> ing coast up to Kismayu, as well as her claims to all other
> territories on the mainland to the north of the River Tana,
> and to the islands of Patta and Manda."

The third result was the absolute cession to Germany of German East Africa, coupled with the recognition of British predominance at Zanzibar and in
Witu. This was effected by Article XI of the treaty.[1]
The indemnity to the Sultan was fixed by an Anglo-
German exchange of Notes on October 27/28. Already
on June 14 the Sultan had placed himself and his
interests entirely in the hands of the British Government. On the mainland and in the island of Mafia all
his rights were permanently ceded to Germany, while
Zanzibar and Pemba became a British Protectorate,
formally notified to the world on November 4, 1890.
Germany gave up her ex-territorial privileges in
Zanzibar in June 1907, under the provisions of the
Convention of November 1899 (the ' Samoa ' Convention).

iv. Material Development

The authority of the German Government over
its East African colony had now been firmly
established. An Imperial Governor was appointed,
and the country was divided into administrative
districts. Dar es-Salaam became the capital. This
place had been founded by Seyyid Majid in 1862;
but Seyyid Bargash had deserted it in 1871. It had,
however, a good position on the Zanzibar Channel, and
a much better harbour than Bagamoyo. Peters founded
a factory there in 1887; and, in the outbreaks of the
following years, it was one of the few places which
were firmly held. It was soon discovered by surveyors
to be the most suitable port for the starting-point of
a railway from the Indian Ocean to Lake Tanganyika.
This railway and its utilization to obtain control over
the commerce of Central Africa, especially that of the

[1] See Appendix II, p. 111.

eastern parts of the Congo State, was one of the principal objectives of German policy; and it is probable that the continuance of the line through the Congo to the Atlantic was part of the scheme.

Even before this main line was undertaken, a beginning had been made of a railway from the port of Tanga, the most northerly in the colony, towards the fertile lands of the Kilimanjaro district. Tanga is the best harbour for security and depth in Tanganyika; a modern town, well laid out, has rapidly developed there. The railway was opened to Moshi in 1912, and has since been connected with the Uganda Railway by the extension to Moshi of the Voi-Taveta branch.

Bismarck's fall and von Caprivi's accession to power did not entail any change in Germany's colonial policy. For the time being no further extension was desired; and in East Africa especially an interval was needed for consolidation and development. Wissmann went on leave, his task of subduing the first outbreak being apparently accomplished. His successor, von Soden, however, had to quell disturbances in many places. The worst of these was among the Wahehes, the warlike tribe of Uhehe in the Usagara mountains, south of Kilossa (now a station on the Central Railway). Here a force of native troops under von Zelewski was surrounded and cut to pieces; the commander himself, with nine European officers and 250 Sudanese soldiers, being killed. About the same time Schmidt was engaged with the Mafitis in the south-west, and Peters was attacked in the mountain country near Kilimanjaro. Wissmann, who was at Dar es-Salaam, was now entrusted with the task of obtaining steamers for the Great Lakes, the control of which was essential to the effectual domination of the country. He succeeded, with British co-operation, in taking a steamer up the Zambezi and the Shire, and reached Lake Nyasa with it towards the end of 1892. The development of railways and harbours was another element in the same problem. The Usambara line from Tanga was begun in August 1891, and harbour works at Dar es-Salaam were undertaken at the same time.

The way for the ultimate construction of the Central Railway was prepared by expeditions against the Sultan of Tabora in 1891, and against the Wahehes near Kilossa in 1892. The Boma (fort) of Tabora was taken early in 1893; and in the autumn of the same year there was severe fighting near Moshi (Kilimanjaro) against the Wajaggas. Von Soden was succeeded by von Schele in September 1893; but, conditions still continuing uneasy, it was thought necessary to recall Wissmann to deal with the situation. During his short period of office Wissmann was engaged in war against Sultan Makhemba and the slave-dealer Hassan-bin-Omari near Kilwa, with success; but ill-health forced him to retire at the end of 1896. Von Liebert, his successor as Governor, held office till 1901.

The war against the Wahehes went on through the latter part of 1896, when it was ended by the taking of their stronghold, Iringa. The chief, Quaqua, killed himself when he found his tribesmen surrounded by the Germans; and the power of the Wahehes was destroyed. At the same time the Masais of the north, who had resisted all efforts to subdue them, were nearly exterminated by a great cattle epidemic, which deprived them of their only means of subsistence. In the north, too, there was an expedition against the warlike tribes of Mount Meru, who had been guilty of killing two missionaries.

v. Native Opposition to German Rule

For the next few years comparative peace seems to have reigned, the more warlike tribes having been for the time being reduced to impotence. Discontent, however, was widespread. The general harshness of the administration and the pressure on the native populations to supply labour for the German plantations was no doubt responsible for this feeling, to which the hut-tax, introduced in 1897, also greatly contributed. This tax was, it seems, introduced not so much for revenue purposes as in order to force the natives to work for the planters so as to obtain money to pay the tax. Besides the forced labour, other causes of discontent are specified by German writers, such as the extortions of Indian traders and the violent conduct of men accompanying caravans; but it is evident that hatred of the hut-tax and of labour on the plantations were the principal causes. Von Liebert was succeeded in 1901 by Count von Götzen, who held office till 1906.

Concerted Rising of Southern Tribes.—It was not till 1905 that the great outbreak of the tribes took place, the most important since the Arab rising of 1888. It differed from all preceding rebellions in that there was concerted action among the tribes; and it was not found possible by the German rulers to utilize ancient enmities to induce one tribe to attack another. The rising began in July 1905 in the Matumbi hills, near Kilwa, and spread rapidly over the southern part of the colony. In debates in the Reichstag it was attributed to the reckless raising of the hut-tax and the enforced labour of all who did not pay it. The rising led to von Götzen's retirement in the beginning of 1906, and the appointment of von Rechenberg as Governor.

To deal with this serious rebellion great efforts were necessary; and naval and military forces co-operated. Missions and military posts had been destroyed, and many persons killed. The fortified post of Livati had fallen; Mahenge and Songea were besieged for many months. The revolt spread northwards to the centre of the colony; but the tribes of the north did not take part in it. After the main rising had been suppressed, a guerrilla war lingered on till 1907. It is admitted that 75,000 persons perished through the war and concomitant troubles.

The loss of life following the suppression of this rebellion was no doubt actually much greater. Sir H. H. Johnston[1] puts it at 120,000, and this is probably

[1] Sir H. H. Johnston, *Colonization of Africa*, 2nd edn., p. 413.

no exaggeration. The crops and herds were deliberately destroyed by the Germans, and the people were left to perish by famine.

vi. Recent Material Development

During the comparatively peaceful periods before and since the rising the development of the country proceeded. This development was mainly material. Communications were the object of unremitting attention, railways being extended, roads and bridges constructed, and steamers placed on the lakes. Experiments in every kind of crop were instituted, and every assistance was given to the planters.

From 1906 to 1910 the office of Colonial Secretary in Germany was held by Herr B. Dernburg, who showed great energy in promoting the welfare of the German colonies; the completion of the railways and the development of trade must be mainly attributed to the policy initiated by him.

III. SOCIAL AND POLITICAL CONDITIONS

(1) RELIGIOUS

THE ancient trade settlements of the Arabs on the coast and the more recent political rule of the Imâm Seyyids, which had its centre at Zanzibar, led to the diffusion of the Mohammedan religion along the whole coast of German East Africa, where the entire population of Arab or mixed origin professes that creed. Away from the coast, however, Islam has made comparatively little progress, and is mainly confined to spots situated along the caravan-routes where there are settlements of Arab slave-dealers. Of these settlements the principal are Tabora and Morogoro. Outside these limits the great majority of the population retain their original forms of belief, which are of an animistic nature, and include ancestor worship. A large number of Christian missions, both Protestant and Catholic, have been established in German East Africa; among the former are German Evangelical, Moravian, and Lutheran Societies, and the University Mission of Central Africa. Among the latter are, or were, the Algerian ' White Fathers,' the so-called ' Black Fathers,' and the Bavarian Benedictines. The English Missions were the strongest in educational work.

(2) POLITICAL

The colony was divided into twenty-four districts, of which nineteen are civil districts, taking their names usually from the principal ports or inland centres, while two were military districts and three were residencies.[1]

The civil districts were the following : Wilhelmstal (including the settled part of the Usambara mountains); the coast districts of Tanga, Pangani, and Bagamoyo; Morogoro (on the plateau above Dar es-Salaam); Dar es-Salaam (a coast district); Rufiyi (principal town Mohoro); Kilwa and Lindi (coast districts); Songea (on the route to Lake Nyasa); Langenburg (on Lake Nyasa); Bismarckburg; Ujiji (on Lake Tanganyika); Dodoma; Moshi (Kilimanjaro and the Masai Steppe); Mwanza (south of Victoria Nyanza); Tabora (on the Central Railway)[2]; Arusha; and Kondoa-Irangi. Iringa and Mahenge in the plateau south of the central railway are military districts.

The residencies, Bukoba, Ruanda (capital Kigali), and Urundi (capital Usumbura), were situated in the country between Lake Victoria Nyanza and Lake Tanganyika.

In 1911 a new regulation regarding the institution of an advisory council came into force, in accordance with which the Governor was assisted by a council of three official and five non-official members (with five substitutes), all of whom had to be natives of Germany. These were selected by the Governor from a list of thirty chosen by the different districts, apparently by the German residents.

(3) EDUCATIONAL

In accordance with German theories, the object of the system of education in force was mainly to teach a sufficient number of natives trades and handicrafts in which they can be of use to European employers. The schools are for the most part in the hands of Protestant and Catholic Missions; but a certain number were under direct Government management. The objects

---

[1] Cd. 7620-51, Diplomatic and Consular Report on German East Africa, 1912-13.

[2] Mwanza and Tabora include the country formerly known as Unyamwezi.

of all seem to have been identical; but very little accurate information on this subject is available.

The figures for the various schools, according to a report prepared in 1911,[1] were as follows:—

	No. of Pupils.		
	Elementary.	Higher.	Industrial.
Government schools ..	3,494	681	137
Mission schools:			
Roman Catholic ..	31,274	724	61
Protestant (6 German, 2 English, 1 American)	29,716	472	88
Total	64,484	1,877	286

A return for 1913 gives the number of pupils in Government schools as 6,177, and in five Protestant and three Roman Catholic schools as 108,557. A comparison with the figures for 1911 shows that much confidence cannot be placed on the accuracy of these returns.

GENERAL OBSERVATIONS

(a) FUTURE OF TANGANYIKA

A review of the history of German East Africa, as given above, proves that, prior to the advent of the Germans, Great Britain, or the British Government of India, was in effect recognised as Protector of all this central East African coast, and that it was not merely British abstention from interfering with German intrusion but active British support of German wishes that brought German East Africa into being. By the permanent establishment of British influence and authority on this coast, the state of affairs would be revived which, prior to 1884, received general acquiescence.

[1] Calvert, *German East Africa*, p. 101.

German East Africa was clearly the most valuable German possession in Africa and by far the most dangerous, in German hands, to the peace of Africa. General Smuts's views on this point, the views of one who has been peculiarly concerned in redeeming Africa from German domination, are familiar.[1]

(b) The Labour Question

The population, numbering between 7 and 8 millions, is very unevenly distributed. It is mainly of Bantu origin, and the languages spoken belong to that family (see above, pp. 16-19). The Swahili of the coast has a large Arabic admixture, and is becoming the *lingua franca* for the whole country. Tribes are numerous and vary much in character. Some are nomadic, pastoral, and warlike; others settled and peaceful. Nearly all are capable of maintaining themselves without working for wages, and object to doing so. Hence the establishment of the plantation system—that of great estates demanding large supplies of labour—must, if continued, lead to perpetual discontent and trouble.

The German view, as stated by Hassert[2], is that " colonization consists in the utilization of the soil, its products, and its men, for the economic profit of the colonizing nation "; or, in G. A. Fischer's phrase, that " colonizing Africa is making the negroes work."

It seems clear that, although the rapid development of the colony as a farm devoted to the cultivation of tropical products required by Germany (which seems to have been the aim of the Government) may be promoted by the German system, the permanent improvement and civilization of the people was incompatible with it, as it led to violence and cruelty on the part of the rulers and revolt or sullen depression among the natives.

[1] See his Address delivered before the Royal Geographical Society on January 28, 1918.
[2] *Deutschlands Kolonien*, 2nd edn., p. 618.

IV. ECONOMIC CONDITIONS

(A) MEANS OF COMMUNICATION

(1) INTERNAL

(a) *Roads, Caravan Routes, and Tracks*

BEFORE 1914 motor roads existed only in the north-eastern corner of the territory. These are now all destroyed, owing to the late war. Wide, well-kept roads, fit for light wheeled traffic, and in some cases provided with rest-houses and stores, ran through all the settled parts of the territory. Metalled roads were found only near the chief European towns, such as Dar es-Salaam and Tanga. From Dar es-Salaam, a coastal road, fit for wheeled traffic on the section beyond Pangani, led northward into British territory. A main road led from Dar es-Salaam across the territory to Kigoma on Lake Tanganyika, with main roads branching off northward to Kondoa-Irangi and to Mwanza, and southward to Bismarckburg and to Neu-Iringa, Neu-Langenburg and Mwaya. Another road branched southward to Mahenge and round to Kilwa Kivinje, which was also connected with the capital by a direct coast road. Kilwa was the starting-point of the main road from the coast through Livale and Songea to Wiedhafen on Lake Nyasa. Main roads connected Lake Nyasa with Tanganyika, and Tanganyika with Lakes Kivu and Victoria. Other important roads were those leading from Wilhelmstal to Moshi and Arusha, from Pangani to Kondoa-Irangi, from Bagamoyo to Itumba and also to Morogoro, from Mahenge to Songea, and from Lindi to the Rovuma and thence to Songea. There were many native tracks, some passable for bicycles. Elephant tracks served in some instances as roads for light traffic.

As the result of military operations, the whole road system of the Government has been destroyed and will have to be reconstructed. On the other hand, military exigencies have led to the opening of fresh tracks, roads, and light-railway routes, most of which may with advantage be maintained or improved and extended.

The introduction of railways has greatly reduced caravan traffic; but there were several important caravan routes still in use in 1913, especially in the native states of Ruanda and Urundi, where they connected Bukoba, on Victoria Nyanza, with Kissenyi, on Lake Kivu, and Usumbura, on Lake Tanganyika. Caravans were a costly and wasteful means of transport, the more so as they withdrew great numbers of natives from agriculture to act as porters. The Germans reckoned that an average day's march for good carriers was 12 to 16 miles. It has been estimated that one railway train, of average capacity and engine power, does the work of 13,000 carriers at about one-twentieth of the cost. Pack-animals were sometimes used, and certain routes were fit for ox- and donkey-waggons. Animals, however, quickly succumbed to the tsetse fly.

(b) *Rivers*

Tanganyika is well watered, and its lakes and rivers should prove of great value in its development. The direction of the river courses is convenient for trade purposes, but there are many rapids and other obstacles, and during the dry season some rivers are very low.

The *Kagera* is the only river among those flowing into the great lakes which is valuable as a means of communication. A proposal to survey the Kagera and its two chief tributaries, the Ruvuvu and Akanyaru, and to improve their channels and furnish them with suitable river craft at a total cost of 2,850,000 marks, was approved by the Government in 1913 in connexion

with the projected railway from Tabora to the Kagera
river bend (see p. 48). The aim of this two-fold project was to open up the rich and thickly-populated
cattle districts of Ruanda and Urundi.

The principal navigable rivers flowing into the
Indian Ocean, named from north to south, are the
Pangani, Wami, Kingani, Rufiyi, Matandu, Mbem-
kuru, Lukuledi, and Rovuma.

The *Pangani* is tidal and navigable for steamers for
22 miles from its mouth; beyond this, even in the dry
season, it might be used by small craft below and above
the falls, which occur 45 miles from its mouth. The
Wami has two mouths, of which the more northerly, the
Purahanya, is navigable for a few miles. The *Kingani*,
or *Ruvu*, on which shipping transport was opened in
1913, is difficult of access by reason of a large shifting
sand-bar near its mouth. At Dunga, which is 35 miles
up the river, there is a depth of about 6 feet. The
river is navigable throughout the year for steam pinnaces up to Mafizi, and for several months for vessels of
heavier draught.

The *Rufiyi*, which was regarded by the Germans as
the best waterway in the territory, has a broad delta
with many mouths. One of the most northerly, the
Simba-Uranga, is navigable as far as Salale for vessels
of 2,000 tons, and all the northern outlets are navigable by revenue cutters and dhows. Above the delta
the river can be navigated by steamers as far as Mtanza
in the dry season, and as far as Kibambove (Kibambwe)
in the rains. A scheme for making the lower section of
the Rufiyi navigable for about 125 miles at an estimated
cost of 5,000,000 marks was approved by the German
Government in 1913. Above Ulanga station (40 miles
from the Shuguli rapids) about 144 miles could be made
navigable at small cost. The Ruaha, the chief tributary of the Rufiyi, is navigable by large canoes at least
as far as Kidatu.

The *Matandu*, the *Mbemkuru*, and the *Lukuledi* are
navigable to a moderate extent. The navigation of
the *Rovuma* is very difficult.

(c) *Railways*

Although the German East Africa railway system was not very highly developed before the war, the policy initiated was progressive and far-seeing. Its main objects were to occupy effectively the inland native states and to draw the trade and mineral exports of the southern and eastern parts of the Belgian Congo to an outlet on the Indian Ocean. The original intention was to construct three railways running across the Protectorate from east to west—a northern line reaching the south of Victoria Nyanza, a central line reaching Lake Tanganyika, and a southern line reaching the north of Lake Nyasa—and to link these together by lines running north and south. Only the second of these lines has been completed; the first has been taken less than half way, and the third has not been begun. The concentration at Dar es-Salaam of the expanding commercial interests of the territory, with the consequent decline of the other ports, led to the postponement of the completion of the northern and southern railways, while a proposal to construct lines branching out from the Central railway came into favour. Opinion, however, continued to be divided as to the advisability of this course. There was much to be said for a system of parallel railways, serving several ports and thus enabling German East Africa to compete for a considerable proportion of the trade to and from the upper Congo, north-east Rhodesia, and Nyasaland.

At the outbreak of war there were, excluding light railways, only two lines in the Protectorate, viz., the Northern or Usambara railway, and the Central or Tanganyika railway. Both were of metre gauge.

The *Northern* or *Usambara railway* runs from Tanga in a north-westerly direction, roughly parallel to the frontier of Kenya (British East Africa), to Moshi (354 km.) at the foot of Kilimanjaro. It is of great commercial importance as giving access to Usambara, the hill region, in which most of the European plantations are situated, and to the healthy cattle-ranching country near Kilimanjaro. The line was begun in 1891, and was opened to Korogwe in 1902, to Mombo in 1904, to Bwiko in 1910, and to Moshi in 1912. It was to have been taken on to Arusha, through country suitable for white settlement, and preliminary earth-work was in progress in 1913. The intention was ultimately to prolong the line to Victoria Nyanza, but with the Uganda railway already serving the lake, a second line seems hardly necessary. The Uganda and Usambara railways were linked during the war by the extension to Moshi of the Voi-Taveta branch of the Uganda line. Further connecting lines might be constructed as needs arise.

The control of the Usambara railway was handed over by the Government in 1908 to the Deutsche Kolonial-Eisenbahn-Bau- und Betriebs-Gesellschaft. The working of the line up to March 31, 1914, was shown in the company's report as follows :—

	1911–12.	1912–13.	1913–14.[1]
	Km.	Km.	Km.
Average length of line ..	268	352	354
	Marks.	Marks.	Marks.
Receipts	1,182,240	1,204,038	1,184,300
Working expenses	791,054	911.092	795,632
Gross surplus	391,186	292,946	388,668

The journey from Tanga to Moshi used to occupy fifteen hours. The fuel consumed in the locomotives was wood. The rolling-stock in 1912 included 18 locomotives, 25 passenger coaches, 6 combined postal and luggage vans, about 280 goods trucks, open and covered, of various sizes, 3 travelling cranes, and 1 derrick.

The *Central* or *Tanganyika railway* runs west from Dar es-Salaam through Morogoro, Kilossa, and Tabora to Kigoma on Lake Tanganyika (1,252 km.). It was

[1] Incomplete; the figures are based upon the average for three months (January—March).

owned by the Ostafrikanische Eisenbahngesellschaft, Berlin, and represented state enterprise in a thinly-disguised form. Its capital was 21,000,000 marks, in 7,000 shares, to be gradually redeemed under a special scheme. By 1913 nine-tenths of the shares had been bought by the Government. The same company owned and operated the electric power-station at Dar es-Salaam, and financed the Ostafrikanische Landgesellschaft, which was formed to deal with the land concession granted to the railway.

The line was begun in 1905, reached Morogoro in 1908, Tabora in 1912, and Kigoma in 1914. The chief engineering difficulty was the bridging of the River Mlagarazi. The total cost of construction was £5,850,000, and the average cost per kilometre £5,000.

This railway is not likely to yield large profits for a long time to come. The regions that it traverses, after the coast section, are practically undeveloped. It was claimed for the line that, in addition to facilitating the interchange of native products, it would enable merchants in many parts of the Congo to obtain their goods more easily from Dar es-Salaam than from Matadi on the Congo river.

The financial position of the railway in 1912 and 1913 can be seen from the following table:—

	1912.	1913.
	Marks.	Marks.
Expenditure	2,939,102	2,703,602
Receipts		
(1) Passengers and baggage	515,684	516,252
(2) General goods	1,392,092	1,531,643
(3) Construction material ..	2,289,834	1,932,158
(4) Miscellaneous	178,127	216,055
(5) Electric works	140,054	148,465
(6) Interest on capital ..	157,550	197,960
	4,673,341	4,542,533

The percentage of working expenses to gross receipts was 66, which was a favourable result for the last year of construction, though it was higher than the average calculated on the aggregate figures for all German colonial railways.

In 1913 the rolling stock included 63 engines, 44 of which were tank engines, 30 passenger coaches, 319 goods waggons, 29 water-trucks, 4 cranes, 39 derricks, and 98 trollies. The station accommodation was excellent.

Light railways.—A number of light railways had also been constructed before the war. The most important of these was the Sigi railway, opened in 1910. This was a 75-centimetre gauge line, running from Tengeni on the Usambara railway to the Sigi saw-mills (23 km.). In 1914 it belonged to the Deutsche Holz-Gesellschaft für Ostafrika, but was managed by the Deutsche Kolonial-Eisenbahn-Bau- und Betriebs-Gesellschaft. Negotiations were in progress with the Colonial Treasury, with a view to adding it to the Usambara railway. The gross receipts from this line in 1912-13 were 38,520 marks, and the working expenses 28,380 marks.

There were also light railways, of which details are lacking, from Mtangata creek to Kigombe; from the Pangani river to Busirihof; at Amboni, near Tanga, where there are sulphur springs and the plantations of the Westdeutsche Handels- und Plantagen-Gesellschaft; from Makuyuni to Ambangalu; and from Mkumbara to Neu-Homow (95 km.). There was a temporary light railway running inland from Lindi for about 24 kilometres.

Two lines branching from the Usambara railway were under construction when war broke out. One was to run from Ngomeni (28 kilometres from Tanga) to Bwiti at the north-east end of the Usambara mountains, and then down to join the main line again at Korogwe. The other was a trolly line from Mombo southward to Nderema near Handeni.

A number of short light railways were latterly constructed to assist the military operations of the invading forces. Some will remain, while the routes taken by the lines that are to be removed may possibly be followed by permanent lines in the future. The extension to Moshi of the Voi-Taveta branch of the Uganda railway was constructed as a temporary line, but has already proved its intrinsic usefulness, and will probably remain as a permanent link between the Usambara and Uganda railways.

Railways projected or proposed.—A large number of railways traversing the territory have been proposed at various times. With few exceptions, these proposals were for branch lines from the Central railway. It is very questionable whether such concentration of the traffic along one main line and through one port, advantageous as it is in the early days of a colony, does not become a serious drawback when the colony begins to develop. The lower part of the line becomes congested, and the port becomes incapable of dealing expeditiously with its traffic.

The six most noteworthy proposals for branches from the Central railway, named from west to east, were as follows:—

(1) A line from Tabora north-westward to the bend of the river Kagera (481 km.), with extensions to Bukoba, Kigali (Kigari), and Mulezi. Its object was to open up the districts of Ruanda and Urundi in such a way as to prevent the Uganda railway from capturing their trade. In the Budget of 1914 a sum of 17,000,000 marks appeared as the first instalment of a loan to the Ostafrikanische Eisenbahngesellschaft for the construction of this line. Construction was expected to take three or four years, and the total cost was to be 50,000,000 marks, including the vote of 2,850,000 marks for surveying and improving the river Kagera with its tributaries and adjacent water-courses (see p. 42).

(2) A line running northward from Tabora by St. Michael to Mwanza on Victoria Nyanza. Such a line would pass through a district said to contain some gold, but otherwise of little value, and its chief source of profit would be the lake-borne trade of the port.

(3) A line running northward from Zaranda (the station for Kilimatinde) to link up the Central railway with Arusha.

(4) A line either from Kilossa (290 kilometres from Dar es-Salaam) or possibly from Mpapwa, farther west, to Bismarckburg at the southern end of Lake Tanganyika. This is an important project, for such a line would tap the cotton district of Usungu, and would be the shortest route from Dar es-Salaam to Katanga and parts of northern Rhodesia; it would come into competition with the existing line from Beira and the projected Benguella railway from Lobito Bay, of which about one-third has been constructed.

(5) A variant on the last scheme was a line from Kilossa through Iringa to Neu-Langenburg and thence to the north end of Lake Nyasa.

The first section of each of these lines would run through important productive areas; but serious difficulties would be encountered in crossing the country between Lakes Tanganyika and Nyasa.

(6) Similar difficulties in construction would attend another scheme, viz., a railway by way of Ulanga (on the River Ulanga, a tributary of the Rufiyi) across the Mahenge plateau to Lake Nyasa.   This scheme was considered in 1913 by the Kolonial-Wirtschaftliches Komitee.

In the north of the territory the chief project has been the continuation of the Usambara railway to Victoria Nyanza. The extension of the line from its railhead at Moshi to Arusha was under construction in 1914. A railway commission reported in that year upon two projects of further extension:—

(*a*) Arusha—Lake Manyara—Mwanza (546 km.); estimated cost, 60,200,000 marks.

(*b*) Arusha—Lake Manyara—Solima Point (Speke Gulf) (477 km.); estimated cost, 55,500,000 marks. The balance of advantages was in favour of the former line, which, however, would run through thinly-populated country, lacking wood and water.

Another proposed line in the north was to branch

from the Uganda railway at Lumbwa station and run to Fort Ikoma, in the north of Mwanza district (about 150 miles, of which 50 would have been through former German territory).

Farther west, a short line was suggested from Victoria Nyanza past Burigi lake to the bend of the Kagera, but this presented grave engineering difficulties. A line was also proposed from Lake Kivu to the north end of Lake Tanganyika, along the eastern bank of the Rusizi.

In the south of the territory the most important line proposed was the Southern railway from Kilwa to Wiedhafen on Lake Nyasa, roughly following the existing caravan route from the coast to the lake. It was to be divided into four sections:—Kilwa–Livale (220 km.), Livale–Mbarangandu (150 km.), Mbarangandu–Songea (180 km.), and Songea–Wiedhafen (120 km.). The total length would have been 670 kilometres, and the cost was estimated at 57,000,000 marks. There are no serious engineering difficulties in the way of such a line, which would open up a very rich area, hitherto undeveloped, and might well become the chief artery for the trade of Nyasaland.

(d) Posts, Telegraphs, and Telephones

Posts.—In 1913 there were fifty-four post offices. Mails to and from Europe were carried direct by steamers of the German East Africa combine and also by ships of other lines which touched at Zanzibar. All coast post offices were visited regularly once a month by Government steamers. Letters reached the Victoria Nyanza ports generally by the Uganda railway. From these points mails were carried by runners to Ruanda and Lake Tanganyika. Runners were commonly employed on postal services in the interior away from railways.

Telegraphs and Telephones.—In 1914 there were thirty-four telegraph offices, operating 2,537 kilometres of land lines. There were three main telegraph systems before the war. The first ran near the line of the Tanganyika railway from Dar es-Salaam to Ujiji and Kigoma. From Kilossa there was a branch line, about 130 miles long, to Neu-Iringa; from Tabora a branch went north to Mwanza; from Ujiji another branch ran roughly parallel with the shore of Tanganyika to Bismarckburg, and was continued into British territory at Kituta (Kitata). The second line ran along the coast from Dar es-Salaam northward to Tanga, and southward to Mikindani. The third, based on the Usambara railway, went through Wilhelmstal and Moshi to Arusha. Eighteen of the telegraph offices had telephone exchanges. The length in 1912-13 of the telegraph and telephone lines together was under 4,000 kilometres—no great length considering the size of the country.

Héliograph communication was much used by the Germans for internal communication in the hill regions. Dodoma, Kondoa-Irangi, Singida, Mkalama, and Kilimatinde, were connected in this way. Thus, too, Mahenge communicated with its sub-stations.

(2) EXTERNAL

(a) *Ports*

(i) *Coast Ports*

At all ports in Tanganyika goods have to be discharged and loaded by means of lighters. The following are the chief seaports:—

Tanga is the terminus of the Usambara or Northern railway, which serves the principal European plantations. In 1913 it owned a small pier where dhows could load and unload by means of two cranes of eight tons capacity, and improvements were contemplated, among them a large deep-water pier. The landing, trans-shipment, and lighterage of goods was let to a contractor under Government regulations.

Pangani has a shallow harbour, and ships drawing more than 3 metres cannot pass the bar at the river mouth. Pangani was served twice a month by a

Government steamer and by a steam lighter of the Deutsche Ostafrika-Linie. It trades especially with Pemba and Zanzibar, exporting ivory and copra, and also refined sugar, produced locally.

Bagamoyo used to be a starting place for caravans, but owing to its inferior harbour facilities was not chosen for a railway terminus. The anchorage for deep-draught vessels is 2 miles from the shore. The position of Bagamoyo at the mouth of the Kingani river brings it a large dhow traffic.

Dar es-Salaam (pop. 25,000) is the terminus of the Central railway and a port of call for European liners. Its harbour, about 3 miles long and half a mile wide, is entered by a channel of $4\frac{1}{2}$ fathoms depth, increasing farther in to a depth of $6\frac{1}{2}$ to 10 fathoms. Ships of more than one hundred tons gross register must carry a pilot on entering and leaving; only Zanzibar vessels and those of the Deutsche Ostafrika-Linie are exempt, since they are well acquainted with the harbour entrance. Hansing & Co. have had a practical monopoly of the lighterage, to the exclusion of non-German interests. Electric cranes transfer cargo from the lighters to the Customs wharves, and the landing-stage is connected by a side line with the railway. A floating dock, built in 1901, was sunk by British cruisers in August, 1914. It belonged to the Ostafrikanische Eisenbahngesellschaft, which in 1913 took over the Imperial flotilla and the coastal steamer service, the charge of Dar es-Salaam docks and workshops, the supply of water to ships in harbour, and also the services on lakes Tanganyika and Nyasa and the Rufiyi river, receiving a subsidy of 250,000 marks per annum, in addition to any profits that might be earned.

Kilwa Kivinje was formerly very useful to slave traders, but its importance has now gone. About sixteen miles south of it is *Kilwa Kisivani*, which has the best natural harbour in the south of the territory.

Lindi, the chief port of the southern districts, lies on the left bank of the Lukuledi river, which is nearly

1,000 metres wide at this point. The harbour is good, but insufficiently protected from east winds. Ocean-going vessels can enter only at high tide, and even then cannot reach the town. Lindi has a healthy climate, and is the centre of a large plantation district.

Smaller ports are Sadani (Saadani), sixteen miles north of Bagamoyo; Kilindoni, on the island of Mafia, which exports copra; Chole, on the same island; Salale, on the Rufiyi, exporting mangrove wood and cotton; Mikindani, which lies in a deep bay, but is very un-healthy; and Kionga near the Portuguese border. These are visited by coastal steamers and steamers of the Bombay service.

(ii) *Lake Ports*

The great lakes form what may be called a second coastline of the territory. In addition to serving the needs of adjacent districts within what was German East Africa, they carried a considerable and increasing traffic to and from the neighbouring protectorates of other countries.

(1) *On Victoria Nyanza.*

Mwanza, on the south, (pop. about 15,000, including 70 Europeans) is unhealthy, but has a good harbour. The construction of the Uganda railway caused the value of the annual trade of this port to rise from £14,000 in 1903 to over £260,000 in 1912. It exported skins, hides, wax, rice, and ground-nuts, and cotton cultivation had recently shown great promise.

Bukoba, on the west, a well-built town, was severely damaged during a British attack. It is healthier than Mwanza, but has a rather poor harbour. It had a large and increasing export trade in hides, ivory, rubber, coffee and ground-nuts, and was practically the only port serving the rich districts of Urundi and Ruanda. The total value of its trade rose from £193,000 in 1911 to £271,000 in 1912.

Shirati, on the east, was the German frontier port and served the Wagaya territories, but its landing is bad. It exported ground-nuts, hides, skins, sesame, samli (clarified butter), and cotton.

Trade on Victoria Nyanza had developed greatly, owing to the Uganda railway, and was severely taxing the existing means of transport.

(2) *On Lake Kivu.*

At the northern end of this lake are Ngoma, Bobandana (Belgian) and Kissenyi (formerly German, now Belgian), and at the southern end is Lukemba, on the Rusizi. The northern region suffers periodically from volcanic outbursts, Kissenyi alone lying outside the volcanic area and possessing a sandy beach.

Ngoma is in danger of eventual destruction by lava flows. It lies about two miles west-north-west of Kissenyi and has no shelter. A little bay (where a small launch might be kept) is formed by the crater of Ngoma hill. The water is so deep that the construction of a pier or mole of wood or stone is impracticable, but a floating landing-stage might be made or a wharf built out from the face of the rock.

Kissenyi may be of importance in the future, as the lakes provide an alternative route to the projected Cape to Cairo railway. The town is well laid out and has good buildings, and the Germans meant to make it an important trade centre. It lies on a wide bay with a gently sloping and sandy foreshore, and the construction of a breakwater is feasible.

(3) *On Lake Tanganyika.*

The Germans looked on this lake as the key to the trade of central Africa. Its chief ports, named from north to south, are Usumbura, Kigoma, Ujiji, Kirando, and Bismarckburg.

Usumbura was suggested as a possible starting-point for the railway line to the south end of Lake Kivu.

Kigoma was chosen as the terminus of the Tanganyika line, because it has a fine well-protected harbour with a depth of nearly fourteen metres. On the southern side of the peninsula forming the bay the station and a quay 250 metres long were built in 1914.

Ujiji was settled by Arabs early in the last century. Its importance lay in its position as a gateway to the Belgian Congo. Its trade was built up on rubber, ivory, and slaves, and when the slave-trade ceased, it still remained a commercial centre for Indians and Arabs and for caravans proceeding to the upper Congo. The town used to be on the water's edge, but owing to the fall of the lake was in 1914 nearly 400 metres distant from it. Though unhealthily situated amongst sand-flats and river deltas, it is free from *glossina palpalis* (tsetse fly), the carrier of sleeping sickness. The port has been transferred to Kigoma.

Kirando has an excellent anchorage, entirely protected by outlying islands; it has substantial station buildings, a large mission, and a sleeping-sickness segregation hospital.

Bismarckburg has only a fair harbour, though steamers can lie close in-shore. The anchorage is exposed and entirely unprotected to the west.

(4) *On Lake Nyasa.*

Lake Nyasa has hitherto had little trade. The two existing trade-routes—(a) from Kilossa to Langenburg and (b) through British Nyasaland—had serious disadvantages, the chief being the prohibitive cost of transport. The mountains of the district are rich in minerals, and the lake adjoins a large agricultural region which it would conveniently serve if the railway between Kilwa and the lake were constructed, and if railway and shipping freights were low enough to make an export trade possible. The natural trade centre for the north-eastern side of the lake is Wiedhafen; but, if mineral development should precede agricultural, the projected railway might be diverted to a terminus at the north end of the lake, where Alt-Langenburg and Mwaya provide harbours within the territory.

(b) Shipping Lines

Passenger and goods traffic with Europe, India, and other parts of Africa was almost exclusively in the hands of the Deutsche Ostafrika-Linie, working in connexion with the Woermann, the Hamburg-Amerika (African service), and the Hamburg-Bremer-Afrika lines. Four steamers sailed each month from Hamburg, two by the eastern and two by the western route round Africa. There were also regular mail and cargo services to Bombay, and coast steamers serving the ports of German and Portuguese East Africa. In 1890 the Deutsche Ostafrika-Linie was paid a subsidy of £45,000 (900,000 marks) for its East Africa service, and in 1900 this was raised to £67,000. The subsidy appears to have sufficed to defray all the Suez Canal dues payable by the company.

The Deutsche Ostafrika-Linie is a Hanseatic shipping corporation. In 1914 this line had 2 large liners of 9,200 tons under construction, owned 25 vessels, and employed 2 vessels of each of the three companies with which it worked in combination. The total tonnage built or building in 1914 was 192,260 tons. (The fleet of the largest British line engaged in the East Africa trade comprised 47 vessels of an aggregate tonnage of 345,765 tons.) The capital of the combine in 1900 was 10,000,000 marks, in 1,000-mark shares. The book value of the fleet on December 31, 1911, stood at 19,110,000 marks, or, including lighters, docks, and other property, at 22,000,000 marks. Dividends of 8 per cent. were paid for many years before the war.

Most of the British goods imported were trans-shipped at Hamburg to German steamers. No British liners called at the coast ports; the Union-Castle Line was under contract not to do so. The whole of the merchant traffic was controlled by German houses, except for a few British coal and oil steamers and Norwegian sailing-ships carrying timber. Native dhows maintained communication with the Comoro Islands, Madagascar, India, Muscat, and African trading ports. Three small Government steamers maintained connexion with the British and French liners calling at Zanzibar.

The following table[1] shows the number and tonnage of ocean-going vessels (excluding native craft) which entered the coast ports in 1913 :—

Port.	No.	Tons.
Moa..	25	11,279
Tanga	229	707,616
Pangani	75	27,752
Bagamoyo	105	222,335
Dar es-Salaam	236	745,415
Salale	56	53,975
Kilwa	55	87,800
Lindi	58	102,803
Mikindani	40	84,270
Other ports..	75	53,729
Total	954	2,096,974

The native craft entering the ports during 1912 numbered 3,457, with a total tonnage of 71,689.

Traffic on the Great Lakes.—On *Victoria Nyanza* the Germans had only dhows for carrying rice from the mills at Ukereve and Nanso to Mwanza, and small steamers belonging to the Deutsche Nyanza-Schifffahrts-Gesellschaft. The latter company, besides carrying on a transport service between German trading centres and the Uganda railway, had rice mills and acted as general traders on the lake. The bulk of the lake trade, however, was in the hands of British steamers of the Uganda Railway Company, six of which are of over 700 tons displacement, and four of

---

[1] From the Consular Report, 1912–13.

over 1,000 tons. The British company owns about a dozen steel barges (the largest of 120 tons capacity) and also a flotilla of small craft.

On *Lake Tanganyika* trade in 1913 was handled by the small German steamer *Hedwig von Wissmann* (sunk on February 9, 1916), a Belgian steamer, two large German-owned dhows, and sundry small craft belonging to Indian and Arab dealers. The *Götzen* (400 tons), the first of three steamers intended to ply in connexion with the Central railway, was launched at Kigoma in August 1915. This was a twin screw steamer, with a draught, when laden, of $7\frac{1}{2}$ ft.

On *Lake Nyasa*, before the war, the Germans had a steamer similar to the *Hedwig* called the *Hermann von Wissmann*, which was destroyed on May 30, 1915; it formerly made nine voyages per annum round the lake, starting from Alt-Langenburg. They had in 1915 a large iron boat, a whale-boat, a steel-built wherry, and many big canoes in Mwaya, and a large whale-boat in Wiedhafen. The English Government steamers on the lake were the *Gwendolen* (*c.* 150 tons), the *Pioneer* (50 tons), and an old gunboat. Two other steamers, the *Queen Victoria* (120 tons) and the *Domira* (80 tons), came once in about five weeks to Mwaya, which was also visited by two large steamers of the Likoma Mission (English), a small steamboat of the Berlin Mission, a privately-owned steamer, and three dhows. The natives use dug-out canoes; they are excellent sailors and boatmen.

The services on Lakes Tanganyika and Nyasa and the Rufiyi river were under the management of the Ost-afrikanische Eisenbahngesellschaft.

(c) Cable and Wireless Communication

Tanganyika is connected with the international cable system by the line of the Eastern and South African Telegraph Company from Dar es-Salaam to Zanzibar *via* Bagamoyo.

The construction of a high-power station at Tabora in 1914 brought the territory into wireless communica-

tion with Togo and what was German South-West
Africa, and through Togo with Nauen in Germany,
thus making it independent of British cables. There
were also wireless stations at Mwanza and Bukoba on
Victoria Nyanza, and at Dar es-Salaam. The first two
were intended for local administrative use; the last
was principally for marine work, and in 1913 could
reach ships as far off as Cape Gardafui. In 1914
the erection of a station at Kigoma on Lake Tanganyika
was contemplated. This was intended to bring the
internal system into communication with the chain of
stations along the Congo river.

(B) INDUSTRY

(1) Labour

(a) *Supply*

White settlement on a large scale is not possible in
Tanganyika, nor does it appear that the Germans
wished to encourage it. The large tracts granted
for plantations had to be worked by native labour, and
the supply of that labour is the chief problem that the
rulers of this territory have to face. The natives
prefer cultivating their own lands to working for
wages on the plantations. German residents have expressed the opinion that a sufficient quantity of native
labour can be obtained only by methods of compulsion,
or by taxing the native until he has to work in order to
pay his taxes. It was certainly upon these principles
that the Germans acted. Yet out of a native population
of some $7\frac{1}{2}$ millions there were in 1912 only about
172,000 engaged as wage earners. Of these 91,892
were employed on plantations. The most populous
part of the country, the north-west native states, is an
untapped reservoir of labour, and it is in that very
region that native civilization and economic development have reached their highest point.

Possibilities of obtaining labour vary greatly in different districts. In districts where there are not
many plantations local labour can be used; where

plantations are numerous planters have to rely upon labour recruited from a distance. In the Tanga interior labour is not plentiful, as the local tribes can make sufficient money for their needs by work on their own farms. One of the chief recruiting areas is the district of Tabora, in which the density of population is not great (4·1 per square kilometre), but from which labour is supplied to more densely populated parts, though this drain on Tabora's resources has helped to check the growth of its own population.

The Germans secured labour by various methods. Licensed recruiters went round to collect labourers, making a separate contract with each man engaged. Regulations governing this recruiting were issued in 1913. The number of recruiters was limited, and a district assigned to each, so that they might be more easily controlled; many abuses, such as systematic deception of the natives, were checked. The period for which workpeople could be engaged was extended from 180 to 240 working days. The new regulations, however, failed to give satisfaction to the planters, who complained that the recruiters were unable to supply enough hands, and that they still engaged men for the shorter period in order to derive profit from re-engaging them when discharged.

In the district of Dar es-Salaam ' labour markets ' had been established. Planters reported the number of hands required; then such natives as were willing to work were collected in centres, where the planters met them and made contracts with them personally. This system, however, was abolished in deference to public opinion in Germany.

Taxation of the native was another method of securing his labour. He was obliged to work in order to have enough money to pay. Sometimes forced labour was insisted upon, ostensibly for default in the payment of the hut-tax.

Labour for certain purposes, such as porterage and local public works, was practically compulsory, though paid.   This forced labour was used indirectly to stimulate 'voluntary' work on the plantations.   In several districts, natives who could produce cards showing that they were employed by European planters were exempt from Government labour, which they would otherwise have been forced to undertake.   The system appears to have had good results in cases where supervision by European officials was possible.

(b) *Labour Conditions*

The native tribes differ very much in point of readiness to work and of efficiency as labourers. The Masais altogether refuse to work on the plantations.   The tribes most popular with European plantation managers, and employed largely in the Tanga district, are the Wanyamwezis, from the Tabora district; the Wasukumas, from the shores of Victoria Nyanza; and the Wairambas, from the Iramba region in the south.

The Swahilis of the coast, though useless as labourers, have considerable commercial capacity, and are found throughout the territory as small traders, servants of the administration, and transport workers.

The appointment of six Commissioners of Native Labour (*Distriktskommissäre*) to superintend the relations of employers and employed had a beneficial influence on labour conditions.

Wages varied in the different parts of the territory.   The highest in 1913 were paid in the older plantation districts, where, as shown in the German official report, they reached an average of 12 to 15 rupees for 30 working days.   The lowest remuneration was given in districts where labour was least in demand and where payments in cash were almost unknown.   In Ruanda the rate per day was 8 to 10 hellers (1½d.), in the interior of Urundi only 5 hellers, and at Usumbura 15 to 20 hellers.   Food was not given in addition.

(2) Agriculture

(a) *Products of Commercial Value*

The *vegetable produce* of Tanganyika is of three sorts. First, there is the wild produce of the forests, collected by the natives; second, there are the crops, chiefly cereals, grown by the natives for their own use; third, the crops grown for export on plantations owned by Europeans and worked by native labour. The number of indigenous plants of economic value is very great, and many plants which have been introduced find in Tanganyika conditions favourable for their growth.

Foodstuffs.—Only three foodstuffs, sorghum, rice, and coffee, have so far attained any importance in the export trade overseas. The value of these exports in 1912 was 150,000, 201,000, and 1,903,000 marks respectively.

Sorghum, a large millet, called by the natives *mtama*, is grown almost everywhere, particularly on the coast, and forms the staple food, except where bananas alone are eaten. The stem contains much saccharine juice; the plant is used for feeding cattle. In 1911 more grain was imported than exported; in 1912 the situation was reversed, only 298,307 kilogrammes being imported, while 1,205,987 kilogrammes were exported. It would be possible so to stimulate cultivation that a large surplus would remain for export after all native requirements had been satisfied. Some other varieties of millet are grown, but are of only local importance.

Rice was being cultivated more and more by natives before the war, and the Central railway was expected to open up fresh rice-producing country. Water rice chiefly was grown; little was exported. In European plantations, which are mainly in the Lindi and Pangani districts, only 466 hectares of rice were being cultivated in 1912. 590 tons of cleaned rice went to Uganda[1] in 1911, and 900 tons in 1912; yet 15,735

---

[1] Imperial Institute Bulletin No. 2, 1917.

tons were imported in 1913 as against 13,213 tons in 1912, and 17,330 tons in 1911.

Maize is grown in preference to sorghum in certain districts of the interior; but natives accustomed to the one take unwillingly to the other. In 1912 the Europeans cultivated only 3,790 hectares of this crop. *Wheat* (chiefly in Langenburg), *oats, rye,* and *barley* are grown in the higher lands by white inhabitants for their own use, but not on a commercial scale.

Cassava (chiefly Madagascan) is the principal tuberous plant in the territory. The root of the bitter cassava yields (1) cassava meal, which is sold widely in France as *farine de manioc*, has much food value, and deserves more attention than it receives, and (2) cassava starch or tapioca, which is of little food value, but supplies cheap starch. Cassava is cultivated chiefly in the south-west and along the coast; it grows easily and is attacked by few pests or diseases.

Sweet potatoes are grown near the great lakes, and form one of the chief articles of diet. In Ruanda alone the annual consumption was reckoned at 2,400,000 cwt. *Yams* and *taro* grow chiefly where bananas grow. English potatoes and vegetables thrive in the higher districts of the interior. Besides peas, beans, and two kinds of spinach, young bamboo shoots, tomatoes, and cucumbers are also grown for food.

Coffee was grown successfully in the Kilimanjaro district by small planters, and by natives in Bukoba and elsewhere. In Usambara it was a failure, though much money was spent on it. Arab coffee chiefly was grown, and its prospects were good, as the quality was satisfactory and the price reasonable. In 1912 there was an export of 1,575,000 kg. (value 1,903,368 marks). In 1910 the export had been 996,000 kg. (value 837,744 marks). Germany took most of the crop, but a little went to England.

The growing of *tea* was dwindling latterly, and little has been exported.

Cocoa was more grown, 120 hectares having been under cultivation in 1912, as against 100 in 1911. The export was not large.   10,000 kg. went to Germany in 1912, and apparently none in 1913.   A little over 1,000 kg. was sent to England.

The natives grow *tobacco,* though not in sufficient quantities to satisfy their wants.   On plantations tobacco-growing was still experimental in 1914. 28,000 kg. was exported in 1911 and 35,000 kg. in 1912.

Poppy-seed was produced for export.   The official export figures, 2,064 kilogrammes in 1912, included hashish, betel-nuts, and poppy-seed, as well as opium. Betel-nuts were grown in the Pangani district, but in 1912 practically the whole crop (26,000 kg.) was taken by Tanga.

Fruits.—*Bananas* are the chief native food in the region between the great lakes, in the Kilimanjaro district, and also in west Usambara.   The bananas grown by the natives are not exported.   Seventy varieties of banana tree are found, of which the commonest is the true banana with a trunk of 20 to 25 ft. in length and a yellow fruit triangular in section.   Many other fruits grow wild, and European fruits are cultivated for private and local consumption.

Date palms exist chiefly in Tabora, where their Arab owners farm them out to people of Indian origin, who pay high rents even for single trees.   After the banana, the date is the most popular of Tanganyika fruits.

Sugar and Spices.—Sugar-cane was much cultivated under Arab rule, notably near the Rufiyi and on the lower Pangani.   There were many small factories.   Sugar is now grown mostly by natives. Urundi is said to be the district best suited for its cultivation.   European sugar plantations existed on a small scale in four districts. and occupied 138 hectares in 1912.   Rum for export was made at a refinery at Pangani.

There are many spices, and the Germans tried without success to break the monopoly of the spice islands of Zanzibar and Pemba. ***Cinnamon*** gives fair promise, but may prove unremunerative owing to the fall in prices. If supplies from the French colonies were cut off from British markets, or if market prices were sufficiently remunerative, *vanilla* might be planted more widely. It was grown formerly for export. The natives grow *cloves* on the island of Mafia. *Ginger* is not indigenous, but is cultivated on a small scale in Mahenge. The growth of *common pepper*, which yields white and black peppers, has not been commercially successful, but chillies have answered well in Wilhelmstal. **Red pepper** grows wild throughout the country.

Oil-yielding Plants.—*Ground-nuts* are extensively cultivated by the natives along the coast and near the great lakes. They yield an oil valuable for cooking, making fats, and conserving sardines; the residue is compressed into feeding-cake. They are exported in considerable quantities to various European countries as well as to adjacent states. The export had increased from 3,099,000 kilogrammes (value 595,961 marks) in 1910 to 6,078,000 kilogrammes (value 1,273,066 marks) in 1912.

Sesame (*sim-sim*), an annual, which costs little labour and gives a generous return, is cultivated by natives in the territory as a foodstuff, and is used largely for local consumption. All the larger coast towns have primitive mills, worked usually by camels, for expressing oil from the seeds. The amount exported in 1912 represented less than 1 per cent. of the world's supply. There is a demand in Europe for sesame oil as a substitute for olive oil in soap-making, and for preparing other edible oils and fats, and the residual cake is much used on the Continent for feeding cattle. The export in 1912 was 1,881,000 kg. (value 523,179 marks), but since then the export has increased considerably, and should continue to grow as new railway sections are opened.

The *Taler gourd* is cultivated by the natives, and the seeds, which contain highly nutritious oil and albumen, are eaten both raw and cooked, but for want of a satisfactory shelling machine have not found a market in Europe.

The *castor-oil* plant (*Ricinus communis*) grows wild everywhere, and is cultivated widely for local needs in Urundi and Bismarckburg.

The *coconut palm* up to 1914 was extensively cultivated by the Arabs for local use, but not much in European plantations, except at Dar es-Salaam and Tanga. The total number of trees owned by Europeans in 1912 was 784,500. Planters were extending existing plantations in preference to planting new areas. Despite a large local demand, the export of copra had become important, as the quality was exceptionally good.

The following table shows the export in 1910-13:—

Year.	Metric tons.	Value in marks.
1910	5,338	1,909,329
1911	5,420	1,844,971
1912	4,241	1,563,042
1913	5,477	2,348,012

Oil palms grow in the Tanganyika district and in other parts of the territory, but not in such profusion as in West Africa. North of Ujiji there are said to be 700,000. The natives make little palm-oil, and in the Tanganyika district the groves are neglected and overcrowded. European cultivation of oil palms was merely experimental in 1913.

Rubber.—The chief rubber-yielding plants native to Tanganyika are *Landolphia stolzii* and *L. tondeensis*; the former is a vine common in Langenburg, the latter a shrubby plant found in the southern parts of the territory. The chief area in which the natives collect wild rubber lies south of a line drawn from Bagamoyo to Ujiji, but collection had decreased partly on account of restrictions and partly through the competition of other industries. The following table shows the export of plantation and wild rubber in 1910-12 (but *cf.* p. 94) :—

Year.	Plantation rubber.		Wild rubber.	
	Kilog.	Marks.	Kilog.	Marks.
1910	413,895	3,291,934	257,034	2,471,821
1911	683,753	3,606,328	152.076	1,658,301
1912	1,017,025	7,233.771	172,699	1,119,006

Of plantation rubber, the variety preferred is *Manihot glaziovii* (Ceará), which in 1912 occupied 44,903 hectares of the 45,317 hectares planted with rubber. This Ceará rubber is seen in areas of 6 or 7 square miles all over the country along the Central railway from Dar es-Salaam to Morogoro and beyond. With commendable forethought the Germans planted these trees at intervals of 8 ft. in rows 10 ft. apart over great tracts of bush country which had been looked upon as waste land. Ceará is not equal to Pará rubber; and, so far, the rubber trade in the territory has not been a complete commercial success; but plantations were largely increasing before the war, and there is good ground for hope for the future, especially when railway extensions make it possible to utilize large areas of bush land. There are rubber plantations in the Usambara district and near Kilwa and Lindi. Rubber cultivation could be widely extended as a native industry. Besides Ceará, Pará rubber (*Hevea brasiliensis*) and *Ficus elastica* have been tried in small quantities. Owing to the fall in the price of rubber in 1912, the 1913 crop of 1,367,000 kilogrammes fetched only a little over six and a half million marks.

Gums and Resins.—*Copal*, the exudation of a tree that grows wild, is found frequently in its fossilized state in the coastal districts. Its small export is not likely to increase. There is plenty in the Belgian Congo, but in Tanganyika the best deposits are becoming exhausted. *Gum acacias* grow wild in some parts, and attempts have been made to introduce them elsewhere. *Acacia catechu*, which grows everywhere, yields a tanning material known as catechu, pegu-catechu, or brown cutch.

Fibre-producing Plants have an important place among the vegetable products of Tanganyika, and their yield is yearly increasing in value. The most important for export is sisal hemp, but there are also kapok, cotton, sanseviera, and others. ·

Kapok grows wild everywhere in profusion, and the great demand for its floss in Germany, together with the fall in the price of rubber, induced many planters in 1912 to undertake its cultivation. The export was small but increasing, and rose from 12,000 kg. (value 13,040 marks) in 1910 to 52,000 kg. (value 62,600 marks) in 1912. Central installations for preparing the fibre for export were recommended by the Kolonial-Wirtschaftliches Komitee.

The chief *cotton* districts are Lindi, in the south, and Mwanza, on Victoria Nyanza. Till 1911 cotton was grown chiefly in the north, but latterly there has been more in the south. The output, though not the price, will be seen to have been rising steadily:—

Year.	Cotton bales at 250 kilog.	Price per kilog.	Total value in marks.	Approximate value in £.
1908	1,081	0·92	249,438	12,471
1909	2,077	0·85	440,461	22,023
1910	3,581	1·21	751,299	37,564
1911	4,322	1·23	1,331,818	66,590
1912	7,526	1·12	2,110,236	105,511
1913	8 768		2,620,000	131,000

Native cultivation was heavily subsidized by the Government and by the Kolonial-Wirtschaftliches Komitee. The latter bought and delivered seed free to the Imperial provincial offices. The value of the seed distributed in 1913-14 amounted to 151,000 marks, but it was doubtful whether the distribution would be continued. Guaranteed prices were maintained for certain cottons in different districts, and prizes were given for the best cultivation, quality, and yield. Efforts were also made to replace imported Egyptian seed by locally-grown varieties and to standardize the variety in each district, so as to facilitate disposal of crops. It has been found that American upland cottons are better suited to native cultivation than Egyptian varieties.

European cultivation was also helped in a similar way, and the area under cotton increased from 1,965 hectares in 1903 to 12,941 hectares in 1912. Even the latter figure represented only about $2\frac{1}{2}$ per cent. of the total area covered by European plantations in the territory. Down to 1913 there had been many failures, and everything points to native cultivation being the more advantageous system. A combination of native and European cultivation was tried in 1912-13 in the Lindi district. European plantations of about 500 hectares were sown with cereals, vegetables, and cotton, and a large ginnery was set up. The planters then let the land round the plantations in small parcels to the natives, prepared the ground by machinery, supervised the manuring, and afterwards bought at the fixed local price the cotton grown by the natives. The motor-driven ginneries set up by the Kolonial-Wirtschaftliches Komitee increased in number from 7 in 1907 to 38 in 1913. There were also many hand machines.

On March 14, 1910, an agreement was drawn up fixing the respective responsibilities of the Reichs-Kolonialamt and the Kolonial-Wirtschaftliches Komitee in furthering cotton cultivation. The Government Agricultural Research Station undertook seed trials, the supplying of water and manure, the repression of pests, the testing of soil, and the meteorological service. At the outbreak of war the Government had five or six experimental cotton stations, with white staff and travelling native instructors. The Komitee dealt with the economic and commercial side, financing light railways for transport, negotiating for the reduction of railway and shipping tariffs, improving waterways, drainage and irrigation, occasionally establishing large ginneries, making agreements for the purchase of cotton, and giving advice. It also supplied planters with machinery and presses at cost price, to be repaid in three yearly instalments.

The cultivation of *sisal hemp* is the premier industry of Tanganyika. In 1913, out of 100,000 hectares of cultivated plantation land, nearly 25,000 were under sisal, while 30 or 40 modern decorticating establishments were run by steam and oil engines, and fed by light field railways. The hemp is obtained from the Mexican plant *Agave sisalana*. The first export, in 1898, was only 3 bales; in 1912 it was 17,000,000 kilogrammes (value 7,000,000 marks). In 1913 the crop represented 19,968,000 kg. of best quality (value 10,342,000 marks), and 1,136,000 kg. of hemp waste (value 368,000 marks). If sisal is to be remunerative to the planter, the price on the Hamburg market must not, according to German commercial calculations, fall below 370 marks per ton, exclusive of capital charges. A general estimate puts the average price for recent years at 500 marks per ton. The hard fibre from agave leaves is preferred for standard binder twine, as it is tough, even and strong, and does not kink when wet. It is also in request for baling twine, ropes, and many other uses. The German sisal owes its superiority to skilful treatment, but there is now excellent English and Australian scutching machinery for decorticating the leaves. The plant needs little care; if the leaves are properly cut, it lasts from ten to fifteen years. Volcanic soil and coral land, such as are found on the coast of Tanganyika, are particularly favourable to it, and stony ground is no disadvantage. Sisal plants can be grown at elevations up to 1,400 metres. The plant has done better in Tanganyika than in its original home, and has overcome the competition of cotton by its greater yield and the quality of its fibre. Before the war there were four large North German sisal companies, one of which has paid as much as 50 per cent.

The Kolonial-Wirtschaftliches Komitee gave a high place amongst other native flosses to *Calotropis*, as being easily cultivated from seed, and fetching nearly as high a price as kapok. They advised that it should be planted alongside the latter, for it bears quickly and yields a return whilst the kapok trees are growing to maturity.

Funtumia elastica floss has also been spun successfully, and *ramie* fibre was experimented with at Arusha. The latter is important in the textile industry and in the manufacture of gas mantles; the leaves could be used as food for silkworms, which were being bred successfully in Morogoro.

Sanseviera grows principally along the upper reaches of the Pangani, in the Mwanza and Bukoba residencies, and round Tabora. The plants grow wild and propagate themselves, requiring no attention; the harvesting may be delayed for a long time, and the leaves stored for a good while before the fibre is extracted. This gives it an advantage over sisal, which must be harvested at the right moment, whilst its fibre must be extracted from the leaves as soon as they are cut.

Dyewoods of several indigenous varieties have been experimented with by the agricultural authorities.

The following figures from the German official report show the distribution of the chief crops grown on European plantations in 1912:—

	Total area under cultivation.	Total area yielding crops.
	hectares.	hectares.
Cereals—		
Maize	3,790	3,790
Rice	466	466
Other cereals	2,350	2,350
Palms—		
Coconut palms	8,178	1,983
Oil palms	104	6
Fruits—		
Bananas	155	155
Other fruits	476	476
Beverages and spices—		
Cocoa	120	70
Coffee	4,803	2,191
Others	71	71
Sugar cane	138	138
Rubber—		
Manihot	44,903	17,044
Other kinds	414	72
Fibres—		
Cotton	12,941	12,941
Kapok	2,632	641
Sisal hemp .. .	24,751	14,359

Live-stock.—Cattle-breeding is firmly established in the north-west districts, but it is prevented in many other parts by the tsetse fly, and also by rinderpest and catarrhal fever. Sir Alfred Sharpe and others look on the vicinity of Lake Kivu as one of the best cattle countries in Africa. The export of living animals through Zanzibar and the Belgian Congo was prohibited. A meat industry might be developed with success now that Victoria Nyanza and Lake Tanganyika have rail communication with the sea. Government figures for cattle in the territory are based mainly on estimate. The official report stated that in 1911 there were 42,927 European-owned and 2,060,490 native-owned cattle in the territory; while in 1912 there were 43,617 European-owned and 3,950,250

native-owned.   The density of herds was greatest in
the sultanate of Ruanda and in the residency of
Mwanza, each of which districts in 1912 contained
over 1,000,000 head, so that together they represented
about 50 per cent. of the total figures.

All the cattle in the territory are of the zebu type.
A large-horned variety is bred by the Watusis only,
and is called after them, while a small-horned variety
is found amongst many tribes, the best known being the
Masais, after whom these cattle are often called. Dr.
Lichtenfeld in 1913 estimated the number of the Masai
cattle at 1,500,000 and of the Watusi cattle at 750,000.
A smaller variety, the Sokotra zebu, found on the coast
near Dar es-Salaam, was introduced by Indian traders,
and is well suited to the climate.

The native methods of cattle-raising are primitive.
Systematic breeding is practised with success only by
the Masais and Watusis, and on a smaller scale by the
Wahehe and Wagogo tribes. The best breeders are the
Masais, who have reared bulls fit for the conditions
of the country and suitable for use by Europeans in
breeding. Official efforts to improve stock were
hindered by the natives' unwillingness to sell their stock,
and by the liability to disease engendered by the over-
stocking of pastures. European cattle are liable to be
attacked by the micro-organisms of Texas fever and
anaphasmosis, which are universally present, though
they do not cause fever in the native cattle. The latter
are hardy and docile; breeds imported for crossing
with them should have like qualities and exceed them
in milk and meat production. The early attempts to
cross with European breeds failed because each settler,
as a rule, chose the breed best known to him in his own
home in Germany, instead of studying the local conditions. By crossing, however, with bulls from the
Italian Campagna, favourable results have been
obtained in Sadani (Bagamoyo). In 1912 cross-bred
cattle were being used to some small extent for
draught purposes.

In most parts of Tanganyika *horses* cannot be used; horse-sickness appears annually between April and July. Europeans owned 202 horses in 1912. *Zebras* have been tried for draught and riding, and have been crossed fairly successfully with horses. In 1912 there were 22,091 native-owned *donkeys*, and 2,543 owned by Europeans. Europeans owned 375 *mules* in 1912, mostly imported.

The figures for the number of *sheep* and *goats* in the territory are based on estimate only. The official report gave the totals for 1911 as 4,930,560 native-owned and 33,406 European-owned, and for 1912 as 6,398,000 native-owned and 41,647 European-owned. The natives rear sheep and goats chiefly in the north, especially near the Belgian Congo frontier; 50 per cent. of those owned by Europeans in 1912 were in the Arusha district. The official report of 1911-12 stated that the breeding of sheep for wool was a failure, partly owing to lack of technical knowledge, and partly because the climate and pasturage were unsuitable.

Pigs do well in all high-lying districts; the number owned by Europeans in 1912 was 5,460. There are fair propects for *ostrich* farming, particularly in Arusha and Moshi, though the number of birds was only 173 on April 1, 1913. Both European and native *fowls* have been successfully reared, but European breeds have suffered through diphtheria.

Animal Products.—*Hides* and *skins* are the chief animal products. In 1913 the export reached a total of 3,456,500 kilogrammes (value 5,500,000 marks).

Samli, a preparation of clarified butter, is made in large quantities by the natives, and a certain amount is exported. Wild bees feed on the bloom of the Ceará rubber tree, and the natives gather *honey* and *wax*.

Since the German occupation the *ivory* industry which once held the chief place, has declined remarkably. The German Government adopted laws similar to those in force in British East Africa for the protection of the game, of which there are vast numbers

The quantity and value of ivory exported increased from 1906 to 1909, and then fell rapidly.

Meat and *dairy produce, hippopotamus* and *boar tusks, rhinoceros* and *antelope horns, cowrie shells, tortoiseshell, swords* of the *sword-fish*, and *wild silk* are exported.

(b) *Methods of Cultivation*

European Cultivation.—The plantation system did not begin to expand unmistakably till within the last fifteen or sixteen years. The three areas of plantations are the Usambara region, with its port of Tanga, the Central Railway region, and the southern region, served by the port of Lindi. Many British firms own interests in these plantations (*cf.* p. 87). In 1912 the total area of European concessions was 542,124 hectares, of which 105,282 hectares were under cultivation and 56,753 yielded crops. The number of Europeans employed on plantations, exclusive of owners, was 498 in 1911 and 606 in 1912.

Native Cultivation.—The low density of the population (about 8 per square kilometre) and the low development of the natives have hitherto prevented intensive culture. In 1914 it was estimated that only 1/800th of the land was under cultivation. Native methods are primitive and wasteful. Land is cleared by cutting and burning forest trees, bush, and vegetation. The ashes render the soil very fertile for about five years, after which a fresh patch is cleared and the old abandoned or planted with bananas or coconut palms. The plough is little used; the customary implement is the hoe. A very elementary system of rotation of crops is practised.

The Government *Referent* for agriculture at Dar es-Salaam was responsible for agricultural administration. Purely scientific research was undertaken by the Biological and Agricultural Institute at Amani. There were other experimental and technical stations at several centres, experts for various purposes, travelling instructors for the natives, trained engineers for visiting plantations and factories, and other machinery for developing agriculture.

The planters formed various agricultural associations, which were finally merged in a National Economic Union of German East Africa and an Economic Union for the Southern Provinces.

Irrigation will undoubtedly play a large part in the development of the native states in the neighbourhood of the lake system.   The Germans had prepared a scheme for drawing water from the south-east corner of Victoria Nyanza through the Mbala plain to the great Wembere plain.   The expert's report pronounced this district to be extremely favourable for cotton-growing, its soil being equal to the best of Texas and the Mississippi region; crops raised by irrigation would repay the cost of constructing a canal; an area of 230,000 hectares of either good or very good cotton soil was to be irrigated by two canals with a capacity of 92 cubic metres per second; 3,000 hectares of good cotton country were to be worked on the Mbala plain. Combined with this scheme was another for using the water-power for electric traction for about 200 kilometres of the proposed Tabora-Ruanda line.   The estimated cost was: canal with power installation, 26,000,000 marks; establishment of the irrigated area, 19,000,000 marks; total, 45,000,000 marks.

(c) *Forestry*

Generally speaking, there seems to be a tendency for the forest area to diminish.   To check the destructive native system of tree-burning, the Government had completed the formation of a number of forest reserves. On March 31, 1913, there were already 161 reserves, totalling 484,417 hectares, or $\frac{1}{2}$ per cent. of the whole area.   During the remainder of the year 274,000 hectares more were to be included.

The German Forestry Service controlled the policing of forests, their protection from fire, the formation and maintenance of reserves, reafforestation, and the valua-

tion and disposal of timber. At Wilhelmstal, Morogoro, and Mohoro there were forestry offices which
served twelve districts, while in other parts a forestry
official was lent to the District Commissioner's staff.
The Forestry Department conducted technical research
in co-operation with the Biological and Agricultural
Institute at Amani.

The three chief forests exploited are the Wiese,
Shume, and Sigi, in the Usambara region. The chief
timbers cut in the Wiese forest in west Usambara
(Wilhelmstal district) are pencil cedar (*Juniperus
procera*), Outeniqua yellowwood (*Podocarpus gracilior*),
and common East African yellowwood (*Podocarpus
thumbergii milanjianus*). The two last are sold in
Germany as 'East African pine.'   Yellowwood is
also exported to South Africa, and the export trade is
likely to develop further. Hardwood timbers are cut
in the Usambara forests, and are used chiefly in the
native school of carpentry at Tanga. The Shume
and Sigi forests produce *mkweo, mkenene, mareka,
mvule, mtamba,* and *kenge,* ornamental woods
employed by coach-builders and decorators, which,
though hard and firm, are light and easily worked.
With improved communication, wood for railway
sleepers and other purposes could be supplied from
the western forests to the Sudan *via* the great lakes.
Timber is also cut in the Rufiyi delta, and round the
ports of Tanga, Pangani, and Kilwa Kisivani. There
are magnificent timber forests on Mount Rungwe and
the Poroto range, north of Neu-Langenburg and Lake
Nyasa.

In 1910-11 there were 16,253 acres of mangroves
under exploitation in large swamps round the mouths
of about eight of the principal rivers, and the bark
was exported for tanning.

The Germans hoped to make large profits from
quinine, which is obtained from the bark of the
Cinchona succirubra. Production costs little, no
machinery being required. The trees were introduced
in 1900, and in 1907 there were already nearly 100,000.

(d) *Land Tenure*

By law, ownerless lands throughout the territory were domain or Crown land, a Government enquiry determining their extent. Natives were to continue to enjoy the land they occupied and were to be allowed at least four times as much as they cultivated. This, however, was a mere official declaration, and is no guide to the actual German treatment of the natives.

Seyyid Bargash, Sultan of Zanzibar, who claimed sovereign rights over the adjoining African coast, renounced these by treaty with the Deutsch-Ostafrikanische Gesellschaft. Under his rule, the actual soil of a property and the buildings or plantations upon it had often been in the hands of different tenants; and this dual ownership, inconsistent with European ideas, survived round Tanga and elsewhere even after the German Civil Code had been introduced. The anomaly became the more noticeable as land rose in value, and as conditions of ownership of the ordinary kind were applied to an increasing extent of territory. Some attempts were made to develop a land reform policy, but these led to many conflicts between the administration and the landholders.

Natives were evicted wholesale from their homes on all kinds of pretexts, while their huts were burnt and their effects destroyed. In Tanga, the Government took possession of the land in the town, having first removed the native population, then planted palms on it, and, as copra oil realized high profits, let out small holdings at high rents. At Dar es-Salaam two-thirds of the natives (16,000) occupied the Sultan's land (*Schollershamba*), covering 24·2 hectares, which included a great part of their reserve and had been acquired by a European association which granted them the right of settlement. In 1915 the municipality received from the Treasury a grant of 500,000 rupees to buy the *Schollershamba*, and the sale contract was signed or about to be signed. There can be little doubt that the natives would have experienced the same treatment as those at Tanga.

Outside the municipal areas, Crown land was not sold outright until at least half was cultivated, but was leased at 5 per cent. of the sale price of from 10 to 100 heller (100 heller = 1s. 4d.) per hectare per annum. The leasehold conditions were that cultivation must begin at once, and must be extended at the rate of one-tenth of the land each year. Pasture land was obtainable on the sole condition of its being fenced with wire or quickset hedge. Native rights on land taken up by Europeans were to be recognized to the extent of 4 hectares per hut.

The Ostafrikanische Landgesellschaft was formed to deal with the land concession granted to the Tanganyika railway, which holds 80 per cent. of its shares. The purchasers were chiefly settlers in search of small or moderate-sized plantations.

(3) FISHERIES

Fish are plentiful along the coast and islands, but the natives, with their very primitive equipment, do not catch enough to supply even an appreciable part of the local needs. The import figures demonstrate the extent of the further demand. Properly organized fisheries with facilities for salting, smoking, and drying would be profitable. Fishing for cowries, pearls, turtles. and ornamental shells is practised on a small scale, and there are a few sponge fisheries owned by Arabs.

Fish abound in the rivers and great lakes, but they are mostly coarse, and are often infested with worms. There are fisheries on the lower Rufiyi, and on the Mkomazi, Rovuma, and Pangani rivers, and also on lakes Mamba and Komba, in the Luengera valley. Lake Tanganyika has 87 species, of which 76 are not found elsewhere. Lakes Victoria, Nyasa, and Kivu have fewer varieties.

(4) Minerals

The mineral wealth of Tanganyika has not yet been fully ascertained. The district round Lake Nyasa, including the Livingstone mountains, where copper, gold, and coal are found in fairly close proximity, appears to be the most valuable; and next, probably, come the Uluguru mountains and the districts of Ruanda, north of Lake Kivu, Lindi on the southern and Mwanza on the northern frontier. With improved transport all could be exploited. In 1912 gold, mica, and garnets were exported overseas, and gold and salt overland. In 1911 the number of persons employed in mining was 2,235, an advance of 320 on the previous year.

Gold.—The most important gold mine is at Sekenke on the Iramba plateau, and is owned by the Kironda Goldminen-Gesellschaft. Some gold was also mined regularly in the Nassa mine in the Mwanza district. In 1912 the amount exported was 234 kilogrammes (value 530,624 marks); practically all went to Germany. The official report of the Kironda output was as follows:—

	1909.	1910.	1911.
Ore recovered ..	3,515 tons.	7,333 tons.	7,132 tons.
Smelted gold ..	176 kg.	429 kg.	395 kg.
Fine gold	134 kg.	347 kg.	316 kg.
Value	400,000 mk.	943,645 mk.	866,188 mk
Fine silver . ..	25 mk.	62 mk.	59 mk.
Average yield of gold per ton of ore ..	38·90 grammes	46·45 grammes	45·92 grammes

There is also gold near St. Michael, near Livale, and near Neu-Langenburg. It is possible that deposits of precious metals will eventually be found in many localities.

The *mica* of Tanganyika, though inferior to the best Indian ruby mica, is highly valued for electrical

insulation. It is found chiefly in the Uluguru mountains, but also on the north-east shore of Lake Kivu
and at Mahenge. In 1911 the export, most of which
went to Germany, was valued at £17,414. There are
deposits also in Usambara, but these have not been
successfully worked.

Iron ore is found in several places, and is smelted
in primitive fashion near Lake Nyasa. There is
also iron ore near Kilimanjaro. Magnetic iron ores
occur in various localities, especially in the Uluguru
range. There is hæmatite iron in the Upangwa district in the extreme south of the Livingstone range,
and near Nyasa. *Copper* is found at Ujiji in the form
of copper quartz (46 per cent. copper), and also north
of Bismarckburg, and at Masazi in Lindi. *Lead* is
found between 15 and 30 miles east of Kondoa-Irangi.

Coal of poor quality is found in several districts,
including the highlands in the Karroo formation, and
especially on the east shore of Lake Nyasa. The coal
to the north-west of the lake on the Songwe and Kivira
rivers is more important, being bituminous and good
for smelting iron ore. There are Karroo strata on the
east of Lake Tanganyika, but it is not known whether
coal exists there.

Carbonate of soda was found in Lake Natron, and
has been obtained in recent years by the Magadi Soda
Co. from Lake Magadi close by in Kenya. A branch
line connects this lake with the Uganda railway and
could be extended to Lake Natron. The soda deposits
of Lake Natron are, however, much more impure than
those of Magadi.

Salt was worked by the Central-Afrikanische Seen-
Gesellschaft (or Bergwerks-Gesellschaft) at Gottorp,
near Lake Tanganyika, where there are brine springs.
There were also small works in the Bagamoyo district.
Deposits of sea-salt are found along the coast.

Insoluble potash, suitable for manure, exists in three
forms—*felspar*, *leucite*, and *muscovite*.

Three minerals containing a high percentage of
uranium are valuable for their radio-active property.

These are *pitchblende*, found in the Lukwangule hills (Mbakana) of the Uluguru range; *rutherfordine* (a yellow carbonate of uranium and a variation of pitchblende); and *samarskite*, found in pegmatite veins in the Morogoro district. *Tourmaline* is reported in the Uluguru mountains, and *graphite* both there and in the Lindi district; the latter is not capable of exploitation under existing conditions. *Asbestos* is reported to occur in Morogoro.

Beryls and *amethysts* have not as yet been mined. *Almandine garnets* have been exported in moderate quantities from the Lindi district.

Mineral Rights.—The Prussian law, modified by an Imperial Decree of February 27, 1906, gave the owner of the soil no claim to its mineral riches. Prospecting was free, subject in native territories to special regulations. Europeans were not allowed in the north-west native districts. Prospecting claims were laid out in squares, not in circles, as in the Belgian Congo. Discoverers could insist on their claims being converted into mining areas (*Bergbaufelder*), which were marked out in rectangles having the lengths of adjacent sides measured in the ratio of 5 to 1. Claims not worked within two years were forfeited. Mining areas were taxed, and the State claimed part of the minerals extracted.

(5) Manufactures

European industrial productions consisted chiefly of material for public and private buildings, and were not on a sufficient scale to bring about an appreciable diminution of imports. Furniture was manufactured on a large scale. There should be good prospects for cement works, roofing-tile factories, glass works, and soap factories. The skilled workmen are mostly Indian. The minor industries are almost wholly in the hands of non-Europeans. Tailors and shoemakers are mainly Goanese; laundry workers, barbers, and glaziers are Indian. There are a few Cingalese ivory and wood turners, and some jewellers. Native work is confined to the production of pottery, iron spears, ornaments, copper and brass work, mats and baskets, wood carvings, brightly-coloured woven fabrics, oil products, cucumber molasses, soap, and salt. Large quantities of rough iron hatchets are exported to neighbouring colonies from Usindya, in Mwanza district. Dhows are built in Kilwa and Dar es-Salaam.

(6) POWER

There are central electrical works, owned by the Ostafrikanische Eisenbahngesellschaft, in Dar es-Salaam. In 1913, on account of prospective extensions in the city and harbour, this company ordered a new power-house and two new dynamos, to cost 250,000 marks.

In 1913 the Governor of German East Africa granted a concession to a Berlin contractor for an electric power-station to utilize the great Mpangani falls on the Rufiyi. The water power available both from the great lakes and the coast rivers, whose steep fall into the Indian Ocean is too rapid for navigation, together with the presence of mica mines and copper deposits, offers opportunities for the erection of hydro-electric installations. Very full regulations as to water rights were drawn up by the German authorities.

(C) COMMERCE

(1) DOMESTIC

(a) *Principal Branches of Trade*

European trade in Tanganyika is for the most part confined to the larger coast towns and ports, though there is a certain amount on the plantations. A great deal of the small trade along the coast is in the hands of Arabs and Indians, who trade with the natives throughout the territory with a success that the European, with his higher standard of living, cannot hope to achieve. There is also internal trade within the Indian communities, and among the natives of the interior.

There are no statistics of the domestic trade of the territory, but its growth is proved by the steady increase of the receipts from the industrial tax. Barter has been superseded more and more by cash transactions; and retail trade has been increasing everywhere, largely owing to the activity of the Indian shopkeeper, who buys hides, skins, and vegetable products from the natives, and sells them cotton clothing and other articles.

(b) *Markets and Towns*

Markets in Africa, when once established, do not readily change; and it is probable that after the war trade will pass through the same district markets as before. These varied in importance and number according to the density of population in the district and the degree of its development. In each of the six northern plantation districts (Kondoa-Irangi, Moshi, Arusha, Wilhelmstal, Tanga, Pangani), large markets were held daily at three points and occasionally at a few other places. The first three districts had in all six large markets, besides smaller ones on caravan routes. There were 23 markets in the Tanga district, besides those established on the plantations. Pangani had several regular markets, and there were smaller markets in the larger coast towns on the caravan routes. Of the north-western districts and residencies (Mwanza, Bukoba, Ruanda, Urundi), Mwanza had a large market in the town which gives it its name, and there were several others in the district. In Bukoba markets were rarer and were found chiefly at the Government posts and the residencies of the sultans. Ruanda had no markets where Europeans could obtain provisions. The caravans requisitioned their supplies from the sultans. Urundi had a principal market at Usumbura, and many others In the western districts (Ujiji, Bismarckburg, Tabora) there were large markets with regular hours at Ujiji, Bismarckburg, Uha, Tabora, and Shinyanga, and small poorly-stocked markets on the caravan routes. In the central districts (Bagamoyo, Morogoro, Dar es-Salaam, Rufiyi, Dodoma, Iringa, Mahenge) the markets were always established near the railway. Dodoma had plenty of well-supplied markets, with settlements of storekeepers, at Government posts and on the railway. The large district of Iringa had a large market at the headquarters of the administration. The quantities of native produce offered for sale were small, since the natives produced little more than they themselves required. Mahenge had a well-stocked market in Mahenge town, and there were dealers in several native places. In Morogoro markets existed only at the chief points on the railway. There were three or four regular markets in the Rufiyi district, where there are large native settlements. The small district round Dar es-Salaam was traversed by the railway and served by the capital, which had regular markets, European shops, and a bank. The districts of Langenburg and Songea towards the south were poorly developed, and had few markets, except at the administrative posts. The two southerly coast districts (Kilwa and Lindi), both well developed, differed largely in population. Lindi had white. planters and Indian and Swahili merchants, besides a large number of natives, and had well-stocked markets in the coast towns. Kilwa had hardly any white people, but many Indian settlements, and possessed a large market at Kilwa town and Indian shops in several places. There were European firms in Kilwa town and one in Livale.

(c) *Organizations to promote Trade and Commerce*

Despite representations made by local planters, the Government declined to establish an agricultural credit bank until the land should come to be of value apart from any work done on it. At present the cultivated land in the territory is tropical plantation, and its value depends entirely on its being kept in a state of cultivation. Where it is neglected, the result of years of work is annulled in a very short time.

A potent influence was exercised by the Imperial Colonial Office in Berlin, and by the Colonial Administration at Dar es-Salaam. Next to these in anxiety to promote German commerce in the Protectorate came the Senate of Hamburg. In addition there was the Hamburgisches Kolonialinstitut, a training college and research institution. All the chief trading interests, such as the Deutsch-Ostafrikanische Gesellschaft, the Deutsche Ostafrika-Linie, the Ostafrikanische Eisenbahngesellschaft, the Deutsch-Ostafrikanische Bank, and private firms such as Hansing & Co., were linked with each other and with Hamburg in such a way as to form parts of a single organization. Berlin had a great colonial propagandist society in the Deutsche Kolonialgesellschaft, with several semi-independent commissions, among them the Kolonial-Wirtschaftliches Komitee, with its cotton-growing committee, rubber-growing committee, oil products committee, and colonial technical committee. Berlin stood for the Government and the military and aristocratic interests; Hamburg for those of the shipowners and merchant-traders. Little scope for organized effort was left to individual initiative beyond participation in the activities of the planters' associations. There was a Chamber of Commerce in Dar es-Salaam and probably one in Tanga. There was some friction and much state control, but all united in the desire to perfect organization, to prevent, as far as possible, any but German goods entering the colony and any but German ships being engaged in the trade, and to ensure a place in the world's markets for the raw materials which it produces.

(d) Foreign Interests

The Germans during their occupation of the territory left little room for foreign interests. Gold mines, salt-works, plantations of sisal, cotton, and rubber, timber forests, and banks were worked by companies with their centres of administration at Berlin, Hamburg, Cologne, Düsseldorf, Wiesbaden, &c. In April 1913, the business undertakings in the territory numbered nearly a quarter of the total in all the German colonies together. Their capital similarly amounted to nearly £5,430,000, i.e., 21 per cent. of the total for all the German colonies combined.

A certain amount of English capital was attracted, especially by rubber plantations. In 1910 eight rubber companies were founded or reconstituted, viz., The East African Rubber Plantation Co., Ltd. (capital £90,000); Muhesa Rubber Plantations, Ltd. (capital £135,000, with an interim dividend of 10 per cent. in the first year); Lewa Rubber Estates, Ltd. (capital £250,000); Kamna Rubber Estate, Ltd. (capital £110,000); Kifulu Rubber Estates, Ltd. (capital £100,000—in liquidation in 1917); Manihot Rubber Plantation, Ltd. (capital £50,000, increased to £110,000); Mkumbi Rubber Plantations, Ltd. (capital £70,000); Mombo Rubber Plantation, Ltd. (capital £150,000). Of these the first four were still existing in 1917, but their amalgamation was then being considered; in the meantime they were working together. The sixth and seventh were amalgamated in 1912, Manihot Rubber Plantation, Ltd., increasing its capital for the purpose. The Mombo company was formed to take over the Kautschuk-Plantage Mombo; it does not appear in the latest directories. Subsequently there was formed the Mroweka Rubber Company, in the

Lindi district, of which no particulars are available; it seems probable that the estate has been absorbed by another company. In 1914 the prosperity of the English rubber plantations was increasing, though their fortunes had been adversely affected by the rubber crisis of 1912-13.

The African Silk Corporation, Limited (London 1910, capital £150,000) was affiliated to the Afrikanische Seiden-Gesellschaft, Berlin, by an agreement stipulating that the London company should hold all the properties and branches in Bukoba, on Victoria Nyanza, and in Uganda, while the German company should hold 35,000 fully-paid preference shares and a guarantee upon a further £20,000 of the London company's capital.

Another English company was the Trepang Company, Ltd., operating in Durban as well as in Dar es-Salaam. Two Anglo-German companies were the Anglo-German Gold-mining and Exploration Company, Ltd., a small company founded in recent years at Entebbe and Mwanza, and the Deutsch-Ostafrikanische Plantagengesellschaft, in liquidation in 1912, whose interests were sold to an English combine.

The total capital represented by British interests probably did not exceed £1,500,000. The number of British private individuals settled long enough in the territory to appear in the directory before the war was less than ten. The liquidator of enemy firms in Kenya points out in his report that no British importing house was working in German East Africa before the war.

Part of the interests of the Westdeutsche Handels- und Plantagen-Gesellschaft were Swiss, and two of its directors in 1912 were Swiss. One or two non-German companies existed at Victoria Nyanza ports. including the Società Coloniale Italiana of Milan. The East African Trading Company, Ltd., an Austrian firm with an English name, had a branch at Bukoba, but its headquarters were at Mombasa. A good many

Greeks, some Dutch, and a few Italians and Portuguese appear in the pre-war list of planters and general traders.

(e) *Methods of Economic Penetration*

In all those districts where the Germans had fully established themselves, they prevented other Europeans from introducing their own trade. In the north-west districts even the Germans had not penetrated effectively. The local Indian and Swahili traders have monopolized most of the domestic trade, and were once regarded by the Germans as constituting a danger to their own commerce; but means were found of ensuring that they should sell German goods, or at any rate receive their wares in German ships and through German export houses.

In the north the districts round the Victoria Nyanza were economically dependent on Kenya for their supplies and for the transport of their goods; but only the internal British transport services benefited, as the German merchants and shippers were firmly established on the coast at Mombasa. The construction of railways within Tanganyika, to compete with the Uganda railway, would greatly diminish even this benefit.

So far as the present British zone is concerned, the best chance of penetration for British interests lies in encouraging the big British-Indian export houses and banks to replace the Germans in accommodating the Indian and Swahili merchants.

(2) FOREIGN

(a) *Trade Returns: Trade with other Countries*

The position of Tanganyika on the western shores of the Indian Ocean, with a long frontier in central Africa, gives it opportunities for wide distribution of trade. During the German occupation only the overseas trade with Germany and the overland traffic on the Uganda railway had been much developed, and there was a marked tendency to concentrate all commercial activity in the Central railway and the port of Dar es-Salaam.

The relative importance of the overseas and overland trade may be seen by comparing the figures in the following table :—

(*a*) COAST PORTS TRADE

Year.	Imports.	Exports.	Total.
	Marks.	Marks.	Marks.
1910	32,594,967	15,818,709	48,413,676
1911	40,356,236	17,122,830	57,479,066
1912	44,691,775	25,079,776	69,771,551

(*b*) INLAND FRONTIERS TRADE

Year.	Imports.	Exports.	Total.
	Marks.	Marks.	Marks.
1910 ..	5,132,143	4,755,495	9,887,638
1911	5,069,923	5,149,071	10,219,194
1912 . ..	5,268,923	6,274,247	11,543,170

The chief overland routes for foreign trade are either by way of the Victoria Nyanza ports and the Uganda railway, or *via* Moshi on the Usambara line and Voi on the Uganda railway. The importance of the first route will be much reduced if the Usambara railway is continued to Victoria Nyanza. In the south there is an outlet *via* the Shire river and by rail to Chinde; but Tanganyika's share of the trade by this route is unimportant.

In the future there should be a much larger overseas trade with India, and direct trade with Australia;

much of the former trade with Germany should be diverted to Great Britain. South Africa and the Sudan both require certain of the products of Tanganyika, and are already working to send their products thither, at first by sea and eventually overland. Italian Somaliland has few needs, and the exports of Kenya are similar to those of Tanganyika; therefore trade with these two countries is less likely to increase. The fact that Tanganyika provides the nearest route from the sea to the rich central Congo region will render its future possession very valuable. But for the war, the total trade of the territory would have amounted to more than £5,000,000 in 1915.

Trade with Germany.—The total trade with Germany rose from £1,870,000 in 1911 to £2,180,000 in 1912, an increase of 16 per cent. Excluding specie, it reached £1,285,000, or 14·4 per cent. over the figures for 1911, while there was an increase of 35 per cent. in the exports to Germany. These figures, however, do not accurately indicate the nature of the trade. Many goods entered as arriving from Germany were merely trans-shipped at Hamburg. Cotton goods from Germany, for example, valued at £175,344 in 1912, were probably not in the main of German manufacture. On the other hand, many imports *via* Mombasa and the lake ports and from India *via* Zanzibar were of German origin, and many exports entered at the Customs under the headings of 'Rest of Africa' and 'Zanzibar' went to Germany.

Trade with Zanzibar.—This trade, which is mostly entrepôt, declined from £331,000 in 1911 to £271,000 in 1912, the decrease of 18 per cent. being due to quarantine regulations following an outbreak of cholera in the island. Almost all imports declined in value except cotton goods, in which there was an increase of £10,000, due to the return to Dar es-Salaam of large quantities by buyers who could not pay for them. The value of exports to Zanzibar fell from £104,000 in 1911 to £82,500 in 1912. Copra declined by £22,500. The principal exports were copra, simsim, ivory, sorghum, copal, coffee, maize, and bags for packing cloves.

Trade with South Africa.—According to the Official Report for 1912-13, podocarpus wood was exported to South Africa. It seems doubtful whether there will ever be an extensive import trade from South Africa, as the whole of the interior trade of the territory has been captured by the Indians; but South African coal might find a market, as it is superior to Bengal coal for steaming purposes. The trade between the Union of South Africa and German East Africa, always small, was entirely interrupted by the war. Exports reached their highest value in 1913, with a total of £390, and imports in 1912 with a value of £4,132, which fell to £3,997 in 1913.

Trade with the Belgian Congo.—The trade with the Congo went by four main routes, viz., Kissenyi, Usumbura, Ujiji, and Bismarckburg, and was limited to the transit of local products, cotton goods, and provisions. Kigoma on Lake Tanganyika, the terminus of the Central railway, will become the entrepôt station for the trade of eastern Congo and north-eastern Rhodesia. In 1912 goods to the value of £57,000, carried in transit, came from or went to the Belgian Congo.

Trade with Kenya.—In 1913-14, of the total receipts of the Uganda railway (Rs. 8,195,182), German East Africa contributed Rs. 1,639,036.

Trade with Rhodesia.—Mr. Hughes, the only white inhabitant of the territory round Lake Mweru in northern Rhodesia, during the late war established between Lake Tanganyika and the Rhodesian railway good motor-road and water communication, which may lead to moderate commercial developments. In 1913 German East Africa, it is recorded, sent goods to southern Rhodesia to the value of £111, but in 1912 the export was worth only £4, and in 1914 nothing was sent.

Trade with the rest of Africa.—Excluding transit trade with the Congo, and considering only the trade *via* the Uganda railway and Mombasa, the imports

from the rest of Africa in 1912 were valued at about
£22,000, and the exports about £300,000, the latter
finding their way principally to America (hides and
skins), Germany (coffee, cotton, ground-nuts, and sim-
sim), and France (ground-nuts and skins).   The imports came from Germany, Great Britain, the Netherlands, America, and Italy.

Trade with India.—According to the British Consular Report for 1912-13, the direct trade with India
rose from £360,000 in 1911 to £440,000 in
1912, and consisted almost entirely of imports.
The chief of these in 1912 were cotton goods
(£155,000) and rice (£139,000).   Generally speaking, more than two-thirds of the cotton goods
imported into German East Africa from India were
of Indian manufacture.   Other imports from India
were flour, samli, teakwood, and spices.   Sugar, glass,
hardware, umbrellas, and silk from India belonged
chiefly to the entrepôt trade.

The total value of the German East Africa goods
sent to India is given in the Indian returns (Cd. 8564)
as follows: 1910-11, £4,000; 1911-12, £2,000;
1912-13, £4,000; 1913-14, £1,000 or less; 1914-15,
£1,000 or less.

*Trade with other countries, including Great
Britain.*—The trade with countries other than Germany, India, Africa, and Zanzibar, rose from £400,000
in 1911 to £670,000 in 1912 (imports £376,500, exports
£294,000).   The value of the direct trade with the
United Kingdom was £291,000 (imports £124,000, exports £167,000).   The chief imports in 1912 were
cotton yarns and manufactures (£71,112), and corrugated iron (£14,683).   The chief export was rubber
(£144,950).   The Netherlands sent cotton, iron goods,
and tobacco, Norway timber, France wine and
olive oil, Italy wine, cotton, oil, and umbrellas, and
Russia petroleum, while America sent petroleum and
took a small quantity of sisal hemp.

(b) Exports

The total value of the exports[1] from 1909 to 1913, exclusive of goods in transit, was as follows:—

					Marks.
1909	...	...	...	...	13,119,481
1910	...	...	...	...	20,805,394
1911	...	...	...	...	22,437,760
1912	...	...	...	...	31,418,382
1913	...	...	...	...	35,551,040

Sisal and *rubber* were the chief exports in 1912, but *skins* and *hides, cotton, copra, coffee,* and *groundnuts* were also important. The value of the exports of each of these, from 1910-12, was as follows[2]:—

	1910.	1911.	1912.
	Marks	Marks.	Marks.
Coffee ..	837,744	1,266,034	1,903,368
Copra ..	1,909,329	1,844,971	1,563,042
Cotton..	751,299	1,331,818	2,110,236
Ground-nuts	595,961	489,738	1,273,066
Hides ..	2,889,133	3,035,183	4,067,350
Rubber	6,194,879	4,780,966	8,426,201
Sisal hemp	3,011,625	4,532,249	7,359,219

The export of *gold* began only in 1911, and fluctuated considerably, as also did that of *dairy produce*, which was first exported in 1912. The Consular Report for 1912-13 states that the total value of exports in that year was £1,570,915, of which £1,253,985 went *via* the coast ports and £316,930 *via* the lake ports. The increase on 1911 was 40 per cent., the coast trade increasing by 46·4 per cent. and the overland trade by 19·2 per cent. There was no export of specie in 1912.

In 1912, 57 per cent. of the exports went to Germany direct, 19 per cent. to the rest of Africa, excluding Zanzibar (which took 5 per cent.), and less than 11 per cent.

[1] From *Die Deutschen Schutzgebiete in Afrika und der Südsee,* 1912-13, and the British Consular Report, 1912-13.

[2] From the British Consular Report, 1912-13.

to Great Britain.   There was a tendency to make less use of Zanzibar for trans-shipment and to increase the United Kingdom's quota.

The exports direct to Germany in 1912 amounted in round numbers to 18,000,000 marks; coffee exceeded 500,000, raw cotton 1,500,000, sisal hemp 7,000,000 (practically the whole crop), and the various rubbers 5,500,000.   A total of 15,500,000 marks' worth of agricultural and forest produce went to Germany, amounting to more than 87 per cent. of the direct export thither.

The following table[1] shows the distribution of the exports among the various countries from 1910 to 1912 :—

	1910.	1911.	1912.
	£	£	£
Germany	629,260	660,351	891,342
United Kingdom	35,637	74,203	167,790
Rest of Europe	38,935	59,565	103,239
Zanzibar	139,225	115,752	82,471
Rest of Africa	193,057	208,499	301,599
India	1,984	1,693	1,251
Other countries	2,171	1,825	23,223
Total	1,040,269	1,121,888	1,570,915

(c) *Imports*

The total value of the imports[2] from 1909 to 1913, exclusive of goods in transit, was as follows :—

	Marks.
1909	33,941,707
1910	38,658,777
1911	45,891,642
1912	50,309,164
1913	53,358,500

[1] From British Consular Report
[2] From *Die Deutschen Schutzgebiete in Afrika und der Südsee*, 1912-13, and the British Consular Report on German East Africa, 1912-13.

Cotton goods are the most noteworthy import, and the demand for cotton clothing of European or Indian manufacture is likely to increase as new districts are opened up and the natives increasingly adopt civilized ways.   The cotton import amounted in 1913 to 28·4 per cent. of the total imports of German East Africa.   In 1912 the Japanese sent ready-made shirts direct from Kobe, and found a quick market.   The direct service of the Austrian-Lloyd steamers between Kobe and Aden may facilitate this trade.   The share attributed to Great Britain in the cotton imports rose from £25,201 in 1910 to £71,112 in 1912.   Other countries contributing cotton were America, the Netherlands, and India; of late years the Lombardy factories have competed; and in 1913 Austria-Hungary and Belgium were also seeking to obtain a share in the trade, the first-named with success.

Of imported foodstuffs *rice* is the most noteworthy, and amounted in 1913 to 6·9 per cent. of the total imports.   The import may decline considerably with increased native production, and the demand can also be met from the surplus of the Belgian Congo, but the large Indian community will always prefer the special varieties of Indian rice.   The import of *flour* in 1913 was 3,000 metric tons (value 999,424 marks), more than half of which came from India.

In 1913, 3,285 metric tons (value 2,519,162 marks) of *unclassified iron goods* and 1,291 metric tons of *machinery* were imported. *Corrugated iron* is used throughout the territory for roofing, and its import amounted in 1913 to 1,591 metric tons (value over 500,000 marks), or just under 1 per cent. of the total import trade.

There is a rising demand for *cement*, of which 15,000 metric tons were imported in 1913 (value 1,080,424 marks).   Almost all was from Germany.

The following table[1] shows the value of the chief imports in the period 1910-12:—

	1910.	1911.	1912.
	Marks.	Marks.	Marks.
Beer, wine, and spirits ...	1,030,473	1,192,067	1,290,930
Cement	444,477	769,369	959,435
Cottons and cotton goods...	10,317,658	12,719,725	14,984,826
Drugs and chemicals ...	542,771	728,371	800,755
Fire-arms, shot, cartridges	562,188	307,425	350,941
Food-stuffs	5,245,394	6,648,277	7,174,511
Glass and china ...	590,782	790,127	877,162
Iron, raw and manufactured	1,283,834	1,462,116	1,445,043
Locomotives, bicycles, &c.	1,184,614	1.439,484	2,483,895
Machinery	1,283,834	1,462,116	1.445,043
Petroleum	507,906	582,185	531,454
Timber	414,742	666,773	751,615
Tobacco	622,473	685,864	893,577

The share taken by each country in the import trade from 1910 to 1912 was as follows[1]:—

	1910.	1911.	1912.
	£	£	£
Germany	983,853	1,212,705	1,290,978
United Kingdom ..	54,290	77,320	124,034
Rest of Europe	92,519	152,907	209,681
Zanzibar	246,739	215,258	188,648
Rest of Africa	245,053	243,748	219,570
India	291,610	359,377	439,615
Other countries	18,872	33,266	42,931
Total	1,932,936	2,294,581	2,515,457

It must be remembered, however, that the goods are entered according to the port at which they were shipped, though they may have originated elsewhere. This is especially noticeable in the case of cotton goods (see above, p. 96).

[1] From the British Consular Report.

(d) *Customs and Tariffs*

German East Africa was not in the German Customs Union. All imported and exported goods were therefore subject to tariff. Specific import duties were imposed on beer, wines, spirits, and all essences and perfumes that contained alcohol; on rice, maize, beans, and other cereals and pulse; on tobacco, cigars, and cigarettes; and on salt; while on all other articles not specifically exempted there was a duty of 10 per cent. *ad valorem*, except on opium, hemp, and bhang, which paid a duty of 25 per cent. *ad valorem*. Duty-free articles included seeds, manures and disinfectants, agricultural machinery, vehicles, medicine and medical instruments, most kinds of printed books, pictures and statues. The principal export duties were on live animals, ivory, horns, hides and skins, wax, tortoise-shell, cowries, fresh meat, rubber, copal, plaiting-grass, wood, sisal, sugar-cane, tobacco, and salt. *Ad valorem* duties ranged up to 15 per cent. On live-stock the duties varied from 25 rupees per horse to 1 rupee per head of sheep, goats, and parrots. There were a number of exemptions of the customary kind.

(e) *Commercial Treaties*

Before the war there was no commercial treaty in existence between the United Kingdom and Germany. The treaty formerly in force had been terminated in 1898, and subsequent attempts to conclude an arrangement acceptable to both sides had failed. The war, therefore, has not had the effect of abrogating any instrument of first importance. Germany, however, had rightly understood that the United Kingdom did not propose to introduce any change of practice to her detriment, and on her side she procured the assent of the German Bundesrat at regular intervals to enactments extending most-favoured-nation treatment to British subjects and products. From 1910 up to the outbreak of war Germany allowed most-favoured-nation treatment to be extended to all British dominions, colonies, and possessions without exception.

In so far as Tanganyika forms part of the original free trade zone (*zone franche*) comprising the basin of the Congo and its extension to the Indian Ocean, the territory is subject to the Brussels Act and the other conventions governing that area, except in so far as later declarations may have expressly withdrawn certain portions of the said area from the operation of those agreements.

In the absence of a commercial treaty, commercial relations between Germany and Great Britain were established by Acts renewed from time to time and published in England every two years.

(D) FINANCE

(1) PUBLIC FINANCE

Like the rest of the German African colonies, German East Africa had both an ordinary and an extraordinary Budget. These were made out in Africa by the Protectorate Administration and submitted to the Budget Committee of the Reichstag in Berlin, where they were often subjected to very drastic reductions. The colony was not entirely self-supporting; it received an Imperial subsidy, employed since 1909 entirely in paying for the military establishment in the territory. The total revenue obtained from German East Africa between 1904 and 1914 was just under 120,000,000 marks (£6,000,000). The total expenditure for the same years, according to the official *Statistisches Jahrbuch* (1915), was about 339,200,000 marks (just under £17,000,000), of which about 167,600,000 marks covered ordinary and about 171,600,000 extraordinary expenditure. Most of the latter was spent in 1908 and 1913-14; there was no extraordinary expenditure in 1904-7

Although the Budget in recent years usually showed a balance between ordinary revenue and civil expenditure, this result was only obtained by crediting the revenue with a little over 3,000,000 marks annually, under the heading 'Savings from former financial years.' No details are forthcoming, and it is therefore impossible to say whether this was a real balance or a specious one merely intended to satisfy the Reichstag.

The heads of ordinary revenue in 1913 and 1914 were as follows :—

	1913.	1914.
	Marks.	Marks.
1. Taxes	5,434,000	6,220,000
2. Customs	4,425,000	5,550,000
3. Miscellaneous administrative services	1,897,000	2,024,000
4. Mint	455,000	571,000
5. Railway	528,000	653,000
6. Harbours	30,000	106,000
7. Railway shares[1]	1,001,000	1,344,000
8. Receipts of the military administration	5,000	10,000
Total	13,775,000	16,478,000

It will be seen from the above table that the principal sources of revenue were taxes (37·7 per cent.), Customs (33·6 per cent.), and miscellaneous administrative services (12·2 per cent.), which together represent more than 80 per cent. of the total.

The hut-tax of 3 rupees a year, which was unsatisfactory and could easily be evaded, was supplemented in 1908 by a poll-tax. According to this, workmen on European plantations paid $12\frac{1}{2}$ hellers a month, and in the interior all adult male natives who were capable of labour and who did not already pay hut-tax were liable

---

[1] Interest and dividends on the shares purchased by the Government from the Ostafrikanische Eisenbahngesellschaft.

to a tax of 1 to 3 rupees a year. It was the intention
of the German Government to develop the poll-tax
further and to let the hut-tax drop. There was also a
small industry tax, which in 1912 produced 1,023,000
marks (£50,000) and in 1914 was expected to produce·
900,000 marks. About 98 per cent. of the poll-tax and
hut-tax was paid by the natives, who also contributed
two-thirds of the industry tax.

The articles on which export duty was levied
were for the most part varieties of native produce, and
most of the import duties were imposed on articles
intended for native use or consumption—principally
textiles.

Minor items of revenue included succession duties,
salt excise duty, a tax on playing-cards, and the profits
accruing from the Deutsch-Ostafrikanische Bank.
The receipts of the mining administration from
licences, &c., amounted to 40,548 marks in 1910, 28,400
marks in 1911, and probably about 50,000 marks in
1912.

The ordinary expenditure, according to the Annual
Official Report, was divided between recurrent and non-
recurrent expenses and reserve fund, as follows :—

	In thousands of marks.				
	1910.	1911.	1912.	1913.	1914.
Recurrent expenses	11,974	13,019	16,461	18,226	20.461
Reserve fund ..	1,021	546	4	87	—
Non-recurrent expenses ..	896	1,103	2,856	2,192	3,282
	13,891	14,668	19,321	20,505	23,743

Of the recurring expenditure, civil administration
cost in 1913-14 over 9,000,000 marks, or 45 per cent.,
military administration over 17 per cent., and the
flotilla a little over 1½ per cent.

The details of expenditure in 1912 and 1913 were as follows :—

	1912.	1913.
	Marks.	Marks.
1. Civil administration	8,476,981	9,308,782
2. Military administration ..	3,568,900	8,615,030
3. Flotilla..	592,274	326,000
4. Savings fund	4,289	87,015
5. Collection of taxes	92,700	209,000
6. Other expenses	3,730,650	4,767,362
7. Non-recurring expenses ..	2,856,118	2,192,126
Total ordinary expenses ..	19,321,912	20,505,315
Extraordinary expenses ..	17,250,000	34,250,000
Total	36,571,912	54,755,315

Until 1911 ordinary expenditure kept fairly level, but after that date rose steadily with the greater development of the territory. The annual extraordinary expenditure was quite irregular, varying largely with the requirements of the schemes in process of execution. It was charged to the Protectorate Loan, which was available for all four German Protectorates in Africa, amounts being allotted according to the requirements of each. Loans were raised annually from 1908 to 1911, but not apparently in 1912 and 1913. Including the loan of 45,000,000 marks placed on the estimates for 1914, the total Protectorate debt seems to have amounted at the outbreak of war to 333,807,000 marks. Of this total 173,551,000 marks (about £8,677,000) represented the share of German East Africa. The interest was calculated at 6,365,000 marks, and the money raised was used chiefly for railway and road construction.

A ten-year programme for the redemption of the 1908 and 1911 loan, extending in the former case to 1924 and in the latter to 1926, was published in the *Deutsches Kolonialblatt*. The details were as follows:—

Year.	Per cent.	Capital.	German East Africa portion.
		Marks	Marks.
1908	4	38,775,000	30,681,000
1911–12	4	38,000,000	17,299,000

Redemption was to take place during this period at a rate of 3—5 per cent.

(2) CURRENCY

The standard coin was the rupee (rupie), of the value of about 1·33 marks (or 1s. 4d.). The heller was a hundredth part of the rupee. Small coins in use were:—

1 heller ...	..	...	copper
10 heller ...	...	...	nickel
$\frac{1}{4}$ rupee ...	...	...	silver (*sumni*)
$\frac{1}{2}$ rupee ...	...	...	silver
1 rupee ...	...	...	silver
2 rupees	...	...	silver

There had also been copper 5-heller and $\frac{1}{2}$-heller pieces, but they proved unpopular, and were recalled in 1913. A nickel 5-heller piece was proposed instead. Cowrie shells were still in use between Victoria Nyanza and Tanganyika, but were being superseded by German small coin. The Deutsch-Ostafrikanische Bank had the right to issue notes of 5, 10, 100, and 500 rupees, but these were little used by the natives. The relation of German rupees to English was approximately 104:100, and consequently English rupees and silver coin were welcomed in the territory, while German rupees and notes were at a heavy discount in British East Africa and Zanzibar. German 20-mark gold pieces were officially changed at 15 rupees in German East Africa.

(3) Banking

Banking was conducted by the Post Office Savings
Bank, the Handelsbank für Ostafrika at Tanga, the
Deutsch-Ostafrikanische Bank, and to some extent by
private mercantile firms, such as Hansing & Co.

The Post Office Savings Bank was worked by the
German Imperial Post Office. Interest at 2 per cent.
was paid on sums up to 1,500 German rupees. Of
1,239 accounts opened by April 1, 1913, 45 per cent.,
representing a value of 99,560 German rupees, were
opened by natives. The Savings Bank's liabilities on
March 31, 1913, were 775,298 rupees.

The Handelsbank für Ostafrika was founded
in Berlin in January 1911 by a group of German financial houses, and was opened at Tanga on
December 1, 1911, with a capital of 3,000,000 marks in
500-mark shares. It had a net profit of 135,381 marks
for 1913 and the dividend paid was 4 per cent.

The Deutsch-Ostafrikanische Bank was founded in
1905. Its capital in 1912 was 2,000,000 marks, in 4,000
shares of 500 marks each, fully paid. Its dividend rose
to 10 per cent. in 1910, but fell to $7\frac{1}{2}$ per cent. in 1914.
The bank had the right to issue notes against a reserve
in silver rupees, and in 1913 increased its note circulation, chiefly in the 500-rupee denomination, by $11\frac{1}{2}$
per cent. as compared with 1912. It has now been
succeeded by several British institutions, including the
Standard Bank of South Africa, the National Bank of
South Africa, and the National Bank of India.

(4) Influence of Foreign Capital

Accurate figures for the foreign capital invested in
German enterprises in the territory are not available,
but it does not appear to have been at all considerable
except in a few plantations (see p. 87). There was
some foreign capital in Italian and Dutch firms; and
the businesses of Arab, Greek, and Indian traders
were not interfered with by the Germans,

(E) GENERAL REMARKS

Tanganyika can never be a white man's country. Before the war the European population was about 5,000 out of a total population of between seven and eight millions. It can never become an outlet for the surplus population of the mother country. The work of the colony will always have to be done by natives, and, since the agricultural resources of the country are very great, its trade might be greatly developed if native labour were properly stimulated and organized by Europeans. Neither the Arabs nor the Germans fully realized the value of this labour, which was wasted by the slave-trade of the one and the harsh labour regulations of the other. The chief reservoir of labour, moreover, is as yet untapped, for the populous sultanates of Ruanda and Urundi have never been fully subordinated to either Arabs or Germans. The future of the country should be economically secured if the native can be assured guaranteed prices for his crops, seed distribution, and improved sanitation, and if he can be given technical assistance in combating the diseases which so frequently attack human beings, animals, and plants.

Tanganyika has the advantage of a long coast-line on the Indian Ocean, and of what is practically a second coast-line on the great lakes. The Germans by various methods kept the commerce almost entirely in the hands of German firms. It was the usual practice of the importing houses to get the goods they required from Germany if possible, or, if they were compelled to turn to other countries, to demand a much wider margin of profit on such goods than they expected to receive on goods from their own country. The Deutsche Ostafrika-Linie was subsidized by the Government, and the value of the traffic in purely German goods conveyed by it rose during the first seven years of the subsidy from £300,000 to £960,000. It was difficult for British companies to compete against such advantages; but, with these restrictions set aside, there is every reason to anticipate a great increase in the trade with British India, Aden, and Australia, particularly as the completion of the transcontinental railway in the last-named country has brought its most populous and important regions into much closer touch with the east coast of Africa. Under new political conditions it might be possible to establish an East African Government line of local coasting and river steamers, with a flotilla on each of the great lakes. The local trade that could be built up between the coastal districts and the adjacent islands, as well as with Aden and the Red Sea ports, would be sufficiently remunerative if the working expenses were kept low and the steamers were not unnecessarily large.

If the Cape to Cairo railway is ever completed, Tanganyika will be an important section of the route. But the railway communications from east to west are likely to be of no less importance. The railway from Dar es-Salaam to Kigoma is already the easiest channel by which the resources of the eastern Congo can reach the sea, and it will probably at some future date constitute the eastern section of a heavily-worked transcontinental line. It may be doubted, however, whether the railway does not run too far north to form the best trade route to the Katanga district. The northern districts of Tanganyika have long lain within the trade sphere of the Uganda railway, though the proposed extension of the Usambara railway to Victoria Nyanza would have been a formidable menace to this connexion. The two railways are now linked together by the Voi-Moshi branch.

APPENDIX

EXTRACTS[1] FROM TREATIES

I

AGREEMENT BETWEEN THE BRITISH AND GERMAN GOVERNMENTS, OCTOBER 29/NOVEMBER 1, 1886, AND ADHESION OF THE SULTAN OF ZANZIBAR, DECEMBER 4, 1886

Recognition of Sovereignty of Sultan of Zanzibar over Islands of Zanzibar, Pemba, Lamu, Mafia, &c.

1. Germany and Great Britain recognise the sovereignty of the Sultan of Zanzibar over the Islands of Zanzibar and Pemba, and over the smaller islands which lie in the neighbourhood of the above within a radius of 12 sea miles, as well as over the Islands of Lamu and Mafia.

Recognition of Sultan of Zanzibar's Sovereignty over certain Territories on the Mainland

On the mainland they likewise recognise as possessions of the Sultan a line of coast which stretches without interruption from the Minengani River at the head of Tunghi Bay to Kipini. This line commences on the south of the Minengani River, follows the course of that river for 5 sea miles, and continues thence on the line of latitude to the point where it strikes the right bank of the Rovuma River, crosses the Rovuma, and runs down its left bank.

The coast-line has an internal depth of 10 sea miles measured from the coast direct into the interior from high-water mark.

Kau

The northern limit includes Kau.

Kismayu, Brawa, Meurka, Magadisho, and Warsheik

To the north of Kipini the said Governments recognise as belonging to the Sultan the stations of Kismayu, Brawa, Meurka, and Magadisho, with radii landwards of 10 sea miles, and of Warsheik with a radius of 5 sea miles.

---

[1] These extracts are here printed as they stand in Hertslet's *Map of Africa by Treaty.*

Leasing to German African Company of Customs Duties at Dar es-Salaam and Pangani.

2. Great Britain engages to support negotiations of Germany with the Sultan for the leasing to the German African Company of the customs duties at the ports of Dar es-Salaam and Pangani, in return for an annual payment to the Sultan by the Company.

Respective Spheres of Influence to be Defined

3. Both Powers agree to establish a delimitation of their respective spheres of influence on this portion of the East African Continent of the same character as that to which they have agreed as regards the territories on the Gulf of Guinea.

Territory referred to in Arrangement

The territory to which this arrangement applies is bounded on the south by the Rovuma River, and on the north by a line which, starting from the mouth of the Tana River, follows the course of that river or its affluents to the point of intersection of the Equator and the 38th degree of east longitude, thence strikes direct to the point of intersection of the 1st degree of north latitude with the 37th degree of east longitude, where the line terminates.

Line of Demarcation

The line of demarcation starts from the mouth of the River Wanga or Umbe, runs direct to Lake Jipé, passes thence along the eastern side and round the northern side of the lake and crosses the Lumi River;

Taveita and Chagga (Kilimanjaro District)

After which it passes midway between the territories of Taveita and Chagga, skirts the northern base of the Kilimanjaro range, and thence is drawn direct to the point on the eastern side of Lake Victoria Nyanza which is intersected by the 1st degree of south latitude.

Mutual Engagements to respect Spheres of Influence

Germany engages not to make acquisitions of territory, accept Protectorates, or interfere with the extension of British influence to the north of this line; and Great Britain makes the same engagement as regards the territories lying to the south of this line.

Kilimanjaro Districts

4. Great Britain will use her good offices to promote a friendly arrangement of the rival claims of the Sultan and the German East African Company to the Kilimanjaro districts.

Witu

5. Both Powers recognise as belonging to Witu the coast-line which commences to the north of Kipini and continues to the northern extremity of Manda Bay.

Invitation to Sultan of Zanzibar to accede to Berlin Act

6. Great Britain and Germany will jointly invite the Sultan to accede to the Act of Berlin, 26th February, 1885, with reservation of His Highness's existing rights under the 1st Article of the Act.

Adhesion of Germany to Declaration between Great Britain and France of 10th March, 1862

7. Germany engages to adhere to the Declaration signed by Great Britain and France on the 10th March, 1862, with regard to the recognition of the independence of Zanzibar.

II

AGREEMENT BETWEEN THE BRITISH AND GERMAN GOVERNMENTS RESPECTING AFRICA AND HELIGOLAND, BERLIN, JULY 1, 1890

East Africa.   German Sphere of Influence

Art. I.—In East Africa the sphere in which the exercise of influence is reserved to Germany is bounded—

German Sphere.   To the North.   River Umba to Victoria Nyanza.

1. To the north by a line which, commencing on the coast at the north bank of the mouth of the River Umba [or Wanga], runs direct to Lake Jipé; passes thence along the eastern side and round the northern side of the lake, and crosses the River Lumé; after which it passes midway between the territories of Taveita and Chagga, skirts the northern base of the Kilimanjaro range, and thence is drawn direct to the point on the eastern side of Lake Victoria Nyanza which is intersected by the 1st parallel of south latitude; thence, crossing the lake on that parallel, it follows the parallel to the frontier of the Congo Free State, where it terminates.

Mount Mfumbiro

It is, however, understood that, on the west side of the lake, the sphere does not comprise Mount Mfumbiro; if that mountain shall prove to lie to the south of the selected parallel, the line shall be deflected so as to exclude it, but shall, nevertheless, return so as to terminate at the above-named point.

German Sphere. To the South. Rovuma River to Lakes Nyasa and Tanganyika (Stevenson's Road)

2. To the south by a line which, starting on coast at the northern limit of the Province of Mozambique, follows the course of the River Rovuma to the point of confluence of the Msinje; thence it runs westward along the parallel of that point till it reaches Lake Nyasa; thence striking northward, it follows the eastern, northern, and western shores of the lake to the northern bank of the mouth of the River Songwe; it ascends that river to the point of its intersection by the 33rd degree of east longitude; thence it follows the river to the point where it approaches most nearly the boundary of the geographical Congo Basin defined in the 1st Article of the Act of Berlin, as marked in the map attached to the 9th Protocol of the Conference.

From that point it strikes direct to the above-named boundary; and follows it to the point of its intersection by the 32nd degree of east longitude; from which point it strikes direct to the point of confluence of the northern and southern branches of the River Kilambo, and thence follows that river till it enters Lake Tanganyika.

Map. Nyasa-Tanganyika Plateau

The course of the above boundary is traced in general accordance with a map of the Nyasa-Tanganyika Plateau, officially prepared for the British Government in 1889.

German Sphere. To the West. River Kilambo to Congo Free State

3. To the west by a line which, from the mouth of the River Kilambo to the 1st parallel of south latitude, is conterminous with the Congo Free State.

East Africa. British Sphere of Influence

The sphere in which the exercise of influence is reserved to Great Britain is bounded—

British Sphere. To the South. River Umba to Congo Free State

1. To the south by the above-mentioned line running from the mouth of the River Umba (or Wanga) to the point where the first parallel of south latitude reaches the Congo Free State.

Mount Mfumbiro

Mount Mfumbiro is included in the sphere.

British Sphere. To the North. River Juba to Confines of Egypt (Uganda, &c.)

2. To the north by a line commencing on the coast at the north bank of the mouth of the River Juba; thence it ascends that bank of the river and is conterminous with the territory reserved to the influence of Italy in Gallaland and Abyssinia, as far as the confines of Egypt.

British Sphere. To the West. Basin of Upper Nile to Congo Free State (Uganda, &c.)

3. To the west by the Congo Free State, and by the western watershed of the basin of the Upper Nile.

Cession to be made by Sultan of Zanzibar to Germany of Possessions on the Mainland and of Island of Mafia

Art. XI.—Great Britain engages to use all her influence to facilitate a friendly arrangement, by which the Sultan of Zanzibar shall cede absolutely to Germany his Possessions on the mainland comprised in existing Concessions to the German East African Company, and their Dependencies, as well as the Island of Mafia.

It is understood that His Highness will, at the same time, receive an equitable indemnity for the loss of revenue resulting from such cession.

German Recognition of British Protectorate over remaining Dominions of Sultan of Zanzibar, including Islands of Zanzibar and Pemba, and Witu

Germany engages to recognise a Protectorate of Great Britain over the remaining dominions of the Sultan of Zanzibar, including the Islands of Zanzibar, and Pemba, as well as over the dominions of the Sultan of Witu.

Withdrawal of German Protectorate up to Kismayu

And the adjacent territory up to Kismayu, from which her Protectorate is withdrawn. It is understood that if the cession of the German Coast has not taken place before the assumption by Great Britain of the Protectorate of Zanzibar, Her Majesty's Government will, in assuming the Protectorate, accept the obligation to use all their influence with the Sultan to induce him to make that cession at the earliest possible period in consideration of an equitable indemnity.

III

AGREEMENT BETWEEN GREAT BRITAIN AND GERMANY, JULY 25, 1893

Section 1. On the coast the line shall start from the high-water mark on Ras Jimbo, and shall run from thence in a straight line to the point where the parallel of 3° 40′ 40·3″ S. (astronomically determined) cuts the eastern bank of Lake Jipe. But on the coast the boundary shall be deflected as follows: It shall run from the Indian Ocean along the northern bank of the Jimbo Creek, making the foreshore in the British sphere, as far as the eastern mouth of the Ngobwe Ndogo. It shall then follow the eastern bank of the Ngobwe Creek to its end, and then run to the point where the above described straight line from Ras Jimbo to Lake Jipe meets the rising ground on which the village of Jasini stands.

Section 2. From the point on Lake Jipe, described in Section 1, the boundary line shall follow the eastern side of Lake Jipe, and round the northern side of the lake crossing the River Lumi, and following the northern bank of the Rufu River (by which is also understood its swamp), as far as the point which is distant 1 English mile east of the German road going from the Marangu station to the coast. From thence it shall run to the summit of Chala Hill in the manner shown in the annexed map. The boundary line shall bisect the Chala Lake. From the north side of the Chala Lake onwards the boundary line shall run parallel to the track, as shown in the annexed map, and 1 English mile west of it as far as the latitude of the so-called Useri Camp. It shall then run at a distance of 1 kilom. south-west of the track shown in the annexed map as going to Laitokitok, as far as the point where it crosses the Ngare Longei (Rongei).

IV

DECLARATION BETWEEN PORTUGAL AND GERMANY, DECEMBER 30, 1886

Art. II.—The Boundary line which shall separate the Portuguese from the German Possessions in South-East Africa follows the course of the River Rovuma from its mouth to the point where the River M'sinje joins the Rovuma and runs to the westward on the parallel of latitude to the shores of Lake Nyasa.

AUTHORITIES

BARK, Lieut. E. W. *Notes from East Africa (Uluguru Moun tains).* (Geographical Journal, October 1917.)

BONN, Professor M. *German Colonial Policy.* (United Empire, vol. V, pp. 126-135, 1914.)

BOURBON DEL MONTE SANTA MARIA, G. *L'Africa orientale tedesca.* 3 vols. Città di Castello, 1915.

BROWN, A. SAMLER, and BROWN, G. GORDON. *Guide to South and East Africa.* London, 1915.

BURTON, Sir R. F. *Zanzibar: City, Island, and Coast.* · 2 vols London, 1872.

CALVERT, A. F. *German East Africa.* London, 1917.

CAMERON, Commander V. LOVETT. *Across Africa.* London, 1877.

CANA, F. R. *Frontiers of German East Africa.* (Geographical Journal, April 1916.)

CROWE, Brig.-Gen. J. H. V., C.B. *General Smuts' Campaign in East Africa.* London, 1918.

FONCK, H. *Deutsch-Ostafrika.* Berlin, 1909.

G., M. L. A. *Landgrabbing (Mafia).* (Blackwood's Magazine, April 1916.)

GUILLAIN, CHARLES. *Documents sur l'histoire, la géographie et le commerce de l'Afrique orientale.* 3 vols. Paris, 1856.

HASSERT, K. *Deutschlands Kolonien,* 2nd edn. (*German East Africa,* pp. 235-318). Leipzig, 1910.

JAEGER, F. *Das Hochland der Riesenkrater und die umliegenden Hochländer Deutsch-Ostafrikas.* Berlin, 1911.

JOELSON, F. S. *The Tanganyika Territory.* London, 1920.

JOHNSTON, Sir H. H. *A History of the Colonization of Africa,* 3rd edn. Cambridge, 1913.

—— *The Nile Quest.* London, 1903.

—— *A Survey of the Ethnography of Africa.* (Journal of the Royal Anthropological Institute, vol. XLIII. London, 1913.)

KAERGER, H. *Tangaland.* Berlin, 1892.

KELTIE, Sir J. S. *The Partition of Africa,* 2nd edn. London, 1895.

KING, NORMAN. *Mafia.* (Geographical Journal, August 1917.)

KOLLMANN, P. *The Victoria Nyanza* (English edition). London, 1900.

KRAPF, J. L. *Travels during Residence in East Africa* (English edition). London, 1860.

LETCHER, O. *The South-West Area of German East Africa* (Geographical Journal, March 1918.)

LEUE, A. *Dar es-Salaam.* Berlin, 1903.

LEWIN, EVANS. *The Germans and Africa.* London, 1915.

LUGARD, Sir F. D. *The Rise of Our East African Empire.* 2 vols. Edinburgh, 1893.

LYNE, R. N. *Zanzibar in contemporary Times.* London, 1905.

MEYER, Prof. Dr. H. *Der Kilimandjaro.* Berlin, 1900.

—— *Die Eisenbahnen im tropischen Afrika.* Leipzig, 1902.

O'NEILL, H. E. *Ancient Civilisations of Eastern Africa.* (Scottish Geographical Magazine, 1886.)

PETERS, K. *Das Deutsch-Ostafrikanische Schutzgebiet.* Munich and Leipzig, 1895.

—— *Wie Deutsch-Ostafrika entstand.* Leipzig, 1912.

SALÎL IBN RAZÎK. *History of the Imâms and Seyyids of 'Omân,* 661-1856. Translated by G. P. Badger (Hakluyt Society, 44). London, 1871.

SCHMIDT, ROCHUS. *Deutschlands Kolonien.* 2 vols. Berlin, 1895-6.

SHARPE, Sir A. *The Kivu Country* (Geographical Journal, January 1916).

SMUTS, General J. C. *East Africa* (Geographical Journal, March 1918).

SPEKE, Captain J. H. *Journal of the Discovery of the Source of the Nile.* Edinburgh, 1863.

STIGAND, Captain C. H. *The Land of Zinj.* London, 1913.

—— *The North Section of the Tanganyika—Nile Rift Valley.* (Geographical Journal, August 1917.)

STRANDES, JUSTUS. *Die Portugiesenzeit von Deutsch- und Englisch-Ostafrika.* Berlin, 1899.

STRONG, A. *The History of Kilwa* (translated from the Arabic. Journal of the Royal Asiatic Society. London, 1895.)

WHITE, S. E. *The Rediscovered Country* (north-east of German East Africa). London, 1915.

ZIMMERMANN, ALF. *Geschichte der deutschen Kolonialpolitik* (*East Africa,* pp. 113-131, 174-183, 194-205, 247-256). Berlin, 1914.

The foregoing list does not include the earlier Portuguese and Arabic authorities on the East Coast of Africa, which will be found in the List of Authorities in *Mozambique,* No. 121 of this series. Reference should also be made to *Kenya,* No. 96, and to *The Partition of Africa,* No. 89, in the Appendix to which the Anglo-German Treaty of 1890 and the German-Portuguese Treaty of 1886 are given; also to Hertslet, *The Map of Africa by Treaty,* London, 1909, and the Atlas which accompanies it.

Maps.

German East Africa is covered by the War Office map (G.S.G.S. General Map 2814), "German East Africa," on the scale of 1:2,000,000 (July 1916); also by six sheets of the War Office International Map of Africa, G.S.G.S. 2465 (1915-19).

The War Office map (G.S.G.S. 2932), "East Africa (former German): Ruanda and Urundi," on the scale of 1:1,000,000 (1919), shows the new Anglo-Belgian boundary and possible railway route.

Larger scale maps are G.S.G.S. 3026, in 35 sheets, scale 1:300,000 (1915-16); and G.S.G.S. 3025, in 5 sheets, 4 of the Usambara (Tanga) district and 1 of Massoko (Neu-Langenburg), scale 1:100,000 (1916). The Kilimanjaro (Moshi and Arusha) district is detailed on G.S.G.S. 1764, sheets 94-I, 94-J, 94-M, 94-N, scale 1:250,000.

The War Office map G.S.G.S. 2896, scale 1:16,000,000 (1918), illustrates the free trade zone mentioned on p. 99 of this book.

HANDBOOKS PREPARED UNDER THE DIRECTION OF THE HISTORICAL SECTION OF THE FOREIGN OFFICE.—No. 114

TREATMENT OF NATIVES
IN THE GERMAN COLONIES

TABLE OF CONTENTS

Wt. 15564/89 1005 9/20 ; F.O.P. [4156]

TREATMENT OF NATIVES IN THE GERMAN COLONIES

I. THE OFFICIAL ELEMENT

" THE question of German colonial policy is a question of native policy. It is not merely a question of how we are to rule them. . . . Owing to the different structure of our colonies, the task will be different in each of the groups. In the Cameroons and Togo we are ruling native States and native tribes by a bureaucracy somewhat on the lines of the Indian bureaucracy. In East Africa we are creating a mixed colony, planting fragments of a white society amongst dense African masses. In South-West Africa we have created a kind of manorial system with a European lord of the manor and an African serf. Each type has its advantages, each has its drawbacks."

In these words Prof. Moritz Bonn, of Munich, briefly summed up the system of colonial administration in the German African colonies. He stated further that—

" Germany had not got the class of men she wanted for the colonies she owned. The German peasant who successfully colonized large parts of the world is not the ideal settler for Africa. For Africa, a country of plantations and large farms, is not a peasants' country. . . . We wanted to build up on African soil a new Germany and create daughter States. We carried this idea to its bitter end. We tried it in South-West Africa, and produced a huge native rising, causing the loss of much treasure and many lives. We tried to assume to ourselves the functions of Providence, and we tried to exterminate a native race, whom our lack of wisdom had goaded into rebellion. We succeeded in breaking up the native tribes, but we have not yet succeeded in creating a new Germany."[1]

Such, in brief, is the history of German colonization in Africa. From the period when South-West Africa

[1] Address on " German Colonial Policy," given before the Royal Colonial Institute, London, on January 13, 1914.

was occupied as a territorial colony—in theory a Protectorate—in 1884, until the present time, Germany has mishandled the native races committed to her care; she has entrusted the administration of vast territories to unsuitable and often venal officials; she has permitted non-commissioned officers, frequently of a brutal type, to acquire too great a preponderance in the actual work of administration; she has allowed her native soldiery an unbridled licence in their dealings with the native races; and, above all, she has degraded, instead of uplifted the natives, disregarded native laws and customs, broken up certain tribes and attempted to exterminate others, and introduced upon African soil the methods of the Prussian bureaucracy.

Bismarck, who in reality was no friend of colonization, foresaw the inevitable course of a colonial policy carried out on the rigid lines of Prussian method. " No success could be hoped for," he said, " from transplanting the Prussian Government official and his bureaucratic system to Africa."   Yet this is exactly what happened.   Men with no knowledge of African conditions, and whose record in the past was not of the best, were sent out to Africa as administrators; and certainly, until recently, the officials chosen by the Colonial Department were often men who for various reasons were not likely to succeed in the Fatherland.

In the early days there were the scandals and atrocities connected with such men as Karl Peters, Wehlan, Kleist, and Arenberg, and more recently there have been those in which have figured G. A. Schmidt, von Brauchitsch and Dr. Meyer, Governors von Puttkamer and Horn, Captain Dominik, Captain Kannenberg, Captain Thierry, Landeshauptmann Brandeis, von Rotberg, and many more, who will be referred to in due course.

In 1906 Dr. Schaedler stated that—

" the story of our colonies contains a whole series of events of a not too pleasant kind : embezzlements, falsifying of evidence, sensual cruelties, assaults on women, horrible ill-treatment— things that do not contribute to a laurel wreath.   It will be

necessary to cleanse and winnow here, to handle matters
severely in the Colonial Department, and abroad among the
officials of our colonies.   The colonies must be no dumping-
ground for second-rate people.   .   .   .   Men with a past, or
who are on the shelf, and officials and officers who are mentally
and morally offensive, are no good to us in the colonies, not
even if they were royal princes, but would only be suited to
drag the German, and I would add the Christian, name in the
dust."[1]

In the same year the Conservative Deputy, Dr.
Arendt, said that—

" It is unfortunately not to be denied that amongst the many
faults which we have committed in our colonial policy must be
included the fact that in the beginning the colonies served as a
dumping-ground for damaged reputations, and that unsuitable
elements were often sent out."[2]

In addition to these unsuitable administrative
elements, use was made of far more unsuitable instruments on the spot. As the Germans became established
in their colonies, they permitted an incredible licence to
the native soldiery in their dealings with the unfortunate natives subjected to their control. Much of the
brutality and many of the atrocities committed in
Africa were due to this favoured element.   A British
officer who travelled along the Nigeria—Cameroon
frontier in 1912-13 informs us that the German native
soldier

" is periodically told on parade that he is a member of the
' greatest army in the world,' and that ' there is only one flag,
the German flag; that all others are as dirt.'   He is told that
he is invincible and can do no wrong : this he firmly believes.
His word is always taken before the word of any number of
natives.   I have often heard him making a report to his officer
which I have known to be an absolute fabrication.   The worst
of it is, he is always implicitly believed.   The German idea is
that a German soldier is *ex officio* above suspicion.   According
to my experience, the average German soldier is an unscrupu-
lous liar, thief, and murderer, and is not to be trusted further
than he can be seen."

---

[1] Reichstag, November 28, 1906.
[2] Reichstag, March 15, 1906.

This licence permitted to the soldiery was a matter of German policy, but it was tempered by severe discipline so far as the actual carrying out of instructions was concerned. It is a profoundly significant fact that immediately on the outbreak of war the Governor of Cameroon, Herr Ebermaier, issued the following proclamation specially addressed to this element :—

> " I decree that corporal punishment shall be done away with for the soldiers of the police force and for coloured Government officials, because they have shown themselves faithful; also for all who have had an honourable discharge from the Service. The Commander decrees the same for the soldiers of the Protectorate. You are to understand this : he who serves the Germans faithfully will be treated like a German, and share in the privileged position of the Germans."[1]

The actual administration of justice (see p. 17 *et seq.*) was in a state of chaos. Each official was a law unto himself. Power was given to and exercised by minor officials, almost without appeal to the higher authorities, who failed to exercise any effective supervision over the proceedings of their subordinates. Even non-commissioned officers, and sometimes native sergeants, were entrusted with powers that are quite foreign to our ideas of administration. One official in Togoland[2] created his native mistress and procuress *Jenufia* (i.e., queen), giving her the power to levy fines and legal dues, and to decide in legal cases in the first instance. Stations were placed in full charge of sergeants. Sergeant Liebert, at the station of Lolodorf, practically left the command of the station to his black wife, as he was ill. This woman had three negroes, accused of highway robbery, arrested, and when Captain Kamptz visited the station she handed over the men to him. They were tied up before a 3.7-centimetre gun and blown to pieces. The powers exercised by the subordinate officials were one of the chief causes of the failure of the Germans to administer strict and impartial justice in their colonies.

---

[1] Proclamation in the *Kamerun Post*, August 8, 1914.
[2] Herr G. A. Schmidt; see *infra*, p. 35.

While the Governors and superior officials failed to exercise proper supervision in Africa, the Colonial Department, at first a branch of the Foreign Office and afterwards a separate Ministry, did not maintain any sufficient control over the colonial officials. There was a systematic policy of hushing up, and such prosecutions of colonial officials as the force of public opinion compelled the Colonial Department to undertake almost invariably resulted in the infliction of a totally inadequate punishment, and that not because they had been guilty of atrocities, but because they had failed in some point of official etiquette. Thus Karl Peters was condemned at first because he had given false reports of his actions to his official superiors, and had thereby committed a grave breach of duty; Wehlan was condemned to a small fine and transferred to another post; Kleist was at first only removed to another post; von Puttkamer was merely fined and reprimanded; Schmidt was at first sent back to Togoland; Brandeis was merely reprimanded; Horn was dismissed, but retained two-thirds of his pension; whilst Dominik does not appear to have been punished at all, but had a statue erected in his honour, as did Peters when he was finally " rehabilitated " after years of controversy. Imperial or other influence was frequently solicited and obtained for the culprits, as in the cases of Peters and Wehlan; and the Colonial Department consistently refused to make public the documents in connection with these cases.

It would not be too much to say that in respect of every official scandal that was revealed through the persistent action of the Clerical and Social-Democratic elements in the Reichstag a hundred secret influences were at work to screen the offenders and to prevent the collection, and certainly the publication, of the scandalous details relating to corruption in the colonies. Deputy Bebel made the following statements :—

" I am absolutely convinced that we should hear much worse things from our colonies than we have heard yet if strict measures were not taken in the colonies to prevent any Euro pean, and especially any German, who has settled there, from telling in public anything about the abuses that come to light there. A man who was long in Cameroon told me that every commercial employé who made public the smallest details about the loathsome conditions was simply ruined, that every means was used to induce his employer to dismiss anyone who had been indiscreet, and that very explicable motives of camaradie make it particularly difficult to induce the officials to bring abuses to light."[1]

" Everything that happens in the colonies is hushed up. . . . Then what have the gentlemen to expect if they are guilty of these abominations and are turned out of the service? Nothing. They are rewarded afterwards."[2]

Deputy Erzberger made similar charges when speaking about the testimony of missionaries; he said :—

" You certainly cannot believe that all is well and in good order when the missionaries are silent. If the missionaries were always to speak according to their true feelings, then we should learn quite different things. But the missionaries must often be silent, because they are under the power of the respective Governors or District Judges."[3]

Herr Scholze, one of the few German missionaries who have dared to speak out, said in a lecture delivered at Carlsruhe in 1904 :—

" I will not say that the Government directly favoured the pernicious excesses in the colonies. . . . There are men who are indignant at the treatment of the natives, but there is hardly ever one who has the courage to disobey the official order against telling friends of anything that occurs in the colonies or making it public."[4]

Father Schmitz and his associates in Togoland, who exposed the atrocities and immoralities of G. A. Schmidt, were directly threatened by Dernburg in the Reichstag. The Secretary of State said that he had written to the Chapter of Cologne Cathedral complaining of the charges brought by their missionaries against officials in the colony of Togoland, and intimating that if what he termed the unfounded charges did not cease

---

[1] Bebel, Reichstag, March 20, 1906.

[2] *Ibid*, December 1, 1906.

[3] Erzberger, Reichstag, December 1, 1906.

[4] Scholze, J., *Die Wahrheit über die Heidenmission und ihre Gegner*, Berlin, 1905.

he would feel compelled to resort to administrative measures against the missions.

> " This campaign against officials must cease, else it would be impossible to get anyone to enter the Colonial Service."[1]

Schmidt himself issued an order that all natives were forbidden to complain any further to the missionaries of the Catholic Mission, and about the same time Governor von Puttkamer forbade officials in Cameroon to visit the Evangelical Protestant missions established there.[2]

Officials, such as Herr Wistuba and Herr Poeplau, who did attempt to make the colonial scandals public, were dismissed from the service for dereliction of duty; but the real offenders were usually maintained in their positions. On this point alone a most damning indictment of German administrative methods could be prepared from the available evidence. There is abundant testimony that many of the instruments of German administration in Africa were " men of low character, *roués*, men with a past."[3] Many officials, too, were deeply interested in concessionary companies.

Such was the type of men employed in the German colonies. Although there were undoubtedly honest and straightforward officials, more especially during recent years, they were hampered and restricted by the action of the Colonial Office in Berlin, which, even during the Dernburg regime, when certain reforms were initiated but never carried through, was not cleared of those who had previously insisted that a veil of secrecy should be drawn over administrative scandals in the colonies.

[1] Dernburg, Reichstag, December 3, 1906.
[2] Rören, Reichstag, December 3, 1906.
[3] Dr. Schaedler, Reichstag, November 28, 1906.

II. FLOGGING IN THE GERMAN COLONIES

IN the treatment of African natives Germany has adopted a standard of her own. General von Liebert, an ex-Governor of German East Africa, a member of the Reichstag, and president of the Anti-Socialist League, declared during the trial of the action brought by Karl Peters against Herr Gruber in 1907, that the acts for which Peters had been condemned were necessary " to open up a black continent to civilization," and that " it was impossible in Africa to get on without cruelty "; and there is ample evidence to prove that von Liebert's view was generally accepted.

In the administration of the German colonies the system of flogging has been one of the chief instruments of oppression. The facts in connection with this degrading system were so notorious and so generally known in adjacent territories that the German African colonies were freely spoken of as the " Colonies of the Twenty-five " (i.e., where twenty-five lashes were the usual punishment) and the " Flogging Colonies."[1]

There is an overwhelming mass of evidence as to the prevalence of this system. On at least two occasions samples of the instruments used have been laid on the table of the Reichstag; on the first occasion a rhinoceros whip,[2] and on the second a cudgel, described officially as

---

[1] Rören, Reichstag, December 3, 1906.

[2] " And with what instruments floggings were carried out," said Deputy Bebel on March 13, 1906, " we had an opportunity of judging some years ago in this House, when a party friend of mine laid a rhinoceros whip on the table of the House."

a " little stick."   Deputy Rören, a Prussian judge, on
the latter occasion said :—

> " meanwhile a 'little stick' of this kind with which the thrash-
> ing took place has been sent to me from Togo, and I take the
> liberty of laying this 'little stick' here on the table of the House.
> Gentlemen, if such an instrument is designated as a ' little
> stick,' then one can have some idea what sort of a bludgeon
> they would not dare to call a ' little stick.' "[1]

The punishments officially recognised as being per-
missible are corporal punishment (flogging and birch-
ing), fines, imprisonment with hard labour, imprisonment in chains, and death.   In the actual administration of flogging a considerable latitude has been
allowed.   As a matter of fact, flogging has been indis-
criminately indulged in.   Rören stated that—

> " this punishment is not ordered merely for grave misde-
> meanours or for crimes by judicial sentence, but it is applied
> on the mere order of administrative officials, even by Station
> Directors, who officially have only the rank of a subaltern, or
> by their assistants, or by some overseers of smaller stations,
> who are taken largely from former non-commissioned
> officers."[2]

In theory all floggings are supposed to be entered in
a punishment book, but in practice this was frequently
not done.   Thus Landeshauptmann Brandeis, of the
Marshall Islands, who " seems to have flogged quite
systematically " for educative reasons, was convicted of
this offence, but received a Prussian Order.   The
Colonial Department wrote to him as follows :—

> " The right of the authorities to order flogging *for general
> educational reasons* is certainly to be denied. You [Brandeis]
> do not seem to have kept always within bounds in this
> direction, particularly not in the case of people who had
> received the punishment of imprisonment imposed by police or
> other courts."[3]

Of the nature of the instrument used and of the atrocious wounds inflicted there is abundant testimony.
Four instruments have been used at different times : a

[1] Rören, Reichstag, December 3, 1906.
[2] *Ibid.*
[3] Dr. Müller, Reichstag, December 4, 1906.

rhinoceros whip or hippopotamus whip, a rope's end, a " little stick " or birch rod, and a salted strap.   In Cameroon the Governor, von Puttkamer, found that the rhinoceros whip was " too cruel," and only allowed a rope's end, but in 1907 the Colonial Office again ordered that the sjambok should be used.

This, the official instrument of punishment, is made of   strips   of   rhinoceros   hide,   80   to   100   centimetres long by 1 centimetre in circumference, and smooth at the whip end; but certain witnesses, amongst whom was King Akwa (Cameroon), stated that they had only seen beating with a rope's end, bound round at the end with wire—an instrument that must have inflicted atrocious wounds.   Herr Bebel described the instrument used as not so much an ordinary rope " but a weapon."   He said :—

> " it is steeped in hot tar, and when well covered with tar it is dipped in sand to produce a very rough surface; and after the whip thus prepared has become stiff and hard enough, with this instrument, which may possibly cause death, men, women, and children, without respect of persons, are punished up to twenty-five strokes.   That is simply barbarous.   That is an act of violence committed in the name of civilization against which we protest with the utmost energy."[1]

Deputy Dasbach described how a missionary had told him that—

> " the flogging was administered in the most cruel way. The soldier who is ordered to give the flogging receives the order to hit with such force that the whip hisses as it comes whirling down, and if the soldier does not flog so hard that the whip hisses he is punished himself."[2]

Consul-General Knappe, of Shanghai, wrote in an official letter :—

> " I have witnessed the carrying out of the punishment of flogging, both in Samoa and in the Marshall Islands.   The impression was a disgusting one, both for white men and black."[3]

---

[1] Bebel, Reichstag, March 20, 1906.
[2] Dasbach, Reichstag, March 26, 1906.
[3] Erzberger, Reichstag, March 13, 1906

Rören described the whole process of flogging as " a form of torture."　He said :—

> " The native, after having been completely stripped, is strapped across a block on a barrel that has been fixed firmly, his hands are bound in front, his feet behind, so that he cannot move, and then he does not get a few blows with an ordinary stick held in one hand, but the strongest among the black soldiers has to wield a plaited rope or a correspondingly thick stick with both hands and with all his strength, and that with such violence that each blow must whistle in the air.　Sometimes, if the blow does not whistle, it has to be repeated, and if this is not done the Hausa gets it himself."[1]

This repetition of blows alluded to by Deputy Rören has been a common occurrence.　The Akwa chiefs complained that they had received many more than the legal number of fifty lashes,[2] which were to be delivered on two separate occasions.

Flogging as administered in the German colonies produced the most unfortunate results on the natives. The results were both physical and moral.　In the case of the Elders of Awete, forty in number, flogged by order of G. A. Schmidt, then Station-Director at Atakpame, so that " pieces of flesh hung from their bodies," the scars were visible three years after the flogging. These men were beaten with four different sticks, which broke one after the other.　One witness stated : " I received three wounds, which caused me to be ill for three months," and others, three years after the punishment, showed scars on their buttocks the size of the palm of the hand.　Many deputies have protested

---

[1] Rören, Reichstag, December 3, 1906.

[2] They complained that "without regarding their repeated representations, the natives, without respect of persons, were flogged for every small offence in civil or criminal matters, receiving twenty-five strokes with the rhinoceros whip or with a thick rope's end soaked in coal tar, rubbed in the sand, and dried stiff.　For greater offences they were often punished with seventy-five strokes, divided between three occasions; three or four weeks at most intervened between two inflictions of punishment."

against these brutalities. On March 26, 1906, Ledebour said :—

" Every flogging becomes barbarous, whether given with a rope's end, the sjambok, or a salted strap. First, it is physically detrimental, causing injury and shaking the nerves; it injures the soul, it brutalizes and blunts it; and it brutalizes the officials who order the flogging. . .   The unfortunate result is that by their administration German officials do not spread ' Kultur,' but produce a servile spirit. . . If that is true, then you have simply worked destruction on the spiritual life of these people."

Rören has stated that—

" it is self-evident that on the portions of the body thus struck the blood congeals and then swells, and so it is not uncommon for a man thus flogged to be ill or sickly for the rest of his life. In some cases, even, weak natives have collapsed after flogging and soon died.   But all, as a general rule, for months, or even for years, find themselves in such a state of nervous tension that if anyone approaches them unexpectedly they cower and scream aloud, from fear and apprehension lest the spot that was beaten may be touched."[1]

Deaths caused by flogging have been very numerous. A few instances, for which there is ample evidence, may be given. District Judge von Rotberg made a journey from Anecho to Atakpame in March 1903. One of the porters fell under his load, and then tried to run away. He was caught. Von Rotberg knelt upon him, pummelled him on the face with his fists, and then had him beaten with twenty-five strokes from a bamboo cane. The man again collapsed, and von Rotberg had him beaten a second time, with the result that he died. One of the most respected and influential natives in Lome testified that the cane used by von Rotberg's orders was a cudgel with which one might have felled an ox. Another case was even more brutal and disgraceful. It concerned a man named Mesa, who was flogged with the usual twenty-five strokes because he was unpunctual with an official's dinner.   Then the official gave him a kick on his private parts, so that the man fell down and remained unconscious for five minutes. Other similar brutalities followed, and another twenty-

[1] Rören, Reichstag, December 3, 1906.

five strokes, so that the following evening the body was
carried through the streets of Lome, under the eyes of
the white officials, to the monotonous dirge of " The
white man has killed the cook."   Rören's comment on
this case is, " And the official has been sent back to
Togoland."

Other cases are connected with Governor Horn, with
Captain Kannenberg, with von Brauchitsch, and with
the Akwa chiefs.   The Akwa chiefs were constantly
flogged, and some of them testified to the deaths of
relatives after flogging. All these cases—and there are
many—are ample evidence of the almost incredible
brutality of German officials in their dealings with the
natives.

It would seem, however, that the climax is reached
when women are flogged.   It is well known that one of
the revolts in Cameroon was caused by the Deputy-
Governor Kleist ordering the flogging of twenty women,
wives of native soldiers, because he considered that they
had been too lazy. Herr Rose, of the Colonial Department, admitted that women had been flogged in New
Guinea;[1] and so recently as May 1914 Deputy Dr.
Müller asked whether it was true that Christian negro
girls had been flogged at certain mission stations in
East Africa to prevent their marrying non-Christian
men.   Dr. Müller received the following answer to his
question :—

" So far nothing is known *officially*.   However, according to
German East African papers of March of this year, at a mission
station in the Mahen district girls of marriageable age have
been flogged for the purposes mentioned in the question."

A non-committal but sufficiently explicit answer.

Moreover, in the report of Mining Assessor Hasslacher, mentioned below, it is stated that not only were
women flogged, but children also:—

" At the Magistracy of Morogoro the flogging punishment of
children is carried out with a 44½-in.-long *kiboko* [i.e.,
sjambok], instead of, as usual elsewhere, with a cane or light
stick."

---

[1] Ledebour, Reichstag, March 29, 1906.

This excessive flogging is admitted by all who know the German colonies, and the constant use of the whip has been noticed even by Dernburg himself.   Speaking to the Budget Committee of the Reichstag on the Colonial Estimates on February 18, 1908, after his visit to Africa. he said :—

> '' On the coast it makes a very unfavourable impression on one to see so many white men go about with negro whips. I even found one on the table of the principal pay office in Dar es-Salaam; it is still the usual thing, and anyone who has been there will confirm what I say. . . The State is always asked to carry a whip in its hand.''

The most biting comment on this statement is afforded by the testimony of a pastor at Dar es-Salaam, who stated that the negroes who went with Dernburg on the expedition from Muansa to Tabora had said: " No, we will not travel with him again; we were never in our lives beaten as in Herr Dernburg's expedition."[1]

The number of floggings officially entered on the punishment sheets probably represents by no means all the cases of brutal treatment by official order, and certainly does not include the many unofficial floggings that took place.   This view is supported by a statement in a Report on Labour Compulsion in the Morogoro District by Mining Assessor Hasslacher, dated 1914.   He states that :—

> '' Nowhere on the estates were punishment registers kept of the punishments by flogging which were executed on the natives by individual planters, at times actually on women and little children, in a shameless—I would almost say blood-lustful—manner. . . . Although, as far as I have ascertained, the punishment by flogging is freely used in the magisterial district of Morogoro and its subordinate centres, still, these official punishments are as nothing compared with the innumerable administrations of the punishment by flogging on the European estates, and would scarcely come into the balance in a complete statistical statement of the flogging administered in the Morogoro district.''

---

[1] Quoted in the Reichstag by Ledebour, on March 17, 1908.

Later in the same report occurs the following :—

> "*Plantation of Dorendorf*: Measureless and senseless flogging was done, according to the statement of my guaranteeing informer, the plantation-assistant Winter. Does Herr Mahnke [the district magistrate] really believe that the labourers who were apportioned to this plantation had voluntarily come to these orgies of flogging?"

Deputy Erzberger on March 19, 1906, said "flogging is used too generally, in my opinion "; and he stated that in 1903 in East Africa 2,293 natives were sentenced to floggings and birchings, and 2,994 natives received floggings as additional punishments. Deputy Noske, on April 30, 1912, gave the figures for 1910 :—

> " The number of natives who are condemned sometimes to very trying imprisonment is most striking. . . . Realise that in East Africa alone in one year 10,144 longer or shorter sentences of imprisonment were given. That, considering the comparatively small district subject to German administration, is a colossally high number of convictions. . . The number of floggings in South-West Africa rose correspondingly. It rose from 928 in 1909 to 1,262 in 1910. In South-West Africa we have from 70,000 to 80,000 natives subject to the German administration. Among this small number of persons no fewer than 2,371 cases of more or less severe punishment were imposed. That is such an enormous percentage that one really does not understand on what principles justice is administered. . . . In Cameroon, besides 54 negroes who were sent out of life into death, 3,516 coloured people were punished with imprisonment; in 881 cases fines were imposed, and in 1,909 floggings. . . A similar increase in the convictions, and, of course, also in the flogging cases, is to be recorded from Togo. That little land had not fewer than 5,206 convictions. . . . Now, surely, there can be no doubt that the Reichstag has no wish that we should make Togo into a flogging area. . . . We have had pretty bad conditions there, and do not want them to be made worse."

In the Morogoro district of German East Africa, according to Herr Hasslacher, the number of floggings has greatly increased. He states :—

> " Since Herr Mahnke has been in charge of the Morogoro magistracy the number of punishments of natives, namely, with floggings, has undergone an alarming increase. The

annual report, to be found in the local records of the magistracy of Morogoro for 1912-13, expresses itself as follows on this matter: ' The Native Criminal Law Administration has considerably grown during the year under review. It ran up from 877 sentences in the preceding year, and 933 in 1910, to 1,812 sentences.   The increase touches chiefly the fourth group of offences; it deals with a more rigorous prosecution of breach of contract.' "

On another occasion Bebel gave the numbers for East Africa.   " According to the Memorandum of 1904-5," he said, "in the district of Kilwa alone there were 434 floggings; in the whole colony 4,783, besides unofficial floggings."[1] It may be taken, therefore, that the number of official floggings has been out of all proportion to the population under German control; whilst the floggings indulged in by planters and settlers, without the intervention of officials, have been exceedingly numerous.

[1] Bebel, Reichstag, March 13, 1906.

III. ADMINISTRATION OF JUSTICE

THE administration of justice in the German colonies has not been placed upon any sure and stable foundation.   It has been, as a matter of fact, the *fons et origo* of most of the troubles that have occurred.   The law itself has also been in a most unsatisfactory and chaotic state.   Under the original charters of some of the colonies, as, for instance, East Africa, the officials were given an absolutely free hand, and were subject only to the ultimate control of the Emperor;[1] and in others the law was administered in an absolutely arbitrary manner, according to the personal ideas of the individual official.

The natives were governed like a conquered people, although, as a matter of fact, in many cases they were (in theory at least) only under the protection of the German Empire.   No man was safe from arrest and imprisonment, and none were able to obtain justice when they dared to complain against the tyranny of officials.   The word of native witnesses was seldom accepted in a court of law, unless it coincided with the official view; and, moreover, natives were not put on oath.[2]

The powers of the subordinate officials were such that they exercised extensive rights of punishment without reference to the higher authorities; and punishments were not infrequently administered without judicial proceedings, as was shown by Rören in the Reichstag on December 3, 1906.   " The real hardship is," he said, " that this punishment is not ordered

---

[1] On this point consult the Charter granted to the German East Africa Company.

[2] Deputy Rören, December 3, 1906.

merely for grave misdemeanours or crimes by judicial sentence." Moreover, those administering justice were subservient to the Governor, as was stated by District Judge von Rotberg, who said :—

> " As the judges in the Protectorates are also administrative officials, they' are also, in the opinion of the Foreign Office, bound in their actions as judges by the intentions of the Governor placed above them."

Rören's comment upon this was :—

> " This certainly is a terrible state of things, and if this idea really exists at the Foreign Office, then it is indeed time that it should be overhauled thoroughly.   In my whole life I have never held any other view than that the judge, in using his judicial functions, was bound by nobody's intentions, neither the Governor's, nor the Minister's, nor those of anybody else, but only by his own conscience."

The intimidation of witnesses is authenticated in instances too numerous to give in detail.   Speaking of the horrible case of Mesa the cook, Rören said that not only had the official concerned not been punished but he had been allowed to return to his duties, " of course, to influence the black witnesses, so that when the enquiry takes place they dare not say any more about it."   In the case of G. A. Schmidt the intimidation of witnesses was notorious and was practised openly; whilst in the case of the Akwa chiefs, intimidation was carried on as an organised system by those who were interested in hushing up the affair.

No special code was used in the German colonies.   On May 1, 1912, Deputy Dr. Müller called attention to this matter as follows :—

> " Our civil and military administration of justice is simply untenable.   I point out that in mixed trials, therefore in the cases between natives and non-natives, there exists a free right of the Kaiser to decide.   With regard to the right of native justice and administration there exists an incredible insecurity concerning the powers of the administrative authorities in this sphere. . . .   One judge uses the German penal code without further ado. . . .   He uses the penal code without turning to the right or the left for the primitive conditions of the colonies.   Another does not use the penal code at all.   Yet another uses something analogous to it. . . .   **In short, our**

criminal proceedings are in a condition which must be stopped as soon as possible, which leaves the natives entirely without rights. That is how it happens that the punishment of flogging is used quite differently in individual colonies, and that in some colonies there is now an immense amount of flogging, whilst in others little flogging has been used. It is just the same as to remands, seizures, carrying out of punishments, and the way of accepting evidence and defence."

Another deputy, so late as May 17, 1914, showed that there had been no improvement. Deputy Dove asked :—

" Wherein does the whole reason for mistrust really exist? In this, that in our colonies the state of justice is so undeveloped that government and administration of justice are in the same hands."

A few years previously Deputy Storz had compared the British and German systems :—

" Nothing shows the difference in the position as to the rights of natives in German and English colonies so much as the administration of justice : the English solemn, earnest, entirely hedged in by guarantees of justice; at the German courts everything without form, and even if the intention to deal out justice be there . . . everything surrounded with the appearance of force and arbitrariness. The English District Commissioner can only act in things of small moment. Appeal can be made to the English judge, who travels about the country and judges cases in the first instance. With us, on the contrary, the officer and agriculturist without judicial training appointed as Director of the station, can decide on the life and death of the natives. True, the sentence needs confirmation by the Governor, but he goes by the report of the official who acted as judge. . . . The consequence is that the reputation of the German race suffers. An urgent demand has been rightly made to end this system of absolute arbitrariness and absolute absence of equity in our colonies."[1]

The most glaring cases of injustice could be adduced to support the contention that the administration was corrupt and venal; but it is only necessary here to state that Governor von Leutwein, of South-West Africa, published a table in his book on that Protectorate, showing the differences in the sentences meted out to Europeans and natives respectively.

[1] Storz, Reichstag, March 24, 1906.

IV. FORCED LABOUR

THE general statement that a system of forced labour, closely akin to actual slavery, has been in operation in the German colonies, is fully borne out by the representations of those who know the actual condition of things with reference to the supply of labour for the plantations and for public works, such as railways, harbours, and roads.

In the German colonies labour must be supplied by the native chiefs when asked for, and upon terms dictated by the local administration.   There is no such thing as an open labour market, where wages are adjusted according to the laws of supply and demand. The wages paid are fixed by the official concerned with the labour administration, and a planter may not pay more than the local rate of wage.

The hut tax has been designed primarily to force the natives to work, German opinion being that. in return for the so-called benefits of European civilization, the natives should render an equivalent service to the State.   This opinion may be gathered from the views expressed by three representative Germans.   Lieutenant-Colonel von Morgen, the leader of an exploring expedition in Cameroon, stated in 1907 that—

" the only real tax, which is also of cultural value, is compulsory labour.   We can do nothing in the tropics without native workmen, and especially cannot make progress in Cameroon, whose future depends on plantations.   As we in Germany have compulsory schooling, so there must be compulsory work in the colonies. . . . As to how this labour is to be supplied, and for how long, the District Judge must decide."[1]

---

[1] *Deutsche Kolonialzeitung* (1907), pp. 318-19.

A similar view was expressed by Major von Wissmann on January 16, 1902; whilst Karl Peters expressed himself as follows :—

" A very good recipe is the demand of a hut tax from every nigger over the age of sixteen—and one of not less than five pounds; so that they are forced to work. Otherwise we shall soon be responsible for a lot of lazy *canaille* from Algoa Bay to the Great Syrtis, who will force Europe to give up the opening up of Africa unless the colonists follow the example of the Tasmanian pioneers and simply exterminate the useless rabble. . . . To me the most advantageous system seems to be one in which the negro is forced, following the example laid down by Prussian military law, to devote some twelve years of his life to working for the Government. During this time he should receive food and shelter and a small wage, say about two shillings a month, like a Prussian soldier."[1]

Prior to the outbreak of the war, the practice in German East Africa and Cameroon is stated to have been as follows :—

Labour was divided into day (or casual) labour and contract (or recruited) labour. The day labourers were not bound to any master, and worked on plantations near their own homes. They were usually given piece-work, and paid for it on the same day. Contract labourers were recruited up-country, and were signed on for 180 or 240 working days. In East Africa thousands of men were recruited yearly in Unyamwezi, Usekuma, Songea, Ungoni, and other back-country districts for the plantations in the coastal belt. Many of these men were " raw natives " who had little idea how far they were going, what work they were to do, and under what conditions they were to live. The recruiting agents paid the native chiefs and headmen one rupee or more for each black man recruited, and naturally the headmen coerced as many of their followers as possible, in order to swell their commission receipts. In some cases

---

[1] Peters, *The Eldorado of the Ancients* (1902), pp. 252 and 278.

the recruiter got into touch with the Government official of the district, and the latter simply announced to the people that so many labourers were required, and his native underlings proceeded to muster the necessary men through the native chiefs and headmen, who were first intimidated.

Not long before the outbreak of war, in October 1913, a new " labour ordinance " was passed, under which time-expired men were entitled to draw their expenses home to the interior from their employers; but formerly men got back again, if they ever did, as best they could. This ordinance stated that in exactly the same way as natives had to pay the hut tax, so they had to perform labour, and, in fact, that labour was a compulsory contribution to the welfare of the State.

The labour thus requisitioned in German East Africa was obtained most frequently by methods amounting to force; and what occurred there went on also in Cameroon, where the conditions seem to have been still worse. In that colony there was constant friction between the planters, the merchants, and the Government with regard to the supply of labour. The merchants complained bitterly that natives who had been in the habit of supplying the traders with the products of their own industry— rubber, coconuts, palm kernels, and the like—were constantly forced to work on the plantations or on the public roads, and were kidnapped from the caravan routes for this purpose. Their charges were laid before the Union of West African Merchants, especially by Herr J. K. Vietor, who laid complaints before the Governor, and was instrumental in having the matter raised in the Reichstag. Herr Vietor wrote:—

" If in former times with us in Germany abuses such as slavery, bondage, and villanage existed, that is no reason to introduce them also in our colonies, where we have the development entirely in our own hands."[1]

---

[1] *Deutsche Kolonialzeitung*, March 6, 1902.

Similarly Herr J. Scholze stated that—

" the desire of the planters, whose wishes the Cameroon Government is only too ready to meet, was completely to impoverish and expropriate the natives living on their domains in order to force them to work at low wages on the plantations. . . . Old men, children, and weaklings were forced to work by Commissioners of the Government and the planters, who shrank from no tricks for this purpose. My heart bled often to see these poor people withering away. I was ashamed that such things could be in a German Protectorate."[1]

The death-rate on the plantations has been very high. On some, which are well managed, it is normal, but on others it is far above what should be the average Thus Herr Scholze has stated[2] that within a year a quarter of the labourers died; whilst Herr Vietor has estimated[3] the death-rate to be at least 20 per cent. :—

" Already in 1902 I was obliged, in consequence of communications received, to demand publicly in a lecture the better treatment of the people, as 20 per cent. of the labourers died yearly. In 1904 I visited Cameroon for the first time, and heard, chiefly from the officials themselves, how bad things looked on the plantations. . . . Whilst I was in Cameroon last year I was told that in six months on the Tiko plantation 50 to 75 per cent. of the workmen had died, as was acknowledged by the manager."[4]

Deputy Erzberger, on March 7, 1914, gave the following figures in the Reichstag :—

" The workmen's death-rate on the Victoria plantation of Cameroon was, in 1909, 7.89 per cent.; in 1910, 3.31 per cent.; in 1912, 10.24 per cent.; in 1913, 9.11 per cent. . . . In Prince Albert plantation I find it to be 26.8 per cent. on the average in 1913."

Owing to the constant withdrawal of natives from their own homes, whole districts in Cameroon were becoming depopulated. Many of these natives never returned to their homes. They either died or were left

---

[1] *Die Wahrheit über die Heidenmission*, 1905.
[2] *Ibid.*
[3] *Deutsche Kolonialzeitung*, May 1, 1902.
[4] Report presented to the Union of West African Merchants, 1914.

stranded on the plantations, in debt to the storekeeper and unable to get away.   The same appears to have been the case in German East Africa, for Hasslacher states in his report, mentioned above, that—

" It is a generally known fact that in the Morogoro district the native who once had taken a worker's ticket with a planter could hardly ever get free from this labour relationship to that particular employer.   The employer did not give the natives their discharge certificates and wages until the men had taken on another work-ticket."

The system in reality is peonage in its worst form. On this point there is the testimony of Father Burgt, quoted by Deputy Erzberger on March 7, 1914. Speaking of conditions in East Africa, he says :—

" Some who ran away from the plantations are supposed to be ' sundowners ' who will return. . . . They will not come back; not a third returns.   Many die of small-pox and dysentery while still on the road; of others their families never hear again.   I know many mothers and wives here who wait seven, eight, ten years, and all in vain, for son or husband."

And speaking of the moral effect on the negroes of this forced labour, Father Burgt says :—

" What do these negroes who have been fetched from the interior take back with them to the neighbourhood from which they came?   What they bring as all their reward is, besides syphilis and other dirty diseases, an unbelievable insolence, vanity, a breath of Islamism, but, above all, an outspoken contempt for all Wasungus—so Europeans are called in the native language.   That is the wood from which one carves rebels, and it is already growing in plenty."

It being plain that large districts have been denuded of their male population, to the detriment of the birth-rate in the villages,[1] some evidence may be given as to

---

[1] On this point there is the testimony contained in the Report presented to the Union of West African Merchants on January 3, 1914.   The writer states :—

" I have sought to test how far the depopulation, which is admitted on all sides as a result of the plantations, has progressed, but have not found any statistics from Cameroon about it.   The only thing is a small return that in the Mahea tribe 167 out of 263 have not borne offspring, and the remaining

the methods adopted to bring the men to the plantations.   On this question there is an abundance of evidence, most of it of recent date.   Thus in a report from Duala, dated September 24, 1913, the writer says :—

> " Against such official recruiting we merchants must protest with all energy. . . . It is simply intolerable that the Government should tear the men from their families, and also, as is clearly proved, arbitrarily take the men recruited against their will to these prescribed plantations. . . . No German Government must be responsible for forcing the people against their will to work on plantations, especially on plantations which have a bad name, where the people know that every third, fourth, or fifth man dies. It is simply iniquitous to tear people who have their own property and who are busy as farmers, from their work, or to take married men against their will from their families. That, in plain German, is simply slavery for a time, instead of, as formerly, for life."

That this view was gradually forcing itself upon the mercantile community, in contradistinction to the plantation owners, is illustrated by the action of a Cameroon Chamber of Commerce, which, in spite of great pressure brought to bear on its members, sent a vigorously worded remonstrance to the Governor of Cameroon on March 18, 1913. Speaking of the unrest in the Edea district, the signatories state :—

> " We do not think that the Government is fully cognizant of the effect which the continuous enlistment of labour and the unrest among the natives has had in this district. Not only the mercantile community, but also the missions, have complained of this to the local Bezirksamt. . . . The bush people are absolutely afraid of coming to Edea, and in various districts the chiefs have declared that they prefer to let the kernels spoil in their houses rather than send them to Edea, as in the latter case they are apprehensive that the people, together with their kernels, may be seized."

---

96 women had 189 children.   Among the Bales, out of 40 Yaunde wives (half the women), 30 per cent. were childless, and the 27 remaining had 53 children.   Only among the Batangas 38 wives had 144 children.   Unfortunately, however, the reasons are not given why so many women have no children. Were so many men really away as porters and workmen, or were there quite other reasons?   Anyway, the question of population appears bad enough in Cameroon."

The Chamber, in particular, protests against a certain Behrens, stating that the name Behrens " is in itself sufficient to fill the natives with a holy terror."

The whole matter was ventilated in the Reichstag on March 7, 1914, when Deputy Erzberger, the leader of the Centre Party, stated in reference to his words in the Budget Committee[1] :—

> " I was quoted just now, without being named, as declaring that if the Secretary of State did not succeed in removing these abuses in our colonial policy as quickly as possible I could no longer bear the responsibility of allowing Imperial money to be voted for colonial policy. I hold to that decision most emphatically, and I am ready to take all the consequences arising from it."

A similar statement had been made by Rören on December 3, 1906, when referring to the atrocities in Togoland. He said :—

> " With this system the colonies cannot develop healthily, and therefore one must have scruples about giving them another *heller* for the development of the colonies, which seems entirely precluded under these conditions."

On March 7, 1914, Deputy Dittmann, a Social Democrat, produced what can only be described as a damning indictment of forced labour in the German colonies. After speaking of the enormous loss of life, Dittmann continued :—

> " The effect on the natives of the exploiting reign of capitalism is simply awful. What has become known in the last few weeks puts a definite end to the naïve representation that since the Dernburg era a good time had dawned for the natives through the reforms introduced; it shows, on the contrary, gentlemen, that an awful decimation of the native population runs parallel with the coming to the fore of the so-called capitalistic ' Kultur.' . . . We Social Democrats have always pointed to this fact, and drawn from it the most telling arguments against the capitalist's colonial policy. This year we live to find a simply overwhelming wealth of proof as to the

---

[1] " If things continue like that Germany can no longer accept the responsibility for its colonial policy. . . . If things go on thus I can vote no more supplies for colonial policy.".

correctness of our assertions, brought from the middle-class side. .... Gentlemen, the natives are dragged by treachery and force from their home districts to places where they die in masses. That concerns Cameroon and East Africa particularly. Ostensibly there is no forced labour there, as the Secretary of State, Dr. Solf, assures us in Committee. In fact, however, the system of work-tickets introduced by the Government in East Africa really means a brutal compulsion to forced work on the plantations, for every black man must prove by this card that he has worked at least twenty days each month for white men. If he cannot he is dragged to the district police station, and there officially flogged with a sjambok, according to the new order regarding work; this is done even without any request from the employer. Gentlemen, surely there we have without doubt the most brutal compulsion to plantation work it is possible to conceive."

On May 12, 1914, Deputy Wels quoted a letter from the Bishop of Cameroon in which the latter showed that—

" Cameroon was suffering from depopulation in a truly terrible degree; the land has only miserable remains of population where twenty years ago there were flourishing villages "[1];

and Dr. Solf, addressing the representatives of the South Cameroon Chamber of Commerce in 1913, said:—

" It is a sad state of things to see how the villages are bereft of men, and how women and children carry heavy burdens; how the whole life of the people appears on the roads. What I saw on the high roads at Jaunde and Ebolowa has grieved me most deeply. Family life is being destroyed; parents, husbands, and wives and children are being separated. No more children are born, as the women are separated from their husbands for the greater part of the year. These are wrong conditions and difficulties which must cease."[2]

In South-West Africa the conditions have been deplorable. Not only were the natives deprived of their lands as a punishment for the Herero Rebellion, but Herr von Lindequist issued a decree placing all Hereros, Hottentots, and Bastards, with the exception

---

[1] The words are those of Wels, but convey the sense of the Bishop's letter.
[2] *Koloniale Rundschau* (1913), p. 740.

because he and his people had dared to complain to the Reichstag about their ill-treatment. This savage sentence, subsequently reduced by administrative orders from Berlin, stands as a permanent record of the way in which local officials have punished in an entirely illegal and arbitrary manner those who have offended them. The German Colonial Office, represented by Dernburg, admitted that "the sentencing of the natives in Cameroon cannot be approved," and, although naturally anxious to shelter Governor von Puttkamer, the nephew of Bismarck and son of a powerful Minister, was forced by public opinion to consent to an enquiry into the proceedings of its officials in Cameroon.

The " Complaints of the Akwa Chiefs " is too long a document to be quoted in full. Briefly, they asked that the persecution by the local German Government of themselves and their King should be brought to an end They represented that their King was the supreme chief for them, and that, if he were treated so brutally, the minds of the people could never rest, and discord was the inevitable result.

> " We beg most humbly," they concluded, " for immediate help on the part of the illustrious German Reichstag ; for such a continuance of abominable treatment of our King is a great and unendurable disgrace to us."

The complaints were about numerous cases of flogging and ill-treatment, the imprisonment of sixty chiefs and heads of families, the spoliation of lands forced labour, disregard of solemn treaties, and the taking of betrothed native girls by high officials. The whole document forms a powerful indictment of German methods in Cameroon.

Of actual brutal treatment of chiefs there are numberless instances. A British officer who was in Cameroon prior to the war relates how the native soldiers were sent out to " visit " certain villages. He says :—

> " Visiting consists of burning, looting, and bringing in the headmen chained together, or trussed up with their arms

behind their backs. . . . The whole party returns to the
' post,' bringing in the chiefs. The corporal is patted on the
back according to the amount of rubber brought in, and no
questions asked."

In German East Africa Captain Kannenberg caused
two village chiefs to be flogged because they would not
tell him the meaning of certain words. One received
75 lashes, the other 100. The first died during the
night.

VI. CHARGES AGAINST INDIVIDUALS

The proved atrocities in the German colonies are so numerous that only a few of the better known can be mentioned here. For purposes of reference they are arranged under the names of the officials chiefly concerned :—

Prince Prosper Arenberg.

This officer, whilst serving in South-West Africa in the year 1900, was condemned at Windhoek for the revolting murder of a native and for violent assaults on native women. The court-martial of the First Guards Division subsequently very properly condemned him to death. The case attracted great interest in Germany. Powerful family and social influences were exerted on behalf of the Prince, and the sentence was commuted by the Emperor to one of fifteen years' imprisonment. Arenberg was removed to the fortress at Tegel, a re-trial was ordered, and the Prince was pronounced of unsound mind and acquitted. Family influence in this case was stronger than the law, and the case proved a favourite weapon in the hands of the Social Democrats.[1]

Dr. Karl Peters.

This man, appointed Imperial Commissary in German East Africa as a reward for his exploring activities, committed numerous atrocities, and is one of the most odious figures in German colonial history.   In

---

[1] See *Prinz Prosper Arenberg und die Arenberge*, No. 1 of *Sozialdemokratische Agitations-Bibliothek*, Berlin, 1904.

his own books he has spoken of these deeds without shame. In an open letter to him Herr Eltz says :—

> " Before God and man, you are responsible for the devasta-tion of fertile country-sides, responsible for the deaths of my comrades von Bülow and Wolfram, of our brave soldiers, and hundreds of Wadschaggas."[1]

In October 1891 Peters arbitrarily caused a native youth, named Mabruk, to be hanged at his station at Kilima-Njaro, and in January 1892 he had a native girl, called Jagodja, hanged at the same place. The former was accused of stealing cigarettes, but the real crime was that he had visited Peters' native concu-bines. The latter was one of Peters' concubines (whom he termed his " princesses "), who had fled for protec-tion to a neighbouring chief. This girl was brutally whipped (with other women) day after day, " so that the blood flowed copiously and the captives were finally unable to scream." The girl Jagodja was flogged until her back resembled " chopped meat."

Peters was brought before the Disciplinary Court at Potsdam on April 25, 1897, six years after these crimes, and condemned to be dismissed the Service, not for the crimes he had committed, but because he had given false reports of his actions to his superiors. He appealed, and the Court of Second Instance at Leipzig confirmed the former sentence Yet, eventually, owing to the pressure of the Colonial Party, Peters was granted his pension by the Emperor, and a statue has since been erected in his honour at Dar es-Salaam. The case created immense interest in Germany, where the " man with the bloodstained hands,"[2] as he was called by the natives, became the centre of a controversy extending over twenty years.

Herr Wehlan.

This official in Cameroon was proved to have been guilty of the most revolting cruelties towards the natives, whom he had caused to be flogged, tortured,

---

[1] *Vossische Zeitung,* October 19, 1892.

[2] Statement by Scavenius, the Danish explorer, in *Politiken* March 1, 1896.

and executed on the slightest pretext. At his first trial in January 1896, before the Disciplinary Court, he was sentenced to a fine of £25 and at the second trial the first sentence was upheld. Wehlan remained an official under the Colonial Department, and was subsequently rewarded with the post of notary in Berlin.

Herr Kleist.

This man, Deputy-Governor of Cameroon, caused a rising in 1893 by flogging twenty women, wives of native soldiers. The men were drawn up on parade to witness the flogging, and—

> " each of the women received ten strokes with a whip made of hippopotamus hide, and Herr Kleist stood by and looked on."

He was tried before the Disciplinary Court on October 16, 1894, charged with undue cruelty and with improper conduct, accompanied by acts of violence, towards other women left in his charge as hostages. The Court held that he had not exceeded his rights. At a second trial on April 7, 1895, he was dismissed the Service because his conduct had " injured the prestige of the German Empire."

Governor von Puttkamer.

This man was nephew of Bismarck and son of a Prussian Minister. He was appointed Governor of Cameroon, although Herr von Soden, a former Governor, had informed the Chancellor, von Caprivi, that he was a gambler and spendthrift.

During Governor von Puttkamer's administration in Cameroon numerous scandals and atrocities occurred. The actions with which he was charged in the Reichstag on December 2, 1906, were the following:—

> (1.) Allowing houses to be built with public money for the concubines of the officials, and also a residence for himself.

<hr>

[1] Statement of an eyewitness writing in the *Berliner Tage blatt.*

   (2.) Receiving gratuitous shares in several colonial
       companies.

   (3.) Conniving at acts of the greatest barbarity com-
       mitted by officers of the colonial forces.

   (4.) Permitting the mutilation of natives killed in
       battle by the cutting off of their private
       parts as trophies.

   (5.) Keeping a German woman at Government
       House, whom he called his " cousin," and sup-
       plied with a forged passport to return home
       in an assumed name.

It was during von Puttkamer's administration that
the Akwa chiefs complained to the Reichstag, and were
therefore sentenced to heavy terms of imprisonment.

Most powerful influences were exerted to screen
von Puttkamer from exposure, but in spite of every
attempt to hush up the affair the Government were
obliged to bring him before the Disciplinary Court,
and he was tried on April 25, 1907, on the following
charges :—

   (1.) Issue of an incorrect passport to a "lady
       friend."

   (2.) Illicit participation in colonial companies.

   (3.) Undue interference with the administration of
       justice.

He was fined £50 and reprimanded; but much of the
evidence was suppressed and pertinent witnesses were
not called.

Herr G. A. Schmidt.

This is one of the most revolting cases in
the annals of German colonialism.   Schmidt, an official in Toguland, began his career by summoning
the native girls at Atakpame to a dance at his station,
and threatening their mothers that if they did not
allow them to appear they would be fined twenty
marks.   The Catholic missionaries intervened, and
Schmidt issued instructions that no complaints were
to be carried to the mission.

Schmidt kept a harem of young native girls, some under the age of puberty. The family of one girl, whom he had kept forcibly, flogged, and otherwise shamefully treated, complained to the missionaries, with the result that, in the words of Deputy Rören[1]—

"at four o'clock in the morning the District Judge, von Rotberg, who had returned meanwhile, came on horseback, as did also his assistant Lang, together with two more, and nineteen black soldiers; came, not to the station building to arrest the criminal, but to the mission. They forced their way into the mission, dragged the Fathers, as they were, out of bed, declared them arrested, without having a warrant, or without even answering their questions as to why they were arrested. They hunted through the mission buildings, even through the chapel, uncovered the altar, rummaged through the sacristy . . . and then the Fathers were surrounded by the nineteen soldiers with loaded rifles, and led off to prison."

Here they remained for twenty-one days, forbidden postal communication with the outside world, and prevented from hearing confession. Meantime all possible witnesses were intimidated, and Schmidt's personal friend, Kersting (who had had a chief shot with a revolver and had afterwards had the man's head cut off), interrogated them before judicial proceedings could be taken. The acquittal of Schmidt became a foregone conclusion, in spite of the evidence of the missionaries as to his immoral relations with the young girls.

The missionary, one Schmitz, who had laid the information against Schmidt, was then cited before the court and given fourteen days' imprisonment for bearing false witness, and it was held that one of the ill-treated children, Adjaro, "had been subject to hypnotic influences or had made her statements in the delirium of fever." Father Schmitz subsequently appealed against his sentence, and was acquitted.

One further fact came out in the evidence. On May 7, 1903, Schmidt proclaimed his black concubine, Sisakbe, formally and officially as *Jenufia* (i.e., queen), invested her with a sword of office, and gave

[1] In the Reichstag, December 3, 1906

her the judicial right to decide in legal quarrels.   Yet
this man, after these proceedings had become known,
was sent back to Togoland by the Colonial Department, and was not dismissed from the Service until the
whole affair had been ventilated in the Reichstag and
the suppression of the revolting details was no longer
possible.

Captain Dominik.

It is asserted that Captain Dominik, then a lieutenant, when in charge of a punitive expedition
against the Bahoho, in Cameroon, attacked a small
village in the neighbourhood of the Nachtigal
Rapids, and either ordered or allowed his black
soldiers to put fifty-two little children, who remained
alive after the general massacre, into baskets and
throw them into the rapids. It is, however, maintained
by the apologists for Dominik that he had not sufficient
control over his black soldiery.

What is certain is that Dominik was responsible for
permitting one of the atrocious customs of native warfare by the troops under his command.   He allowed
his men to cut off the privy parts of fallen foes. Deputy
Bebel on December 1, 1906, said :—

> " Formerly the order had been given to cut off their ears, but
> the soldiers cut off the women's ears also to increase artificially
> the number of fallen foes.   In order to overcome this, Dominik
> gave orders for their heads to be cut off, but this proved incon-
> venient."

For this practice Dominik, after representations
from the British Government, sent through the German Embassy in London on August 10, 1902, was
reprimanded.   A monument to Dominik was sent to
Cameroon in 1912, and a replica was unveiled at
Yaunde on May 5, 1914.

Lieutenant Schennemann.

Lieutenant Schennemann, the Station Director at
Yaunde, Cameroon, had a black wife, and hearing
rumours that she was too intimate with certain natives,

he ordered a native sergeant, named Duara, to punish the three blacks whom he suspected in such a manner that they should not have the power to repeat the offence.

The sergeant went to the wrong village, and fearing that if he could give no proof of having obeyed his orders he would be soundly thrashed, he seized the first three negroes he met, threw them to the ground, and, lying as they were, had them mutilated in the fashion ordered by Schennemann.   The men thus mutilated were left to their fate.[1]

Captain Kannenberg.

This horrible case was revealed by three deputies in the Reichstag—Bebel, Erzberger, and Ledebour—on March 13 and 15, 1906.   One night in 1898 at Kongwa, German East Africa, Kannenberg was disturbed by the crying of a child.   He left his tent, put his gun through the grass wall of a hut, where a woman and a child lay, and shot the woman in the back.   He then fired further shots.   An enquiry was instituted, but no proceedings followed.

The second case, mentioned on page 31, was the excessive flogging of two chiefs.   One of the men died during the night, and Kannenberg was prosecuted, received three years' imprisonment, and was ordered to be dismissed from the Service.   Almost immediately he was granted imprisonment in a fortress, and shortly afterwards he was pardoned and given his full pension

Landeshauptmann Brandeis.

This official, when in charge of the Marshall Islands, contrary to legal decrees, ordered natives to be flogged repeatedly, and did not allow the floggings to be entered in the punishment book.   Although this was admitted by the Colonial Office, he was subsequently granted an Order for his meritorious services.

---

[1] Bebel, Reichstag, December 1, 1906.

Captain Kamptz.

This case illustrates "summary justice" in Cameroon. Kamptz was in command of the Protectorate troops, and passing through the station of Lolodorf he found that Sergeant Liebert, who was in charge, had fallen ill, and that his black wife was acting in his stead. This woman had arrested three negroes accused of highway robbery. Kamptz had the men brought before him and condemned them to death. The execution was carried out in the most barbarous fashion. A cannon was loaded, the prisoners were placed one after the other at one metre's distance in front of the gun, and shot to pieces.

Captain Thierry.

It was commonly reported, stated Deputy Ablass on December 15, 1905, that Thierry "had simply shot down the natives like game, and that he was notorious in the whole of the Protectorates for his cruelty." The particular crime with which he was charged was that he had shot down the father of a pupil of the Catholic Mission at Lome, who, for fear of Thierry, had fled up a tree. His crimes were brought to the notice of the Colonial Department on November 22, 1904, but no action was then taken.

Governor Horn.

Waldemar Horn was Governor of Togoland during the period when the numerous scandals connected with Schmidt, Metzger, Kersting, von Rotberg, and other officials occurred. His case was discussed in the Reichstag on March 19, 1906, by Dr. Ablass and others. From the speeches then made it appears that Horn was warned at the end of 1903 by his subordinates that if he did not resign his conduct would be denounced. He returned to Berlin on leave, and requested an enquiry. Yet it was not until March 1906 that Legationsrat Rose informed the Reichstag that the charges brought against him had proved to be true.

His trial took place before the Disciplinary Court on May 6, 1907, upon the main charge of causing the death of a native in 1902. It appeared in evidence that a native had been sentenced to a term of five years in chains and to two floggings of twenty-five lashes each for petty theft. By the Governor's orders, after the first flogging he was bound to a post fully exposed to the heat of the sun. From time to time the man was unfastened in the hope that he would confess where he had hidden the money. Then he was tied to the post for a further period of twenty-four hours, without water or food. The next morning the Governor noticed that the native looked " rather exhausted," and he expired shortly afterwards.

For this crime the High Court of Togoland and Cameroon had sentenced Horn in 1905 to a fine of 900 marks or three months' imprisonment. The Disciplinary Court sentenced him to be dismissed the Service with the loss of one-third of his pension.

Chief Justice Dr. Meyer and Regierungsrat von Brauchitsch.

In the " Complaints of the Akwa Chiefs " these two officials in Cameroon are accused of forcibly taking two young girls, betrothed to natives, as their concubines.   The complaint is—

> " that Regierungsrat von Brauchitsch had bought and taken to wife the betrothed of Rudolph Masako, and Supreme Judge Dr. Meyer the betrothed of a young man, Diberabari."

This complaint was made by Chief Akwa Elma, who stated that—

> " von Brauchitsch had declared repeatedly on palaver days that it was forbidden to take the wife of another for oneself."

A further complaint was that before a Court consisting of von Brauchitsch, Assessor Reichhof, and others, King Akwa had been forced to put his mark to a document. In the report of the Committee of the

Reichstag on these proceedings and on the sentencing of the Akwa chiefs is the following:—

" The impression produced is that the officials seem to be those really accused. Apparently they were unable to adapt themselves to the customs and habits of the natives, and to judge them from that standpoint. Several officials, as seems to result from their own statements, appear to have been guilty in their official handling of the matters of the worst kind of mistakes, and even of punishable offences, namely, misuse of official power, robbing others of freedom, inflicting bodily injuries, and, in one instance, forcing a signature against the decree of the Imperial Chancellor of February 27, 1896."

As illustrating how officials in Cameroon regarded sensual crimes with violence, the following case may be cited. The representatives of two commercial depots in Cameroon, stated Dr. Ablass, were walking one day on the Akwa road, when they met the wife of a chief, " who is an educated man, having attended a gymnasium in Germany." These men went up to that chief's wife in broad daylight and forcibly made an indecent assault upon her, but natives ran to her assistance and set her free.

" Thereupon a complaint was made to von Brauchitsch, and he decided that the two representatives of commerce should be punished. But no punishment is recorded. On the contrary, all that could be ascertained was that the two gentlemen had a very pleasant social meeting with Herr von Brauchitsch a few days later."[1]

---

[1] Deputy Dr. Ablass, Reichstag, March 19, 1906.

VII. BRUTALITIES IN SOUTH-WEST AFRICA

The brutalities committed by German farmers and settlers in South-West Africa have been so numerous as to be out of all proportion to similar cases that occur from time to time in newly settled countries where the arm of the law is weak.

In March 1907 a young German farmer in the Ontjo district was condemned to three years' imprisonment for killing a native woman and causing the deaths of two others. One woman who fled from her employer in consequence of his brutalities was pursued and shot, while another woman and a girl were tied to trees and left to their fate.

In 1915–16 ten cases of extreme brutality were dealt with by the British administration. These cases afford some evidence of what has been going on in this colony for many years :—

1. A farmer, Walter Böhmer, shot at a number of natives who had deserted from their employment, and killed two. He had already been condemned by a Protectorate Court in 1912 for beating to death a native who was in a weak condition and consumptive.

2. Carry Venuleth, a farmer at Okajati, caught two bushmen, a man and a woman, brought them before a mock court, consisting of himself and two others, and had them shot.

3. A farmer named Holtz murdered a native who had deserted from his service by striking him on the head with a very heavy knife and afterwards shooting him in the back and stomach.

4. A farmer, Karl Georg Schroeder, killed a native servant with three shots from a revolver.

5. Stoetzer, a farmer at Gobabis, killed a native herd by firing at him, buried the body, and made no report of his proceedings.

6. Antonius Setecki punished a young native herd in a most atrocious manner. The boy had lost two calves. He was locked in a room, tied with reins round his neck and hands, the latter being secured by placing behind the knees a stick to which the rein was attached. Next day the boy was taken out and tied to the farmer's horse with the rein round his neck. He was beaten with a stick, and Setecki then threw the rein over the branch of a tree, hoisted the boy up till his toes just touched the ground, and kept him in this position, repeating the torture three of four times during his journey.

7. A German woman, Freifrau von Werder, shot an aged native.

8. Johann Binkowski, a police sergeant, shot a native and left his body lying unburied.

9. A police officer, Frank Juzek, killed a native at Okhambahe. The boy, who was in custody for theft, had got away, and was recaptured and tied up by Juzek, who had him knocked about and thrashed. Next day the boy, whose hands were tied behind him and whose feet were in leg-irons, was unable to move. He was kicked severely and stamped upon, and the following day he died.

10. Two farmers, named Nauhas and Jakubowski, captured a bushman, put a chain round his neck, tied him to a cart-wheel, and ordered a native to flog him with a twisted rein. The man was thrashed for nearly an hour. Then Jakubowski recommenced the thrashing, and the man was left tied to the cart-wheel all night. In the morning he was dead.

Cases of a similar character were reported by a party of 'Boers and others who had offered their services as transport riders during the Herero Rebellion. Their testimony was contained in the *Cape Argus* for September 25, 1905.   It referred to the deliberate killing of the wounded, the inhuman thrashing of women, their employment upon excessively hard labour so that at Angra Pequeña five or six women died every day, and other similar atrocities. Mr. Griffiths, one of the party, related how a petty chief, who had dared to lift his hand as if to strike a soldier, was tied to a waggon-wheel in such a manner that he was practically hanging by the wrists, and was left there for three days and nights without food or water.   The man was then hanged, after having been brutally kicked and clubbed by rifles.   Another case was connected with a native woman and her baby.   The woman was carrying a heavy burden on her head and the baby on her back. She fell forward in the sand, and the sergeant thrashed her and the baby for five minutes.

More recently Dr. Walker has stated[1] :—

" I have seen photographs of executions and floggings, all very barbarous.   Natives are generally hanged to trees with their arms free, so that they linger a long time, preventing suffocation by holding on to the riems with their hands.   On one occasion our troops found some bodies hanging from a branch by means of barbed wire round their necks; bodies, too, were found fastened together in graves, with every indication of being buried alive."

---

[1] H. F. B. Walker, *A Doctor's Diary in Damaraland*, London, 1916.

VIII. RISINGS AND REBELLIONS

THE numerous risings that have occurred in the German colonies afford the best commentary on German methods of administration. They have been due to a variety of causes, such as expropriation of the tribal lands, seizure of sacrificial cattle, maladministration of justice, excessive floggings and general severity of treatment, invasion of native rights and customs, flogging of women, forced labour and recruiting of natives by means of forced levies, or to a combination of all; but in every case they have been suppressed with a ruthless barbarity that, if committed by a less powerful nation, would have roused a storm of indignation throughout the civilized world.

Three of these rebellions were of an exceedingly serious nature, and resulted in the massacre of whole tribes of natives. Various estimates have been made of the number of natives killed in these unnecessary wars, and there is no reason to doubt the correctness of that made by Professor Schillings, the naturalist, at one time an official of the German Colonial Depart ment, who stated that " by this barbarous method of warfare 200,000 people were shot down in a few years."[1] In the Herero Rebellion, the best known of these wars, the greater part of the tribe—men, women and children—was exterminated, and out of a total of 80,000 only about 20,000 escaped from the ruthless barbarity of the Germans. In the Majimaji Rebellion in German East Africa 75,000 persons succumbed to

---

[1] Quoted from a speech by Deputy Noske, Reichstag, May 1912.

German ferocity;[1] and in the previous Bushiri Rebellion large numbers of natives and Arabs were slain. All of these risings could have been prevented.

German methods of warfare are well illustrated in a letter quoted by Bebel on March 13, 1906. The writer said:—

> " On August 23, at 5 A.M., we surprised the rebels at Kibata as they were attempting to cross the river. There was a long, narrow bridge there, which they had to cross, so that we could pick them off comfortably. There were seventy-six dead, besides those who fell wounded into the river. Many wanted to swim the river, but were torn to pieces by the crocodiles. In the middle of the river was a sandbank where they wanted to rest; but here too the shots caught them. That was a sight! I stood by the river behind a fallen tree and shot 120 rounds. The prisoners were always hanged."

The details of the Herero Rebellion in South-West Africa are too well known to need recapitulation here.[2] This tribe was ruthlessly driven into the desert to perish of slow starvation, after General von Trotha had issued his proclamation of October 2, 1904, stating that Hereros, with or without arms, would be shot, and that the whole nation must leave the country. No attempt was made to negotiate with the rebels. No quarter was given. Women and children were shot or hanged.

" We tried to assume to ourselves the functions of Providence," stated Dr. Bonn, of Munich University, " and we tried to exterminate a native race whom our lack of wisdom had goaded into rebellion." One of the leading German anthropologists, Professor Dr. Luschan, has said:—

> " I am entirely convinced that our late war in South-West Africa might have been avoided, and that it was simply the result of neglect of the teachings of ethnology on the part of the leading officials."

In other words, the Germans did not take the trouble to understand the natives. And, alluding to this,

---

[1] Statement by Deputy Ledebour, on the authority of Dernburg, March 17, 1908.

[2] See *South-West Africa*, No. 112 of this series, p. 16.

another eminent anthropologist, Dr. Dietrich Wester-
mann, said : " Those are wrongs of which the onus
rests directly on our colonial policy."

With regard to the Herero Rebellion, the Germans
have been convicted many times by their own
speeches and writings. Probably the most telling picture of this horrible campaign is that written by Gustav Frenssen, a German pastor, entitled *Peter Moors
Fahrt nach Südwestafrika*. As a realistic study of
German warfare, every word of which can be substan-
tiated, this book is of the highest value.

The Bushiri Rebellion, which was the first serious
rising in East Africa, caused much bloodshed all along
the coast, and Kilwa especially was a scene of great
carnage. This rising amongst the Arabs was caused by
the overbearing behaviour of the German officers and
officials, who went into the Arab houses whenever they
liked and walked through the harems of the principal
Arabs.

The Majimaji Rebellion of 1905 was an even more
serious affair. It started in the coastal district and
spread inland as far as Uhehe; but the behaviour of the
Wahehes, who remained loyal to the Government and
formed a barrier to the spread of the rebellion west
ward, prevented a general conflagration throughout the
colony. The rising was suppressed with the greatest
barbarity. Large districts were denuded of their food
supplies and the crops burned, and the natives who had
escaped from the devastated areas were driven back
again to their homes, where some thousands died of
actual starvation.

What is true of the larger rebellions is also true in a
greater or less degree of every campaign which the
Germans have undertaken in Africa. In certain
colonies these revolts have been incessant. The record of
Cameroon from 1891 to 1903 is stained with needless
bloodshed; and since 1904 there have been in the
same colony no fewer than seventeen military expeditions of one kind and another. That of East Africa
includes many such expeditions between 1891 and 1903,

culminating in the suppression of the Majimaji Rebellion of 1905.[1]   In South-West Africa the years 1893 and 1894 brought the expeditions of von Leutwein against the Witboois, and between 1894 and 1901 there were four other campaigns.   In November 1903 the Bondelzwarts rose in rebellion, and thereafter came the Herero rising.

[1] *La Dépêche coloniale*, July 31, 1914.

AUTHORITIES

BARKER, J. ELLIS. *The German Danger to South Africa*
(Nineteenth Century, October 1905).
BIGELOW, P. *Children of the Nations.* London, 1901.
BONN, M. J. *German Colonial Policy* (United Empire, 1914,
vol. 5, pp. 126-42).
—— *Nationale Kolonialpolitik* (Schriften des sozialwissenschaftl.
Vereins der Universität München. No. 5.) Munich, 1910.
BRIGGS, J. H. *German East Africa during the War* (Journal of
the African Society, 1917, vol. 16, pp. 199-205).
DAWSON, W. H. *Evolution of Modern Germany. London,* 1908.
*Deutsche Kolonialzeitung: Organ der deutschen Kolonialgesell-
schaft.* Frankfurt a/M., 1886 *to date.*
*Deutsches Kolonialblatt: Amtsblatt für die Schutzgebiete in
Afrika und in der Südsee; herausgegeben im Reichs-Kolo-
nialamt.* Berlin, 1902 *to date.*
FRANCOIS, H. von. *Nama und Damara.* Berlin, 1914.
FRENSSEN, G. *Peter Moors Fahrt nach Südwestafrika* (English
edition, translated by M. M. Wood, London, 1914).
GIESE, F. *L'organisation judiciaire des Colonies allemandes*
(Bulletin de Colonisation comparée, 1912, pp. 1-30).
Gold Coast Leader. Accra, 1911-1914.
HARTMANN, M. *Mission und Kolonialpolitik* (Koloniale Rund-
schau, 1911, pp. 167-95).
HILDEBRAND, G. *Die Stellung der Sozialdemokratie zur Kolo-
nialpolitik* (Koloniale Rundschau, 1911, pp. 22-31).
IRLE, I. *Die Herero: ein Beitrag zur Landes-, Volks-, und
Missions-Kunde.* Gütersloh, 1906.
Koloniale Abhandlungen. Berlin, 1905-1913. Heft 1-67.
*Koloniale Rundschau: Monatsschrift für die Interessen unseren
Schutzgebiete und ihrer Bewohner.* Berlin, 1911-1914.
Koloniale Zeitschrift. Leipzig, 1908 *to date.*
LEUTWEIN, T. G. von. *Elf Jahre Gouverneur in Deutsch Südwest-
afrika.* Berlin, 1906.
LEWIN, EVANS. *The Germans and Africa.* London, 1915.

MEYER, Prof. Dr. HANS. *Das deutsche Kolonialreich.* 2 vols. Berlin, 1910.

Papers relating to certain trials in German South-West Africa (Cd. 8371). 1916.

PETERS, KARL. *New Light on Dark Africa.* London, 1891.

POWELL, E. A. *The Last Frontier.* London, 1913.

Prinz Prosper Arenberg und die Arenberge. (No. 1 of *Sozialdemokratische Agitations-Bibliothek.*) Berlin, 1904.

Reichstag: Stenografische Berichte. Berlin, 1905-1914. (Especially debates on December 11, 1905; March 13, 15, 16, 17, 19, 20, 23, 24, 26, 1906; May 22, 1906; November 28, 29, 1906; December 1, 3, 4, 1906; May 3, 6, 8, 1907; March 17, 20, 1908; April 30, 1912; May 1, 2, 7, 8, 1912; March 7, 1914; May 13, 17, 1914.)

Reichstag: Aktenstücke (1907, No. 323, vol. 241. Contains '' Complaints of the Akwa Chiefs '').

SASSEN, F. *La situation juridique des fonctionnaires coloniaux allemands* (Bulletin de Colonisation comparée, 1911, pp. 93-111).

SCHOLZE, J. *Die Wahrheit über die Heidenmission und ihre Gegner.* Berlin, 1905.

SHANTON, E. F. *In German Gaols.* London, 1917.

Times, London, 1896-1907. (Especially February 19, 1896; March 14, 16, 19, 27, 1896; July 8, 1896; January 11, 1897; April 27, 29, 1897; November 16, 1897; March 5, 1904; March 21, 1906; June 23, 1906; December 1, 3, 4, 5, 10, 24, 1906; March 25, 1907; May 6, 17, 1907.)

TONNELAT, E. *L'expansion allemande hors d'Europe.* Paris, 1908.

VIETOR, J. K. *Geschichtliche und kulturelle Entwicklung unserer Schutzgebiete.* Berlin, 1913.

—— *Kolonialpolitik und Bodenreform.* (Heft 58 of *Soziale Fragen*, edited by A. Damaschks.) Berlin, 1912.

WALKER, H. F. B. *A Doctor's Diary in Damaraland.* London, 1916.

The figures in heavy type give the number of the book referred to, those in lighter type the page.

B.

Ba-ngandu, Sudan tribe, **111**, 9.

Babinga tribe, **111**, 10.

Bafilo, **110**, 51; captured by Germany, **110**, 22.

Bafut tribe, **111**, 19.

Bagamoyo (Sadani), **113**, 21, 32, 53; cable, **113**, 58; old trade route, **113**, 21; port, **113**, 52, 53; protection of, against native risings, 1888, **113**, 31; road, **113**, 41; rubber, **113**, 66; shipping, **113**, 57.

Bagamoyo district, administration, **113**, 38; markets, **113**, 85; population, **113**, 20; salt works at, **113**, 81.

Baghirmi, French expeditions from, **111**, 20.

Bagida, German flag hoisted at, 1884, **110**, 17.

Bagielli tribe, **111**, 10.

Bags, export, **113**, 92.

Bahnfelder Abbau-Gesellschaft, **112**, 79.

Bahnfelder Diamantgesellschaft, **112**, 79.

Bahoho, punitive expedition against, atrocities during, **114**, 37.

Bahr-el-Ghazal, **111**, 74.

Baibanjedda, occupied by Germans, **111**, 20.

Baibokum hills, graphite, **111**, 61.

Baikie, exploration of Benue river by, 1854, **111**, 18.

Bakasi peninsula, **111**, 1 note.

Bakers, **112**, 81.

Bakoko tribe, **111**, 10.

Bakundu tribe, **111**, 10.

Bakwiris, attack on, by von Gravenreuth, 1892, **111**, 19.

Bali, climate, **111**, 7, 8; iron ore near, **111**, 61.

Bali country, exploration, **111**, 19.

Bali tribe, Cameroon, **111**, 19; birth rate, **114**, 25 note.

Balinga, **111**, 20.

Bambimbi, caravan route, **111**, 31.

Bamboo, cultivation, **113**, 63.

Bamenda district, administration, **111**, 25, 27; cotton cultivation, **111**, 57; iron ore, **111**, 61.

Bamum, market and trade centre, **111**, 63, 65; proposed railway, **111**, 39.

Bamum district, proposed railway extension, **111**, 44.

Bananas, **113**, 53, 62, 63, 64, 72; export, **110**, 33, **111**, 66.

Bandeng tribe, **111**, 19.

Bangalla language, **111**, 10.

Bange river, **111**, 64.

Bangui, **111**, 42.

Bania, **111**, 20, 35.

Bank of British West Africa, **110**, 49.

Bankhaus Bleichröder, **112**, 32.

Bankhaus Sal. Oppenheim und Gesellschaft, **112**, 32.

Banking, Cameroon, **111**, 69–70; South-West Africa, **112**, 101; Tanganyika, **113**, 87, 104; Togoland, **110**, 49.

Bantu language, **111**, 9–10, **113**, 19, 40.

Bantu race, **111**, 9, 9–10, **112**, 7, 59, **113**, 16, 17, 19.

Banyeli, iron ore beds, **110**, 40, 41.

Banyo, **111**, 22; cattle breeding, **111**, 59; paths, **111**, 30; trade centre, **111**, 63.

Banyo district, **111**, 12, 61; administration, **111**, 25, 27; cotton cultivation, **111**, 57; honey and wax production, **111**, 58.

Baptist mission, Cameroon, **111**, 15, 18.

Barawa island, sovereignty of Sultan Said admitted, **113**, 26.

Barbers, **112**, 81.

Bare, proposed railway extension, **111**, 44.

Bare district, population, **111**, 12.

Bargash, Sultan, **113**, 27; accession, 1870, **113**, 26; Dar es-Salaam deserted by, 1887, **113**, 32; treaty with Deutsche-Ostafrikanische Gesellschaft, **113**, 78.

Barley, cultivation, **113**, 63.

Barmen mission, *see* Rhenish mission.

Barombi, *see* Johann-Albrechts-Höhe.

Barter system, **111**, 69.

Barth, explorer, **111**, 18.

Basket-work, industry, **113**, 83.

Bassa river, **110**, 6.

Bassari, cotton market, **110**, 44

Bassari country, iron ore, **110**, 40; population, **110**, 41.

Bassila, **110**, 51.

Bastard race, **112**, 7, 18, 42, 45, 59; labour, **112**, 43, **114**, 27–8; protected by proclamation of Herero chief, 1904, **112**, 15; treaty with Germany, 1885, **112**, 13.

Batanga, British shipping service, **111**, 49; fishing, **111**, 60.

Batanga tribe, Cameroon, birthrate, **114**, 25.

Batunga, **111**, 19.

F.

Government Agricultural Research Station, improvements of cotton cultivation, **113**, 69–70.

Government Land Bank, **112**, 64–5, 102, 104.

Government stores, exempt from duty, **110**, 47; import, **112**, 90.

Grain, import, **112**, 90.

Granville, Lord, and Ambas bay, **111**, 16.

Grape-vine, cultivation, **112**, 47.

Graphite, **111**, 61.

Gravenreuth, — von, attack on Bakwiris, 1892, **111**, 19–20; killed, **111**, 20.

Great Asia mine, **112**, 70.

Great Britain, agreement with France, 1862, **113**, 109; agreements and treaties with Germany, **110**, 18–9, 50, 51–2, **111**, 17, 32, 72–4, **112**, 1, 11, 13, 96, **113**, 29, 31, 107–9, 112; and Ambas bay, **111**, 15; annexation of Walvisch bay, 1878, **112**, 11; Ashanti expedition, 1895–6, **110**, 20; boundary commission, **110**, 53; boundary protocol with Germany and Belgium, 1910, **113**, 24; cession of Ambas bay to Germany, 1887, **111**, 16; chiefs demand German protection against, 1884, **110**, 17; commercial treaties with Germany, **113**, 98–9, terminated, 1898, **112**, 95; currency, **113**, 103; declarations, *re* Ambas bay, 1885, **111**, 16, *re* commercial travellers, 1869, **112**, 95, *re* financial associations, 1874, **112**, 96, to respect independence of Zanzibar, 1862, **113**, 26, 29; definition of boundary, 1904, **110**, 52; division of Togoland between France and, 1914, **110**, 22; emigration, **112**, 41; enterprise in Togoland, **110**, 16; exchange of notes with Germany *re* indemnity to Sultan, 1890, **113**, 32; influence on East African coast, **113**, 39; interests in Tanganyika, **113**, 87–8; negotiations with, regarding Togoland frontier, **110**, 17; occupation, of Togoland, 1914, **110**, 22, of Yendi, Aug. 22nd, 1914, **110**, 22; palm kernel trade, **111**, 56; protectorate over remaining dominions of the Sultan of Zanzibar, 1890, **113**, 111; protest against Portuguese treaty with Germany, 1887, **112**, 97; recognition of German protectorate of Cameroon, 1885, **111**, 16; Samoa

Great Britain—*cont.*
Treaty with Germany, 1899, **110**, 21; shipping, **110**, 1, **113**, 56–7, 58; and South-West Africa, **112**, 10–2, 18; suppression of pirates in Persian Gulf, 1819, **113**, 25; trade, **110**, 45, 46, 47, **111**, 67, 68, **112**, 92, 94, **113**, 63, 93, 95, 96, 97.

Great Fish bay (Tiger bay), **112**, 32; proposed railway, **112**, 31.

Great Fish river (Oub), **112**, 3, 4.

Great Lakes, **113**, 27, 33.

Great Namaqualand, German Protectorate declared, 1884, **112**, 13.

Greeks, in Tanganyika, **113**, 22, 89, 104.

Green Likwala river, **111**, 34, 75.

Grenfell, Rev. George, discovery of Ubanghi by, **111**, 18.

Griffiths, Mr., evidence *re* German atrocities, **114**, 44.

Gröben, — von der, expedition under, 1683, to Guinea coast, **110**, 15.

Groceries, import, **112**, 90.

Grootfontein, climate, **112**, 6; customs, **112**, 94; forestry, **112**, 58; orange plantations, **112**, 47; orchardist appointed, **112**, 46; railway, **112**, 22, 24; water supply, **112**, 56.

Grootfontein, administrative district, **112**, 17; Bushmen, **112**, 44; copper and lead, **112**, 69, 69–70.

Grootfontein, Ein-und Verkaufsgenossenschaft, **112**, 86.

Grootfonteiner Verwertungs-Gesellschaft, **112**, 86.

Groot Otavi mine, **112**, 69, 70.

Grossfriedrichsburg, fort built, 1683, **110**, 15.

Grote Doden tribe, *see* Ogei.

Ground-nuts, cultivation, **110**, 33, **111**, 53, **113**, 65; export, **110**, 33, **113**, 53, 54, 65, 93, 94.

Gruber, Herr, action brought against by Karl Peters, **114**, 8.

Gruner, expedition under, 1894–7, **110**, 20, 22.

Guam tribe, **110**, 10.

Guano, **112**, 67; export, **112**, 83, duties, **112**, 94.

Guano islands, guano, **112**, 67.

Guchab mine, **112**, 69, 70.

Guillain, Capt., **113**, 28.

Guinea, Gulf of, **110**, 1, **111**, 1, 72, **113**, 108.

Guinea coast, Portuguese on, in 15th century, **110**, 14.

Guinea worm disease, **110**, 9.

N.